T0270949

The Intellectual Foundations of Alfred Marshall's Economic Science

This book provides a contextual study of the development of Alfred Marshall's thinking during the early years of his apprenticeship in the Cambridge moral sciences. Marshall's thought is situated in a crisis of academic liberal thinking that occurred in the late 1860s. His crisis of faith is shown to have formed part of his wider philosophical development, in which he supplemented Anglican thought and mechanistic psychology with Hegel's *Philosophy of History*. This philosophical background informed Marshall's early reformulation of value theory and his subsequent wide-ranging reinterpretation of political economy as a whole. The book concludes with the suggestion that Marshall conceived of his mature economic science as but one part of a wider, neo-Hegelian social philosophy.

Simon J. Cook is a Postdoctoral Fellow at the Cohn Institute for the History and Philosophy of Science and Ideas, Tel-Aviv University. He previously taught for five years at Duke University. Dr. Cook received his Ph.D. from the Faculty of History at the University of Cambridge.

Historical Perspectives on Modern Economics

General Editor
Craufurd D. Goodwin, Duke University

This series contains original works that challenge and enlighten historians of economics. For the profession as a whole, it promotes better understanding of the origin and content of modern economics.

Other books in the series:

William J. Barber *Designs within Disorder: Franklin D. Roosevelt, the Economists, and the Shaping of American Economic Policy, 1933–1945*

William J. Barber *From New Era to New Deal: Herbert Hoover, the Economists, and American Economic Policy, 1921–1933*

Filippo Cesarano *Monetary Theory and Bretton Woods: The Construction of an International Monetary Order*

Timothy Davis *Ricardo's Macroeconomics: Money, Trade Cycles, and Growth*

Anthony M. Enders and Grant A. Fleming *International Organizations and the Analysis of Economic Policy, 1919–1950*

Jerry Evensky *Adam Smith's Moral Philosophy: A Historical and Contemporary Perspective on Markets, Law, Ethics, and Culture*

M. June Flanders *International Monetary Economics, 1870–1960: Between the Classical and the New Classical*

J. Daniel Hammond *Theory and Measurement: Causality Issues in Milton Friedman's Monetary Economics*

Samuel Hollander *The Economics of Karl Marx: Analysis and Application*

Lars Jonung (ed.) *The Stockholm School of Economics Revisited*

Kyn Kim *Equilibrium Business Cycle Theory in Historical Perspective*

Gerald M. Koot *English Historical Economics, 1870–1926: The Rise of Economic History and Mercantilism*

Continued after the Index.

The Intellectual Foundations of Alfred Marshall's Economic Science

A Rounded Globe of Knowledge

SIMON J. COOK

Tel-Aviv University

CAMBRIDGE
UNIVERSITY PRESS

32 Avenue of the Americas, New York NY 10013-2473, USA

Cambridge University Press is part of the University of Cambridge.

It furthers the University's mission by disseminating knowledge in the pursuit of education, learning and research at the highest international levels of excellence.

www.cambridge.org
Information on this title: www.cambridge.org/9781107514126

© Simon J. Cook 2009

First published 2009
First paperback edition 2015

A catalogue record for this publication is available from the British Library

Library of Congress Cataloguing in Publication data
Cook, Simon J.
The intellectual foundations of Alfred Marshall's economic science : a rounded globe of knowledge / Simon J. Cook.
p.   cm. – (Historical perspectives on modern economics)
Includes bibliographical references and index.
ISBN 978-0-521-76008-9 (hardback)
1. Marshall, Alfred, 1842–1924.   2. Economics – Great Britain – History.
I. Title.   II. Series.
HB103.M3C6 2009
330.15′7–dc22   2009004014

ISBN 978-0-521-76008-9 Hardback
ISBN 978-1-107-51412-6 Paperback

"Backwards or forward, it's just as far. Out or in, the way's as narrow." "Who are you?" "Myself. Can you say as much?" "What are you?" "The Great Boyg.... Go round about, go round about."

Henrik Ibsen, *Peer Gynt*

Contents

Contents   xi

Acknowledgments

During the years that it has taken to produce this book, I have incurred many debts and obligations. It is a pleasure, finally, to acknowledge them. My motivation for engaging in this study was in no small measure born out of conversations with Stephen Kingston and Julian Hone, two fellow undergraduate students of economics at Kings College, Cambridge. I am also indebted to the Fellows of Kings for their patience and support over many years (and here I am glad of the opportunity to acknowledge a deep debt of gratitude to Tess Adkins). As a graduate student, David Palfrey taught me to appreciate the profound if often subterranean influence of Coleridge's writings within mid-Victorian Cambridge. Four teachers at Cambridge have played a prominent role in my education and have helped to make this book what it is. It was my privilege to be introduced to economics by James Trevithick. Iwan Morus and Simon Schaffer taught me how to do history of science. From Gareth Stedman Jones I am still trying to learn the history of political thought. Finally, I am very grateful for the kind assistance of the staff of the Marshall Library in Cambridge. If it was not for the help of Rowland Thomas, the head librarian, and Alex Saunders, who was the archivist of the Marshall papers, the research for this book could not have been completed.

In more recent years, a number of institutions and individuals have provided the support and intellectual nourishment that have made it possible to write this book. The British social security system helped keep body and soul together during some difficult years. A Lady Davis Fellowship at the Hebrew University of Jerusalem proved slightly more generous in terms of financial support and, more importantly, facilitated some extremely valuable conversations with Alon Kadish. For five years I was lucky enough to teach at Duke University, where I was graciously received by Crauford Goodwin, Roy Weintraub, and Neil De Marchi at the weekly History of

Political Economy seminars. To Neil in particular I am indebted for intellectual stimulation, encouragement, and razor-sharp criticism. During my
first year at Duke, it was my pleasure to make the acquaintance of Gregory
Moore, of Notre Dame University in Australia, with whom I have since
maintained an e-mail correspondence that, on my part at least, has been
a source of instruction, edification, and amusement. I am particularly
indebted to Greg for drawing my attention to the important, if indirect
and therefore easily overlooked, significance of Leslie Stephen in the history of later-nineteenth-century political economy. Finally, the last stages
of the writing of this book were facilitated by a postdoctoral fellowship at
the Cohn Institute for the History and Philosophy of Science and Ideas at
the University of Tel-Aviv.

The most important intellectual debt that I incurred in undertaking
the present study is the one I owe Tiziano Raffaelli. Without his exegesis
of Marshall's early philosophical paper "Ye Machine," my own attempt to
make sense of Marshall's early intellectual life could never have advanced
beyond the first step. At a later date my thinking was considerably advanced
by innumerable e-mail conversations that arose out of his editing of my
contributions to *The Elgar Companion to Alfred Marshall* (2006). It was
also Tiziano who first suggested that I transcribe Marshall's early historical writings for publication in the *Marshall Studies Bulletin*. In this book
I diverge from some of the arguments developed by Tiziano in his earliest
interpretations of Marshall's philosophical papers. It seems to me, however,
that the arguments developed in the last part of the book converge, by way
of an investigation of the idealist side of Marshall's thought, with the position that Tiziano has more recently articulated as a result of his thorough
study of Marshall's evolutionary economics. This, of course, is not necessarily a view shared by Tiziano.

A number of individuals read and commented on some or all of the chapters of this book. Donald Winch, Roger Backhouse, and Rachel Stroumsa
read earlier drafts of the whole, and the comments of each were extremely
valuable (if, at the moment of receipt, also extremely vexing). Each, in his
or her own way, earned the particular merit of motivating me to cut several thousand words from different parts of the book, while Rachel also
pushed me to rewrite parts of almost every paragraph. Michael Cook read
the whole of the second half of the book and prompted me to clarify certain economic concepts as well as to rewrite a large number of ill-phrased
sentences. Gregory Moore provided valuable advice on earlier drafts of the
first half of the book. Sarah Stroumsa offered useful comments on Chapter
Two. David Palfrey, Andrew Holgate, and Yair Wallach read what, in light

of their comments, became earlier drafts of the introduction. This book has also benefited from the grammatical, logical, and stylistic insights of Mary Racine, Cambridge's sharp-eyed copy editor. None of these individuals is responsible for the remaining errors.

Finally, I wish to express my thanks to my immediate family for putting up with an obsessive Marshall scholar for so long. Neither my wife, Rachel, nor our two sons, Yotam and Yair, have ever known me not engaged in the research for, or the writing of, this book. But each one of them has been busy while I have been working on Marshall (some, of course, for more years than others). Two of Rachel's productions, in particular, have been a source of wonder and amazement. It is to Rachel that my deepest obligations lie, and it is with pleasure as well as relief that I now leave this book behind and (as may once have been done in Odessa) turn to building with her a house beyond the place where the train tracks end.

Abbreviations

CAM   *The Correspondence of Alfred Marshall, Economist*, 3 vols., edited by John K. Whitaker (Cambridge: Cambridge University Press, 1996)

ECAM   *The Elgar Companion to Alfred Marshall*, edited by Tiziano Raffaelli, Giacomo Becattini, and Marco Dardi (Northampton, Mass.: Edward Elgar, 2006)

EEW   *The Early Economic Writings of Alfred Marshall*, 2 vols., edited by John K. Whitaker (London: Macmillan & Co., 1975)

EHC   "Alfred Marshall's Essay on the History of Civilization," edited by Simon J. Cook, *Marshall Studies Bulletin* 9 (2005) (http://www.dse.unifi.it/marshall/welcome.htm)

EI   Alfred Marshall and Mary Paley Marshall, *The Economics of Industry* (London: Macmillan & Co., 1879)

EPW   "The Early Philosophical Writings of Alfred Marshall," edited by Tiziano Raffaelli, *Research in the History of Economic Thought and Methodology, Archival Supplement* 4 (1994): 51–159

FWC   Alfred Marshall, "The Future of the Working Classes," in *Memorials of Alfred Marshall*, edited by A. C. Pigou, pp. 101–18 (London: Macmillan & Co., 1925 [1873])

LTW   Alfred Marshall's *"Lectures to Women": Some Economic Questions Directly Connected to the Welfare of the Laborer*, edited by Tiziano Raffaelli, Eugenio Biagini, and Rita Tullberg (Aldershot: Edward Elgar, 1925 [1873])

Mill CW   *The Collected Works of John Stuart Mill*, 31 vols., general editor, John M. Robson (Toronto: Routledge, 1965–91)

MTV   Alfred Marshall, "Mr Mill's Theory of Value," in *Memorials of Alfred Marshall*, edited by A. C. Pigou, pp. 119–33 (London: Macmillan & Co., 1925 [1876])

Principles   Alfred Marshall, *Principles of Economics*, 9th (variorum) ed. 2 vols. (London: Macmillan & Co., 1961 [1890])

RCP   *Reform Club Papers* (London: Macmillan & Co., 1873)

Stewart CW   *The Collected Works of Dugald Stewart*, 11 vols., edited by William Hamilton (Edinburgh: Thomas Constable and Co., 1854–60)

The following standard abbreviations refer to volumes of *The Glasgow Edition of the Works and Correspondence of Adam Smith*, 6 vols. (Oxford: Clarendon Press; Indianapolis: The Liberty Fund. 1976–87):

Corr   *Correspondence*, edited by E. C. Mosner and I. S. Ross (1987)

LJ   *Lectures on Jurisprudence*, edited by R. L. Meek, D. D. Raphael, and P. G. Stein (1978); containing LJ(A): Report of 1762–3; LJ(B): Report of 1766

LRBL   *Lectures on Rhetoric and Belles Lettres*, edited by J. C. Bryce (1983)

TMS   *Theory of Moral Sentiments*, edited by D. D. Raphael and A. L. Macfie (1976)

WN   *Wealth of Nations*, edited by R. H. Campbell, A. S. Skinner, and W. B. Todd (1976)

Introduction

This book is a study of the intellectual foundations of Alfred Marshall's economic science. It makes no attempt to evaluate Marshall's contributions to economic science by the lights of current economic thinking. Nor is it conceived as a step toward the reformation of contemporary economic theory, showing what one of its founders "really meant." Even the most historically minded of contemporary neo-Marshallian economists are likely to find this study "backward looking," with little connection to contemporary research.[1] Yet these disclaimers are not intended to justify a study of 'ideas for ideas' sake. "We need history," Nietzsche once wrote, "but not the way a spoiled loafer in the garden of knowledge needs it." Intellectual history can, on occasion, lead us not only to the roots of our present beliefs, but also to fresh perspectives on current problems. But the contemporary problems that this book points toward are not specifically economic ones. They relate rather to the connection between our economic reasoning as a whole and our various political, moral, and cultural values; for the primary concern of the following chapters is not the development of Marshall's economic thought as such, but the intimate and intricate connections that can be traced between his work in political economy and the development of his philosophical thinking.

Marshall's earliest philosophical writings date to the late 1860s, when he first became associated with the moral sciences as taught and developed at the University of Cambridge. As will be told in detail in the third chapter of this book, these writings reflect Marshall's efforts to navigate his way through a rather messy Victorian philosophical dispute. In this dispute orthodox Anglicanism was defended by the argument that the gulf between the human mind and the divine mind could not be bridged by human reason and that only revelation allowed us knowledge of God's

---

[1] See the editorial introduction to *ECAM*, xvi.

purposes for humanity. The philosophical framework of this orthodox position, however, became the basis for a new "agnostic" creed developed by "scientific naturalists" who, by passing over revelation, now separated a knowable domain of nature from an unknowable realm of the "Absolute." The champion of utilitarianism, John Stuart Mill, opposed the philosophical framework adopted by both orthodox and agnostics, and defended a secular moral philosophy. Finally, a number of liberal Anglicans insisted that reason granted humanity access to the divine mind and its purposes on earth. Some of the fiercest fighting in this contest occurred between advocates of a version of common sense philosophy that supported orthodox Anglican theology and proponents of a new "incarnationalist" theology that rested on a Coleridgean version of German idealism. As will be argued in Chapter Three, Marshall's earliest philosophical writings show that he came to accept the mental dualism articulated by those liberal Anglicans in Cambridge, whose thought derived from Coleridge.

The basic argument developed in this book is that this early philosophical dualism provides the key to a significant swath of Marshall's subsequent intellectual development. As we shall see in Chapter Three, Marshall began with Mill's attempt to show that our idea of the self, rather than resting on an intuition, could be accounted for by the association of ideas. Seeing that Mill had failed in this attempt, Marshall nevertheless rejected the common sense intuitionist alternative to Mill's associationist psychology developed by William Hamilton and Henry Mansel (and therefore also the philosophical basis of "agnosticism"). Marshall concluded rather that Cambridge liberal Anglican philosophers had been correct to distinguish between a higher and a lower sphere of the human mind. According to this Coleridgean mental dualism, a higher "Self" was identified with the activity of self-consciousness, while Mill's associationist psychology could be accepted as providing the basis for a physiological account of the workings of a lower animal self. Marshall's distinctive mechanical rendering of an associationist model of the lower self is outlined in Chapter Four. In Chapter Five we shall explore some of the ways in which Marshall's philosophical dualism informed his earliest efforts in political economy, most significantly by shaping the methodological procedures by means of which he sought to reformulate and advance this science.

In the early 1870s, Marshall's discovery of Hegel's *Philosophy of History* led him to develop further the idealist facet of his psychological dualism. As we shall see in Chapter Six, Hegel provided Marshall with a vision of self-consciousness as a subject of historical development. This development, Hegel had argued and Marshall now concurred, had occurred in two broad stages.

First of all, a moral order composed of self-conscious human agents had gradually emerged out of the natural world ("subjective freedom"). Second, social institutions that realized, protected, and fostered the further advance of self-consciousness had come into being ("objective freedom"). Modern economic life, Marshall now concluded, required for its precondition both subjective and objective freedom. But reconciling this idealistic philosophy of history with his earlier study of the evolution of the lower self described by associationist psychology was not entirely straightforward. Initially, and as told in Chapter Seven, Marshall concluded that a liberal dose of higher education was needed to bridge the gap between the spiritual potential and the problematic mental actuality of the majority of the population. But in the last chapter of this book we shall see how, over the course of two decades, Marshall would develop and revise the categories of Hegel's *Philosophy of History*. The resultant social philosophy, which constituted a "rounded globe of knowledge" of which economic science was but one part, was founded on a dialectical vision of a distinctly modern form of progress.[2]

This book, then, can be read as an account of how Marshall's specifically economic ideas were developed against the background of an idealist philosophy. From this point of view, the present study reveals the intimate connection that existed on all levels between Marshall's economic and philosophical thought. But if this book recounts an episode in the history of political economy, it does so by focusing primarily not on Marshall's economic science, but on the intellectual foundations of that science. Hence it perhaps makes more sense to approach it in the first instance as an exercise in the history of philosophy rather than the history of political economy. Ultimately, however, such distinctions are somewhat artificial; as the following pages argue, the economic and the philosophical components of Marshall's thought constituted but two halves of a single "rounded globe of knowledge." It was indeed Marshall who, at the beginning of the twentieth century, took political economy out of the Cambridge Moral Sciences Tripos and established a separate and autonomous faculty of economics. But what the present book demonstrates is that, for this founder of modern economic science, there could be no question that economics provided a complete perspective on modern social problems. Economic science might warrant institutional autonomy, but intellectually it remained subordinate to that higher philosophy on which it was founded.

---

[2] The expression a "rounded globe of knowledge" derives from Keynes 1925: 48. Keynes, however, applied it solely to the economic science set out in Marshall's *Principles of Economics*.

Today, however, economics appears to have broken free of these philosophical chains. This development has significant repercussions for our
own political thinking. At one extreme of current political debate stands
a libertarian philosophy that appears to deny the reality of any public values not determined by the market. At another extreme we find atavistic
Marxists who simply reject the workings of the market as false and fetishis-
tic. Between these two extremes we encounter a political debate conducted
in two languages – the language of economic science and the language of
moral, political, and cultural values – and these two languages appear to
be mutually unintelligible. The situation is perhaps not dissimilar to that of
the early nineteenth century when, in Britain, no consensus existed between
those who employed mechanical and those who employed organic metaphors in their discussions of social issues. This early-nineteenth-century
state of affairs in fact forms a crucial part of the wider context within which
we should situate Marshall's Herculean efforts to reconcile apparently conflicting philosophical positions and thereby achieve a platform for political
consensus. If, once again, we today find ourselves unable to reconcile economic and political values, this does not, of course, entail that we need to
resurrect Marshall's rounded globe of knowledge as a whole. One important
step that we can take, however, is to bring into view both the merits and the
limitations of Marshall's particular intellectual synthesis. This book contributes to this task by way of a detailed study of how and why that synthesis was
first developed. In the remainder of these preliminary remarks, however, an
attempt will be made to place Marshall's efforts in a wider historical perspective in order to formulate an initial evaluation of the intellectual presuposi-
tions of Marshall's project.

We can begin by noting that the very choice of the historical method
in the following pages implicitly signals dissent from one part at least of
Marshall's rounded globe of knowledge. According to today's academic terminology, the present historical study falls under the label of "contextualist."
This is because it engages in a close reading not only of Marshall's texts, but
also of his contexts. Behind such a procedure stands an assumption that the
meaning of Marshall's texts can be usefully framed in terms of his authorial
intentions and a conviction that we are aided in interpreting what Marshall
meant to do in composing these texts by paying close attention to both the
language he employed and the concrete situations within which he so acted.
The adoption of such a methodology should certainly not be mistaken for
the claim that a contextualist strategy constitutes the only valid approach
to the history of ideas. A contextualist methodology does, however, stand
in direct opposition to an approach that derives the meaning of a text by

situating it within a series of canonical texts. The latter method generates a teleological meaning from any particular text by ascertaining its place in a seemingly inevitable march of thought from error to truth. From this point of view, neither the particular languages found within the text nor the specific historical backgrounds that informed its composition are of any intrinsic interest. One of the claims advanced in this book is that Marshall's innovations in political economy were inextricably bound up with just such a teleological approach to the history of ideas.

Marshall's version of the history of ideas will occupy us at a number of points in this book (specifically in Chapters One, Five, Six, and Seven). What we shall find is that his approach combined two distinct historical narratives, each of which stemmed from a different stage in his early philosophical development. To begin with, by 1871, Marshall had formulated a distinction between thought and its expression in the history of political economy. On the basis of this distinction, he proceeded to dismiss variations in terminology as superficial compared with an underlying continuum of economic thought (which he discerned from the Physiocrats through Adam Smith to David Ricardo and John Stuart Mill). Such a distinction between thought and words was itself founded on Marshall's philosophical mental dualism, which saw words as the product of the lower, creative ideas of the higher self. As we shall find, Marshall's approach to the use of language was, in some ways at least, compatible with the contextualist method employed in this book. Writing for Marshall was, in the first instance, a communicative act, the performance of which presupposed both specific circumstances and specific intentions. Nevertheless, a significant gap remains between even this perspective on the use of language and that which is utilized in the present study.

The interpretations developed here rest in part on the assumption that language shapes, propels, and circumscribes the possibilities of thought. Such an assumption is typical of the intellectual history of the last third of the twentieth century and has its roots in the antipsychological linguistic turn taken by philosophy at the beginning of the twentieth century. Not surprisingly, perhaps, this assumption was quite alien to Marshall. Marshall's starting point is the individual mind, and he regards language as simply the expression of ideas that are formed independently of language. In other words, Marshall views communication as an activity whereby two or more minds happen to make use of some particular system of signs for the purpose of exchanging ideas. From such a perspective, the activity of communication is based on the separate and independent mental activities of two or more private selves. But Marshall's distance from today's social conception of language becomes even more marked when we turn from his approach to the ordinary ideas of everyday mental experience to what he regards as those creative or "constitutive ideas" embodied in philosophy or the sciences. In these cases, writing and speech become not simply separate from but actually inferior to an activity of spirit, which follows its own teleological development quite unrelated to particular concrete situations or individual acts of will. From this standpoint and as illustrated in Chapter Five, language becomes a barrier that we must overcome to arrive at that truth which belongs in the higher realm of reasoned thought.

This idealist kernel of Marshall's history of ideas was broadened and deepened in the wake of his discovery of Hegel. By associating the thought of the eighteenth century with ancient pagan philosophy, Marshall was able to project his Hegelian philosophy of history onto the history of social thought since the time of Turgot and Smith. Eighteenth-century social thought, Marshall now supposed, had identified society with a natural order with which it was wrong for human institutions to interfere. Over the course of the century separating Turgot and Smith from John Stuart Mill and himself, however, Marshall believed that this laissez-faire natural law philosophy had given way to a moral and, ultimately, idealist social philosophy. Thus at the heart of this book stands the argument that Marshall's intellectual project as a whole can best be understood as founded on two convictions: that J. S. Mill had correctly pointed to the need to recast the social thought of the eighteenth century in light of the new social philosophy of the nineteenth, but that Mill's associationist psychology had, unaided, been unequal to the task. As we shall see in Chapter Seven, by 1873 these two convictions had led Marshall to attempt to reformulate political economy as a properly moral science. Such a reformulation rested on a version of the history of ideas that, for our purposes, it is instructive to contrast with the findings of more recent intellectual history.

In the writings of the historian of philosophy Knud Haakonssen, early modern moral philosophy is presented as a long-running three-cornered contest.[3] One of these corners was occupied by the defenders of the various orthodox confessional creeds. Opposed to such religious orthodoxy, but also to one another, stood the new "voluntarism" initiated by Thomas Hobbes and a mainstream "moral realism" that was in key ways continuous with scholastic metaphysics (these terms, we might note, are derived from modern as opposed to early modern philosophy). Both orthodox and

[3] This account is culled from a variety of Haakonssen's papers, but see in particular Haakonssen 2004, 2008. For a cogent justification of his noncontextualist employment of modern terminology, see the introduction to Haakonssen 1996.

voluntarist emphasized the gulf between the human and the divine mind, but where the former sought moral guidance in revelation, voluntarists saw morality in terms of conventions established by social interaction. Moral realists, in contrast to voluntarists, held that moral duties or virtues were objective facts about the universe, but in contrast to the theologically orthodox they argued that the human mind, unaided by revelation, had the cognitive ability to discern these facts. With regard to the Scottish Enlightenment, Haakonssen identifies David Hume and Adam Smith as continuing the voluntarist tradition of Hobbes, while he considers the common sense philosophy of Thomas Reid and Dugald Stewart to be a development within the mainstream tradition of moral realism. As should already be apparent, Haakonssen's sketch highlights elements of both continuity and change with regard to that Victorian dispute that we have identified as forming the background of Marshall's early philosophical writings.

To begin with, it is clear that sometime in the first part of the nineteenth century, a mutation occurred in common sense philosophy. In the hands of Stewart, Reid's philosophy had proved the crucial intellectual resource in establishing an optimistic moral philosophy grounded on the conviction that the divine law is both written in our own hearts and constitutes the underlying order of the social world. In other words, Stewart took for granted that the finite human mind could know the nature of the divinity.[4] In the Victorian dispute, however, common sense philosophy provided intellectual support for the orthodox theological position that the human mind cannot know God, and so must rely on revelation for moral guidance. Hence it is Cambridge Coleridgeanism rather than Hamilton and Mansel's version of common sense philosophy that appears to be a continuation of mainstream Enlightenment moral realism. This continuity begins from a shared belief in our ability to discern God's moral purposes and extends to a relative indifference to specific forms of worship in light of a conception of society as the domain of God's providence. In other words, our real duties to a God who we know desires and works for our moral improvement are discharged in the course of ordinary life. Thus both Stewart and the Cambridge Coleridgean F. D. Maurice believed that the proper study of moral philosophy can elevate us in our social activities to the status of "fellow workers with God."[5] Here, we might add, lies a clue to the striking similarity in the tone of moralizing optimism found in the economic writings of both Stewart and the mature Marshall.

[4] See *Stewart CW*, VII: 120–60 (especially 121–2).
[5] *Stewart CW*, I: 489, 491–2.

Any underlying continuity between the moral philosophies of the eighteenth and nineteenth centuries was, however, radically obscured by a change in language. The early modern debate between moral voluntarists and realists was conducted using the terms of natural law theory. That is, both traditions employed juridical concepts, such as duty, obligation, right, and property, which derived from Roman law. Following the use to which natural rights language had been put in both the American and the French revolutions, however, nineteenth-century British public moralists self-consciously spurned the framework provided by the language of natural law. But in doing so they also lost sight of the philosophical distinctions that, in the preceding century, had been drawn by means of this language. British philosophers from Jeremy Bentham onward now projected onto the seventeenth and eighteenth centuries a single monolithic natural law tradition. The resulting amalgam of two opposing moral philosophies allowed for criticism that drew on often incompatible elements of both. Bentham, for example, attacked the idea of "natural rights" by rejecting as "nonsense on stilts" the metaphysical arguments that had in fact supported a conception of rights as derived from duties. In 1870 the historical economist T. E. Cliffe Leslie would perform a similar fusion by identifying a providential teleology as one of the foundations of Adam Smith's political economy. Marshall's reading of eighteenth-century thought followed in the footsteps of Bentham and Cliffe Leslie, with the difference that he emphasized the importance of both the Roman juridical tradition and the Stoic philosophy by means of which it had been interpreted, both in the ancient world and in the early modern period. As we shall see in Chapter Six, when welded to his Hegelian vision of history, this interpretation of eighteenth-century natural law theory allowed Marshall to regard Adam Smith as representative of an era that uniformly founded its account of the moral world on a pagan conception of nature.

Judged by the light of more recent scholarship, then, the history of social thought around which Marshall conducted his reformulation of political economy was seriously flawed. The mutation of common sense philosophy and the construction of an erroneously monolithic reading of the natural law tradition served to obscure important underlying continuities between eighteenth- and nineteenth-century moral thought. Supplemented by elements of German idealism, the mainstream moral realism of early modern philosophy was maintained far into the nineteenth century. Because he saw transformation rather than continuity, however, Marshall was able to conceive of his own reformulations of political economy as the last acts of a modern project responsible for placing a mechanical and ultimately pagan science on properly moral foundations. But once we locate Marshall's moral philosophy as a further development of that mainstream moral realism that can be traced back through Stewart and Reid to Richard Hooker and before him Thomas Aquinas, a different picture emerges. Put simply, Marshall now appears to be a moral philosopher who, like Stewart before him, was determined to situate a version of Adam Smith's science of political economy firmly within an enduring tradition of moral realism – a tradition to which Smith himself definitely did not subscribe.

It was Marshall's philosophy of mental dualism that allowed him to tame Smith's moral philosophy while advancing his political economy. In his mature thought, Marshall identified economics as a physical science that, as such, treated of the lower but not of the higher self. In the first instance, then, economic science and "higher philosophy" were to be separated. At the same time, however, economic science maintained an intimate connection with a higher philosophy that provided its foundations and its underlying telos. This connection can be illustrated by Marshall's mature conception of "economic organization." For Herbert Spencer, organizations were natural entities. Marshall adopted a version of Spencer's model of the evolution of organizations, but placed it within the framework provided by his philosophy of history. An *economic* organization, for Marshall, develops not within a natural but a moral environment. A physicalist economic science was therefore not a "natural science"; if it passed over it also presupposed those moral foundations of the modern social world that were properly studied by a higher philosophy. The connection was reinforced by Marshall's ubiquitous emphasis on education. Participation in either markets or economic organizations (as factory workers or as managers) served to educate different aspects of character. In this way the economic sphere, in theory at least, fit neatly into an overall social philosophy that conceived of progress in terms of the ethical education of both higher and lower selves. In practice, of course, Marshall experienced tremendous difficulties in reconciling economic science with his higher social philosophy. The economic many were continually threatening to burst asunder the overreaching hold of a philosophical one. It is a tribute to Marshall's strength of character, that as illustrated by successive editions of his *Principles of Economics*, he neither abandoned his unifying philosophical vision nor compromised the integrity of his science of economics.

The question arises, however, as to how valuable this remarkable unified vision actually was. The first two chapters of this book are dedicated to an examination of some of the contexts informing Marshall's early work. In Chapter One, in particular, it will be argued that Marshall's philosophical and economic projects can be related to the specific political and social situation in which academic liberals found themselves in the late 1860s and early 1870s. Put simply, Marshall's early intellectual efforts can be seen as attempting to arrive at two distinct but related goals: the construction of a new public role for university academics as nonpartisan authoritative experts and the establishment of that authority on a reconciliation of opposing philosophical positions. The hope fueling such a project was that a reformulated science of political economy might command the consensus of liberal Anglicans and romantic social critics as well as secular academic liberals. The problem was, however, that the reformulation of political economy that Marshall unveiled in 1873 was seriously and fairly obviously incomplete. Marshall's tragedy, one might say, was that by the time he had worked his thought into a comprehensive shape some two decades later, the social and political situation had changed irrevocably. Indeed, by the time of his death in 1924, Marshall appeared to have bequeathed a divided legacy. As J. M. Keynes insisted in his obituary memoir, Marshall had been "endowed with a double nature," half scientist and half religious pastor.[6] Keynes here set the tone for the subsequent twentieth-century reception of Marshall's thought, which basically consisted of the development of various parts of his scientific legacy, and the dismissal of the underlying philosophical framework as an uninteresting vestige of religious faith and Victorian moralizing.

Keynes's judgment was no doubt well received in the twentieth century in large part because it accorded with the perspectives of an academic world increasingly under the spell of logical positivism. Today, however, it is no longer possible simply to dismiss metaphysics out of hand as meaningless. Nor does it seem helpful to place an iron curtain between technocratic scientific expertise and discussion of political and moral values. After a century of quietude, political philosophy has once again become an ongoing academic concern.[7] Marshall's metaphysical positions thus warrant renewed examination. But while there can be no doubt as to the intellectual power of Marshall's philosophical system, we also need to be clear as to its limitations. Both can be usefully illustrated by a comparison of aspects of Marshall's thinking with the moral philosophy of Adam Smith; for by means of his mental dualism, Marshall (quite unconsciously) managed to replicate at least some aspects of Smith's naturalistic moral philosophy,

---

[6] Keynes 1925: 11–12.
[7] On the revival of political philosophy and its relationship to the twentieth-century histories of the disciplines of economics and the history of political thought, see Tuck 1993.

while at the same time adhering to the mainstream tradition of moral realism. To appreciate just what this entailed, however, we need to acquaint ourselves briefly with the basics of Smith's voluntarist moral theory.

For Smith, the morality found at any time in any particular nation is, in general, "that which is most suitable to its situation."[8] As situations change, argued Smith, so do our moral judgments. Behind this conception of moral adaptation stands Smith's fundamental concept of sympathy. Sympathy, as Smith uses the term, is an imaginative act whereby a spectator puts her- or himself into the situation of an actor, compares the resultant "sympathetic feelings" with those observed in the actor, and on the basis of the convergence or divergence of these two sets of sentiments, approves or disapproves of the behavior of the actor. Crucially, Smith insists that sympathy "does not arise so much from the view of the passion [of another], as from that of the situation which excites it."[9] Now, Smith further insists that human beings not only desire to approve of the actions of others, but also strive to be the fitting objects of sympathetic approbation. What this means is that the desire for mutual sympathy leads to appropriate modifications in social behavior. Mutual sympathy, in other words, provides a mechanism for the selection of behavior suitable to new social situations. Morality, for Smith, is thus constructed in the process of social life.

Marshall's conception of the evolution of social conventions among primitive human beings has certain affinities with Smith's naturalistic account of moral evolution. For Marshall, human beings, before the advent of self-consciousness, are motivated solely by the desire to obtain pleasure and avoid pain. They achieve this goal primarily by following routine behaviors. When faced with an unprecedented situation, however, these primitive humans act either at random or upon deliberation. In either case, a successful outcome will generate a new routine that in the future may be enacted automatically. The selection mechanism at work here is the Darwinian one, whereby unsuccessful behaviors lead to extinction. Successful behaviors, by contrast, become habits and are then passed on to offspring in the form of instinctual routines. Such a model is readily expanded into an account of social evolution. The social unit for Marshall is that of the individual "race." The survival of any one race depends on the evolution of a set of customary practices that maintain and foster collective life. These may arise by chance

---

[8] *TMS*, 209 (V, 2, 13). This interpretation follows Haakonssen 1981: ch. 3. For the sake of brevity, I have passed over Smith's account of "the impartial spectator." The notion of such a spectator, however, provides not only an important component of Smith's model of moral evolution, but also provides his moral theory as a whole with a normative component.

[9] *TMS*, 12 (I, i, I, 10).

or by way of deliberation but, once established, can be passed on through education and social sanctions. Races that do not arrive at a set of workable social customs will perish. Again, environmental changes may demand an alteration of customs, and those races that do not evolve appropriately face extinction. Thus Marshall, like Smith before him, provides us with an open-ended vision of the evolution of behavioral conventions. That is to say, neither posits a set of universally correct customs or an ideal set of conventions toward which all actual societies are moving.

There are, of course, some fundamental differences in the approaches of Smith and Marshall. For a start, Marshall does not actually regard these open-ended customs as properly moral; they are merely the social equivalent of animal instincts. Morality as such arises only once human beings have separated themselves from nature by way of the development of self-consciousness; and Marshall's approach to morality itself was anything but open-ended. But there is also a significant divergence in the naturalistic explanatory strategies adopted by Smith and Marshall. Smith begins with a social fact – the desire for mutual sympathy among humans. Marshall, by contrast, begins with the relationship between an individual mind and its environment (which may include other individual minds). As such, each thinker is representative of his age. As Hans Aarsleff has pointed out, Smith's conception of mutual sympathy is part and parcel of the same eighteenth-century fascination with sociability that gave rise to a dramatic interest in all forms of communicative activities.[10] Marshall's psychological starting point, however, was indicative of a century in which furious disputes over whether sociability was natural to humanity had given way to bitter disagreement over the nature of the individual human mind. Thus, in place of the social perspectives found in the writings of Smith, we find in Marshall a fusion of historical metaphysics and evolutionary psychology.

This book demonstrates that Marshall did not see economic science as constituting the whole of social philosophy. Rather, almost all aspects of Marshall's economic thought were grounded in his wider philosophical concerns. Today, as illustrated by our difficulties in formulating a political theory that embraces but is not colonized by economic science, Marshall's

---

[10] See Aarsleff 2006. According to John Millar, Smith's early Glasgow lectures were informed by the conviction that the "best method of explaining and illustrating the various powers of the human mind, the most useful part of metaphysics, arises from an examination of the several ways of communicating our thoughts by speech, and from an attention to the principles of those literary compositions which contribute to persuasion or entertainment" (see *Stewart CW*, 10: 11). For Smith's view of economic exchange as a form of rhetorical persuasion, see *LJ(B)*, 493–4.

unified vision surely merits reexamination. This introduction, however, suggests that reexamination will not lead to resurrection. The contrast with Smith's thought alone seems to be decisive here; for while Marshall's dualistic philosophy did indeed allow him to fuse elements of Smith's naturalism with an opposing philosophy of moral realism, such a synthesis came at too high a price. At least, such a conclusion seems unavoidable given the presuppositions of the present study. Smith's thought begins with social relationships established between human beings who, in a variety of ways, communicate with one another. Broadly speaking, this is also the starting point of the contextualist study of Marshall's thought set out in the following pages. But this kind of social perspective disappears in Marshall's thought. On the one hand, he presents an organic vision of an economy composed of individuals who, because they participate in similar industrial practices, therefore develop similar mental routines. On the other hand, he situates these individuals within a historical process that is the result not of human agency, but of abstract spiritual forces. The kind of communicative social sphere that preoccupied Smith is, as it were, cut in two and flattened on either side of Marshall's mental dualism. This is not to say that Smith necessarily provides the answers to our concerns here. What does seem clear, however, is that the emphasis on social communication found in Smith has at least a certain affinity with the philosophical concerns of our own day. Whatever the merits or the limitations of this study, one thing is clear: its presuppositions simply have no place in Marshall's rounded globe of knowledge.

PART I

THE CONTEXTS OF MARSHALL'S
INTELLECTUAL APPRENTICESHIP

ONE

Continuity and Consensus

The State of Long-Term Memories

INTRODUCTION

Although economists continue to discuss many of Marshall's economic ideas, core elements of his early economic thought, not to mention its metaphysical, historical, and psychological grounds, have disappeared from view over the course of a little more than a century. This collective amnesia is related to the fact that key contexts of Marshall's thought – such as the struggle for cultural authority at a moment of Anglican disestablishment – have by now passed beyond our cultural horizons. But it is also an illustration of the fact that a society remembers its past selectively. The Victorians lost sight of the particularities of eighteenth-century political and intellectual life as a whole, and indeed consistently and systematically misinterpreted Adam Smith.[1] But just as in the twentieth century, where the various constructions of the history of political economy served divergent disciplinary and wider polemical purposes, so Victorian formulations of this history were the product of nineteenth-century intellectual and political developments. This chapter points to a number of those developments in order to provide a context for our subsequent investigation of Marshall's early intellectual life. It explores these developments by way of a discussion of some of the Victorian versions of the history of political economy.

Much of the discussion of this chapter is organized around the thought of two prominent Cambridge liberals, Leslie Stephen and Henry Sidgwick. These two "lights of liberalism" provide useful focal points, not least because

---

[1] Victorian anachronism was by no means confined to the intellectual history of the eighteenth century. On Erskine May's misunderstanding of the political history of the reign of George III, see Butterfield 1959: 151. We may note here that May's *Constitutional History of England* (3rd ed., 1871) was used by Marshall as a historical guide in his notes on Smith's *Wealth of Nations*.

the secondary literature that has been constructed around them has cast long shadows on the history of Cambridge moral science in this period, shadows that have obscured much that is distinctive about Marshall's early thought. In his memoir of Marshall, J. M. Keynes quoted from Marshall's own 1900 memorial tribute to Sidgwick, in which he declared that in the late 1860s and early 1870s he had been "in substance" Sidgwick's "pupil in Moral Sciences."[2] Following this lead, and despite the well-known animosity that later developed between the two men, standard commentaries have tended to assimilate accounts of Marshall's early Cambridge years into the "golden age" portraits of "Henry Sidgwick's Cambridge" painted by F. R. and Q. D. Leavis. Yet in the same commentaries we almost invariably find a sketch of Marshall's early loss of religious faith and subsequent conversion to agnosticism that draws heavily on Noel Annan's picture of Leslie Stephen as a "godless Victorian" – a portrait that, we should note, was developed in opposition to the Leavises' account of Sidgwick.[3] Drawing uncritically (and often unconsciously) as it does on the work of both Annan and the Leavises, the conventional picture of Marshall's early Cambridge years is, not surprisingly, somewhat hazy. By explicitly situating Marshall's early thought in terms of its divergence from the opinions of both Sidgwick and Stephen – which themselves were far from identical – it should be possible to come closer to developing a historical image of Marshall's early thought, rendered without the various mythological distortions that have proved so appealing to so many associated with twentieth-century Cambridge.

This chapter has four sections, each of which explores an aspect of the nineteenth-century construction of the history of political economy.[4] The first three sections explore various contexts and resources relevant to Marshall, while the fourth provides an overview of the position that Marshall had arrived at by around 1873. The first section will survey some aspects of the transformation of Adam Smith's intellectual legacy in the first half of the nineteenth century and, in the process, provide an account of the consensual mid-Victorian interpretation of Smith's intentions as a moral

---

[2]   Keynes 1925: 7.
[3]   See Q. Leavis 1947 and F. Leavis 1952. Rothblatt 1968 replicates key contours of the "golden age" portrait, for which he is duly criticized by Annan 1984: ch. 12. But as John Gibbins has pointed out, all of these interpretations share the common fault of exaggerating the significance of the break between agnostic academic liberals and the liberal Anglicans who shaped Cambridge thought in the 1860s (Gibbins 2001: 61).
[4]   There has been insufficient attention to the role of histories of political economy in the history of political economy, but useful surveys can be found in Backhouse 2004 and Craufurd Goodwin's entry, "The History of Economic Thought," in *The New Palgrave Dictionary of Economics*.

philosopher. The second section situates the changing attitude of Stephen to political economy in the third quarter of the nineteenth century. As an undergraduate at Cambridge in midcentury, Stephen had taken J. S. Mill's *Principles of Political Economy* (1848) as his bible and had assumed that within its pages he could find sure grounds for his radical political ideas. After 1868, however, Stephen grew disillusioned with the current state of liberal social thinking and, by way of his in-depth study of eighteenth-century thought, came to the conclusion that the science of political economy as founded by Adam Smith now needed to be integrated into a broader evolutionary science of sociology. The third section examines the way in which Sidgwick sought to bolster the authority of J. S. Mill's version of political economy by means of a philosophical notion of consensus. Sidgwick was concerned to show that Mill's political economy remained valid, while Stephen went back to Smith in order to explain why, in recent years, political economy had lost its authority. Both, however, were agreed that the history of political economy had involved no substantial changes in either doctrine or methodology. In the concluding section, we briefly survey how, by 1873, Marshall had come to the conclusion that continuity in the history of economic thought meant continuous development rather than continual stasis.[5] Such a conclusion, it will be suggested, related to the ways in which, unlike either Stephen or Sidgwick, Marshall made use of history to conduct a reformulation of the doctrines and the methods of political economy.

MID-VICTORIAN IMAGES OF ADAM SMITH

Shortly before his death, Adam Smith ordered the destruction of sixteen volumes of unfinished work. Consequently, for well over a century commentators interpreted Smith almost exclusively in terms of the two works published in his lifetime, the *Theory of Moral Sentiments* (1759) and the *Wealth of Nations* (1776). But the discovery of two different sets of student notes on Smith's lectures on jurisprudence, first in 1896 and then in 1958, has recently fueled an increasingly sophisticated revision of the conventional image of Smith's thought that had been forged over the course of the nineteenth century.[6] In light of this recent scholarship, Smith can now be seen as engaged in the gradual development of an overarching "science of the

---

[5] Marshall's strategy with regard to the history of political economy replicates an earlier nineteenth-century development in Whig political history (see Burrow 1981: ch. 2).

[6] For revisions of the nineteenth-century image of Smith, see especially Haakonssen 1981, Hont and Ignatieff 1983, and Winch 1978. See also Haakonssen 1982, Pocock 1985, 2003: ch. 16, Rothschild 1994, and Winch 1991, 1992, 1996. But for a revisionist revisionism that

legislator," within which political economy formed an important, but by no means dominant branch.[7] Within this science of the legislator, a historically conceived theory of jurisprudence provided a crucial link between moral philosophy and political economy. As we saw in the introduction, Smith's naturalistic theory of moral judgment was framed in terms of the sympathetic response of a spectator, who related any action to the specific circumstances within which it was performed. Of such moral judgments, however, Smith insisted that those relating to the violation of the rights of another person were more certain, and so formed a category apart from those judgments relating to virtuous actions. This distinction, which was itself a reformulation of Grotius's distinction between perfect and imperfect rights, allowed Smith to separate his theory of jurisprudence from the rest of his moral philosophy.[8] It was this separate theory of jurisprudence that came to provide the organizing framework for his subsequent study of political economy. Once this missing jurisprudential link is recovered, much of the *Wealth of Nations* can then be read as an extended treatise on the relationship between commercial activity and the provision of justice.[9]

In his biography of Adam Smith (first published in 1794), Dugald Stewart described Smith's decision to burn the vast bulk of his unpublished papers as an "irreparable injury to letters."[10] As the Edinburgh Professor of Moral Philosophy between 1785 and 1810, whose lectures were attended not only by future founders of the *Edinburgh Review* such as Henry Brougham and Francis Horner, but also by that future radical polemicist James Mill, Stewart played a pivotal role in the shaping of Smith's posthumous reputation as well as his intellectual legacy. But as Haakonssen has pointed out, Stewart's changes to the content of Smith's political economy, which stemmed from his different philosophical commitments, effectively brought about the dissolution

presents Smith's *Wealth of Nations* as marking the point where a tradition of Gladstonian liberalism emerged from the limits of the civic humanist tradition, see Robertson 1983.

[7] Winch 1983: 256–7.

[8] This interpretation is derived from Haakonssen 1981. For further discussion of Smith and natural law, see Forbes 1982, Haakonssen 1996, Hont and Ignatieff 1983: 26–44, and J. R. Moore 2006. For a summary of recent scholarship on the more general history of Protestant natural law, viewed as a series of responses to Richard Tuck's 1987 call to rescue "modern" natural law from its assimilation to neo-Thomism and its marginalization by neo-Kantianism, see Hunter 2001: 356.

[9] See Winch 1978: 70. Hont and Ignatieff take the jurisprudential interpretation further by arguing that because of his emphasis on the productivity of specialized labor, Smith was able to overcome the traditional natural law antithesis between the private individuation of God's dominion and the rights of the propertyless to adequate provision (Hont and Ignatieff 1983: 26–44).

[10] *Stewart CW*, 10: 74.

of Smith's conception of a science of the legislator.[11] Stewart's concern was to fashion the common sense philosophy of Thomas Reid into a pedagogical tool for the virtuous mental cultivation of Scotland's future leaders.[12] He therefore rejected Smith's voluntarist moral theory, the emphasis on the circumstances of an action of which accounted for the historical component running through Smith's science of the legislator. Stewart turned rather to Reid's theory that moral judgments relate directly to objective moral qualities in actions. But from such a common sense perspective, the ground of Smith's differentiation of jurisprudence from the rest of moral philosophy vanished, and political economy became for Stewart a direct extension of moral philosophy. Furthermore, Stewart now insisted that political economy was concerned with the factors on which the happiness of the people directly depends and as such should be cultivated before any study of forms of government.[13] In Stewart's hands political economy, previously a branch of Smith's science of the legislator, not only lost its historical form and its jurisprudential foundations, but was now declared independent of any science of politics.

Stewart not only coupled political economy directly to moral philosophy, but also bequeathed to the later nineteenth century a revised classification of the sciences and a revised formulation of the correct procedures of Baconian induction in the moral sciences. Objecting to Smith's agreement with the ancient division of philosophy into natural philosophy, ethics, and logic, Stewart insisted that "*Matter* and *Mind* ... are the two most general heads which ought to form the ground-work of an Encyclopedical classification of the sciences and arts." In this twofold division, political economy was to be considered a part of "the inductive Philosophy of the Human Mind."[14] By "inductive," Stewart here meant the kind of introspective philosophical examination of human consciousness developed by Reid. Such introspection was necessary, Reid had insisted, because the realm of mind was fundamentally distinct from that of matter and could not be explained by analogy with the external world (the mistake, Reid insisted, of David Hume's theory of ideas). The moral sciences must adopt their own method, that of mental introspection. What this method revealed, Reid held, was a

---

[11] Haakonssen 1996: ch. 7.

[12] Phillipson 1983: 96–7.

[13] See, e.g., *Stewart CW*, 8: 21. But as Haakonssen points out, Stewart elsewhere effectively denies that political philosophy is capable of scientific treatment at all (Haakonssen 1996: 226).

[14] *Stewart CW*, 1: 17–22, emphasis in original; see also *Stewart CW*, 8: 17, and *WN*, 766 (V. i. f. 23). Smith's commitment to the ancient arrangement cannot have been particularly strong given that he substituted rhetoric for logic in his early teaching at Glasgow.

variety of innate powers of the mind together with a number of self-evident "first principles of common sense." Smith had eschewed metaphysical accounts of human nature and claimed that, as a matter of fact, in different social situations human beings generate different moral conventions. But where Smith had looked to the different forms of social life in order to explain the variety of moral sentiments generated in history, Stewart now insisted that the political economist must rest his reasoning on an introspective account of the universal principles and powers of human nature.[15]

As Neil De Marchi has pointed out, John Stuart Mill's enormously influential essay "On the Definition of Political Economy" (1836) follows "the pure methodological tradition of Dugald Stewart."[16] Mill divided "the whole field of human knowledge" into "physical science, and moral or psychological science," and insisted that the methodology of the moral sciences was distinct from that of the physical sciences.[17] Experiment in a moral science such as political economy was not possible, because irregularly operating disturbing causes could neither be isolated nor accounted for by repeated observations. The implication was that history must be rejected as the ground of reasoning in political economy and replaced by a set of a priori assumptions, which were themselves derived from the physical sciences and from the introspective inductions of the mental science of psychology.[18] Of course, and as we shall see, Mill founded this Baconian methodology on an account of the human mind derived from a science of psychology that stood in direct opposition to the mental philosophy embraced by Stewart. Nineteenth-century debates between associationist psychologists, such as Mill, and intuitionist mental philosophers, like Stewart, turned on disagreements over the correct conclusions to be drawn from the introspective observation of mental experience. But in the dust raised by these philosophical disputes, the distinctive historical rendering of Grotius's natural rights theory, which constituted the "Newtonian" moral philosophy of Adam Smith, simply disappeared from view.[19]

---

[15] I am indebted to Knud Haakonssen for criticism of an earlier draft of this paragraph.

[16] De Marchi 1983: 166. De Marchi criticizes Hollander 1985 for omitting the role of Stewart in his account of the history of method from Smith to Ricardo and J. S. Mill. For an account of methodological reflection in political economy between Stewart and Mill, see Fontana 1985: ch. 3. Corsi argues that the influence of Stewart on J. S. Mill was mediated by way of the Oxford Noetics, particularly Richard Whately (Corsi 1987: 136–7). On Stewart's political science and its diffusion, see Winch's "The System of the North" in Collini, Winch, and Burrow 1983.

[17] *Mill CW*, 4: 316, and see De Marchi 1983: 169, 174.

[18] Cf. *Stewart CW*, 8: 13.

[19] For Smith's discussion of Newton's method, see *LRBL*, 146.

It was in England in the early nineteenth century that political economy became known as "the dismal science." In contrast to Smith's ambivalence concerning the future, Stewart's moral and scientific objectivism allowed him to present a cautious yet glowing picture of "continually accelerating" progress as, aided by the printing press and the education of all orders of society, the human mind accumulated and disseminated not only mental illumination but also enlarged sentiments of humanity.[20] But such an optimistic vision proved impossible to sustain in the face of the political and social impact of the French Revolution and Napoleonic Wars.[21] It was also unpalatable to a generation increasingly influenced by an Evangelical religious awakening that emphasized sin, hellfire, and both personal and collective divine punishment. A key moment in the transformation of Scottish into English political economy was the insistence by T. R. Malthus that humanity, while driven by sexual passion, was otherwise "inert, sluggish, and averse from labour, unless compelled by necessity."[22] On this reading of human nature, productive labor beyond that of animal reproduction was driven by fear and need, far more than by imaginative desire and social vanity. In order to explain the motivations that propel commercial society, Smith had looked primarily to that "desire of bettering our condition" that "comes with us from the womb, and never leaves us till we go into the grave."[23] But to those radical political economists who had absorbed the languages of the Benthamite utilitarian calculus and associationist psychology, Malthus taught the lesson that, in stimulating social labor, pain and fear of punishment were at least as efficacious as pleasure and hope of reward.

Boyd Hilton has taught us to see that the bleak prognosis of Ricardian political economy was in many ways but a secular version of the then-prevalent Evangelical vision of mortal life. Malthus's initial assertion that subsistence can be expanded only arithmetically was subsequently developed into a law of diminishing returns in agriculture and combined with

---

[20] *Stewart CW*, 2: 487. On Stewart's optimism, see Haakonssen 1996: ch. 7 and Hont 1983: 310–13. Smith's ambivalence centered on his conviction that the various European nations would be ruined by their national debts (*WN*, 911 [V, iii, 10]). For the British and European context of Smith's concerns, see Hont 2005: ch. 5 and Sonenscher 2007.

[21] For aspects of the transmutation of Scottish into English political economy in the period just before and after the French Revolution, see Burrow 1988, the first three chapters of Collini et al. 1983, Hilton 2006, Jones 2004, Rothschild 2001, Teichgraeber 2000, and (especially) Winch 1996. On Christian political economy, see Hilton 1988, the very clear statement of Evangelical economics in Hilton 2006: 183–4, and Waterman 1991, and for the wider Evangelical awakening, see Ward 1992.

[22] Malthus 1976: 120.

[23] *WN*, 341 (II, iii, 28).

the further assertion that population grew geometrically. When formulated by Ricardo into a system in which three classes of landlords, capitalists, and laborers competed for income derived from a single fund, the result was a very dismal picture of human prospects indeed. Ricardian political economists saw in the future a "stationary-state" in which accumulation had ceased and wages fallen to subsistence levels. Here was a secular version of the Evangelical expectation of the immanent arrival of a catastrophic future in which the sins of both individuals and society would be chastised by divine retribution. For both Benthamites and Evangelicals, the world was ultimately a machine for the enforcement of moral education by means of an exact and exacting system of justice. Where Evangelicals saw human nature as bestial, corrupt, and sinful, philosophical radicals such as Ricardo's mentors Jeremy Bentham and James Mill conceived of man as born "dissocial" – but, as Carlyle put it, strove to promote "man's salvation as a social being."[24] Evangelicals embraced a retributive theology, in which free trade and laissez-faire social policies were advocated so as not to interfere with a divine machinery of providential punishment. In this mechanistic theology, moral failing received its just reward – poverty and bankruptcy. For philosophical radicals, it was the state and the market that provided the instruments of moral correction and education. But whether the system of rewards and punishments was conceived of in secular or religious terms, in the visions of both philosophical radicals and Evangelicals, punishment was far more visible than reward.

The role of J. S. Mill's 1836 essay on method in this story of the development of early-nineteenth-century English political economy is Janus-faced. Mill's essay was in part a response to Thomas Babington Macaulay's 1829 assault on James Mill's a priori method. John Stuart was forced to conclude that much of Macaulay's case against his father's method was simply unanswerable. Nevertheless, by 1836 he was convinced that because political economy (unlike the science of politics) dealt with just one class of human actions, it could indeed rest arguments on the a priori psychological premise that such actions were governed by self-interest.[25] What economic agents qua economic agents were interested in, according to Mill, was acquiring wealth and luxury and avoiding labor. Adam Smith had characterized commercial agents as "prudent" – a virtue that, according to

---

[24] Quoted in Hilton 2006: 333. This discussion is derived from various works by Hilton, but see in particular Hilton 1989: 60–2, 2006: 326, 520.

[25] De Marchi points out that Mill nevertheless replaced his father's syllogistic method with one derived from the science of mechanics in which multiple premises were to be composed and resolved (De Marchi 1983: 167–70).

Smith, "commands a certain cold esteem, but seems not entitled to any very ardent love or admiration."[26] "Economic man" (as Mill's abstraction was soon christened) appeared to be simply selfish and lazy. Inevitably, moralists from Thomas Carlyle and S. T. Coleridge to John Ruskin and beyond castigated Mill and his disciples in political economy as practitioners of an amoral and even immoral science. Certainly, Mill could be said to have taken all that was most dismal in the Benthamite characterization of human nature and packed it into the science of political economy. But by explicitly insisting that such a package was an abstraction, Mill implicitly pointed to a more noble, cultured, and self-sacrificing side of human nature. As we shall shortly see, Mill in this way laid the grounds for an optimistic interpretation of the pessimistic tendencies deduced by political economy. At the same time, and by the same means, Mill also provided the framework for what would become the conventional mid-Victorian reading of Adam Smith's intentions as a moral philosopher.

After Mill had established the a priori method of political economy on an account of economic motive derived from psychology, it evidently became hard to imagine that any other approach had ever existed. In Marshall's copy of Buckle's extremely popular *History of Civilisation in England*, first published in 1858, we find a vertical line drawn in the margin adjacent to the following explanation of how, in the *Wealth of Nations*, Smith had obtained his results by

arguing from principles which the selfish part of human nature exclusively supplied, and he omitted those sympathetic feelings of which every human being possesses some share, but which he could not take into consideration, without producing a problem, the number of whose complications it would have been hopeless to unravel.[27]

Buckle thus explained how in the *Wealth of Nations* Smith employed a deductive method that was based on psychological principles derived from the selfish part of human nature. But such a reading of Smith's method in political economy was in essence no more than a projection onto Smith of J. S. Mill's formulation of the methodology of political economy. Buckle further insisted that in his *Theory of Moral Sentiments* Smith had also employed deductive reasoning, but in this case from principles supplied by the sympathetic or altruistic part of human nature. Such an interpretation of the *Theory of Moral Sentiments* rested on a gross misreading. For Smith, "sympathy" was

[26] *TMS*, 216 (VI, i, 14).
[27] Buckle 1867: III, 318.

a basic *mechanism* or constituent of moral judgment, by means of which we use our imagination to put ourselves into the situation of another and judge how we would have acted. Buckle, however, took Smith to be using the term in its more standard mid-nineteenth-century usage to refer to a benevolent or non-self-regarding *motivation*.[28] Nevertheless, Buckle's was the unchallenged consensus reading until around 1870 and, despite challenges from Cliffe Leslie and indeed also Marshall, in many ways continued as the dominant interpretation of Smith far into the twentieth century.

Buckle's reading of Smith's method was in fact indicative of a new moral and political climate: from midcentury onward, nascent confidence and guarded optimism came to replace anxiety and pessimism. In the decades after 1850, the obsession with original sin and hellfire declined, while political stability was no longer felt to be under threat. At the same time, earlier industrial uncertainties gave way to a long boom, and reaction to the Irish famine produced a retreat from policies of unmitigated laissez-faire. In such an environment, an earlier expectation that future prospects amounted to either immanent catastrophe or impending stagnation began to give way to a more optimistic convention in which gradual and continued social progress was perceived to be the norm. This revised attitude toward the future went hand in hand with a widespread rejection of the tendency of Evangelicals and Benthamites to focus exclusively on the bestial and selfish features of human nature. Future progress came increasingly to be seen as a consequence of moral improvement, and human goodness now became as much an object of public discourse as a moral failing. But such revised expectations of the future and amended conventions concerning human nature also went hand in hand with a revised reading of the past: in the more confident and forgiving climate that arose around midcentury, it seemed only natural that if the political economy founded by Smith was indeed solely concerned with the selfish part of human nature, then in his other great treatise, on moral sentiments, Smith *must* have concerned himself with the selfless and benevolent side of human nature.

Stefan Collini has pointed out that in associating Smith's two treatises with a basic division within human nature itself, Buckle spoke with the "voice of the mid-nineteenth-century."[29] Buckle's reading of Smith, he argues, was

---

[28] Buckle's formulation appears to have contributed to the subsequent construction in Germany of "Das Adam Smith Problem." On the confusion at the heart of the "Adam Smith problem," see the various accounts in Haakonssen 2006 (especially Broadie, pp. 164–5, and Mehta, p. 246), and Raphael 2007: ch. 13, where Buckle's picture of Smith's work is described as "absurd."

[29] Collini 1991: 67.

indicative of the way that, after midcentury, educated Victorians habitually divided their substantive moral universe into two exhaustive classes of actions and motivations: selfish and altruistic. Such a division, Collini further explains, while articulated according to different intellectual idioms, arose in the first instance not from the principles of this or that moral philosophy, but from the cluster of moral assumptions that, from midcentury onward, informed the everyday experience of educated middle-class existence.[30] Thus, by the end of the 1850s, both secular liberals and romantic liberal Anglicans regularly contrasted the lower self with a higher, "non-self-regarding" self, and both associated the higher self with an ideal of "manliness." As will become clear in subsequent chapters, there existed key differences between the romantic and the liberal interpretations of "manly character." Nevertheless, the considerable common ground in the moral sensibilities of midcentury secular liberals and romantics has led Collini to write of a "moralizing of political economy" in this period and to suggest that "the temper" of mid-Victorian liberalism had more in common with that of its romantic critics than it did with that of later liberalism.[31] Although we should guard against exaggerating the theoretical convergence of liberal and romantic positions, it is certainly the case that in the decades after midcentury secular liberals increasingly came to agree with the long-standing liberal Anglican insistence that social progress rested on the continued victory of the higher self in its struggle with the lower part of human nature.

Liberal Anglican attitudes toward political economy in the first half of the century can be illustrated by the views of the Coleridgean churchman Maurice. When he applied for the Oxford Chair of Political Economy in 1837, Maurice declared that "political economy is not the foundation of morals and politics, but must have them as its foundation or be worth nothing."[32] Maurice was not elected to the chair, and so did not commence the arduous task of placing political economy on properly moral foundations. Nevertheless, the basic approach that he intended to take with regard to reformulating political economy is clear enough from his later

---

[30] Collini 1991: 74.
[31] Collini 1991: 84; see also Collini 1989: 54 and Hilton's comments on p. 60 of the same volume.
[32] Maurice 1884: I, 209–10. If he was successful in his candidacy, Maurice went on to explain, he would "of course endeavour to master the details of the subject – with its principles, alas! I am not acquainted, for I cannot call the notions which I find in the books about it by that august name." Maurice was not successful in 1837, and neither was the Mauricean clergyman J. B. Mayor, who in the 1863 election to the Cambridge Chair of Political Economy was defeated by Henry Fawcett.

pronouncements as a Christian Socialist. In concrete terms, Maurice was convinced that the church of England embodied a principle of cooperation that had the potential to counter the competitive principle at work in modern society.[33] But on a more abstract level it is clear that Maurice, like other romantic critics, wanted a science of political economy founded on an ideal of the higher as opposed to the lower self. The construction of such a reformed science, however, would have involved more than the mere substitution of a self-regarding economic machine by a charitable, cooperative, and cultured human agent. Where Mill's orthodox formulation of political economy was founded on the attempt to identify lawlike relations within existing states of society, Maurice's vision of Christian political economy was of a teleological science that would strive to establish a moral ideal toward which society could progress. Whether with regard to the individual or society, Maurice and other liberal Anglican thinkers opposed Ricardian pessimism and Evangelical simplicities with a vision of moral and social improvement. In the years after midcentury, Maurice and other liberal Anglicans would find that a newly optimistic approach to orthodox political economy among secular liberals, while by no means constituting the looked-for moral reformation of the science, at least established some common ground between them.

The methodological practices of orthodox political economists after midcentury reflected the same moral dualism that informed Buckle's reading of Smith. Mid-Victorian liberals subscribed unhesitatingly to Mill's definition of the science of political economy as founded on hypothetical deductions concerning the behavior of an abstract "economic man," and yet in their practical engagement with social issues consistently looked to the moral improvement of the working classes in order to derive from Ricardo's pessimistic doctrines an optimistic vision of the future.[34] Henry Fawcett, for example, had no doubt that, as a science, political economy dealt only with the wealth-begetting characteristics of human nature, and yet consistently insisted on a connection between moral strength of character and economic betterment. In Chapter Five we shall see the extent to which Fawcett was following directly in the footsteps of Mill in his *Principles of Political Economy*. Nevertheless, it seems worthwhile to anticipate some of this later discussion by examining here the juxtaposition of two polar opposite characterizations of human nature as illustrated in the chapter entitled

---

[33] Jones 2003: 179.
[34] On Mill's *Principles*, see Chapter Five of this book.

"Political Economy" in Leslie Stephen's *Life of Henry Fawcett* (1885).[35] At one point in this chapter, Stephen described how the wages of the laboring class are determined by the supply and demand for labor. If "the labouring class chooses always to multiply up to the verge of its means of subsistence," he explained, the rule determining wages "is greatly simplified and gives rise to what has been called the 'iron law' of Ricardo." Ricardo's critics, Stephen continued,

> sometimes speak as if he had intended to demonstrate the absolute impossibility of a permanent rise in wages. That is only true on the assumption of the improvidence of the labouring class. His argument is substantially that they can only raise the price of their services by limiting the supply – that is, by keeping down their own numbers. Assuming that they have sufficient self-command to raise the standard of comfort, the action of supply and demand will be in their favour, as, in the contrary case, it will be against them.[36]

Stephen's assertion to the contrary notwithstanding, an emphasis on the farsightedness and self-control of the working class was not prominent in the writings of Ricardo. It became a dominant part of the orthodox tradition only through the optimistic interpretation of the doctrines of Ricardo and Malthus set down in Mill's *Principles*. In addition, and as Collini observes, Fawcett's generation emphasized the morally educative impact of the discipline imposed by economic activity to a much greater extent than had Ricardo and his contemporaries.[37] In the passage just quoted, Stephen posited a causal connection from working-class self-control to improvements in working-class wages. But for a midcentury political economist like Fawcett, a causal connection in the opposite direction was equally significant, and the fluctuations of the labor market could be expected to gradually inculcate among the working classes the moral virtues of responsibility and self-control. Put simply, the market created self-reliant and self-restrained economic agents, and such moral characteristics provided the keys to material improvement. This was particularly so in the case of the labor market, where a Malthusian perspective entailed that the self-control characteristic of a higher "manly" self could be seen to translate into a positively altruistic and self-sacrificing attitude toward the material conditions bequeathed to future generations. Thus, by so emphasizing the general interaction between

---

[35] Harvie singles out this chapter as "probably the best account of the economic beliefs held by Fawcett's generation" (Harvie 1976: 305, n. 82). For an account of Stephen's *Life* as "an appeal from the old to the new Liberals," see Collini 1991: 173.

[36] Stephen 1885: 155–6.

[37] Collini 1991: 184.

the "manly" character of the higher self and the mechanisms of a market economy, midcentury political economists transformed Ricardo's dismal vision of an impending stationary state into an optimistic vision of gradual social advancement, amelioration, and progress.[38]

AN ACADEMIC LIBERAL HISTORY

By the mid-1870s the orthodox method of political economy had come under sustained attack, and Buckle's reading of Smith had been revised in a number of directions. For our purposes, these related events can be usefully approached by way of a discussion of Stephen's intellectual development after midcentury. In the 1850s and early 1860s, Stephen had been part of a small clique of radicals in Cambridge who had embraced the logical, political, and economic writings of J. S. Mill. By the late 1860s, these "Cambridge Millites" were no longer a fringe sect, and it had become clear to the nation at large that both of England's ancient universities were now the new and apparently permanent home of advanced liberal political thought. The high-water mark in the fortunes of what has come to be called "academic liberalism" was the publication in 1867 of the democratic manifesto *Essays on Reform*, a collection of essays by academic liberals, positivists, and liberal Anglicans in support of franchise reform. Following his loss of religious faith and the subsequent resignation of his fellowship, Stephen had by this time left Cambridge for London and begun to earn his living as a writer for the periodical press. Nevertheless, he was still marching in step with the academic vanguard of advanced liberal opinion, as is indicated by his contribution to the *Essays*. In the wake of the events that followed the passage of the Second Reform Bill in 1868, however, Stephen and many academic liberals came to the conclusion that the political analysis contained in the *Essays* had been woefully inadequate. In Stephen's case, the resultant crisis in his political thinking led not only to disillusionment with orthodox midcentury political economy, but also to a sophisticated reconstruction of the place of Adam Smith in the history of "English" social thought.

Stephen's contribution to *Essays on Reform* can be considered a representative sample of academic liberal thinking just before the passage of the Reform Bill. Stephen argued that rather than giving rise to the direct parliamentary participation of the working classes, the extension of the franchise to the working classes would in fact bring about the election of

---

[38] Hilton 1989: 60–2.

radical intellectuals like Stephen and his university friends.[39] If such a view was widespread among academic liberals in 1867, so too was the sense of disappointment, when in the general election of 1868 the new voters conspicuously failed to return more than a handful of academic liberals to Parliament. Academic liberal disillusionment was complete when it subsequently became apparent that the manipulations, dishonesty, and compromises of party politics had succeeded in substantially derailing the radical agenda of the Gladstone administration (the most acrimonious issue of the time, it is worth noting, being the role of the established church in the education of the nation's youth). As Christopher Harvie points out, the academic liberal contributions to *Essays on Reform* had, in general, amounted to a political intervention rather than a deeply distilled philosophical analysis of democratic politics.[40] By the early 1870s, this had indeed become clear to many of the essayists. The root problem with the kind of political argument that informed the *Essays*, as Stephen's own contribution amply illustrated, was a deep-seated failure to adequately theorize the role that academic liberals would henceforth play in the wake of any successful agitation on behalf of electoral reform.[41] Stephen's response to the emerging crisis of academic liberal political thought was to withdraw from active political life and to rethink the theoretical basis of his understanding of modern society.

Some of the fruits of this reflection were harvested in Stephen's *History of English Thought in the Eighteenth Century*, first published in 1876. As Jeffrey von Arx has shown, Stephen's *History* as a whole can be read as a prolegomenon to a theory and practice of intellectual leadership capable of meeting the dangers posed by organized religion in the late nineteenth century. In his introduction, Stephen explained that social progress was founded on intellectual progress, that such intellectual progress was the product of a small elite, but that a belief accepted by that elite must also be impressed on "the imagination of the ignorant and the stupid, or it will remain forever an esoteric doctrine" incapable "of becoming an important factor in the intellectual development of the race."[42] The conclusion that Stephen drew from his study of eighteenth-century thought was that because the rationalism of the deists and other free-thinkers had been isolated from social life, advanced English thought as a whole had been unable to resist the popular

---

[39] von Arx 1985: 18.

[40] Harvie 1976: 151–2.

[41] Harvie regards this lack of theory of political leadership as the central failure of academic liberalism (Harvie 1976: 13, 142).

[42] Stephen 1962: I, 60.

religious awakening at the end of the century. Behind this historical conclusion stood Stephen's growing conviction that the passage of the Second
Reform Bill had opened up a new struggle for the hearts and minds of the
masses. Such a struggle, Stephen believed, would be waged between clerical
forces of superstition and reaction, on the one hand, and progressive secular intellectuals, on the other.[43] The political disputes of the early 1870s over
the role of the church in the education of the nation's youth were thus, for
Stephen, indicative of the cultural politics of the modern age.

Stephen drew two contemporary political lessons from his study of the
eighteenth century. First of all, he concluded that eighteenth-century English
rationalism had lost the cultural battle to the forces of religion in large part
because it had remained on a purely intellectual level and had made no contact with the "vulgar multitude." The radical intellectuals of Stephen's own
day should therefore take pains to conscript the arts to the cause of secular
culture, and so engage the imagination of the masses.[44] But Stephen further
argued that not only had eighteenth-century rationalism failed to engage
the masses, it had also failed to understand them. The rationalism of the
eighteenth century, in other words, had been devoid of sociological insight.
Radical intellectuals in the later nineteenth century must therefore work to
understand the forces that mold the history of society. For this task, Stephen
concluded, orthodox political economy was wholly inadequate. Political
economy as received from the pen of Mill was, for Stephen, essentially the
same science that had been first developed by Adam Smith. It was, in other
words, a characteristic product of eighteenth-century "English" rationalism.
Where Stephen in his radical youth had rested his political analysis on the
tenets of orthodox political economy, an older and possibly wiser Stephen
now sought to ground his revised political thought in a new evolutionary
science of society.

It is conventional to interpret Stephen at this time as simply under the
general evolutionary spell to which so many succumbed in these years. But
if Darwin and Spencer provided him with an evolutionary model in the
image of which a nineteenth-century science of society was to be made, it
was Henry Maine who provided Stephen with the grounds of his historical depiction of Adam Smith's thought. Maine's *Ancient Law* had generated
interest and excitement from the moment of publication in 1861. Within
a decade, however, critics of mainstream political economy had perceived
that Maine's scholarship had provided them with a useful stick with which

---

[43] von Arx 1985: 21–2.
[44] von Arx 1985: 60.

to beat the reigning orthodoxy.[45] As we shall discuss further in Chapter Six, in *Ancient Law* Maine had contrasted the "historical method" of the nineteenth century with the eighteenth-century adoption of an ancient natural law tradition that (or so Maine claimed) identified society with a static state of nature. Maine's work thus provided a framework in which Smith's *Wealth of Nations* could be criticized as founded on a static and now-discredited conception of nature. Given that it was generally accepted that the basic shape and structure of political economy had remained constant since its formation by Adam Smith, such a criticism of the *Wealth of Nations* was effectively an attack on the mainstream political economy of the day. Thus Maine provided Stephen with a useful historical map in his search for the roots of the problems with contemporary liberal social thought.

Stephen was by no means the only thinker who found in Maine's work a means to reconceptualize the thought of Adam Smith and, in so doing, to draw revisionist lessons with regard to contemporary political economy. Buckle, it will be recalled, had stated that in the *Wealth of Nations* Smith had employed a deductive method with principles derived from the selfish part of human nature. In his 1870 *Fortnightly Review* essay, "The Political Economy of Adam Smith," the Anglo-Irish political economist Cliffe Leslie seized on Maine's account of eighteenth-century social thought to argue that Smith had in fact employed two methods: an inductive, or historical, method derived from Montesquieu and a deductive, or a priori, method derived from jurisprudence and founded on an ancient conception of "nature." What we witness here, which indeed would soon become characteristic of the revised approaches to Smith developed in the 1870s, is a new recognition of the importance of jurisprudence in Smith's overall project, combined with a fundamental misconception as to the actual nature of Smith's historicist reworking of the natural law tradition. What mattered to Cliffe Leslie, however, was that in Maine he had now found a means of criticizing the reigning orthodoxy of his own day. Maine's scholarship, he explained, had revealed that the deductive method rested on "that theory of Nature which, descending through Roman jural philosophy from the speculations of Greece, taught that there is a simple Code of Nature which human institutions have disturbed." He hardly needed to add that Maine had "explored the fallacies lurking in the terms Nature and Natural

---

[45] That the potentially subversive implications of Maine's work were not perceived earlier is illustrated by the way that many of the contributions to *Essays on Reform* combined elements of J. S. Mill's social philosophy with elements of Maine's historical scholarship (on which, see Collini 1991: 178 and Harvie 1976: 155).

Law."[46] The implication of Maine's scholarship, therefore, was that political economy must reject the deductive method and turn instead to the historical method that Smith had derived from Montesquieu.[47]

In the discussion of Adam Smith's economic thought in Stephen's *History of English Thought in the Eighteenth Century*, we see another form of appropriation of Maine's arguments. Like Buckle, before him, Stephen insisted that "from the appearance of the 'Wealth of Nations' the main outlines and chief methods" of political economy had been "distinctly marked out."[48] In other words, Stephen did not depart from the midcentury convention that there existed an identity of method and basic doctrine from Smith through Mill. But like Cliffe Leslie, Stephen insisted that the eighteenth-century identification of society with an unchanging natural order, and its associated doctrine of natural rights, was "everywhere in the background" of the *Wealth of Nations* and was responsible for the fact that in Smith's treatise there is "a whole side of the question which is left in obscurity."[49] Stephen was not referring to altruistic motivations or inductive inferences, but rather to an analysis of the historical forces that shape the evolution of society. Thus Stephen differed from Cliffe Leslie in identifying the modern (i.e., nineteenth-century) "historical method" not with inductive historical inquiry, but with a science of society founded on a philosophy of progress. Given this formulation, Stephen could reject Mill's proclamation of the methodological independence of political economy and assert that any development of social thought past the point reached by Smith necessitated that political economy henceforth "be regarded not as a separate study, but as a department of sociological theory."[50] What might appear to us at first sight to be a call to return to a position not too far removed from Smith's historically oriented science of the legislator was in fact perceived by Stephen as a new beginning that necessitated the rejection of the main

---

[46] Leslie 1870: 552.

[47] In 1879 Cliffe Leslie would declare that "the English economist of the future must study in the schools of both Mr Stubbs and Sir Henry Maine, as well as in that of Mr Mill" (see Leslie 1969: x). But Cliffe Leslie was determined to regard Mill as really a historical economist, albeit one who had been led astray by Ricardo's deductive methodology. For Cliffe Leslie's historical challenge see Koot 1975, 1980, 1987 and Moore 1995.

[48] Stephen 1962: II, 269. On Stephen's *History*, see Bicknell 1962 and von Arx 1985, 34–50. For Stephen's earlier economic writings (including discussion of a now-lost diagrammatic treatment of supply and demand), see G. Moore 2006. Stephen took issue with Buckle's interpretation of Smith as distinguishing between selfish and selfless activities in his two works. The morality analyzed in the *Theory of Moral Sentiments*, he argued, was "a kind of reflected selfishness," while altruism "was never contemplated by Smith" (Stephen 1962: II, 272–3).

[49] Stephen 1962: II, 272, 276.

[50] Stephen 1962: II, 278.

part of Smith's intellectual project (i.e., his moral and jurisprudential theories) and the subordination and assimilation of the economic part to a new evolutionary science of sociology.

Stephen drew on Maine's distinction between a static eighteenth-century conception of nature and a historical nineteenth-century mode of social thought in order to characterize political economy as pre-evolutionary. His notion of evolutionary progress itself was derived from Charles Darwin, Herbert Spencer, and Auguste Comte. By "sociology" Stephen had in mind an evolutionary version of the social dynamics proposed by Comte and discussed by Mill in his *System of Logic*.[51] For Stephen, "the underlying law of development" was a process that involved "the gradual adaptation of the race to its environment."[52] Such adaptation constituted an evolution of both human nature and society. In other words, looking at recent scientific formulations of evolutionary theory, Stephen countered what he took to be an eighteenth-century (but ultimately ancient) static conception of nature with the nineteenth-century scientific discovery that nature was in a constant state of flux. From this evolutionary perspective, Stephen looked askance at even the great historical triumvirate of the eighteenth century, dismissing as "crude" because "divorced from philosophy" the histories of Hume, Robertson, and Gibbon.[53] But Stephen's evolutionary philosophy of history also led him to diverge from the views of his old friend Fawcett. As he noted in his *Life of Fawcett*, his friend was not interested in the "influence of evolutionist doctrines" within philosophy, "nor did he, I think, care for any applications of the same ideas to questions of political theory."[54] It would seem that, in Stephen's mature opinion, Fawcett's intellectual limitations and his continued adherence to orthodox political economy were in many ways but two sides of the same coin. By 1876 it had become clear to Stephen that political economy was inherently limited by its pre-evolutionary eighteenth-century origin and that a modern practitioner of political economy was therefore inevitably limited to a static and partial perspective on the laws of social development.

[51] In looking at sociology to replace political economy, Stephen can, of course, be seen as attempting to develop J. S. Mill's ideal of a social science at the expense of his actual work in political economy. Mill himself was quite clear that the proper development of a scientific sociology would have substantial repercussions on political economy (see Collini et al. 1983: 137).
[52] Quoted in von Arx 1985: 35.
[53] Stephen 1962: I, 48.
[54] Stephen 1885: 102.

Stephen's *History* constitutes a seminal work in the history of thought and a natural terminus for this discussion of the conventional mid-Victorian interpretation of Adam Smith. Stephen expanded Buckle's midcentury identification of the methodology of Smith with that of Mill into a general historical picture that systematically assimilated the economic thought of the Scottish Enlightenment into that of the early-nineteenth-century philosophical radicals. Only in the wake of recent scholarship has it become clear how deeply flawed is this mid-Victorian notion of a stable methodology extending from Adam Smith through Ricardo to J. S. Mill. Thus it is only in the past few decades that scholars have begun to appreciate that Smith was no utilitarian, that his political presuppositions were those of a skeptical Whig rather than those of a Gladstonian liberal, and that far from practicing a deductive methodology divorced from history, Smith actually subscribed to a sophisticated historical vision of the relationship between the development of property rights, law and government, and the improvement of civil society. As John Pocock reminds us, early-nineteenth-century orthodox political economy, founded as it was on a restrictive and reductionist theory of the human personality, constituted not a methodological continuation of but a radical philosophical departure from Adam Smith's synthesis of "moral sentiment" and the "wealth of nations."[55] But as we have already begun to see, later Victorian obfuscation of the discontinuities that arose in the passage of economic thought from Smith to Ricardo and Mill, contributed to a vision of the history of political economy that could provide an important resource in the various efforts to revise social thought in light of current political concerns.

THE PRINCIPLE OF AUTHORITY IN MATTERS OF OPINION

Stephen's turn from political economy to sociology was propelled by his perception of the inadequacy of existing liberal political thought in the face of modern democratic political reality. On the whole, academic liberals still in Cambridge shared Stephen's concern with the apparent failure of the newly enfranchised voters to recognize academics like themselves as the natural representatives of working-class interests. Indeed, Stephen's sense of a need to rethink the theoretical basis of liberal politics was indicative of a more general unease in the late 1860s and 1870s concerning the current state of liberal thought. Nevertheless, academic liberals in Cambridge were by no means sympathetic to the actual solutions that Stephen came to propose.

[55] Pocock 1983: 251.

Stephen emphasized the importance of methods of nonrational persuasion in a mass democracy. In the introduction to his *History*, for example, he explained that the "great mass of the population does not think, but feels," and he elaborated on this point with regard to the eighteenth century:

Below the social stratum accessible to philosophical thought, or even to its remotest echoes, lay the great masses, agitated by a rapid growth of material prosperity, increasing and multiplying so as to strain to the uttermost the powers of the old social framework, and ready, as the recognised leaders of thought became incompetent, to listen to any who could speak with authority. For authority in some shape – the authority of sound reason, or the authority of blind tradition, or the authority of some powerful wielder of imaginative symbols – must always guide the masses of mankind.[56]

By and large, however, academic liberals who still resided in Cambridge refused to abandon a faith in the fraternity and potential equality of a republic founded on reason and chose rather to emphasize the need to accompany any extension of the franchise with an extended provision of education. As Marshall's friend J. F. Moulton declared in 1872, delivering the first talk at the newly founded Cambridge Reform Club, it was the duty of every citizen to acquire "at least a primary political education."[57] In fact, and as Harvie observes, all of the early talks delivered at the club were "preoccupied with supplementing political participation by instruction in the laws of social development."[58] And from such discussions emerged the university extension movement, which sent numerous young Oxbridge dons out to lecture in various provincial towns and in which Cambridge liberals took a leading role. But in addition to embracing a new faith in mass education, Cambridge liberals also began to construct a new self-image of themselves and their university as the font of expert opinion. Rather than embracing Stephen's idea of manipulating the masses through emotional symbols, academic liberals came to see themselves as shaping a popular opinion that was – or soon would be – educated enough to recognize in academic consensus what Stephen called "the authority of sound reason."

In February of 1873, Sedley Taylor delivered an address to the Cambridge Reform Club entitled "On the Principle of Authority in Matters of Opinion." His talk illustrates the way in which Cambridge liberals were now seeking to fashion a position for themselves as leaders of public opinion. In the talk Taylor discussed the fact that, in a modern political democracy, citizens are called upon to give their opinion on complex matters in which

---

[56] Stephen 1962: I, 60.

[57] *RCP*, 3–5.

[58] Harvie 1976: 204–5.

they are unlikely to have much expertise. He began with the observation that the "exigencies of common life are constantly placing us in a position where, of two or more alternative modes of action, we *must* adopt one." But "though the *formation* of an opinion is unavoidable, the opinion itself may be arrived at in two extremely different ways": by private judgment or through the authority of others. For Taylor, Protestantism and Liberalism (as opposed to Catholicism and Toryism) had always placed private judgment above received authority and, by doing so, had ensured the progress of liberty in the modern world. Yet in a complicated world, it is highly unlikely that an individual will always possess the requisite knowledge for "forming a really *independent* opinion," and nothing "is more certain than that in nine cases out of ten he *must* take the opinions of other men on trust, i.e. adopt the principle of authority." In short, while holding private judgment to be morally and politically superior to the following of authoritative social convention, Taylor acknowledged that in practice, private judgment is constantly forced to rely on external authority. Therefore, he declared, we stand "in urgent need" of "a test by which to discriminate between trustworthy and untrustworthy authority." Taylor found such a test in the notion of "independent consensus," the "great principle of *agreement among independent investigators*."[59] Independent and knowledgeable investigators, Taylor indicated, were to be found in the modern university. Thus, if Moulton had declared at the first Reform Club talk that it was the duty of every citizen to obtain a "primary political education," Taylor was now suggesting that one of the lessons of such an education must be that the formation of authoritative opinion should be placed in the collective hands of academic experts.

Taylor's notion of expert consensus applied to the arena of mass politics an epistemic conception of consensus already developed within Cambridge's philosophical circles. In his *Methods of Ethics* (1874), for example, Henry Sidgwick would declare that the agreement of other minds constituted a necessary, if not sufficient, warrant for regarding an ethical proposition as established "in the highest degree of certainty attainable."[60] With regard to intellectual inquiry in general, Sidgwick's criteria for epistemic warrant were that a proposition withstand critical reflection, that it be coherent, and agreed on by other experts. As his biographer, Bart Schultz, observes, Sidgwick always insisted that "the special characteristic of *my* philosophy is

---

[59] *RCP*, 15–18, emphasis in original. Note that when he visited America in 1875 Marshall adopted a methodological variant of this principle: "I made a rule not to accept any important statement as trustworthy until I had had it confirmed by several independent authorities" (*EEW*, II: 356).

[60] Sidgwick 1890: 338–42.

to keep the importance of the others in view." For Schultz, this "deceptively simple statement" points directly to the social dimension of Sidgwick's philosophical endeavor; for behind this ideal of a consensus of experts stands the Cambridge discussion society (and, most importantly for Sidgwick, that of the Apostles). At the same time, Schultz points out, Sidgwick's social ideal – nonpartisan inquiry conducted openly within a closed and self-selecting fellowship – informed his strong dislike of what he described as the "demoralising effects of politics under the party system."[61] Civilized conversation behind college walls was for Sidgwick eminently preferable to the histrionics of party bickering on the national political stage. But the agreement arrived at by means of such elite conversations also contained an epistemic warrant unavailable in the noise, dishonesty, and manipulations of a national political debate that was orchestrated by parties struggling for power as opposed to fellow philosophers searching for truth. In his Reform Club talk, Taylor was advocating a variant of Sidgwick's academic ideal of elite consensus to the citizen body at large.

Yet an ideal of expert academic consensus stood in apparent conflict with certain undeniable realities of change and transformation that were occurring at that moment within England's ancient universities. As we shall explore further in the next chapter, the five years following the Second Reform Act witnessed the definitive steps in the transformation of Cambridge University from an Anglican seminary into a lay center of scientific research and secular education. Such a transformation involved more than the formal disassociation of the university from the propagation of Anglican doctrines in the rising generations. It included the extension of the student body to non-Anglicans and women, and the systematic overhaul and reform of the university's teaching structures. Even within established subjects such as classics and theology, an older ideal of amateur proficiency now gave way to a new demand for professional expertise. Furthermore, this period saw an intensive advance in scientific knowledge claims. From the varieties of evolutionary theory, to recent developments in thermodynamics, the construction of new symbolic systems of logic, the reception in Britain of non-Euclidean geometries, and the excitement generated by the new method of comparative historical scholarship, a wave of intellectual advance challenged hitherto stable consensuses and threatened to sweep aside Cambridge conventions. In the wake of such a wholesale transformation of their university, it makes sense that a notion of consensus and its implication of a continuity of intellectual development would be appealing

---

[61] Schultz 2004: 192, emphasis in original; see also pp. 262, 595–7.

to many academics. What is harder to fathom is how, in the wake of such social and intellectual changes, consensus and continuity could appear to be appropriate descriptions of the processes and progress of knowledge.

Such a tension within the university between ideal consensus and actual disagreement is perhaps nowhere as marked as in the case of political economy. Although the science had been taught within Cambridge since early in the nineteenth century, there had been little in the way of a university-wide consensus on the subject before the 1870s. In 1828 George Pryme had been elected the first professor of political economy at Cambridge and had proceeded to teach a course culled mainly from the economic writings of Smith and Ricardo. But in the words of David Palfrey, William Whewell, who would later become the first head of the Moral Sciences Tripos, regarded "Old Man Pryme" as "a dangerous Ricardian contamination within his ancient university," and his response to Pryme's election was to deliver a mathematical critique of Ricardian orthodoxy the following year. By 1831, Palfrey observes, as Whewell delivered his second critique and his friend and ally Richard Jones published his anti-Ricardian book on systems of rent, "the battle-lines between Cambridge Ricardians and anti-Ricardians" had been drawn.[62] A number of events might have been expected to change this situation after midcentury. In 1848 political economy became one paper within a new Moral Sciences Tripos. Then, in 1863 and after a hard-fought campaign, Henry Fawcett, an ardent disciple of J. S. Mill, succeeded Pryme in the Cambridge chair. Finally, in 1855 Whewell became master of Trinity College and the Cambridge moral sciences passed into the more liberal Anglican hands of the Rev. John Grote (who in 1866 was succeeded by Maurice). As already noted, in the years after midcentury there was a convergence between secular liberal and liberal Anglican social attitudes. But such convergence did not amount to intellectual consensus. Until Marshall began to seriously study the subject in the early 1870s, political economy remained isolated from the other moral sciences to which it was institutionally attached.

But by the early 1870s, secular liberals in Cambridge were confronted not only by ambivalent attitudes toward orthodox political economy from their Anglican colleagues, but also by the apparent collapse of the authority of the science throughout the nation as a whole.[63] The introductory pages

---

[62] Palfrey 2003: 272–4.

[63] Hutchison 1953 argued that the crisis of confidence of political economy was brought about not by marginalism but by the criticisms of Ruskin, Cliffe Leslie, and others. But Hutchison did not attempt to link these criticisms to the wider crisis of confidence in liberal political thought in this period. There is now a considerable body of literature

of Sidgwick's 1883 *Principles of Political Economy* provide a retrospective account of this breakdown of confidence. As Sidgwick stated, the mid-Victorian generation that had been "taught by J. S. Mill" had regarded political economy "as unique among moral sciences for the clearness and certainty of its method and the admitted trustworthiness of its conclusions." By 1871, however, "these halcyon days of Political Economy had passed away" in the wake of a tidal wave of criticism that had washed away a generation's "undoubting confidence." Sidgwick attributed this breakdown in confidence to a variety of theoretical challenges, most notably Mill's 1869 recantation of the wages-fund theory, Cliffe Leslie's 1870 essay "The Political Economy of Adam Smith," and the mathematical formulations of W. S. Jevons's 1871 *Theory of Political Economy*. In addition, he identified a growing feeling during this period that in the context of the developing strife between labor and capital, Mill's methodology was inadequate to establish the laws that determine the relationship between work and wages.[64] If in the early 1870s Cambridge liberals had come to believe that public opinion should be formed by expert consensus, they were faced with a very serious problem because expert authority regarding political economy, hitherto a stable foundation stone of the whole liberal edifice, had apparently collapsed.

In Cambridge in the early 1870s, the fortunes of liberal political and economic thought were thus intimately connected. This fact is crucial for understanding the context of Marshall's early economic thought. In the retrospective view of twentieth-century economists, it was the introduction of a mathematical theory of value that led to a revolution in economic theory in this period. From the point of view of Cambridge academics in the early 1870s, however, Jevons's new mathematical approach to economics was but one small factor in a more general breakdown of confidence in the authority of orthodox political economy. One cause of this crisis of confidence, as should now be clear, was simply the exacerbation of the tension that had existed between the methodology of the science and the practice of the art of political economy since midcentury – an underlying friction between inherently pessimistic method and doctrines, on the one hand, and optimistic interpretation and moralistic application, on the other. But the problem was also intimately bound up with the current crisis in liberal political thought. In the 1860s academic liberals had implicitly accepted

dealing with the breakdown in confidence in political economy in the 1870s. See, e.g., Coats 1954, Kadish 1982, 1986, 1989, Koot 1975, 1977, 1980 1987, Maloney 1976, 1985, and Schumpeter 1986: 821ff.

[64] Sidgwick 1887: 1–6.

Mill's version of political economy as providing an account of the basis of social life.[65] The breakdown of consensus regarding the authority of political economy thus threatened the core intellectual framework employed by academic liberals in their analysis of society and in their political judgments. But the connection could work both ways. For Stephen, as we have seen, political frustrations fueled theoretical dissatisfaction and criticism of orthodox political economy. For Cambridge liberals who were not prepared to follow Stephen's historical analysis and sociological conclusions, it was nevertheless imperative to come up with a strategy for reestablishing some kind of expert consensus in political economy on which the authority of their liberal political opinions could be seen to rest.

The most straightforward of such strategies was taken by Fawcett, while a more subtle and sophisticated version of the same strategy was developed by Sidgwick in the late 1870s. Fawcett, who in the half-serious words of his close college friend and biographer Stephen "had read no book except Mill's 'Political Economy,'" simply refused to acknowledge the existence of a crisis in the authority of political economy.[66] He continued, for example, to subscribe to the wages-fund theory even after Mill's recantation in 1869.[67] Sidgwick's more sophisticated version of this same strategy can be gleaned from the introduction to his *Principles of Political Economy*. Sidgwick began this work with the account of the breakdown of the midcentury consensus that was quoted earlier. But as he went on to explain, his primary purpose in publishing his treatise was to demonstrate that the various theoretical criticisms of the 1870s had ultimately been so much sound and fury, their significance amounting to little more than the need for a restatement of "the really sound and valuable results of previous thought" in "a more guarded manner."[68] Sidgwick maintained that careful philosophical reflection on the terms and doctrines of the science would allow one to "eliminate unnecessary controversy." Once this was achieved, he suggested, it would be clear that expert opinion in the 1880s differed little from the consensus views of the "generation whose study of Political Economy commenced about 1860" – which was, of course, about the time that Sidgwick himself had begun the study of Mill's *Principles of Political Economy*.[69]

[65] Harvie 1976: 159.
[66] Stephen 1885: 97. Stephen goes on to tell us that Fawcett also read Smith, Malthus, Ricardo, and Tooke's "History of Prices."
[67] Stephen 1885: 157.
[68] Sidgwick 1887: 7.
[69] Sidgwick 1887: 3.

Sidgwick's analysis of the state of political economy illustrates the practical value that Cambridge philosophers could attach to notions of consensus and continuity in an era of intellectual turmoil and political transformation. Taylor had argued that the agreement of independent experts was a test for the trustworthiness of authority in matters of opinion. But for Sidgwick, the average citizen was not always capable of gauging the actual state of expert opinion; for it was only through calm philosophical reflection that underlying positions could be discerned amid the noise of scientific bickering and disputation. Indeed, the public arguments of political economists could not be wholly separated from the distorting noise of national political debate. Only once philosophical reflection had eliminated "unnecessary controversy" could it be seen whether there was consensus or real controversy regarding any opinion. Sidgwick's discussion of the recent history of political economy implied that scientific experts themselves were often unable to bring the requisite philosophical method to their disputations.[70] Economists, Sidgwick observed in his chapter on value, frequently "underrate the importance of *seeking*" and "overrate the importance of *finding*." Their problem, "as most readers of Plato know," was a faulty conception of true philosophical method.[71] For example, Jevons and Cliffe Leslie had been so enthused by the apparent novelty of their formulations that they had failed to appreciate that their positions entailed relatively little substantive disagreement with the orthodox position they were so concerned to discredit. Consensus might indeed confer authority on opinion, but it is clear that Sidgwick did not believe that either layman or expert was necessarily able to determine whether grounds for consensus actually existed. The palpable divergence of the ideals of consensus and continuity with academic reality thus constituted, in Sidgwick's case at least, the strength rather than the weakness of these ideals; for the gap between appearance and reality provided Cambridge moral philosophers with grounds for regarding themselves as the ultimate court of appeal in matters of both technical expertise and political opinion.[72]

---

[70] In his *Methods of Ethics*, Sidgwick conceded that he had not properly discussed "how we are to ascertain the 'experts' on whose 'consensus' we are to rely, in this or any other subject," but maintained that in this work his "scientific conclusions are to so great extent negative, that I thought it hardly necessary to enter upon this discussion" (Sidgwick 1890: 343n). But the same could hardly have been said about the conclusions drawn in his *Principles of Political Economy*.

[71] Sidgwick 1887: 49, emphasis in original.

[72] Sidgwick's strategy of reestablishing consensus by passing over the significance of the historical (but not the mathematical) criticism of older orthodoxy was continued, and given

CONCLUSION: SITUATING MARSHALL

Philosophical reflection rarely has the last word. In concluding this introductory discussion, it will be instructive to begin by comparing Sidgwick's
brief survey of the recent history of political economy with that provided
but four years later by Herbert Foxwell. In his 1887 essay "The Economic
Movement in England," Foxwell observed that around midcentury the science "attained its zenith of popularity and authority." But, he acidly added,
"perhaps at no period in its history was such a position less deserved." For
Foxwell it was not theoretical criticism but "the facts of every-day experience" and the "rough but inexorable logic of events" that had discredited the
"old doctrines." Beginning around 1870, Foxwell went on to explain, three
independent theoretical departures had led to the "correction" and "development" of economics by a new generation of economists. First, the "scientific instrument of mathematical analysis" had introduced a new precision
into economic reasoning, and had thus been responsible for an overhaul of
"the whole system of definitions and assumptions." Second, a new appreciation of historical scholarship had led to the abandonment of a method
of deduction from assumptions deemed "in some sense 'natural,' or common to all ages." In place of the deductive method, economists had been
led to the study of "social evolution." Finally, economists had taken to heart
the criticisms of such romantic moralists as Carlyle, Maurice, and Ruskin.
The older generation of economists, Foxwell explained, had propagated a
"distinctly unmoral" science, for they "claimed that economic action was
subject to a mechanical system of law, of a positive character, independent
of and superior to any laws of the moral world." But the new generation of
economists had replaced such materialism with a "healthy estimate of the
real objects of existence."[73] In a nutshell, Foxwell's expert opinion flatly con-
tradicted the conclusions Sidgwick drew from philosophical reflection. Far
from constituting "unnecessary controversy," mathematical, historical, and
moral criticism had served to correct a system of doctrines already discredited by their patent inability to explain social reality.

As we shall see in following the development of Marshall's thought in subsequent chapters, each of the three theoretical departures that Foxwell held
to have transformed midcentury political economy had been developed by
Marshall during the early 1870s. Foxwell had been taught political economy
by Marshall in the early 1870s and then joined him as a college lecturer in

---

definitive form, by John Neville Keynes in his 1891 *The Scope and Method of Political
Economy* (see Moore 2003).
[73] Foxwell 1887: 84–90.

the moral sciences. The two were thus colleagues at St. John's until Marshall left Cambridge in 1877, and close friends for the rest of the decade and beyond. Thus one can read Foxwell's 1887 essay as reflective of positions that he had absorbed from his old teacher and therefore also as indicative of the deep gulf that separated Marshall's early thought on political economy from that of Sidgwick.[74] It is indeed clear that Marshall took the theoretical criticisms of Mill's formulation of political economy much more seriously than did Sidgwick, and his own *Principles of Economics*, first published in 1890, did not so much attempt to restate the old thought in "a more guarded manner" as reformulate the method and doctrines of economics in order to reconcile the old thought with new theoretical developments. Nevertheless, in the first paragraph of the preface to this treatise, Marshall insisted that the "new doctrines have supplemented the older, have extended, developed and sometimes corrected them, and often have given them a different tone by a new distribution of emphasis; but very seldom have subverted them."[75] In other words, Marshall, no less than Sidgwick, insisted that continuity was the defining feature of the recent history of political economy.

There would appear to be something paradoxical in Marshall's position. To believe, as Foxwell did, that mathematical, historical, and moral criticisms had transformed midcentury political economy, and yet to insist along with Sidgwick on the continuity of recent doctrinal history, seems at first sight to be contradictory. The starting point for the resolution of this apparent paradox is to be found in the fact that in the early 1870s Marshall developed a conception of philosophical method quite different from that advocated by Sidgwick. To begin with, while holding with Sidgwick that progress in economics was dependent on achieving clarity and precision in terms, definitions, and assumptions, Marshall also held that if philosophical reflection could achieve this goal, it was aided by both historical inquiry

[74] It is usually assumed that Foxwell's seemingly idiosyncratic insistence on the harmony and mutual importance of mathematics, morality, and history in the development of economics after 1870 is to be explained in terms of his simultaneous admiration of both W. S. Jevons and Arnold Toynbee, and is unrelated to his early relationship with Marshall. Although Foxwell's later divergence from Marshall is undeniable, the fact is that in the 1870s Marshall was working on precisely those elements that Foxwell would later characterize as distinctive to the "new" economics. For example, while Foxwell's historical interests are normally assumed to have been developed in opposition to Marshall, we find Foxwell commencing his historical studies by asking for Marshall's advice on the secondary literature (see the letter to Foxwell of July 1878 in *CAM*, I: 99–100).

[75] *Principles*, I: v. For a hint of at least some aspects of the early rift, see Sidgwick's 1871 letter to Marshall as reproduced in *CAM*, I: 13–4. For Sidgwick's subsequent opposition to the enthusiasm of Marshall and others for evolutionism and historicism in the moral sciences, see Sidgwick 1876, 1886.

and the employment of mathematical or diagrammatical techniques. But if Marshall insisted on a rather different methodological approach than that of Sidgwick, he certainly did not deny philosophical method any role in the advance of economic thought.

Marshall, it could be said, opposed Sidgwick's Socratic ideal of philosophical dialogue to a Platonic ideal of philosophical dialectic. J. B. Schneewind, in his study of Sidgwick's moral philosophy, writes of the Knightbridge Professor of Moral Philosophy, F. D. Maurice, that he was "a true Coleridgean in his insistence that there is something of value to be learned from the deepest views of any thinker on religious matters. Each in his own way has seen a part or an aspect of the truth. So far as each has done so, each is right: it is only their denials, Maurice teaches, that are wrong."[76] In his biography of Sidgwick, Schultz quotes Schneewind's description of Maurice in order to illustrate how much Sidgwick's notion of consensus owed to the ideal of philosophical discussion that he learned from his membership in the Apostles, and also from Maurice himself in their discussions at the Grote Club. But while Schultz is certainly correct to emphasize Sidgwick's debt to both Maurice and the Apostles, Schneewind's description of Maurice's method points equally to that aspect of Maurice's Coleridgeanism that was systematically developed by Marshall rather than Sidgwick. In the opening sentences of his 1876 essay on Mill's theory of value, for example, Marshall explained that a man is "trustworthy" when he writes of the truth that he perceives, but not when he criticizes errors in the truths of others.[77] Again, in a note in the *Academy* in 1874, he declared that with regard to "the whole of the wages-problem it may be said that Mr. Jevons and Mr. Cairnes in general see vividly each that class of considerations which the other almost ignores."[78] And again, in a letter of 1891 Marshall explained that his *Principles* had been written to express only one idea: that in the dispute about value each party had "been right in what he affirmed but wrong in what he denied."[79] These and many similar such statements point directly to the very particular lesson that Marshall learned from Maurice and the tradition of liberal Anglican philosophy.

Consensus, Marshall came to believe, was not the end product of philosophical conversation, but an end product of the application of a philosophical method.[80] As we shall discover as we follow the course of Marshall's

---

[76]   Schneewind 1977: 99; Schultz 2004: 49–50.
[77]   *MTV*, 119.
[78]   Whitaker 1994.
[79]   *EEW*, I: 97–8.
[80]   Backhouse 2006 points to the shared emphasis placed on an ideal of consensus by Marshall and Sidgwick but does not investigate the fundamental differences in their formulation of

early thought in subsequent chapters, a dialectical conception of consensus formation stood at the very heart of the method by which Marshall accomplished his early reformulation of political economy. This method, which had its roots in the thought of Coleridge as developed by Maurice and other Cambridge liberal Anglicans, generated progress in the history of ideas by fusing within a higher synthesis the constructive elements of opposing points of view. Such a dialectical method provided Marshall with his own version of Sidgwick's assertion that the philosophical economist could perceive continuity where even the ordinary economic expert saw only discord. Furthermore, and related to their divergent ideals of consensus, Sidgwick and Marshall constructed different readings of the recent history of political economy. While Sidgwick asserted the continuing validity of Mill's midcentury formulation of the methods and doctrines of political economy, Marshall asserted a continuity of development from one consensus position to another. Here, we might note, Foxwell would dissent from the point of view developed by his old teacher: while Foxwell was content to learn economics from Marshall, he was evidently far less sympathetic to Marshall's philosophical ideas about consensus and continuity. Indeed, at the root of nearly all of Marshall's disagreements with his liberal Cambridge colleagues stood his commitment to a form of romantic metaphysics.

Marshall's metaphysical beliefs also led him to propose a reading of the history of political economy that departed from the conventional mid-Victorian picture of the relation of Smith to the subsequent history of economics, for Marshall would insist on a history of continual development *within* economic thought since the time of Smith. By so doing, he was able to subsume within his own vision of economic science much of the rationalist evolutionary science that for Stephen formed the groundwork of a new dynamic science of sociology. In other words, Marshall's insistence on the development of economic doctrine and method went hand in hand with an assertion that political economy had itself become a dynamic science. But in Marshall's early metaphysical philosophy of history, materialist evolution was itself posited as subordinate to a deeper spiritual development of human nature. Such a spiritual development involved the gradual emergence of moral freedom and the consequent development within humanity of a self-consciousness of its essential separation from the natural world.

this ideal. The common assumption in the literature that Marshall's notion of moral philosophy can be assimilated to that of Sidgwick has been bolstered by Collini 1975; Collini, with little evidence or even argument, recruited Marshall to supplement his argument that Sidgwick did not develop a "Cambridge Idealism."

As we shall find in Chapter Six, this idealist philosophy of history was constructed by way of a reading of Maine's *Ancient Law* through the lens of Hegel's *Philosophy of History*. Through this Hegelian reading of Maine, Marshall would eventually arrive at the conviction that Smith's tendency to identify the social order with an unchanging natural order had, in the nineteenth century, been superseded by an understanding that the object of study was the kind of social organization that emerged within a moral realm characterized by freedom. Here, again, we see Marshall's dialectical method of consensus at work: in adopting this romantic philosophy of history Marshall did not thereby deny the validity of Stephen's evolutionary perspective; rather he sought in his philosophy of history to reconcile both materialist and idealist accounts of progress.

The political intentions that stood behind Marshall's ideal of achieving intellectual consensus are most clearly brought to light if we compare his attitude toward the church with that of Stephen. Marshall, as we shall see in later chapters, lost his Anglican faith some time in the late 1860s or early 1870s. But whereas Stephen had arrived at a militant form of agnosticism, in which the fundamental political issue of the day involved a struggle with the church for the symbols of cultural authority, Marshall arrived at an accommodating and metaphysical philosophy of history, and was content for the church to maintain a moral mission within society. Thus, in the most fraught political issue of the early 1870s, the role of the established church in the provision of national education, Marshall made no objection to a continuing clerical role in the provision of education to the working classes.[81] Collini has entitled a discussion of J. S. Mill's place in English culture after his death in 1873 "From Dangerous Partisan to National Possession."[82] The same title could be given to a discussion of Marshall's reforming intentions in the early 1870s with regard to Mill's version of the science of political economy. Marshall's method of consensus was ultimately intended to give rise to a reformulated economic science as a broad church, in which the Anglican and secular elements within his university, and within the nation at large, could come together in agreement on the moral, material, and intellectual factors that would give rise to a continual progress of the working classes and of the material and cultural wealth of the nation as a whole.

---

[81]   On Marshall's tacit support of the Anglican position in 1873, see Biagini 1995.
[82]   Collini 1991: 311–41.

TWO

A Liberal Education

INTRODUCTION

In 1853 a French guest at Trinity College naively asked his hosts if a college fellow was an "*élève*." The professor of geology, Adam Sedgwick, put the visitor right. A fellow of a Cambridge college, he explained, is "a Protestant monk, a *frère*, and nothing more."[1] Within two decades of this conversation, women students were attending lectures in Cambridge and the religious tests that had discriminated against non-Anglicans were abolished. At the same time, a number of dons were now earnestly engaged in a systematic overhaul of university teaching practices. Furthermore, and as we saw in the preceding chapter, by 1873 Cambridge had become not only a home of advanced liberal political thinking, but also the site of an attempt to construct a new academic self-image as the font of authority in matters of social and political opinion. The transformation of this Anglican monastery had been long in the making, but the critical moment of disestablishment, and the emergence of the University of Cambridge as a secular institution of teaching and research, occurred in the late 1860s and early 1870s. This transformation of Anglican seminary into modern university thus coincided with the first period of Alfred Marshall's association with the Cambridge Moral Sciences Tripos.

A central theme of this book is the relationship between Marshall's developing thoughts on education, on the one hand, and his social philosophy, on the other. Marshall's earliest writings on university reform are discussed in the last part of the present chapter. In subsequent chapters it will become clear that as his early ideas on the nature of a liberal education were developed, revised, and extended, so a foundation was put in place for some of the most distinctive elements of Marshall's more mature political, social,

---

[1] Reported in a letter from F. A. Hort to the Rev. G. Blunt, July 1853 (Hort 1896: I, 257).

and economic thought. This chapter as a whole consists of an exploration of a handful of the many positions advanced over the course of a century of discussion and controversy as to the proper business of a university. Such an exploration will allow us to situate Marshall's early writings on higher education in the context of a wider history of political and social thought. The survey of attitudes and approaches to a liberal education from Adam Smith through Henry Fawcett can thus be seen as an elaboration of some of the key themes presented in the preceding chapter.

In 1876 Adam Smith considered a university education to be more an ornament than a foundation of civil society. By 1873 (as we shall see in the penultimate chapter of this book), Marshall had come to identify the extension of higher education as the key to the future progress of society. Behind Marshall's identification stands his synthesis of two distinct nineteenth-century streams of thought. First, a liberal education was supposed to foster within the student certain traits of character (just which ones was, of course, a matter of dispute). Second, the scientific research conducted at modern universities increasingly came to be seen as providing a foundation for British industrial strength.[2] If in 1873 Marshall would hold up the modern university as the source of both moral and technological progress, the kernel of his fusion of these two streams of nineteenth-century thought is to be found in his earliest writings on education of the 1860s. But to understand what was involved in this synthesis, it is necessary to appreciate the diverse ways in which one or another or both of these traditions had been used, over the course of the preceding century, to support a variety of opposing political and social philosophies. As we shall see, within any one nineteenth-century formulation of the proper ends of a university can be found a particular ideal of character, a conception of the relation of the world of industry to that of culture, and a vision of the role an educated elite should play in the progress of society.

ADAM SMITH ON THE INSTITUTIONS OF EDUCATION

In book V of the *Wealth of Nations*, Smith discussed the expense of justice and defense in four distinct stages of society. His procedure was to relate such

---

[2] Compare Thomas Huxley's claim that Prussian industrial might was due to the fact that every "third-rate, poverty-stricken German university" carried out more scientific research than did Oxford and Cambridge (quoted in Desmond 1998: 387) with Smith's discussion of invention in *LJ(B)*, 346–7. Smith was quite certain that the invention of "wind and water mills," as well as of the "fire engine," was the work of "an ingenious philosopher," yet it does not seem to have occurred to him that this might have provided a reason to endow research.

expense to the particular needs that arise according to whether subsistence is procured by hunting and gathering, pastoralism, agriculture, or the mercantile activities of a commercial society. But in the same book, Smith discussed the expense of institutions of education – schools, universities, and churches – by way of a different historical framework. Smith here did not make use of the four-stages theory because, in his opinion, before the advent of commercial society all requisite skills are taught in the process of everyday life. Once the growth of commerce introduces specialization and opulence into a society, however, there is a demand for certain forms of higher education, producing separate institutions with their attendant expenses. Smith's discussion of the institutions of education was built around a comparison of the respective educational regimes and characters of the inhabitants of ancient and modern commercial societies. Such a comparison replicated aspects of what has been called "the Enlightenment narrative" of the emergence of modern commercial society out of the "barbarism and religion" of a feudal past.[3] In Smith's formulation of the history of civilization, the intensive division of labor characteristic of modern commercial societies, combined with the particular religious conditions of modern Europe, generated certain contemporary social problems that were best remedied by the provision of education.

To understand Smith's distinctive contribution to the "Enlightenment narrative," it is important to appreciate the use he made of a tradition of early modern political thought that viewed luxury and refinement as corrosive to the virtue on which the security of a polity rested. In his Glasgow lectures on rhetoric and *belles lettres*, Smith had explained to his students that literary and other arts arose only in the wake of commerce and opulence. For example, he claimed that the only arts known in ancient Greece before the Persian Wars were arms and music. By the time of Demosthenes, however, the Athenians had embraced commerce and cultivated eloquence. But this was by no means an unmitigated blessing; for Smith accepted the widespread civic humanist conviction that commerce and the arts corrupt the martial spirit. Hence all of Demosthenes' eloquence had been unable to stir the now-corrupted citizens of Athens to defend their liberty against the predatory designs of Philip of Macedon.[4] This history of the fall of Athens provided but one instance of what for Smith, and indeed for many of his contemporaries, was a basic cycle of pre-modern history. In this schema martial virtue is a prerequisite for liberty and the preservation

---

[3] Pocock 1999.
[4] *LRBL*, 135–8, 149–51; see also *LJ(A)*, 231–2, 242–4.

of wealth, and yet wealth gives rise to luxury and the arts, which in turn corrupt military virtue and so lead to the decline and eventual collapse of the social order. The distinctive twist that Smith gave to this analysis was to provide an account of Europe's emergence from the barbarism and religion of its feudal past – an account suggesting that modern commercial societies had found a means of reconciling political stability with the progress of the arts.

Smith's explication of the genesis of modern commercial society began with a picture of the feudal past dominated by the Catholic Church and a handful of barons. Both of these orders were extremely wealthy, but before the cultivation of commerce and the arts, surplus from the land could be spent only on "rustic hospitality," a practice that guaranteed a large army of idle retainers for the barons and the genuine gratitude of the poor to the church. With the "gradual improvements of arts, manufactures, and commerce," however, both church and barons began to spend their agricultural surplus on luxuries for themselves. Consequently, the power of both church and barons disintegrated.[5] Rather than giving rise to anarchy and chaos, however, this led to an end to the clerical monopoly of letters, an extension of the power of the crown, and the imposition of national systems of justice throughout much of Europe. Such administration of justice in turn provided the requisite security for the further development of commerce and the arts. At the heart of Smith's understanding of this unique development of modern history stood that most distinctive of modern institutions, the standing army. With the modern establishment of standing armies, the hitherto all-important corrupting influence of commerce and the arts had been neutralized. For sure, the populations of modern commercial societies lacked the martial virtues of nomadic horsemen and warrior-peasants. But Smith was convinced that a professional army equipped with modern weapons was a force of unprecedented military power, more than a match for a modern citizen militia. With the rewards of their labor secured by the two institutions of a system of justice and a standing army, the populations of modern commercial societies were now free to dedicate the whole of their labor to the pursuit of riches, the cultivation of the arts, and the subsequent enjoyment of luxuries such as, for those in the higher ranks at least, a liberal education.

One further strand of social analysis is interwoven into Smith's discussion of the institutions of education. The educational institutions founded by the Catholic church – "the most formidable combination that ever was

---

[5]   *WN*, 802–4 (V. i. g. 24–5) and book III, ch. IV.

formed against the authority and security of civil government, as well as against the liberty, reason, and happiness of mankind" – had cultivated only casuistry and superstition. But the Protestant Reformation had fostered an antinomian enthusiasm deeply threatening to the civil order. The civil magistrate, therefore, must keep a close eye on all institutions of religious education. Smith was not unsympathetic to his friend David Hume's argument in favor of an established church that by guaranteeing the incomes of the clergy (thereby removing the need for them to court popularity with the people), would effectively "bride their indolence."[6] It was science, however, that in Smith's view provided "the great antidote to the poison of enthusiasm and superstition." It was in the interests of society, he argued, that the "superior ranks" be taught the rudiments of the modern sciences – "for where all the superior ranks are secured" from superstition and enthusiasm, "the inferior ranks could not be much exposed to it."[7] Nevertheless, Smith in the *Wealth of Nations* went so far as to insist that the common people too must receive at least some basic education; for "the understandings of the greater part of men are necessarily formed by their ordinary employments," and the modern system of the division of labor generated "gross ignorance and stupidity" among "the inferior ranks of the people." The more the common people are instructed, however, "the less liable they are to the delusions of enthusiasm and superstition, which, among ignorant nations, frequently occasion the most dreadful disorders."[8]

Smith's discussion of the institutions of a liberal education in the *Wealth of Nations* amounted to a sophisticated and nuanced combination of historical and economic analysis. Early on in his discussion, he laid it down as a general rule that in "every profession, the exertion of the greater part of those who exercise it, is always in proportion to the necessity they are under of making that exertion." In both ancient Greece and the Scottish universities of his own day, where the income of professors derived in part from the fees of their students, the natural growth of specialization and opulence had generated a demand among the upper ranks for a liberal education, and this demand had in turn been met by a competitive educational

---

6 *WN*, 791 (V. i. g. 6) and see Hume 1983: I, 134–6. Smith ultimately came down in favor of a competitive religious regime in which the weakness of the many sects would oblige each to learn candor and moderation.
7 *WN*, 796 (V. i. g. 14).
8 *WN*, 781 (V. i. f. 50), 788 (V. i. f.–g. 61). For the argument that Smith's views on education flowed from the natural jurisprudential side of his thinking in addition to that of civic humanism, see Haakonssen 1982: 207, 209. For a comparison of Smith's views with those of Ferguson, see Winch 1996: 120–1.

regime which ensured that teaching duties were executed "with a certain degree of exactness."[9] The lesson here was that both the demand for and the provision of education were natural products of the growth of civilization. As we have seen, Smith fused this economic analysis with the historical argument that, in modern Europe, the higher education of those in the upper ranks of society no longer posed a threat to the military capabilities on which the security of society depended. Furthermore, the provision of such a liberal education to the upper ranks was to be welcomed as providing an antidote to the peculiarly modern poisons of superstition and enthusiasm.

Smith's blend of economic and historical analysis allowed him to make some stinging criticisms of certain contemporary institutions of liberal education. In the "unnatural" feudal world, education had been provided not because of an interest in the arts and letters among the upper ranks of society, but in order to offer theological training to future clerics. The result had been the corruption of the ancient system of philosophy.[10] But it was just this feudal past that had given rise to the universities of Europe. Furthermore, because the medieval universities of Oxford and Cambridge had been endowed with large tracts of land, the "prosperity and revenue" of their professors remained "in a great measure independent of their reputation, and altogether independent of their industry." With no incentive to cultivate the new sciences and the new learning that had blossomed since the revival of letters in the sixteenth century, these surviving relics of the feudal past continued, at their best, to teach "an exploded and antiquated" system of ecclesiastical philosophy, now "universally believed to be a mere useless and pedantic heap of sophistry and nonsense."[11] In fact, because their salary constituted the whole of their revenue, the professors at England's ancient universities had no incentive to fulfill their teaching duties at all. At the University of Oxford (which Smith had attended for five years after his graduation from Glasgow), "the greater part of the public professors have, for these many years, given up altogether even the pretence of teaching."[12]

[9]   *WN*, 759 (V. i. f. 4).
[10]   *WN*, 765 (V. i. f. 19), 770–2 (V. i. f. 28–32).
[11]   *WN*, 780–1 (V. i. f. 46).
[12]   *WN*, 761 (V. i. f. 8). On Smith's time at Oxford, of which very little is known, see Ross 1995: ch. 5 and Smith's letter to William Smith (*Corr*, 1). Edward Gibbon described his fourteen months at Oxford as "the most idle and unprofitable of my life" and suggested that Smith had been correct to blame Oxford indolence on monopolistic professorial practices (see Gibbon 1984: ch. 3).

FROM THE SCOTTISH ENLIGHTENMENT TO
VICTORIAN ENGLAND

Adam Smith's analysis of the causes of the corrupt state of the English universities would seem to have been as applicable to early Victorian Cambridge as to late-eighteenth-century Oxford. By the nineteenth century, the colleges of Cambridge had become extremely wealthy institutions. The vast bulk of college wealth consisted of land, much of which had originally derived from estates owned by the monasteries dissolved in the Reformation.[13] The Protestant monks of the Cambridge colleges did not, however, follow any arduous monastic rule. In fact, once he was elected to a college fellowship, very little was required of a Cambridge don. To be sure, a fairly regular attendance at the college chapel services was expected, and until 1882 college fellows, unlike their clergymen brethren in the parishes, were required to observe the celibate life. In part because of this requirement of celibacy, a college fellowship was seen by many as a temporary position, to be resigned as soon as a suitable parish living was obtained and marriage therefore became a possibility. But those who remained within the college walls could rest content in the knowledge that neither teaching undergraduates nor pursuing their own research would be required of them. As late as 1876, Lord Salisbury could complain to the House of Lords that a "sum of £250 or £300 is attached to fellowships to which no duties are attached, and the man who receives it may, if he chooses, remain in idleness for life."[14] As Smith had put it exactly a century earlier, there was no connection between academic industry and academic revenue.

It is not surprising that nineteenth-century England witnessed prolonged and bitter complaints over the state of the ancient universities. Yet Smith's analysis of the corrupt condition of teaching at Oxford hardly had an impact on these English debates. This was no doubt in part because the English arguments were conducted within a historical framework very different from that of Smith's Enlightenment narrative. With the Elizabethan settlement, England's two medieval universities had been defined as "national institutions," charged with defending the Anglican order of state and church. In the years following the Reform Bill of 1832, however, the status of these bastions of the English Reformation became the focus of

---

[13] For details of college revenues and expenditures, see Garland 1980: 137, n. 11, Howard 1935, and Huber 1843: II, 576–80, and for the expenditure of college revenues on fellowships, scholarships, sizars, rectories, vicarages, curacies, and the like, see Cooper 1861: II, 339–42.

[14] Quoted in Winstanley 1947: 270.

intense controversy. Gladstone, for example, speaking in opposition to a bill of 1834 that proposed opening Oxbridge to dissenters, informed the House of Commons that the whole purpose of the colleges was to cultivate Anglican doctrine "in the rising generation of the country." Only through their connection with the established church, he insisted, could the ancient universities of England be regarded as "national institutions."[15] Gladstone's nonconformist opponents, by contrast, compared the notoriously wealthy Oxbridge colleges to the monasteries dissolved by Henry VIII and insisted that these institutions could not be regarded as national institutions, precisely because they excluded non-Anglicans. Thus the nineteenth-century English debate about the reform of Oxford and Cambridge had no place for an eighteenth-century contrast between modern commercial society and a barbarous and religious feudal past. What was at stake was rather the meaning of England's Protestant Reformation in an era of political reform. The growing calls for the "nationalization of the universities" were calls not for state ownership, but rather for the separation of the universities from the control of the established church.[16]

But the failure of Smith's discussion of education to resonate in the nineteenth-century English debates can also be traced to certain deep-seated cultural and intellectual shifts that occurred in the wake of the French Revolution. In their enduring anxiety over the threat to the civil order posed by religious antinomianism, Scottish moral philosophers like Smith and Hume stood side by side with both eighteenth-century Whig politicians and latitudinarian Anglican churchmen. For all these supporters of the Whig order, commerce was understood to foster polite social intercourse and, by so doing, to dissolve the enthusiastic tendencies of prophetic puritan religiosity.[17] Such social analysis evaporated in the early nineteenth century in the face of a remarkable rehabilitation of "enthusiasm." Enthusiasm now came to denote a state of moral energy in which devotion to a higher good had overcome the self-absorbed passions and interests of the lower self.[18] Initially the product of an Evangelical religious awakening that combined an ideal of inner religious fervor with a pietistic aspiration toward social respectability, an enthusiastic ideal was soon disseminated throughout educated Victorian society. Thus Coleridge, the great romantic critic of

---

[15] Quoted in Harvie 1976: 30.
[16] See Garland 1980: 14, 153 for early Victorian dissenting calls for the "nationalization" of the universities. For later and nonsectarian discussion of nationalization, see, e.g., Campbell 1901 and Paley 1869.
[17] Pocock 1985: 234–9.
[18] See Houghton 1957: 263–5 and Hilton 1989: 62–3.

Evangelical simplicities, drew a distinction between the enthusiast and the fanatic, and went on to decry the absence of enthusiasm in the philosophical thought of the eighteenth century.[19] Even J. S. Mill in his *Autobiography* (1873) explained that the bleak state of mind which befell him during his youthful mental crisis was connected to an utter absence of enthusiasm for those social reforms that had hitherto constituted the defining purpose of his life. In such a climate, Smith's analysis of education as the great antidote to enthusiasm lay neglected on the shelves, passed over by the various streams of Victorian public moralism as but one more example of the soulless rationalism of eighteenth-century social philosophy.

At the same time, many nineteenth-century public moralists came to reject the standard premise of both the English and Scottish Enlightenments that civilization was the child of commerce. For Smith, like many of his contemporaries, the increasingly complex social relations caused by the growth of commerce were what fostered the progressive refinement of the passions, the development of sympathies, and the general growth of manners. In the last years of the eighteenth century, however, Edmund Burke argued that the church and the nobility were necessary to the growth of manners and that manners formed a precondition of the growth of commerce.[20] In thus reversing the causal connection between commerce and manners, Burke anticipated, and in many ways cultivated, a distinguishing feature of nineteenth-century romantic political and social thought: Burke paved the way for the standard romantic conviction that trade and industry were hostile to the progress of the arts, and that culture in fact stood in need of protection from the anarchic and philistine energy of the commercial classes. Thus, as Pocock has written, "at the point where Burke's revision of perspectives forces scientific Whiggism to redefine itself as Tory stands Coleridge's *Constitution of Church and State*, a study of how a static landed and a dynamic commercial class must discipline themselves by endowing a clerisy charged with the perpetuation of culture."[21] Some of Adam Smith's indolent English clerical fellows were about to discover a social role for England's ancient Anglican seminaries. Henceforth, such national institutions could be envisaged as fortresses of culture that might

---

[19] See, e.g., Coleridge 1983: 30–1, 147, 197; 1993: 8.
[20] Hampsher-Monk 1992: 276–82; Pocock 1985: 188–9. Burke's position was developed out of Robertson 1825: 62–4; cf. Hume 1983: I, 371, 486–7.
[21] Pocock 1985: 282. On nineteenth-century ideas of a clerisy, see Knights 1978, especially chapters 2, 5, and 6. For a useful discussion of the relationship between the thought of Burke and Coleridge, and the relationship of both to eighteenth-century thought, see Morrow 1986, 1990: 69–72.

provide not only protection from, but perhaps also a light of learning onto, the barbaric commercial hordes. Indeed, and as we shall now see, by the mid-nineteenth century an enthusiasm for a version of such an ideal of a clerisy had informed a moderately systematic overhaul of one of England's ancient universities.

WILLIAM WHEWELL

It is well known that Coleridge's thought had a profound impact on early Cambridge Apostles and future Broad Churchmen, such as Connop Thirlwall, Julius Hare, and Maurice. As Peter Searby writes, Hare was "the first man in Cambridge to be influenced by the philosophical writings of Samuel Taylor Coleridge," and "as Maurice's teacher he introduced Coleridge's ideas to the man who was to diffuse them more widely in the Church of England than anybody."[22] (In his turn, Maurice, together with John Stirling, introduced the writings of Coleridge to J. S. Mill.) But a Coleridgean conception of the university as a bastion of Anglican culture was also upheld, albeit in somewhat modified form, by moderately enthusiastic clerical dons such as Adam Sedgwick and William Whewell, who were students with Thirlwall and Hare in the 1810s, fellows of Trinity College a decade later, and the leading lights within Cambridge by midcentury.[23] Whewell, in particular, differed from Coleridgeans such as Hare and Maurice, both in his attempt to codify what he took to be the constitutive ideas of culture and in his underlying conviction that the nation's cultural tradition comprised scientific as well as moral ideas. Nevertheless, by midcentury Whewell would instigate a series of reforms designed to establish Cambridge as the home of the torch bearers of right reasoning in both the natural and the moral sciences.

Whewell's initial concern had been to reconcile the teaching of Anglican doctrine with an image of Cambridge as the university of Newton. From the late 1820s onward, and in opposition to dominant Coleridgean, High Church, and Evangelical attitudes, Whewell insisted that natural philosophy constituted a fitting object of research and instruction. Adopting an inductive Baconian methodology, Whewell argued that because older scientific truths were not replaced but rather subsumed within newer theories,

---

[22] Searby 1997: 352. On Maurice's debt to Coleridge, see Chapter Three of this book.
[23] On Whewell and Sedgwick, Garland 1980 is useful but overstates Whewell's reforming aspirations and fails to emphasize the Coleridgean dimension of Whewell's vision. Hofstetter, by contrast, does not sufficiently emphasize Whewell's differences with such then-nonresident Cambridge Coleridgeans as Hare and Maurice (see Hofstetter 2001: ch. 5).

so the teaching of the sciences led not to a constant revolution in opinions, but rather to intellectual humility and respect for tradition.[24] In the 1830s, and newly inspired by Adam Sedgwick's "Discourse on the Studies of the University of Cambridge," Whewell absorbed Coleridge's reading of Bacon, and so supplemented his initial inductive methodology with an idealist epistemology. In his version of Coleridge's uncritical form of German idealism, Whewell proposed that both moral and natural sciences rested on "fundamental ideas." This idealist philosophy was clearly designed to counter radical London utilitarianism, but it is evident that Whewell also intended to establish Cambridge as a center of idealist moral philosophy to rival the common sense intuitionism of Edinburgh. At the heart of Whewell's philosophical system stood a "fundamental antithesis" between "Idea" and "Fact." Such an antithesis existed between moral ideas and positive legal frameworks, and between scientific ideas and empirical observations. Relations of duty and the affections, Whewell claimed, were "as fundamental a part of man's thoughts as the relations of time and space."[25] But such idealist foundations of his thought notwithstanding, Whewell's systematic form of epistemological idealism set him apart from the Coleridgean tradition of Hare and Maurice. Against their more liberal Coleridgeanism, with its pronounced aversion to systematic thought and a corresponding ideal of education (clearly inspired by the meetings of the Apostles) as a communication of minds by means of informal conversation, Whewell developed a systematic idealist philosophy and then worked to embody it within a carefully structured program of undergraduate study.[26]

Whewell's ideal of a liberal education also involved an Evangelical component absent in the more Socratic or conversational mode of education cherished by the Apostles Hare and Maurice. In Whewell's writings, a liberal education was presented as a ladder to the salvation of the soul, a pathway along which enthusiasm could meet with right reasoning in order to lead the student upward toward grace. Cambridge students were to be taught to reason inductively, which meant placing faith in God's works. To reason deductively, as did the followers of Ricardo and those mathematicians who employed symbolic analysis (as opposed to traditional

---

[24] See Palfrey 2003: 142. For the connection between Whewell's Anglican theology and his philosophy of science, see Yeo 1979, 1993. A good composite portrait of Whewell is supplied by Fisch and Schaffer 1991.

[25] Quoted in Palfrey 2003: 149.

[26] Palfrey 2003 observes that Maurice's antisystematic challenge became "a dividing line between resident Cambridge moral theorists and their Coleridgean correspondents." He relates the dispute in part to respective training in mathematics and classical philology.

Cambridge geometric reasoning), was to reason internally, to place one's faith in oneself and spurn the aid of external authority (the Scriptures and the teaching of the church). Thus, for Whewell, enthusiasm countered the self-absorption of materialist science, while an Anglican clerisy provided the external authority that could lead toward grace.[27] This Christian pedagogy was reinforced by an application to the classification of the sciences of Coleridge's distinction between "permanent" and "progressive" classes of society. In Whewell's scheme, permanent sciences had already established fundamental ideas; progressive sciences had not, and so were still being developed by research. Only permanent sciences could form a part of a liberal education, because only these could instill a proper respect for tradition. Progressive sciences, Whewell feared, would lead students to question the authority of their teachers. In a series of midcentury reforms, Whewell proceeded to integrate this clerical vision of a liberal education into the Cambridge curricula.

A series of Senate resolutions passed in midcentury provides evidence of a concerted effort within the university to standardize, reform, and regulate university teaching practices.[28] Most of these reforms bear Whewell's stamp. For example, while the Mathematical Tripos was reformed, thermodynamics and electromagnetics, the most exciting areas of midcentury physical science, were excluded from the reformed curriculum because they were deemed "progressive sciences." A further innovation was the establishment, also in 1848, of a new Natural Sciences Tripos and a new Moral Sciences Tripos.[29] While Whewell continued to insist that classics and mathematics constituted the proper objects of study in a liberal education, he was nevertheless also determined to establish Anglican authority over a wider field. Thus once the new Moral Sciences Tripos had been established, Whewell placed himself at its head and attempted to subordinate the relations of the various moral sciences to his version of Anglican philosophy. But his

---

[27] For Whewell's voluminous discussions of a Cambridge liberal education, see Whewell 1835, 1837, 1845. For a contrast of symbolic and geometrical reasoning in mathematics, see Whewell 1845: 40–1. For the spiritual and religious significance of Whewell's philosophy of science, see Yeo 1979. See also the relevant chapters of Fisch and Schaffer 1991 and chapter 1 of Richards 1988.

[28] For details see Winstanley 1935: 208–13. Palfrey 2003 argues that Whewell was motivated less by reforming zeal than by a concern to preempt and head off the threat of parliamentary-directed reform.

[29] See Winstanley 1947: 185–90. The first examinations for these two triposes were conducted in 1851. The *Cambridge Calendar* of 1855, p. 26, gives details of the "Regulations for the Moral Sciences Tripos, adopted by the Senate, Oct. 31, 1848" and also reproduces a part of the Report of the Syndicate, which led to this innovation.

attempt to use the new tripos as a vehicle for integrating law, history, and political economy with Christian moral philosophy proved too ambitious, and within a decade this part of his university project had collapsed. Under his successor in the Knightbridge Chair, the Rev. John Grote, the Moral Sciences Tripos was reorganized: history and law were ejected and logic and psychology introduced.[30] This renovation of the tripos would have important repercussions for the subsequent development of the moral sciences within Cambridge: as we shall see in Chapter Three, it was within Grote's reconstituted Moral Sciences Tripos that Marshall first found his bearings as a moral scientist.

In the history of economics, Whewell is known primarily as an early critic of the orthodox deductive method and as the author of a couple of mathematical treatments of economics in 1829 and 1831.[31] But it is primarily his subsequent construction of an idealist philosophy of the moral and natural sciences that necessitates attention to Whewell in this study of Marshall's early thought. The emphasis on natural sciences such as mechanics at Cambridge – the university of Newton – effectively allowed Whewell to turn on its head the eighteenth-century belief that the progress of commerce drove the advance of the arts. In an industrializing society, in which machines were increasingly understood to be the engines of progress, a clerisy that preserved and taught the science of machines could represent itself as the guardian not only of cultural values, but also of material economic progress. When in 1866, for example, the liberal Anglican Rev. F. Farrar counseled that "the important question for England was not the duration of her coal," but rather the number of her science teachers, he was indicating his acceptance of Whewell's identification of scientific culture as the foundation of the nation's wealth.[32] And because Whewell embodied this cultural vision within his midcentury reform of the Mathematical Tripos, crucial elements of Whewell's vision were inevitably absorbed by the young Alfred Marshall when, as an undergraduate between 1861 and 1865, he studied mathematics at Cambridge.

---

[30] Note that in Cambridge in this period the terms "psychology," "mental science," and "mental philosophy" were often synonyms.

[31] For Whewell's economic writings, see Campanelli 1982, Cochrane 1975, Henderson 1985, 1990, and 1996, and Rashid 1977. There is an interesting discussion of the development of Whewell's thinking concerning the methodology of economics in Maas 2005. Note that before 1833 Whewell, while firmly opposed to "Ricardites," "Milleans," and "McCullochites," did not place any emphasis on rebutting utilitarian moral philosophy (Palfrey 2003).

[32] Quoted in Desmond 1998: 350.

JOHN STUART MILL

As Perry Williams has observed, Whewell's writings embody a fundamental shift from eighteenth century assumptions concerning the nature of a liberal education; for while "in the eighteenth century a gentleman's education had been directed towards the acquisition of taste and polite manners, a liberal education for Whewell now meant the cultivation of the basic faculties of the human mind." Such a redefinition of the idea of a liberal education went hand in hand with a redefinition of the term "civilization"; as Williams points out, it no longer meant for Whewell "the process of acquiring polite manners or 'civility,' but the state of a nation's culture, the general level of development of the higher faculties of the mind."[33] Whewell's idealist conception of the human mind was forcefully and consistently challenged by J. S. Mill. Nevertheless, when placed in contrast to Adam Smith, Mill and Whewell stand side by side in their shared emphasis on the mind in and of itself as the foundation of philosophical, political, and social thought (as opposed to the sociable mind in concrete historical circumstances investigated by Smith). As Mill put it in 1840, Bentham and Coleridge, the two seminal thinkers of the age, had both agreed "in perceiving that the groundwork of all other philosophy must be laid in the philosophy of mind."[34]

Mill, of course, declared the "Germano-Coleridgean doctrine" of the mind to be not only erroneous but, as he wrote in his *Autobiography*, "the great intellectual support of false doctrines and bad institutions."[35] Nevertheless, his own avowed adherence to "the school of Locke and Bentham" did not prevent him from finding value in some aspects of Coleridge's vision of the proper relationship between culture, institutions of learning, and society. Whatever philosophical and political differences existed between Mill and Whewell, their shared identification of education with mental cultivation went together with a dismissal of Smith's arguments against the endowment of institutions of higher education. Mill's position was clearly set out in the first part of his 1835 review, "Professor Sedgwick's Discourse on the Studies of the University of Cambridge."[36] Although the main part of this essay consisted of a scathing assault and point-by-point refutation of Sedgwick's

[33] Williams 1991: 122–3.
[34] *Mill CW*, 10: 121. This sentence was underlined by Marshall in his copy of Mill's essay (Mill 1859: I, 396 [ML]).
[35] *Mill CW*, 1: 233 (see also pp. 269–71).
[36] *Mill CW*, 10: 31–74. Although Sedgwick had intended to do little more than point to the need for an alternative to utilitarian moral philosophy (a challenge subsequently taken up by Whewell), Mill insisted on treating Sedgwick's criticisms of utilitarianism as stemming from a fully developed nativist moral philosophy.

recent attack on utilitarian moral philosophy, Mill introduced his review with a brief discussion of the purpose of a university and of the means of evaluating the state of the English universities. He began in a manner reminiscent of Smith in his article on education:

Whatever individual competition does at all, it commonly does best. All things in which the public are adequate judges of excellence are best supplied where the stimulus of individual interest is the most active; and that is where pay is in proportion to exertion: not where pay is made sure in the first instance, and the only security for exertion is the superintendence of government; far less where, as in the English universities, even that security has been successfully excluded.[37]

Mill saw the University of Cambridge as a corrupt institution, failing to make proper use of its not inconsiderable resources. Nevertheless, such a conclusion was established only by the subsequent demonstration that Sedgwick's arguments were little more than moral sophistry. In other words, the failings of the university were to be exposed not by its paying customers, but by a philosopher. The key to Mill's position was his insistence that Smith's principle of payment according to results applied only to cases in which the public was indeed a competent judge of a commodity. Mill proceeded to argue that this was not the case with regard to "the education by which great minds are formed."

To rear up minds with aspirations and faculties above the herd, capable of leading on their countrymen to greater achievements in virtue, intelligence, and social well-being; to do this, and likewise to educate the leisured classes of the community generally, that they may participate as far as possible in the qualities of these superior spirits, and be prepared to appreciate them, and follow in their steps – these are purposes, requiring institutions of education placed above dependence on the immediate pleasure of that very multitude whom they are designed to elevate. These are the ends for which endowed universities are desirable.[38]

J. S. Mill, heir to the legacy of philosophical radicalism and future author of the bible of midcentury political economists, implicitly signaled his dissent from Smith's arguments on the endowment of education by stating his belief in the existence of values that stood above the judgment of the general public and that could not therefore be determined by the marketplace. Where Smith looked to a principle of economic competition by which to regulate the universities, Mill was concerned to remove the realm inhabited by "great minds" from the arena of the marketplace. Mill's dissension from

---

[37] *Mill CW*, 10: 33.
[38] *Mill CW*, 10: 33.

Smith's arguments can be readily related to the influence of Coleridge's writings on his thought. As he would explain in his essay "Coleridge" five years later (in a sentence carefully underlined in Marshall's copy), Coleridge had "vindicated against Bentham and Adam Smith and the whole eighteenth century, the principle of an endowed class, for the cultivation of learning, and for diffusing its results among the community."[39]

This Coleridgean side of Mill's thought would prove of supreme importance to the young Alfred Marshall. Henry Sidgwick regarded Mill's essay on Coleridge, as well as the essay on Bentham with which it was paired, as a product of what he described as Mill's "most eclectic phase."[40] Marshall, however, found in these two essays a profound statement of Mill's grasp of contemporary thought, an insight into the architecture of Mill's own philosophical project, and a yardstick against which to measure the limitations as well as the strengths of Mill's concrete achievements. Put simply, Marshall took the aim of these two essays to be the reconciliation of the schools of Bentham and Coleridge, and he saw this not as an exercise in eclecticism, but rather as *the* philosophical challenge facing the second half of the nineteenth century. It is not surprising that his copies of Mill's essays on Bentham and Coleridge contain more underlinings, marginal annotations, and markings than any other surviving text from this period. Indeed, if we turn to Marshall's loose-leaf notebook from the late 1860s, we find that he has transcribed from Mill's essay on Bentham the statement that the "two systems of concentric circles which the shock given by Bentham and Coleridge is spreading over the ocean of mind have only just begun to meet and intersect."[41] Many of Marshall's most important early writings, philosophical, historical, and also economic, can be read as attempts to further this meeting and intersection.

Nevertheless, and as we shall see in the following chapter, Marshall concluded early on that Mill had not achieved anything like a successful reconciliation of the schools of Bentham and Coleridge.[42] In light of the wider arguments of this book, it is important at this point to establish just how far and to what degree Mill embraced Coleridgean ideas. We may begin by noting that the views of both Sidgwick and Marshall stand in opposition to those of Mill's recent biographer, Nicholas Capaldi, who hails Mill as

---

[39] Mill *CW*, 10: 150 (Mill 1859, I: 445 [ML]).
[40] See Sidgwick 1877: 628. For a different view, see Maurice 1862: 664–5.
[41] M 4/1, f. 183. Marshall's transcription, which is given in main the text, is not an exact quotation; for the original, see *Mill CW*, 10: 78 (Mill 1859: I, 331 [ML]).
[42] Hence Marshall's early thought as a whole amounted to an attempt to carry out just that reconciliation that Mill had called for but, in his opinion, failed to enact.

"the greatest of the English Romantics."[43] Capaldi regards Mill's essays on Bentham and Coleridge as a declaration of Mill's conversion to romanticism. At the heart of this interpretation stands Mill's assertion in the essay on Coleridge that "in almost every one of the leading controversies, past or present, in social philosophy, both sides were in the right in what they affirmed, though wrong in what they denied."[44] For Capaldi, this statement is "both a reflection of Romanticism and an indication that the nature of that reconciliation must itself be Romantic."[45] In the preceding chapter, very similar Coleridgean statements by Marshall were quoted in order to illustrate Marshall's commitment to a form of Coleridgean philosophy. Nevertheless, I want to argue here that it is simply wrongheaded to identify a similar Coleridgean commitment with regard to Mill. Capaldi, it appears to me, has failed to distinguish between the attempt to establish common ground between two seemingly polar opposite systems of thought and the endeavor to reconcile two opposing systems within a single unified whole. The former was Mill's intention, the latter Marshall's. A review of certain key episodes in his early biography will enable us to clarify this point with regard to Mill.

The winter of 1826 saw the beginning of a crisis in Mill's mental history. In seeking a way out of his depression, Mill began to read romantic poetry and, in so doing, came to the realization that human experience included aesthetic feelings and moral sentiments of which he had hitherto hardly been aware. As he put it in his *Autobiography*, recovery from mental crisis involved an awakening to the importance of "the internal culture of the individual." Subsequently, the "cultivation of the feelings became one of the cardinal points in my ethical and philosophical creed."[46] Moral and aesthetic feelings, Mill was now convinced, constituted potential pleasures of a qualitatively superior order than did those purely physical pleasures that Bentham and James Mill had understood to be the sole motivating ends of human life. Thus, and in opposition to the attenuated conception of human nature found in the writings of his father, J. S. Mill came to embrace an ideal of individuality and self-cultivation that, in the pages of his 1859 *On Liberty*, he placed at the heart of his liberal philosophy. Ultimately Mill believed that the conditions that fostered or held back the development of individual character became the crucial factors in determining the future progress or

---

[43] Capaldi 2004: 365. See Winch 2004 for critical discussion of Capaldi's thesis.
[44] *Mill CW*, 10: 122–3. Cf. *Mill CW*, 18: 252, 254, 258 (*On Liberty*).
[45] Capaldi 2004: 89.
[46] *Mill CW*, 1: 147.

stagnation of society.[47] Thus far there is clearly a case for claiming that Mill came to embrace at least certain elements of romanticism.

At this point in our account of Mill's early mental history, we need to switch focus from personal to political considerations; for the lessons that Mill derived from his personal mental crisis were fused into his reading of the new political landscape that emerged into view in the wake of the passage of the 1832 Reform Bill. After 1832 Mill came to see as inevitable the future political dominance of the middle or commercial classes. But as the traditional authority in matters of opinion hitherto held by a landed aristocracy dwindled in the face of an emerging public opinion, governed by newspaper editorials and the idols of the marketplace, Mill came to fear that the authority of blind tradition would be replaced only by conformity to a crushing mediocrity. In de Tocqueville's *Democracy in America*, he found a seemingly prophetic articulation of such concerns. In his 1840 review of de Tocqueville's second volume, Mill summarized the author's message as a warning that the inevitable tendency toward equality in modern societies presented a danger "not of too great liberty, but of too ready submission; not of anarchy, but of servility; not of too rapid change, but of Chinese stationariness."[48] Yet against de Tocqueville's identification of democracy as the potential agent of such social stagnation, Mill insisted that the real problem, in Britain as much as in America, was the increasing dominance of the commercial classes and the consequent "unbalanced influence of the commercial spirit" within society. The real danger, Mill explained, was that the variation and diversity fostered by free discussion and toleration were under threat from a commercial order that threatened to impose "upon all the rest of society its own type; forcing all, either to submit to it or to imitate it."[49]

Here, then, are the roots of what has been called Mill's "liberal elitism." The term is John Skorupski's, who has forcefully argued that Mill shared with Coleridge the conviction that "there can be substantive and not merely instrumental deliberation on moral, cultural, and spiritual questions, that some individuals are more penetrating judges of these questions than others" and, furthermore, "that such individuals are socially vital and must exert a due influence through the recognition of their authority in their

---

[47] On Mill's revision of his father's associationist psychology and its implications for his philosophy of the moral sciences, see Wilson 1998: 203–54. For Mill's debt to von Humboldt in *On Liberty*, see the introduction to Burrow 1993, and on Mill's concern with character, see Collini et al. 1983: 158. For a general discussion of Mill's ideal of self-cultivation, see Capaldi 2004: 252–7.

[48] *Mill CW*, 18: 188.

[49] *Mill CW*, 18: 196–8, and see Capaldi 2004: 152.

sphere."[50] Skorupski nevertheless insists that Mill's "moderate elitism" differed from the "strong elitism" of Coleridge, in which a clerisy was to be endowed with formal authority in matters of opinion. In *On Liberty*, Mill decisively rejected Coleridge's call for such a clerisy. As Sheldon Rothblatt puts it, in Mill's pluralistic vision intellectuals are to be scattered throughout the institutions of Victorian society rather than gathered together into a formal clerisy. But as Rothblatt notes, such a solution did not answer all of Mill's social concerns. Scattering intellectuals throughout society might provide a safeguard against the tyranny of conformity, but it did not guarantee the establishment of high cultural standards. Nor did it offer any solution to the problem of cultural leadership in a democratic age.[51] For both of the latter needs, Mill continued to look to endowed institutions of higher education. In other words, Mill rejected Coleridge's idea of a clerisy, yet remained convinced that education must be removed from the realm of economic competition.[52]

The question remains, however, just how far Mill's liberal social philosophy differed on fundamental matters from the romantic social philosophies developed by the followers of Coleridge. In the wake of his mental crisis, Maurice and John Stirling introduced Mill to the writings of Coleridge.[53] Yet Mill wrote of these two Coleridgean friends in an early draft of his *Autobiography*, "If I agreed with them much more than with Bentham on poetry and general culture, I was as much opposed to them as ever on religion, political philosophy, ethics and metaphysics."[54] Mill might have added political economy. In his essay on Coleridge, he declared that on economic matters the sage of Highgate "writes like an arrant driveller, and it would have been well for his reputation had he never meddled with the subject."[55] The fundamental point, however, is that even while coming to recognize the importance of the role of aesthetic feelings and moral sentiments in social and political life, Mill remained convinced that such feelings were not innate.[56] Ultimately, Mill was inoculated against the more

---

[50] Skorupski 1999: 195.
[51] Rothblatt 1968: 114–15. For Mill's enduring idea of education as self-cultivation, see his 1867 inaugural address at St. Andrews (in *Mill CW*, 21: 215–57).
[52] See the 1868 essay "Endowments" for evidence of Mill's long-standing commitment to university endowments (*Mill CW*, 5: 628).
[53] Capaldi 2004: 76.
[54] *Mill CW*, 1: 162.
[55] *Mill CW*, 10: 155. For a discussion of Coleridge's views on political economy, see Winch 1996: 325–32.
[56] Mill's emphasis on higher feelings led him to revise the relationship between parts and whole set down in the associationist psychology of James Mill (see Wilson 1998: 214–17).

fevered speculations of Coleridgean idealism by his enduring commitment to associationist psychology.[57] In short, Mill's rejection of the "Germano-Coleridgean" philosophy of the human mind ensured that his revision of the heritage of Bentham and his father remained conceptually distinct from, and ultimately opposed to, the romantic social thought that in England was developed out of the writings of Coleridge.

In the 1860s Mill entered into an alliance with Coleridgean public moralists such as Mathew Arnold over the need to reform England's ancient universities. This alliance was formed despite fundamental disagreements over mental philosophy, and therefore over political and social theory. It was, as Rothblatt puts it (borrowing a phrase from Mill's essay on Bentham), an alliance formed by way of agreement over the "secondary ends" of elite higher education. But in Mill's case, the grounds of such an alliance had been laid more than two decades earlier. The essays on Bentham and Coleridge belong to that period of Mill's life in which, following the death of his father in 1836 and the waning of the political fortunes of the philosophical radicals, he had renounced political partisanship and embraced the role of a public moralist.[58] At the basis of this political reorientation stood the conviction that as aristocratic dominance gave way to a democratic commercial society, consensus among the educated elite was the necessary condition for the establishment of authority in matters of political opinion. Yet Mill also recognized that the grounds for such a consensus did not yet exist. This had been amply demonstrated by his fundamental disagreements with Coleridgeans like Maurice and Stirling over such matters as psychology and the philosophy of history. Mill therefore set about fashioning a political philosophy in which respect for opposing positions was fused with the belief that free discussion might eventually lead to a consensus over fundamental political principles. Mill's essays on Bentham and Coleridge were not manifestations of a conversion to romanticism. Rather, they were evidence of an attempt to reach out to philosophical opponents and thereby establish the grounds for a continuing discussion that might, one day, arrive at consensus.

Mill's new liberal philosophy alienated many of his former radical friends and allies who were deeply engaged in the day-to-day struggles of

---

[57] This is why Mill had no time for the liberal Anglican idea of history developed out of Coleridge's idealist psychology by Thomas Arnold and Hare. Against the liberal Anglican idea of history Mill would counter a version of Augustus Comte's "Social Dynamics" (see *Mill CW*, 8: 917–30). As Duncan Forbes has observed, these two Victorian approaches to history were "ultimately divided by psychological theory" (Forbes 1952: 132; see also p. 15).

[58] Thomas 1979: 204.

parliamentary politics. For many academic liberals in the late 1860s, however, Mill's moderately elitist liberal philosophy was extremely attractive. Newly disillusioned with parliamentary politics, facing a practical need to cohabit with liberal (and not so liberal) Anglican college fellows, and looking to construct a new self-image of academic authority in a democratic age, they found that Mill's version of liberalism had much to offer. It is not surprising, however, that different academic liberals developed different aspects of Mill's liberal philosophy and blended it with different philosophical traditions – traditions to which Mill was either opposed or only partially sympathetic. Before turning to one of these philosophically sophisticated renderings of Mill's liberalism, however, we must take note of the more straightforward "Cambridge Millites," who first preached the word of Mill in Cambridge. These "manly fellows" were sublimely unconcerned with the higher aesthetic feelings cultivated by their master and had little interest in Mill's liberal politics of consensus. In the person of Henry Fawcett, this "unreconstructed" form of Mill's liberalism set the tone of Cambridge political economy in the years of Marshall's intellectual apprenticeship.

HENRY FAWCETT

J. S. Mill's writings first entered Cambridge in midcentury, where they were avidly consumed by a circle of "Cambridge Millites."[59] This small group of undergraduates, with the young Henry Fawcett and Leslie Stephen at the center, might be described as radical in their political philosophy. They had no interest in the romantic undercurrent apparent in much of Mill's writings and certainly did not share their master's Coleridgean leanings. Stephen, as we have seen in Chapter One, came to identify the church, rather than the marketplace, as the primary threat to progressive culture in a democratic age.[60] As for the onetime Cambridge Professor of Political Economy, Henry Fawcett, Stephen himself observed that believers "in 'Culture' naturally set him down as a Philistine."[61] Thus it is no surprise that Fawcett was hostile to Whewell's vision of a Cambridge clerisy, consistently celebrated the virtues of a competitive educational regime, and actively campaigned to remove

---

[59] G. Moore 2006.

[60] Although his admiration for many of Mill's writings remained, Stephen in these later years came to regard Mill himself as an intellectual prig, whose overly "feminine" nature was responsible for the lamentably emotional character of his less hardheaded writings. See Gregory Moore, "Stephen and the Clubbable Men of Radical London" (unpublished paper, 2007).

[61] Stephen 1885: 92.

what he saw to be the barriers to free competition within the University of Cambridge. Yet on closer inspection we find that Fawcett's idea of a liberal education was far removed from the advocacy of professorial competition found in Smith's *Wealth of Nations*. As we shall see, Fawcett had no interest in paying professors according to results, nor was he particularly concerned with the efficiency of collegiate instruction. Rather, he celebrated an existing competitive examination system because it had the effect of improving the moral character of the student body.

Fawcett's pedagogy and his social philosophy were but two sides of the same coin. As Stephen tells us, the competitive system of examinations and prizes meant that, for Fawcett, Cambridge was "almost the only place where a man won his position exclusively on his merits."[62] Thus, as a university reformer, Fawcett insisted that his "primary object was to do away with all restrictions which hampered the full efficiency of the prizes offered to intellectual excellence ... the more open the field, the greater would be the success of the system."[63] This is the conviction that stood behind Fawcett's agitation against the university religious tests that discriminated against non-Anglicans. Precisely the same conviction also stood behind his support for national electoral reform and extension of the franchise. Fawcett's guiding principle, that free trade would give "free play to all men's intellects and faculties," applied equally to commerce, politics, and pedagogy. Participation in the market, in the Cambridge Mathematical Tripos, or indeed in the machinery of government constituted a moral training. In each case, competition propelled the individual out of a weak and childish self-absorption and fostered the virtues of responsibility, foresight, and independence. In a word, Fawcett's attitude toward a Cambridge liberal education was reflective of that same mid-Victorian temperament that, as we saw in Chapter One, was responsible for the "moralizing of political economy" in this period.

A comparison of the pedagogical ideals of Whewell and Fawcett reveals the daylight between Anglican and secular liberal ideals of a "manly character" in the mid-Victorian era. In contrast to Smith, both Victorians routinely understood human nature in terms of a higher and a lower self. But whereas Whewell's higher self was spiritual and its growth fostered by a study of the inductive sciences under the tutelage of an authoritative clerisy, Fawcett's higher self was robustly athletic and developed by way of healthy

---

[62] Stephen 1885: 105–6, 96; on open competition as the mainstay of university reform, see pp. 105–6, 114.
[63] Stephen 1885: 162.

competition between peers. There is, however, a certain irony in this contrast, for Fawcett's ideal of character improvement was in many ways the product of his undergraduate experiences studying for a Mathematical Tripos designed by Whewell. In 1848 Whewell had set in motion a tripos intended to provide that careful geometric and inductive study of natural and artificial mechanisms that, Whewell believed, would serve to educate the spiritual faculties of students. In practice, however, Whewell's tripos proved an increasingly arduous and stressful exercise that called forth great strength of nerve but drilled students to mechanically perform standardized problems at a rapid pace. To understand how this happened, we must explore briefly certain aspects of the history of the Mathematical Tripos that provided the core component of the undergraduate education of Fawcett, Stephen, and also Marshall.

Commenting on the English universities in the first decades of the nineteenth century, the German scholar Huber noted:

Our Universities produce learned men in the several sciences, or men for practical life. ... The English Universities on the contrary, content themselves with producing the first and most distinctive flower of the national life, the well educated "Gentleman."... We scarcely need add that even during the University residence the studies are by no means the only thing that brings about this result. A complicated machinery of reciprocal influences lies in the manners, habits and other relations peculiar to the English college life, bearing upon the education of the youth and the development of their feelings and characters.[64]

Cambridge certainly continued to provide a finishing school for the aristocracy throughout the nineteenth century and beyond.[65] But by midcentury, two systems of education existed side by side at Cambridge. Within the walls of the endowed colleges there continued among the college fellows a traditional and noncompetitive regime, very similar to that encountered by Smith at Oxford a century earlier. But outside the college walls, unofficial teachers competed for the fees of ambitious students, who themselves competed for a high position in the list of examination results. Behind this transformation of undergraduate life stands the gradual replacement of the traditional Latin disputation with written examinations in the vernacular – a process that had begun in the mid–eighteenth century and that gave rise to the Cambridge Mathematical Tripos, the "oldest and most famous written

[64] Quoted in Garland 1980: 2.
[65] A statistical survey of the social backgrounds of students entering Sidney Sussex College is given in the appendix of Rothblatt 1968. See also Groenewegen 1995: 72, 74 and Miller 1961: ch. 1 and p. 92.

competitive examination in England."[66] After the tripos examinations, those students who had achieved honors were ranked in order of merit. Those who achieved a first-class honors degree in mathematics were known as "wranglers," and the student who topped the order of merit earned the title of "senior wrangler" (Marshall in 1865 was "second wrangler"). By mid-century the Mathematical Tripos had contributed to the establishment of an educational regime that turned out graduates who, if not the "flower of national life," were at least highly efficient calculating machines.

The potential social advance open to those who ranked high in the order of merit fostered an intense competition for tripos distinction. Over the years the examinations for the tripos became more and more competitive, and ambitious students found themselves regulating their time and efforts with an ever-greater level of mechanical precision. The examinations were open-ended (i.e., candidates solved as many problems as the time allowed), and thus an ever-increasing number of points could be gained as students became more and more efficient in grinding out routine answers to stan-dardized questions. Yet collegiate instruction remained minimal; univer-sity professorial lectures bore little or no relationship to the content of the exams and were for this reason but sparsely attended.[67] Consequently, there emerged, outside the formal structures of the university, a system of pri-vate coaching. A Cambridge coach drove his "team" of students through what the historian of science Andrew Warwick describes as "a carefully contrived course of ordered topics and graded examples."[68] The purpose of such coaching was not to offer useful knowledge, still less to impart a cultural heritage, but simply and solely to enable students to achieve the greatest possible success in the tripos examinations.

George Pryme, Fawcett's predecessor in the Cambridge Chair of Political Economy, was sixth wrangler in 1803. This was despite spending half his time reading for classics, a situation that would have been unthinkable in Cambridge

---

[66] Rothblatt 1968: 181; see also Warwick 1998: 291.

[67] Each college student at nineteenth-century Cambridge was assigned to a college tutor, whose role was to stand *in loco parentis*, responsible for his ward's intellectual and moral development. The practice, however, does not seem to have matched the theory (see Garland 1980: 12, Rothblatt 1868: 197, and Winstanley 1947: 408–10). By midcentury the most intimate intellectual relationship that a student could expect with his seniors was not with any member of his college, but with his coach.

[68] See Warwick 1998: 293. Coaches were already starting to appear in the late eighteenth century. William Paley, who was senior wrangler in 1763, had a private coach in his last year (Searby 1997: 296). According to Warwick, the term "coach" was coined by under-graduates in the 1830s from the mail or stagecoach, "to capture the way a tutor drove his 'team.'" See also Ball 1889 and Palfrey 2003: 61. On the origins of the order of merit in the late medieval *Ordo*, see Searby 1997: 282, n. 14.

some fifty years later, when any serious and ambitious student – a "reading man" – would have engaged the services of a coach and could never have so divided his time between triposes in such a competitive environment.[69] In his autobiography, Pryme commented about undergraduate life in Trinity College around 1800 that "the system of private tuition had not then become common, and the lectures of the tutors during term-time were by many of the students (myself included) deemed sufficient."[70] Pryme also followed the advice of the master of Trinity, Dr. Mansel, "not to shut myself up with my books, but to mix in society, and so relax the strain upon my mind."[71] For Henry Fawcett, who occupied the Chair of Political Economy between Pryme and Marshall – and indeed for Marshall himself – a liberal education at Cambridge was essentially a grueling marathon that culminated in an intensely stressful period of examinations, so stressful, in fact, that Fawcett's nerves failed him in the tripos of 1856.[72] If such an education did little for the manners, tastes, and feelings of young men, it did, at least in the opinion of Stephen and Fawcett, provide "a sound masculine training" that turned out "intellectual athletes."[73]

According to his old college friend Stephen, Fawcett "felt, I have no doubt rightly, that his own mental fibre had been invigorated by the mathematical course, though he had derived no knowledge useful in the ordinary sense. His gratitude to the University for this service was unfailing. He held that it had turned him out, and, of course, had turned out others, thoroughly well equipped for the battle of life."[74] Thus, although Fawcett was not interested in paying professors according to results (even before he himself became a professor), in the late 1860s he resolutely defended the prize fellowship system at Cambridge against the gathering momentum for the endowment of research. As Stephen explained, such proposals ran the danger that "instead of the old strenuous competition, the students would be encouraged to listen to professors spinning fine phrases and creating sham sciences to justify the existence of their chairs."[75] Such condemnation clearly echoed the words of Adam Smith, but as Collini has commented, the emphasis on *strenuous* competition as the positive alternative to endowed sophistry indicates a distinctly mid-Victorian temperament.[76]

[69] See Marshall's letters to the *Cambridge University Gazette* (discussed pp. 77–9 below).
[70] Pryme 1870: 48–9.
[71] Pryme 1870: 54.
[72] Warwick 1998: 314.
[73] Stephen 1885: 91.
[74] Stephen 1885: 91, 92.
[75] Stephen 1885: 115.
[76] Collini 1991: 191.

What mattered to Fawcett was not useful knowledge but character, and Fawcett clearly regarded the mixed economy of Cambridge, in which professors did little but students competed intensely, as a perfect training ground for young character. The purpose of a university for Fawcett was the cultivation of "manly character" in the rising generation of the country. The rationale for a competitive regime within a university was not to keep the professors on their toes in their research and teaching, but to develop moral strength of character among the students.

If Fawcett and Smith were agreed on the virtues of a competitive university regime, they understood those virtues quite differently. For both men, a liberal education prepared the student for participation in the competitive world of the market, and it achieved this end by cultivating within him the same character traits as those inculcated by the market itself. But these traits were construed quite differently. Smith in his article complained that in the present corrupt state of the English universities "a gentleman, after going through, with application and abilities, the most complete course of education" that the times afford, could nevertheless "come into the world completely ignorant of every thing which is the common subject of conversation among gentlemen and men of the world."[77] Implicit in this complaint is the assumption that one purpose of a liberal education was to polish the manners and refine the tastes of a young man, so that he was rendered fit for that polite conversation that was the axis around which the wheels of commercial society revolved. If the self-consciously gruff Fawcett ever consciously engaged with this aspect of Smith's vision of the nature of commercial society, it was surely to dismiss it with a snort as "sentimental" and "effeminate." For Fawcett the commercial world, like the Cambridge tripos, both called for and called forth such "manly" characteristics as self-control, courage, and an upright and independent spirit.[78] For the second holder of the Cambridge Chair of Political Economy, it was not polite manners but an enthusiastic and robust vitality that ensured success in the "battle of life"; and it was "effeminate" weakness and "dependency," not sectarian enthusiasm, that constituted the chief threat to social well-being.

THE YOUNG ALFRED MARSHALL

Alfred Marshall both matriculated at and graduated from the university of William Whewell. He thus not only absorbed certain intellectual aspects of

---

[77] *WN*, 781 (V. i. f. 46).
[78] See Collini 1989: 53.

Whewell's idea of a liberal education, but also imbibed much of the same athletic educational ethos as had Fawcett and Stephen. But Whewell died in 1866, and the following year Marshall returned to a university stirred up by the imminent prospect of both internal and external reform of its institutions and practices. Not long after Whewell's death, the young Trinity don Henry Sidgwick wrote to his mother from Cambridge, "We are in a considerable state of agitation here, as all sorts of projects for reform are coming to the surface, partly in consequence of having a new Master – people begin to stretch themselves, and feel a certain freedom and independence."[79] From the moment of his return to Cambridge in 1867, Marshall appears to have become an enthusiastic participant in this internal movement of university reform. Such enthusiasm went hand in hand with a rejection, or at least modification, of the different educational values propagated by Whewell, on the one hand, and Fawcett, on the other.

Marshall's reforming activities within the university brought him into the same alliance that, on the national stage, Mill had recently formed with public moralists such as Matthew Arnold. Many accounts of the transformation of Cambridge after 1866 overlook the fact that a great many of the organizational changes that now occurred, and are usually associated with the "reforming dons" of the late 1860s, were first proposed in the 1850s by the "party of reform" that emerged within Trinity College. Midcentury liberal Anglican fellows of Trinity such as B. F. Westcott, D. J. Vaughan, and J. L. Davies may be seen as the Coleridgean heirs of Julius Hare and Connop Thirlwall, founders of the Broad Church movement. Looking to Maurice for leadership, they had advocated a more flexible approach to church dogma and opinion within the university, and a greater social role for the university within the nation as a whole.[80] As Harvie observes, during the 1860s the shared political perceptions of secular and Anglican liberals proved more important than their divergent philosophies.[81] Liberal Anglican reformers found common ground with a number of academic liberals, among whom Marshall should be included, not only in a shared support for national political reform, but also on a range of fundamental issues related to the reform of the university.

[79] Sidgwick and Sidgwick 1906: 145. Compare Sidgwick's comments with Kingsley's more immediate reaction: "Whewell is dead! It is only a question of hours now. The feeling here is deep and solemn. Men say he was the leader in progress and reform, when such were a persecuted minority. He was the regenerator of Trinity; he is connected with every step forward that the University has made for years past" (Kingsley 1877: II, 221).
[80] See Harvie 1976: 46–7, 35.
[81] Harvie 1976: 20.

It is instructive to compare the reforming activities of Fawcett and Marshall in these years. By the late 1860s, Fawcett had emerged as one of the most energetic agitators in the campaign to persuade Parliament to abolish the University Test Acts. Yet voting with his feet, Fawcett demonstrated an indifference to the internal teaching reforms of this period. Indeed, despite being the professor of political economy, Fawcett shared Whewell's view that classics and mathematics constituted all that need be studied in a liberal education, and therefore disapproved of the midcentury innovation of a Moral Sciences Tripos. Marshall, by contrast, though no doubt sympathetic to the agitation against the religious tests, does not appear to have actively supported the campaign to abolish them. On the other hand, once he was appointed a college lecturer in the moral sciences in 1868, he became one of several dons who, after training with a private coach for his own tripos examinations and then himself coaching students in order to pay off his student debts, participated in the attempt to replace such private-sector instruction with a new regime of intercollegiate lectures. In short, if Fawcett and Marshall were both university reformers, the different directions of their reforming efforts are suggestive of underlying differences in their conceptions of the value of a liberal education.

Marshall in these years can be described as a critical but enthusiastic disciple of J. S. Mill. Yet Fawcett was one of the most loyal of Mill's followers. Clearly, there were salient differences in the versions of liberal social philosophy that Fawcett and Marshall derived from Mill's writings. Such a divergence can be placed within a wider frame; for if there were two tides that washed the thought of Mill into nineteenth-century Cambridge, the second intersected with the second wave of practical Coleridgean reforms within the university. In the Cambridge of the 1850s Whewell, on the one hand, and Fawcett and Stephen, on the other, had articulated polar opposite political and philosophical positions. But by the late 1860s and early 1870s, liberal moral scientists such as Sidgwick, John Venn, and Marshall could find much of their basic intellectual orientation in the writings of Mill, and yet find also a good deal of practical and in some cases theoretical agreement with those liberal Anglicans whose primary philosophical orientation derived from the writings of Coleridge. In the following chapter, we shall examine the theoretical developments within Cambridge Anglican thought in the 1860s that fostered this intellectual meeting, cohabitation, and even, in some cases, fusion. For the present it is sufficient to repeat Rothblatt's statement that this generation of academic liberals could at least agree with Maurice, who headed the tripos between 1866 and his death in 1872, on a number of "secondary ends." That is, both Coleridgeans and this second generation of Cambridge Millites could agree on the proper role of their university in producing cultivated minds, on the need to establish high moral and cultural standards, and on the necessity of leadership by the best educated.[82]

Marshall's early reforming sympathies are illustrated in four letters written to the *Cambridge University Gazette* between late 1868 and 1869. In these letters he demonstrated an underlying conviction that the business of a liberal education was the development of cultured minds. Culture, as Marshall presented it, was the property of a mind that grasps ideas, methods, and principles. Thus, in his vision of a reformed examination structure, the aspiring mathematical student was "to read Latin in that liberal and appreciative manner which an Honour Examination can foster," because only such a reading would allow him "to obtain much of that culture which arises from real acquaintance with the great minds of a nation." Under the present system of "cram," by contrast, there was little hope that a student would "ever acquire any grasp of the ideas, to the expression of which the chief value of the languages is owing." Equally, it was "mere cram" to learn a "new method of investigation" in mathematics "without a thorough grasp of the idea of that method." But if aspiring classics men took mid-university honors in applied mathematics (i.e., competed in a tripos examination), as Marshall urged, they would be likely to gain "a real insight into the main principles of Physics," and so speedily be "initiated into the chief methods by which the world has attained its present knowledge."

Two points can immediately be made concerning these letters. First, while Marshall evidently subscribed to some version of the Coleridgean ideal of the university as a guardian and perpetuator of culture, it is also clear that he adhered to some components of Whewell's midcentury vision of a Cambridge clerisy as the guardians and teachers of scientific as well as humanistic culture. Second, although as an educational product "cram" represented the antithesis to "culture," Marshall believed that it constituted a major product of the present unreformed system. The basic argument made in these letters was that there was a need to institute mid-university honor examinations both in Latin and in the applications of elementary mathematics to physical science.[83] In making his case, Marshall at one point

---

[82] Rothblatt 1968: 132.
[83] *CAM*, I: 1–8. The discussion of Marshall's early letters on university reform in this and other chapters has developed out of, but should now be understood to have superseded, those first set out in Cook 2004.

noted that the "general tendency to specialisation" that existed at Cambridge
as elsewhere meant that even the best students were likely to compete in
only one of the two major triposes. Yet under the present system, he further
observed, all students were required to sit for non-honors "Pass" examinations in both classics and mathematics midway through their studies.
Under such a system, he argued, the private tutor could scarcely be blamed
for hinting to the student "that it was only virtue that can be its own reward"
and for exhorting him not to allow the secondary "Pass" examination to
"interfere more than is absolutely necessary with his 'work.' " In other
words, under the present unreformed system, an honors student's midca-
reer studies for his non-honors subject amounted to little more than superficial cram. It is this condemnation of an educational regime that fostered
cram as opposed to liberal study that stands behind Marshall's participation
in what Rothblatt describes as the "revolution of the dons." At the heart of
this revolution was a determination to institute a new system of intercollegiate lectures that would replace the old regime of private coaches.[84]

From the shared point of view of many academic liberal and liberal
Anglican college fellows, the system of private coaching represented, as
Harvie puts it, the "cash nexus in academic life."[85] Under the old regime,
coaches drilled students to a single end: maximum success in the tripos
examinations. Such a system of cram might meet the demands of the
undergraduate market, but it did not supply the kind of liberal education that the reforming dons saw as the duty of a national institution to
provide. The assault on the system of private coaching and the establishment of a new system of intercollegiate lectures thus amounted to a direct
rejection of Smith's identification of competition with desirable teaching
practices. It was an expression, in fact, of a conviction that the activities of teaching and learning could not be evaluated by the market and,
indeed, were at present being corrupted by the market. Such divergence
from the point of view set down in Smith's analysis of education in the
Wealth of Nations was, of course, but a manifestation of a deeper historical fissure. As we have already noted, from Addison to Smith it had
been taken for granted that polite culture was the child of commerce.
When mid-Victorian luminaries such as J. S. Mill and Mathew Arnold,
and Cambridge moral scientists such as the aged Maurice and the young
Alfred Marshall, could come together in agreement as to the inherent

---

[84] See Rothblatt 1968: 114–15, 132, 207–11, and on the teaching revolution itself, see
   pp. 209–47.
[85] Harvie 1976: 62.

philistinism of modern commercial culture, we may, as Pocock puts it, "regard the Scottish Enlightenment as effectively dead."[86]

Victorian dissent from Smith's article on education was not always implicit. Sometime, probably in 1868 or 1869, Marshall composed four folios dealing with Smith's discussion of education in the *Wealth of Nations*, or rather on the "principal questions wh[ich] Smith seems to have overlooked."[87] This manuscript sheds light on Marshall's early social thought. The first point that Marshall raised concerned the ends of a liberal education. He questioned whether it was sufficient merely to dwell on the pecuniary advantages that derive from the "increased *direct* efficiency" of the graduate of higher education.[88] A liberal education, Marshall suggested, would give rise to indirect civic benefits by increasing the graduate's "services as a citizen." Smith had looked to primary education to secure the lower orders from public disturbances born of religious enthusiasm. Marshall now looked to higher education to enhance the value of citizenship in a dawning democratic age.

Marshall's second point of disagreement concerned the efficacy of competitive principles in the special case of education. In his opinion, Smith had overlooked the fact that in matters of education the public was not "able to distinguish between work well done & work badly done" – this because the public "have no special means of forming a right judgment on the subject." Therefore, he argued, "the method, applicable to almost all other cases, of paying according to results" could not be applied in the case of education. What Marshall proposed instead was that, "in view of the welfare both of students & teachers," it was "on many accounts advisable that advanced classes should be taught by those who are engaged in extending the limits of the science." Quite why Marshall was convinced that his intellectual vanguard would not succumb to indolence is a question to which we shall turn shortly. The more immediate question facing him was how to evaluate research, and so identify those who truly were extending the limits of knowledge. Here, again, Marshall insisted that the market did not provide an appropriate method of evaluation: is "it not even more impossible

---

[86] Pocock 1985: 310; also pp. 50, 281.

[87] M 4/12, ff. 87–90. The pages are numbered by Marshall according to a dual system such that each folio is marked first by a "1" and then below by a series from 1 to 4. One folio numbered "1, 2" is found in M 4/5, f. 33 and deals with a separate aspect of Smith's article (a comparison of Greek and Roman educational practices and character). All the other folios of M 4/12 deal with medieval history, and it is clear that these four folios, which are found at the very end of the manuscript, have at some point been misfiled.

[88] M 4/12, f. 88, emphasis in original.

to reward thinkers according to their performances than to reward teachers in this manner?" Marshall was here following – almost certainly self-consciously – in Mill's Coleridgean footsteps, footsteps that led directly to the support of endowed institutions of higher education.

In the final paragraph of his notes, however, Marshall did offer one reason for going along with Smith's arguments against endowments. Yet if the conclusion was the same as Smith's, his reasoning was, if anything, even more distant from the worldview of Smith than the claim that the world of the university should be separated from the competition of the marketplace. Marshall wondered whether his teacher-scientists, "if the endowments awarded are more than barely sufficient to enable them to continue their studies," were not likely to "become servile in their habits of thought." Behind this question stands the conviction that the supply of ideas cannot be enhanced by either the prospect or the guarantee of material comfort; for the "best work" of "true men of learning" is "generally done by men of strong will," irrespective of their pecuniary situation:

[I]s it not a necessary condition for the most effective thought that the teacher should be wedded heart and soul to his study, that he should entirely forget himself for her, that save when his attention shall be distracted by some duty which for the time is more pressing, his thought should be ever recurring to her[?] Is not the student's frame of mind an essentially non-self-regarding frame of mind; or as some people would say a religious frame of mind? And can such a frame of mind be purchased by large endowments?

Some things in this world, such as a scholarly or religious frame of mind, money apparently cannot buy. Nor, therefore, can the market price of such things be regarded as a true measure of their real value. We have traveled a long way from the world of Smith's indolent Oxford professors, whose interest it was to live as much at their ease as they could. Indeed, we seem to have turned the pages of Smith's *Wealth of Nations* and discovered that religious enthusiasm, not expectation of financial reward, is the chief motivation of scholarly activity. And in fact there is a telling mistake contained in Marshall's four folios of notes on Smith; for while the content of these folios unambiguously refers to Smith's discussion of the education of youth in his second article, Marshall has nevertheless headed each of his folios "art III," which is the article in book V of the *Wealth of Nations* in which Smith deals with religious institutions. Perhaps this was no more than a simple error on Marshall's part. Nevertheless, it is hard not to suspect that behind such a mistake stood an awareness that Smith's article on religious instruction was just as relevant to the debates over the reform of mid-Victorian Cambridge as was his article on the education of youth, and indeed that Marshall's own distance from Smith related as much to Smith's attitude to religious enthusiasm as to his analysis of education.

It is clear that at least at this point in his Cambridge career, Marshall identified the academic ideal with some notion of enthusiasm – a yearning to transcend the self through an altruistic absorption in scholarship. Such enthusiasm generated true research and was therefore a characteristic of those best suited to provide liberal education. It is interesting to compare Marshall's description of the enthusiastic scholar with the young Henry Sidgwick's religiously saturated utilitarian musings of but a few years earlier. "I desire only studies that however abstract in … reasonings have for their end human happiness," Sidgwick wrote in his commonplace book in the period just before the onset of his full-blown religious doubts sometime in the mid-1860s. "Thus Political Economy to make men happier and better en masse. … The strongest conviction I have is a belief in what Comte calls 'altruisme': the cardinal doctrine, it seems to me, of Jesus of Nazareth."[89] Where Marshall was to emphasize the losing of self in scholarly thought, Sidgwick's academic ideal focused rather on the overcoming of self through a commitment to social well-being. At root, however, these different formulations sprang from the same kind of enthusiasm that in 1854 Mill had identified as forming the "essence of religion." Such a state of enthusiasm, Mill had explained, consists in "the strong and earnest directions of the emotions and desires towards an ideal object recognized as of the highest excellence, and as rightfully paramount over all selfish objects of desire."[90]

Nevertheless, we should be wary of leaping to the conclusion that Marshall's ideal of scholarship rested on some as yet unchallenged aspect of his early Anglican faith. In Chapter Three we shall begin the task of setting Marshall's early intellectual development in the context of a youthful crisis of religious faith. Such an inquiry will occupy us, directly or indirectly, for the rest of this book. Rather than attempt to preempt the conclusions of

---

[89] Quoted in Schultz 2004: 42. Compare J. S. Mill's insistence that "the morality of self-devotion" belongs to the utilitarian as much as to the Stoic or transcendentalist, and that in "the golden rule of Jesus of Nazareth, we read the complete spirit of the ethics of utility" (*Mill CW*, 10: 218). In her copy of this work, Mary Paley wrote in the margin next to the latter statement that Mill here incorporates the "whole doctrine of human sympathy & sociality" (Mill 1871: 24 [ML]). For Sidgwick's mature views on "political economy and private morality," see Sidgwick 1887: ch. 9.

[90] J. S. Mill, "The Utility of Religion" (1854), quoted in Collini 1991: 73. For Mill, the object of enthusiasm could as readily be identified with society as with God. Note that Marshall's notion of "non-self-regarding" motivations carries echoes from J. S. Mill's *On Liberty*, echoes that would also reverberate in Sidgwick's *Methods of Ethics*.

this inquiry, let us pass over for the time being any further discussion of the nature of the seemingly religious overtones of Marshall's early academic enthusiasm. A more fruitful interpretive approach at this stage is to relate Marshall's ideal of scholarly enthusiasm to what, in Chapter One, we saw to be a conventional mid-Victorian dichotomy between selfish and selfless actions and motivations.

If we compare the language of his notes on Smith with that of his early letters on university reform, it becomes clear that some basic dichotomy between higher and lower moral states informs Marshall's thinking on university life. At one point in his letters, Marshall had argued in support of the minor triposes now starting to proliferate in Cambridge. If the student was "but an ordinary man," Marshall claimed, the traditional system of classics and mathematics led him to become "narrow and lethargic in his intellectual habits." Indeed, the "intrinsic values of Classical or Mathematical studies" were not in Marshall's opinion sufficient to compensate for the fact that "Cambridge may safely defy any University in the civilized world to produce a set of men who, without being specially idle or stupid, have made less of their advantage than these men."[91] By "these men," Marshall meant "ordinary men," whose underlying motivations were clearly different from the enthusiasm of those "true men of learning" eulogized in the notes on Smith. Yet however sluggish "ordinary men" might become, Marshall does not describe them as selfish. Thus, at first sight at least, it is unclear whether the contrast of ordinary and scholarly minds is a variation on, or simply of a different order than, the conventional educated mid-Victorian opposition between selfish and selfless states of mind.

On closer inspection, however, it becomes clearer how Marshall's contrast of ordinary and scholarly minds was related to the conventional dichotomy between selfish and selfless states of mind. First of all, it is evident from Marshall's language that the enthusiastic scholar is selfless in his commitment to learning. Indeed, it is precisely because he is so motivated that economic competition at the level of advanced teaching and research is at best pointless, and at worst destructive. For the ordinary student, by contrast, a tendency to become lethargic and narrow in habits of thought suggests a need for some form of external stimulus. The "ordinary man," in other words, needs the spur of competition and external reward if he is not

---

[91] Marshall in these letters argued that "some knowledge of the more prominent physical phenomena" was increasingly becoming a general cultural requirement "from every rank in life" and "from either sex." Consequently, he suggested, the "motive of an honest shame" would lead even "ordinary" students to study hard for a mid-university honors examination in applied mathematics.

to stagnate in his mental activity. Marshall's contrast between ordinary and scholarly students is certainly not reducible to Buckle's reading of Smith's division between the selfish economic and the sympathetic moral components of human nature. Nevertheless, his distinction between ordinary and scholarly minds performs a role similar to Buckle's dualistic division of human nature in situating different mental and moral states on either side of a binary division of motivations and actions. Furthermore, only on one side of this division can the competition of the market provide a useful spur to industry and efficiency.

Marshall's criticism of Smith's advocacy of competition within the world of the university thus points to an underlying conviction that only lower states of mind can be analyzed by political economy. In contrast to the "ordinary man," "true men of learning" have transcended desire for wealth, desire for luxury, and aversion to labor. Such students and scholars, in other words, are not motivated by any of the self-regarding drives that propel the abstract "economic man" who forms the subject matter of orthodox political economy. Furthermore, such a division of motivations corresponds to a division within social activities. It appears, then, to be the belief of the young Marshall that cultural activities, which is to say the discovery and advanced teaching of ideas, stand apart from those activities that make up the ordinary business of life. In 1868 Marshall began teaching political economy to moral sciences students at St. John's College. But according to his thinking around 1869, the very business of teaching political economy was an activity that belonged to a realm apart from the sphere of life that it studied. Culture, for the young Marshall, included the principles and the method that made up the science of political economy, but that science of the values of ordinary life was itself unsuited and unable to pronounce on the cultural value of a scholarly university life. Over the course of the next two chapters, we shall uncover the philosophical grounds on which Marshall established this distinction, while in later chapters we shall come to see how the development of Marshall's social thought in the early 1870s turned on a revision, if not quite a wholesale abolition, of this division.

PART II

DUALIST MORAL SCIENCE: 1867–1871

THREE

Mental Crisis

A "CRISIS IN HIS MENTAL DEVELOPMENT"

Marshall's early Cambridge career began "just at the date which will ... be regarded by the historians of opinion as the critical moment when Christian dogma fell away from the serious philosophical world of England, or at any rate of Cambridge."[1] Such, at any rate, was the opinion expressed by John Maynard Keynes in his 1924 obituary memoir of Marshall in the *Economic Journal*. After his graduation from the Mathematical Tripos in 1865, Marshall briefly taught mathematics at Clifton public school, but then returned to Cambridge to take up coaching in mathematics. Upon returning to Cambridge, he came into contact with the world of the Cambridge moral sciences. In 1867 Marshall began attending the weekly meetings of the Grote Club, whose members were involved in the moral sciences. According to Keynes:

It was at this time and under these influences that there came the crisis in his mental development, of which in later years he often spoke. His design to study physics was (in his own words) "cut short by the sudden rise of a deep interest in the philosophical foundation of knowledge, especially in relation to theology." ... after a quick struggle religious beliefs dropped away, and he became, for the rest of his life, what used to be called an agnostic.[2]

Keynes's concise and apparently informative account of Marshall's early "crisis" of "mental development" provides something of a challenge for the twenty-first-century historian of opinion. Keynes was interpreting Marshall's reminiscences, and the memories of youth by a man in his old age are notoriously unreliable. Furthermore, as a member of the Cambridge

[1] Keynes 1925: 7.
[2] Keynes 1925: 6–7.

generation that reveled in atheism and delighted in mocking the earnest struggles with belief of their eminent Victorian forebears, Keynes was not, perhaps, the most objective interpreter of such reminiscences. (Keynes once wrote of Henry Sidgwick, for example, that he "never did anything but wonder whether Christianity was true and prove it wasn't and hope that it was.")[3] All things considered, we should not be too surprised if we discover that Keynes's narrative proves to be unsatisfactory on a number of points. But before turning to his further account of the course of Marshall's struggle with religious belief, it is useful to anticipate some of the arguments that will be developed over the course of this and subsequent chapters.

There are good reasons to suspect that in the passage just quoted, Keynes – and quite possibly he was here simply following the aged Marshall's lead – conflated (at least) two distinct elements of the young Marshall's mental development.[4] Marshall's memory appears to have been shaped by what had become, for his generation, a topos; for if "in later years he often spoke" of a "crisis in his mental development," in these later years he was echoing the words of J. S. Mill's *Autobiography*, the fifth chapter of which is entitled "A Crisis in My Mental History." In this chapter Mill recounted how in the winter of 1826–7 he had fallen into a "dull state of nerves," "unsusceptible to enjoyment or pleasurable excitement." In this dejected state he found himself performing his occupations "mechanically, by the mere force of habit. I had been so drilled in a certain sort of mental exercise, that I could carry it on when all the spirit had gone out of it."[5] Mill's *Autobiography* was published in 1873, and the words just quoted must have touched a chord with many graduates of Cambridge's Mathematical Tripos. As we saw in the preceding chapter, the examinations for the tripos became increasingly competitive, routine, and standardized as the century progressed. Although a code of stoicism prevented public discussion of the trials and tribulations of the tripos, the examination system, in the words of a modern historian, "clearly worked ambitious undergraduates to the limits of their emotional

---

[3] Quoted in Schultz 2004: 4. For an account of Sidgwick's struggle with Christianity, see Schultz 2004, especially chapter 2. For Keynes as a member of the first atheist generation in Cambridge, see Berman 1990.

[4] It is also possible that Keynes was following a narrative provided by Mary Paley Marshall, for conversations with her provided much of the biographical material for his memoir of her late husband. Mary Paley, it should be borne in mind, came up to Cambridge only after Maurice had died and a division between secular and reactionary Evangelical religious thinking – quite absent but half a decade previously – had come to characterize the Moral Sciences Tripos.

[5] *Mill CW*, 1: 137, 143.

and intellectual tolerance."[6] We have already noted how Fawcett's nerves failed him in the tripos of 1856. Such a condition was by no means unusual. In letters home to his father in the 1840s, Francis Galton described how the three best mathematicians in the year above him were graduating as "poll men" because their health had collapsed. Galton himself subsequently suffered a breakdown that forced him to leave Cambridge for a term.[7] To achieve the position of second wrangler in the tripos of 1865 must have cost Marshall many weary hours of mechanical mental drill. When two years later he returned to Cambridge, his initial study of philosophy was conducted in a no less strenuous manner, and as Marshall later reported, he became physically ill.[8] In the following chapter it will be suggested that such a breakdown in his health, rather than some spontaneous appearance of theological doubt, initiated Marshall's mental crisis.

But the full significance of Marshall's echo of Mill's autobiography is found not so much in any shared cause of mental crisis as in the apparent nature of the solution. His problem, Mill came to believe, was that his education not only had failed to cultivate his feelings, but had exclusively developed just that "habit of analysis" that "has a tendency to wear away the feelings."[9] A way out of the crisis was offered by Maurice and Stirling, Mill's former "Coleridgean adversaries" with whom he now "fell more and more into friendly discourse." In Maurice's conversation, Coleridge's writings, and the poetry of Wordsworth, Mill now discovered romanticism; as he characteristically put it, the "influences of European, that is to say, Continental, thought, and especially those of the reaction of the nineteenth century against the eighteenth, were now streaming in upon me."[10] Whatever the young Marshall's mental difficulties may have been nearly half a century later, they clearly led him into an engagement with Coleridgean philosophy. When in 1873, having just arrived at the end of his own philosophical odyssey, Marshall first turned the pages of Mill's *Autobiography*, we may surmise that he read much of his own recent mental experiences into Mill's account not only of mental crisis, but also of its resolution.[11] Half a century later

---

[6] Warwick 1998.

[7] See Warwick 1998: 295–301. Groenewegen reports that after becoming the senior wrangler in 1859, James Wilson, Marshall's fellow Johnian and later friend in Bristol, suffered a nervous breakdown, the result of which was that he was to make "the discovery that my illness had swept away all my higher mathematics" (Groenewegen 1995: 87).

[8] See Chapter Four of this book.

[9] *Mill CW*, 1: 141.

[10] See *Mill CW*, 1: 159–69.

[11] That Marshall read Mill's *Autobiography* in the year that it was published is demonstrated by his references to it in his 1873 talk "The Future of the Working Classes."

Marshall was quite certain that he, too, had experienced a youthful "crisis in his mental development."

I would argue that the "crisis" in Marshall's early mental life is a story that culminates not so much with loss of faith as with its discovery. This is not to say that Keynes was incorrect to describe Marshall's religious beliefs as dropping away (although in neither his published nor unpublished writings of this period does Marshall ever describe himself as an "agnostic"). There can be no question, for example, that Marshall early on ceased to believe in the historical veracity of the gospel narratives or, indeed, that around this time he discarded much of the Evangelical creed of his childhood.[12] More significantly, perhaps, by 1873 at the latest he was convinced that the grounds of the sciences (economic science included) were not to be found in theology. But if Marshall lost his childhood faith sometime between 1867 and 1873, he nevertheless gained another faith during the same period. The nature of this new faith was metaphysical, and it came to provide the grounds, and even to some extent the content, of his subsequent reformulation of economic science. But though it was not theological, such a faith owed much to Cambridge liberal Anglicanism and the English romantic philosophy that derived from Coleridge. Whether such a faith should be characterized as a "religious faith" is a moot point, discussion of which is best postponed until after we have traced its genesis and examined its nature over the course of the next few chapters; for as yet this argument has not been developed beyond an assertion. As a first step in the movement from speculation to reasoned conclusion, then, let us return to Keynes's account of the theological nature of the crisis in Marshall's mental development.

"Marshall was wont to attribute the beginning of his own transition of mind," Keynes explained, "to the controversy arising out of Mansel's Bampton Lectures," which, Marshall claimed, first came into his hands in 1867. What was the nature of this controversy? Quoting from Leslie Stephen's *English Utilitarians*, Keynes explained that in 1858 the Oxford don Henry Mansel became a champion of religious orthodoxy when he "adopted from Hamilton the peculiar theory which was to enlist Kant in the service of the Church of England." Then, continued Keynes, in 1865 "appeared Mill's *Examination of Sir William Hamilton's Philosophy*, which included a criticism of Mansel's extension of Hamilton to Christian Theology. Mansel replied.

---

[12] By 1875 Marshall could write, in a letter to Foxwell, that a short while ago he had become "*absolutely* convinced that Christ neither taught nor believed any of the leading dogmas of Christianity" (*CAM*, I: 34, emphasis in original).

Mansel's defense of orthodoxy 'showed me,' Marshall said, 'how much there was to be defended.' "[13] But this was not yet the end of the road:

Meanwhile in 1859, the year following the Bampton Lectures, the *Origin of Species* had appeared, to point away from heaven or the clouds to an open road on earth; and in 1860–62 Herbert Spencer's *First Principles* (unreadable as it now is), also born of the Hamilton–Mansel controversy, took a new direction, dissolved metaphysics in agnosticism, and warned all but ingrained metaphysical minds away from a blind alley.[14]

This is all very well – at least until we inquire into the actual positions of Mill and Spencer in this "great controversy" with Mansel. As we shall see later, Mill's intention was not to derive some secular creed of agnosticism, but simply to demolish Mansel's entire philosophy. Spencer's "new direction," by contrast, was derived *from* Mansel's philosophy. Mansel's intention had been to establish "the separate provinces of Reason and Faith." This he attempted to do "by showing that Reason itself, rightly interpreted, teaches the existence of truths that are above Reason." Such truths cannot be conceived, but "it is our duty, in some instances, to believe that which we cannot conceive."[15] In other words, our finite reason cannot discern God's nature or purposes, and for moral guidance we must look to revelation. For "scientific naturalists" with dissenting roots or sympathies, such as Herbert Spencer or Thomas Huxley, Mansel's philosophical defense of Anglican orthodoxy provided a perfect framework for their own attempt to free scientific speculation from theological interference. Science was now held up as the domain of evidence and reason; theology, by contrast, was presented as a domain governed by faith and revelation. In his *First Principles*, Spencer established the separation of science and theology by simply translating Mansel's term for God, the "Absolute," as "Unknowable." Then, in 1869, Huxley coined the term "agnostic," a maneuver that allowed him to sidestep all theological debate as "metaphysical," while his materialist explanations of the mind relentlessly pushed scientific naturalism into areas hitherto regarded as sacrosanct. Huxley had in fact already rejected Spencer's version of Mansel's "Unknowable" as a "last remnant of idolatry," but his own distinction between metaphysical speculation and scientific

[13] Keynes 1925: 8.
[14] Keynes 1925: 9.
[15] Mansel 1859: 69, 85. Such an endeavor had its roots in book 4, chapter 18 of Locke's *Essay Concerning Human Understanding* ("Of Faith and Reason, and their Distinct Provinces"). But by turning to Hamilton's marriage of Scottish common sense philosophy and Kantian criticism, Mansel avoided the anti-Trinitarian implications of Locke's argument.

knowledge was clearly but a further derivation from Mansel. As Leslie Stephen would put it in his "Agnostics Apology" of 1876, the "whole substance" of Mansel's argument "was simply and solely the assertion of the first principles of Agnosticism."[16] But if, as Keynes seems to imply, Marshall followed the same route as Spencer and Huxley, does this mean that he had now rejected Mill's onslaught on the philosophy that provided the foundation of agnosticism?

The significance of this question is heightened if we turn to a serious lacuna in Keynes's account of Marshall's religious crisis. Marshall is reported to have talked of the significance of "the controversy arising out of Mansel's Bampton Lectures." After so quoting Marshall, Keynes proceeds to identify this controversy with Mill's book on Hamilton. But the "great controversy" that arose out of Mansel's Bampton Lectures was initiated not by Mill but by Maurice (the same clergyman who had led Mill to Coleridge in the wake of *his* mental crisis). Now, Maurice was Knightbridge Professor of Moral Philosophy at Cambridge between 1866 and 1872, and therefore head of both the Moral Sciences Tripos and the Grote Club during the period of Marshall's crisis of faith. Yet this Coleridgean Broad Churchman, with whom Marshall must have had regular intercourse during this period, is written out of Keynes's narrative. To the nature of the dispute between Mansel and Maurice we will turn later. For the present it is sufficient to observe Maurice's response upon reading the attack on Mansel contained in Mill's 1865 book on the philosophy of William Hamilton. Mill had managed to state with great emphasis, wrote Maurice in a letter to Charles Kingsley, and "in a few words what I was trying to say in a long series of letters." Furthermore, Mill had achieved in the conclusion to his discussion of Mansel's arguments "a grand and affecting theological statement."[17] The range and relationship of the positions that marked the "great controversy"

---

[16] Stephen 1903: 9. Lightman 1987 describes Mansel as the "missing link" connecting scientific agnosticism with Kantian skepticism. This was also the opinion of many nineteenth-century churchmen (see, e.g., Hitchcock 1891: 637). The link between Mansel and agnosticism was something that, for once, Stephen and Maurice could agree on. Editing his father's *Life and Letters*, Maurice's son observed how his father "had warned the Orthodox that the sword of Agnosticism which they had clutched at from Dean Mansel, would become a much sharper one in the hands of their opponents." And as he went on to explain, what Maurice "had predicted actually followed. ... Mr. Huxley and Mr. Spencer adopted the same tone towards all thought but their own, which before had been held by the various religious sects" (Maurice 1884: II, 608–9).

[17] Maurice 1884: II, 498–9. Keynes suggests that Mill's *Examination* constituted a "divergence from received religious opinions" (Keynes 1925: 7). Indeed, but it was a divergence quite in keeping with that general Anglican reaction to Evangelicism associated particularly with Maurice.

stirred up by Mansel's Bampton Lectures were clearly not as straightforward as Keynes's smooth prose might lead us to believe.

The simplicity of the picture drawn by Keynes is further disturbed when we observe that in Cambridge in the 1860s Darwin's *Origin of Species* was welcomed by those who regarded themselves as followers of Maurice. Keynes, it will be recalled, presented Darwin's book as another blow to the religious faith of the inhabitants of the "serious philosophical world of England." Within Cambridge, Darwin's work met with a hostile reception from the old guard of clerical dons such as Adam Sedgwick (who had once taught Darwin) and from the now-dwindling group of Evangelicals, whom the Regius Professor of History, Kingsley, described in 1861 as the remaining "scraps of the Simeonite party, now moribund here."[18] Yet by 1863 Kingsley could write to Maurice from the university that "Darwin is conquering everywhere, and rushing in like a flood, by the mere force of truth and fact."[19] Maurice himself "never tired of quoting the spirit of Mr. Darwin's investigations as a lesson and a model for Churchmen."[20] Fenton J. A. Hort, then a young Cambridge disciple of Maurice, described Darwin's *Origin* as "a book that one is proud to be contemporary with" and wrote to a friend that "I am inclined to think it unanswerable."[21] The general tenor of this liberal Anglican response to Darwin is perhaps best captured in a letter written to "Darwin's bulldog," Huxley, by Kingsley. Commenting on his supposed descent from the apes, Kingsley told Huxley, "I accept the fact fully and care nothing about it"; what really matters, he declared, is our moral nature – which is, he insisted, "nearer to God than to a Chimpanzee."[22] Given the importance of evolutionary thought in Marshall's philosophical development, it is worth noting that Kingsley was here expressing views by no means dissimilar to those that were consistently held by Marshall.

In Keynes's failure to consider the possible relevance of Maurice and liberal Anglicanism to Marshall's youthful crisis of mental development, it is

---

[18] Kingsley 1877: 183. "Simeonites" (or "Sims") were followers of the great Cambridge Evangelical Charles Simeon, fellow of Kings and curate of Holy Trinity Church, who had died in 1836.

[19] See letters to Maurice in Kingsley 1877: II, 172, 175, 218. See also Kingsley's letter to Darwin of 1867 (Kingsley 1877: II, 283). After Maurice died, the Knightbridge Chair was occupied by the Rev. Birks, whom James Moore describes as "Britain's foremost evangelical anti-Darwinist" (Moore 1979: 20–2).

[20] Maurice 1884: II, 608; see also p. 452.

[21] See Hort 1896: I, 415–16, 430–1. For Hort's less enthusiastic feelings toward Huxley, see Hort 1896: I, 475.

[22] Desmond 1998: 288. Kingsley's correspondence with Huxley is detailed in Desmond 1998: 263, 288–9.

possible to detect the long shadow cast by Leslie Stephen's writings over the subsequent histories of this period of English (or at any rate, of Cambridge) intellectual life. As noted in Chapter One, in the early 1860s Stephen's own crisis of faith had culminated in the rejection of the Evangelicism of his childhood and the resignation of his Cambridge fellowship. For Stephen, Christianity was always identified with the Evangelical doctrine of the Atonement. Therefore, when in a series of articles written between 1867 and 1873 he examined a Broad Church movement that had turned away from a theology founded on the Atonement, he accused its members of being unbelievers who hid their abolition of Christianity behind a veil of historical interpretation of scripture and contradictory Coleridgean metaphysics.[23] Stephen was particularly unsympathetic to Maurice, who in a letter of 1874 he described as "the most utterly bewildering" of "all the muddle-headed, intricate, futile persons I ever studied," a judgment that in the twentieth century enjoyed wide if perhaps undeserved circulation.[24] In these articles, his later *Dictionary of National Biography* entries on both Coleridge and Maurice, and his book *The English Utilitarians*, Stephen established the framework that Keynes later used to recount Marshall's crisis of faith. Such a framework passed over not only Maurice, but also more generally the liberal Anglicanism of the Broad Church movement and, in doing so, reduced the diversity of a generation's struggles with religious faith to a simple binary choice between orthodox Evangelicism and agnostic unbelief.

In the remainder of this chapter, an attempt will be made to improve on Keynes's account of Marshall's early mental history. Our first task will be to place liberal Anglicanism into the picture of the dispute that arose out of Mansel's Bampton Lectures. This will involve, first of all, identifying the nature of Maurice's theological thought. But it will also involve identifying the nature of the liberal Anglican philosophy of the Rev. John Grote, who shaped the Moral Sciences Tripos that Maurice subsequently headed and the young Marshall joined. We will then turn to the earliest of Marshall's philosophical writings from this period. In 1991 the Italian philosopher and Marshall scholar Tiziano Raffaelli meticulously transcribed, edited, and published four philosophical papers that Marshall composed between

---

[23] See Stephen 1873; also Searby 1997: 382–3 and Annan 1984: 172–85.

[24] Quoted in Sanders 1940. Stephen's aversion to Maurice was so great that in 1894 he broke his own rule that only sympathetic biographers write entries in the *Dictionary of National Biography* and composed the entry on Maurice. The root problem with Stephen's account of Maurice, and indeed with much of the subsequent literature on Maurice that derives from Stephen, is that Maurice's explicit and self-conscious Coleridgean aversion to systematic thought is presented as mere "muddle-headedness."

around 1867 and 1869, almost certainly for presentation to the Grote Club. These papers, together with his early notes on Hegel and his essay on the history of civilization of the early 1870s, enable us to reconstruct much – if by no means all – of the course of Marshall's philosophical development in these crucial early years. In this chapter, however, we will examine only the first two of Marshall's Grote Club papers, as they provide the crucial evidence of Marshall's initial response to what Keynes called "the Hamilton–Mansel controversy." The picture that will emerge of Marshall's struggles with Christian faith is by no means comprehensive. What should become sufficiently clear, however, is that by around 1868 Marshall had taken as his own the basic framework of the liberal Anglican philosophy of John Grote.

LIBERAL ANGLICANISM: RESOURCES, OPPONENTS, ALLIES

Traditionally the authority of the Church of England has been understood to rest on two foundations. On the one hand, it is a national church instituted by the king-in-Parliament. On the other hand, it conceives of itself as an apostolic church, the body of Christ, and, as such, the medium of spiritual power on earth. Much of the history of the Church of England, both doctrinally and politically, and indeed also the wider history of religion in England after the Reformation, can be told in terms of the tension generated by these two grounds of Anglican authority.[25] In the later years of the seventeenth century, the restoration of church and crown left a considerable body of the population outside the reestablished order. Furthermore, toleration of public worship was extended only to Trinitarian sects, for a denial of Christ's divinity was tantamount to a denial of the apostolic authority of the established church. But in the peace that followed victory over Napoleon, suppression of "rational dissent" gave way to a series of parliamentary reforms of the Anglican establishment. By 1835 the Test Acts excluding non-Anglicans from positions of political power had been repealed, a Catholic emancipation bill had been passed, and a new ecclesiastical commission had commenced the practical reform of the Church of England. Such Erastian measures inevitably upset the delicate balance maintained for well over a century between the two poles of authority within the Anglican Church. In the acrimonious dispute over church rates between 1834 and 1868, for example, the High Church emphasis on

---

[25] See Clark 2000: 256–83, 501–5 and Pocock 1995, 1999: ch. 1.

apostolicity over nationality was understood by opponents as a determination to transform Anglicanism from the national religion into an exclusive sect.[26] Maurice and the nineteenth-century Broad Church movement, by contrast, responded to the shift in relations between church and state by smothering the flames of sixteen centuries of doctrinal dispute in a blanket of Coleridgean metaphysics and by identifying the nationality of Anglicanism with a new vision of England as a socially harmonious religious community.[27]

The writings of Coleridge can be detected behind much that is distinctive in Broad Church theology. We have already encountered in Chapter Two Coleridge's argument, in his *Constitution of Church and State*, for the necessity of an endowed clerisy charged with preserving and disseminating the nation's culture. Because Coleridge believed that theology provided the ground not only for the sciences, but also for civic duties, he looked to the Anglican clergy to provide the nation's "clerisy."[28] Nevertheless, Coleridge drew a distinction between the clerisy, or "national church," and the church of Christ, or universal church. Such a distinction between the visible and the invisible church can be related to his fundamental metaphysical distinction between the faculties of reason and understanding. Simply put, understanding for Coleridge is the faculty of reflection, discursive thought, and judgment, while reason "is a direct aspect of truth, an inward beholding," which "in all its decisions appeals to itself as the ground and *substance* of their truth."[29] This division of the faculties into an ineffable, self-conscious reason and a more superficial and at times contradictory understanding allowed Coleridge to construe the dogmatic disputations of the different creeds as so much noise, arising from the clash of opposing notions of understanding that, nevertheless, were rooted in the same principles of reason. These notions of understanding were not entirely empty, but it was only through the employment of reason that their underlying substance could be detected: the deeper "we penetrate into the ground of

---

[26] See Ellens 1987: 242–4.

[27] In the long run, Maurice's vision here, as elsewhere, would be victorious. As Sachs 1993 argues, over the course of the nineteenth century the identity of Anglicanism underwent a fundamental shift, as an ideal of an Apostolic tradition gave way to an ideal of modern religious community and social mission.

[28] See Coleridge 1976: 46–57. Coleridge insisted that the national church or clerisy was coterminous with human society and therefore had not always been Christian. Furthermore, he warned that non-Anglicans constitute "a numerous party" that had already won "ascendancy in the *State*" and, unless checked, "*will* obtain the ascendancy in the *Nation*" (see Allen 1985).

[29] Coleridge 1993: 223, emphasis in original. See also Coleridge 1969: II, 77–8n.

things, the more truth we discover in the doctrines of the greater number of the philosophical sects." Reason, then, could lead us from sectarian partiality to the general ground of the universal church.

The spirit of sectarianism has hitherto been our fault, and the cause of our failures. We have imprisoned our own conceptions by the lines, which we have drawn, in order to exclude the conceptions of others. J'ai trouvé que la plupart des sects ont raison dans une bonne partie de ce qu'elles avancent, mais non pas tant en ce qu'elles nient.[30]

For a High Churchman like John Henry Newman, Coleridge "indulged a liberty of speculation ... which no Christian can tolerate."[31] But for more latitudinarian members of the Anglican clergy, Coleridge's deeply Christian rendition of German romanticism carried an evident appeal. By 1828 both Maurice (not yet baptized into the Church of England) and his Cambridge tutor, Julius Hare, had embraced Coleridge's distinction between reason and understanding. In his sermon "The Children of Light," which has been said to mark the advent of the Broad Church movement, Hare dismissed Kant's argument that reason could evaluate the evidence for or against theological beliefs. The task of reason, Hare insisted, was rather to discern the truth found within the "instinctive voice of human nature."[32] In like manner, Maurice would come to explain the method of reason as not the building of a system, but the uncovering of "the underlying principles in which every thought must find its root if it would be a thought that is true for humanity."[33] Such a conception of the role of reason dissolved an entire history of bitter ecclesiastical disputes over creeds and dogmas into a history of merely conflicting opinions. The truth of the Trinity, however incomprehensible it might appear to the understanding, was now to be unearthed by the candle of reason within. Once so discerned, the apparently competing dogmatic opinions of the various sects could now be seen for what they were – myriad reflections and mediations of the one

---

[30] Coleridge 1983: 245–7. Coleridge quoted with approval Leibniz's description of "true philosophy" as at once explaining and collecting "the fragments of truth scattered through systems apparently the most incongruous."

[31] Quoted in Rule 1964: 293.

[32] Quoted in T. Jones 2003: 142. Although not received into the church of England until 1831, Maurice in 1828 also praised Coleridge's distinction between reason and understanding (see Sanders 1938: 233, 1936). Maurice's initial statement of indebtedness to Coleridge is contained in his *Kingdom of Christ*, where he states that Coleridge taught him to discriminate between that which "belongs to our artificial habits of thought, and that which is fixed and eternal" (Maurice 1842: I, 10).

[33] Maurice 1884: II, 136–7; see also Jones 2003: 151.

underlying yet ineffable truth. As Hort would explain to the bishop of Ely in a letter of 1871:

Mr. Maurice has been a dear friend of mine for twenty-three years, and I have been deeply influenced by his books. To myself it seems that I owe to them chiefly a firm and full hold of the Christian faith; but they have led me to doubt whether the Christian faith is adequately or purely represented in all respects in the accepted doctrines of any living school.[34]

That he learned from Coleridge to place his faith in reason as opposed to dogmatic opinion did not, of course, mean that Maurice refrained from attempting to express in words the certainties of his faith. At the heart of his Platonic theology stood a vision of the Trinity in Unity and a conviction that, as he put it in a letter of 1860, "mankind stands not in Adam but in Christ."[35] Departing from Coleridge, who had claimed that philosophy "cannot be intelligible to all," Maurice insisted that just as Christ was in every man, so too was the faculty of reason that would humbly open the doors of faith to every man.[36] Reason, for Maurice, allows mankind to confront a reality beyond the mind; individual self-consciousness discovers, as its ultimate ground in reality, a divine self-consciousness – the "I AM" that is the divine name. Such a discovery is open to all humanity, and therefore Christ, who is the incarnation of the divine name, is the savior of all humanity, not merely of those who accept the creeds and sacraments of some particular sect. By the same token, the universality of reason establishes the social bond of the universal church within which all of humanity is united, irrespective of opinions or special revelations.[37] But reality for Maurice has a dual nature: it is at once an unchanging fixed ground (Christ as Logos) and an active force, the divine will (Christ incarnated), which continuously works toward the realization of the universal church on earth. Such a vision of the incarnation and continual embodiment of Christ in the material world provided the theological grounds of Maurice's midcentury participation in the Christian Socialist movement. But such a social and pantheistic-leaning theology also led him into direct and sustained, if

---

[34] Hort 1896: II, 155. As a young man, Hort published an essay entitled "Coleridge" (in *Cambridge Essays, Contributed by Members of the University* [London: John W. Parker, 1856]), which Leslie Stephen apparently hailed as "the only serious attempt known to him to give a coherent account of Coleridge's philosophy" (see Hort 1896: I, 306).

[35] Maurice 1884: II, 358.

[36] Coleridge 1983: 243; see also Brose 1971.

[37] Clayton 1972: 308. Clayton (p. 318) observes, "Rationality for [Maurice] is similar to what we mean by sanity: being in touch with reality, as distinguished from a world which the mind creates for itself." See also Morris 2005: 170–4, 187–92 and Sanders 1941: 36.

ultimately victorious, confrontation with an Evangelical Anglican orthodoxy that emphasized the chasm separating God from a fallen humanity.

From the mid-1850s through the late 1860s, Broad Churchmen such as
Maurice and Benjamin Jowett became embroiled in an increasingly bitter
dispute with Evangelical and High Church opponents within the church of
England. The result of this internecine theological struggle, according to
Boyd Hilton, was that through the efforts of Maurice and other liberal theologians, an Anglican orthodoxy centered on the Evangelical doctrine of the
Atonement was, over the course of roughly fifteen years, transformed into
what Hilton regards as a more "vapid" theology centering on the Incarnation.
This mid-Victorian transformation of Anglicanism can be viewed as the
theological expression of that midcentury shift in the attitudes, expectations, and temperament of England's middle classes from anxiety to confidence that was discussed in Chapter One. Indeed, Hilton regards Maurice's
theology as the "religious equivalent" of the secular optimistic enthusiasm
of mid-Victorian liberals such as Stephen and Fawcett.[38] In the wake of the
Irish famine and amid a new concern for the social condition of the working
classes, Maurice and J. S. Mill, each in his own way, signaled a retreat from
the conventional faith of both Anglicans and radicals in the moral efficacy
of a system of unmitigated laissez-faire.[39] By around 1870, the theological
beliefs of the typical Anglican clergyman no longer reflected the stern presuppositions of Evangelicism.[40] An Evangelical God of justice and righteous
anger had been replaced by a liberal Anglican God of mercy and love.

The victory of Maurice's incarnationalist theology did not come without
a struggle. Mansel's philosophical and religious teaching can be seen as an
orthodox reaction to the liberal theology that in the first decade after midcentury was already gaining ground within the church. In other words, Mansel's
"defense of orthodoxy" (to quote Keynes) was not a defense of religious belief
against some infidel creed of unbelief. Rather, it was a defense of an earlier
nineteenth-century orthodoxy founded on the Atonement against the rising tide of incarnationalist theology and Coleridgean philosophy within the
Church of England. The immediate context of Mansel's lectures was provided by the publication in 1855 of Jowett's edition of the *Epistles of St. Paul*,
in which Jowett argued that man cannot be punished for what he never did,
and therefore Christ cannot have atoned for what we have not done. This was
a direct assault on the orthodox position, and a flurry of criticism inevitably

---

[38] Hilton 1989: 63.
[39] See Hilton 1988: 283.
[40] Hilton 1988: 3–6, 288–9; cf. Hort 1896: II, 157. See also Hilton 1988: 271.

followed, the "sophisticated climax" of which, as Hilton puts it, was Mansel's Bampton Lectures.[41] Against Jowett, Mansel argued that, from its finite perspective, humanity cannot know, and therefore cannot judge, the morality of divine providence. But such a conclusion emerged as but one implication of a more general philosophical argument that the human mind cannot know God because there are necessary *limits* to our religious knowledge. Against a Coleridgean faith in the candle of reason, Mansel invoked the authority of St. Paul: "For now we see through a glass darkly. … Such is the Apostle's declaration of the limits of human knowledge."[42]

The dispute between Mansel and Maurice has traditionally been viewed as marking a pivotal point in the troubled history of the Anglican reception of Kant's *Critique of Pure Reason*. Writing of the controversy in 1891, the liberal theologian Henry Hitchcock described the Broad Church theology as deriving from Coleridge, who himself had imbibed "the honey of the German hive, without its poison."[43] Mansel, for his part, was adamant that Kant had "contributed, perhaps, more than any other person to give a philosophical sanction" to the erroneous theological beliefs of the day. Nevertheless, he explained in his Bampton Lectures, from Kant's "speculative principles, rightly employed, might be extracted the best antidote to his conclusions, even as the body of the scorpion, crushed upon the wound, is said to be the best cure for its own venom."[44] Thus Mansel's starting point was to insist on what might be called a Copernican revolution in theology: "The primary and proper object of criticism is not Religion, natural or revealed, but the human mind in its relation to Religion."[45] But the limits of religious thought discovered by such criticism were in fact "but a special manifestation of the limits of thought in general."[46] That is to say, in the words of the quote from Hamilton that Mansel placed as a motto at the head of his published lectures, "No difficulty emerges in theology, which had not previously emerged in philosophy."[47] In short, this Anglican controversy

[41]　Hilton 1988: 289–90.
[42]　Mansel 1859: 65 (*1 Corinthians* [13: 12]).
[43]　Hitchcock 1891: 634.
[44]　Mansel 1859: 55. Maurice naturally charged Mansel with failing to "distinguish between a Principle and a Notion" (Maurice 1859: 198) and with imposing "the Logic of the Understanding upon the Conscience and the Reason" (Maurice 1860: 185). See also Maurice's subsequent exegesis of Kant's distinction between reason and understanding in Maurice 1862: 629.
[45]　Mansel 1859: 61.
[46]　Mansel 1859: 62.
[47]　Two quotes served as mottoes for Mansel's work. The first was from Berkley: "The objections made to faith are by no means an effect of knowledge, but proceed rather from ignorance of what knowledge is."

can be interpreted as a clash between two quasi-Kantian approaches to the mind, the one critical and the other romantic.

But the controversy can also be seen as pitting a Coleridgean idealism against a mid-nineteenth-century reworking of the common sense philosophy of Thomas Reid. Reid's aim had been to refute the skepticism that he found in Hume's writings and that he concluded ultimately from Locke's account of ideas as the intermediary connection between the mind and the material world. But as Dugald Stewart explained in his *Elements of the Philosophy of the Human Mind* (1792), "Dr. Reid, who first called the Ideal Theory in question, offers no argument to prove that the material world exists; but considers our belief of it as an ultimate fact in our nature."[48] In the same way, Reid insisted that our belief in the continuous existence of the mind is simply an ultimate fact of consciousness of which "every man who has common sense is a competent judge."[49] But as Stewart went on to explain, in his dispute with the theory of Hume and Locke, Reid had "thrown no light whatsoever on what was generally taken to be the great object of the inquiry – the mode of communication between the mind and the material world; all Reid has provided is a precise description of the fact such as to provide a distinct view of the *insurmountable limits* which nature has prescribed to our curiosity."[50] From one perspective, then, Mansel can be seen as simply developing Reid's basic mode of argumentation.[51] From Reid's insistence on our necessary ignorance as to the nature of the communication between mind and matter, Mansel now argued that the nature of any connection between the human mind and the divinity stood equally beyond the limits of our curiosity.

The core of Mansel's rendering of common sense philosophy was set out in his 1857 *Encyclopaedia Britannica* article "Metaphysics," which was soon published as a book of the same title. Here Mansel explained that metaphysics as a whole pertained to "the facts of consciousness." These facts constituted a unified whole but could be considered from two points of view: subjectively in relation to the mind (psychology) or objectively in relation to the "realities known" (ontology).[52] He accordingly divided his study of metaphysics into a first part, "Psychology," and a second, "Ontology." From

[48] *Stewart CW*, II: 37.
[49] Reid 1863: 422.
[50] *Stewart CW*, II: 78, emphasis in original.
[51] For the suggestion that in developing Reid's common sense philosophy, Hamilton and Mansel also subverted it, see p.7 above.
[52] Mansel 1875: 26–7.

this starting point, Mansel went on to develop the key arguments that would later be deployed in his Bampton Lectures. One of the conclusions drawn in the "Psychology" was that the infinite could not be an object of human consciousness.[53] From this it followed that there was no place for a discussion of the nature of the divine being in the section "Ontology." In "Psychology," we further learn "the important lesson that the provinces of reason and faith are not coextensive; that it is a duty, enjoined by reason itself, to believe in what cannot be comprehended."[54] And in the last paragraph of this section, Mansel triumphantly declares that he has demonstrated that "the function of thought is in all cases the same." Thus, while the "hypothesis of a faculty of reason distinct from understanding may indeed be necessary, as an assumption, to support the systems of those philosophers who aim at constructing a philosophy of the absolute and the infinite," such a distinction between reason and understanding is nevertheless "unnecessary, and therefore untenable."[55]

While it was Mansel's Bampton Lectures that initiated the public confrontation with Maurice, the 1857 article "Metaphysics" served to alert liberal Anglican theologians to the storm that was brewing. Already in that year we find Maurice describing his lectures on the *Epistles of St. John* as putting him in "direct antagonism to Mr. Mansel and his school":

seeing that I maintain – on St. John's authority … – not only that the knowledge of God is possible for men, but that it is the foundation of all knowledge of men & things; that science is impossible altogether if He is excluded from the sphere of it.… Atheism is the only alternative for an age which demands science, if we cannot 'know that we know' God, and if to know Him is not eternal life.[56]

But Maurice was by no means the only liberal Anglican who, in the late 1850s, became concerned about the theological implications of Mansel's psychology. Between 1855 and 1866, the Rev. John Grote was Knightbridge Professor of Moral Philosophy and thus head of the Moral Sciences Tripos. Grote's thought as set down in the first volume of his *Exploratio Philosophica* (1865) has an important claim on our attention, not least because he provided an overview of the key issues in the dispute with Mansel in a purely philosophical form (as opposed to Maurice, who wrote first and foremost as a theologian). Furthermore, and as will be argued later, not only did the young Marshall evidently study Grote's *Exploratio* very carefully, but by

[53] Mansel 1875: 278.
[54] Mansel 1875: 278.
[55] Mansel 1875: 280–1.
[56] Maurice 1884: II, 311; cf. Kingsley 1877: II, 105.

around 1868 Marshall had arrived at a philosophical position very similar to that of Grote.

Grote succeeded Whewell in the Knightbridge Chair of Moral Philosophy. We have already noted in Chapter Two how the Moral Sciences Tripos was reorganized under Grote, with history and law removed to form a separate tripos, and logic and mental philosophy (or psychology) introduced as new subjects. Such reorganization was accompanied by a repositioning of Whewell's intellectual legacy. Grote insisted that the "semi-Kantist or Kantiodic doctrine, with its almost inevitable results of notionalism and relativism, does not properly belong to the right portion of Dr Whewell's views."[57] By "notionalism" Grote meant the tendency to "realize" the abstract logical concepts of understanding, a tendency that he regarded as the key error of Hamilton's philosophy. By "relativism" he meant the "theological relativism" that Mansel was building on Hamilton's philosophy. In other words, Grote saw Kant as standing at the root of the pernicious teachings of Hamilton and his disciple Mansel, and was determined to place the foundations of Cambridge Anglican philosophy on quite different grounds. In opposition to Hamilton and Mansel, Grote's intention as head of the tripos was to fashion a philosophy conducive to both theology and science. His underlying concern was laid out in the introduction to his *Exploratio*, where he explained that with regard to the younger generation,

what I want more than anything is to prevent their enterprise being damped by their being told, whether on the grounds of notionalism or positivism, that to know about God, to form a notion of an ideal of what should be done or what they and the human race should aim at – that this and much like it is visionary and beyond the reach of the human faculties.[58]

"Positivism," for Grote, was that philosophy which mistook phenomena for the whole of reality. But while positivism itself was akin to atheism, Grote saw a constructive role in the moral sciences for what he called "phenomenalism," or the study of material facts. He characterized Mill's *System of Logic* (1843) as "a Phenomenalist Logic," which is to say that he considered it a logic of evidence that outlined the rules of the study of the

---

[57] Grote 1865: 240. Venn 1866 (and elsewhere) would adopt Grote's terminology and follow him in accusing conceptualist thinkers such as Hamilton of "realizing" logical terms, a sin that, for Venn, was also committed by Quetelet and Buckle with their notion of "normal man" (see Cook 2005).

[58] Grote 1865: xxxii. A useful account of Grote's life and thought can be found in Gibbins 1998 (I have not had the opportunity to consult Gibbins 2007).

behavior of phenomena in time.[59] Grote did not belittle the importance of such a study, and indeed actively encouraged John Venn's development of Mill's phenomenal or "materialist logic."[60] Nevertheless, he insisted that there was more to human history than positive facts and laws. Grote could even agree with Mill that there may be a phenomenalist science of human nature, according to which actions are determined by circumstances and character, and character is itself determined largely by circumstances.[61] Nevertheless, Grote insisted, "Before we can *act* ... we must know what we *want*," and so while it is all very well to know what circumstances will produce this and that character, this is not the same thing as knowing what kind of character we want to produce from any particular regime of education. In short, and in direct contrast to the physical sciences, "the logic of the moral sciences, or what Mr Mill considers such, will not at all in the same degree stand alone without Teleology."[62]

Such a "Teleology" Grote identified with what he called "Real Logic," which was the product of a "higher philosophy." Real logic was developed by way of a reflection on the movement of the mind in the processes by which positive knowledge was advanced. It was thus "able to take into account the *growth* of knowledge, whether in the individual or the race."[63] Grote looked to Whewell's *Novum Organon Renovatum* (1858) as an exemplary case of real logic. He insisted that phenomenological logic should be subordinate to real logic, but he nevertheless accorded value to the former. So where Whewell himself had implicitly presented his *Novum Organon Renovatum* as a superior rival to Mill's *System of Logic*, Grote now insisted that the two represented different kinds of logic, both of which had their place in the study of the moral sciences. Essentially, then, Grote's position that man could be considered both from the point of view of his phenomenal behavior and as a self-conscious and self-reflecting being was the same as that of both Coleridge and Maurice: but such a mental dualism was to be placed within a Cartesian as opposed to a Kantian framework. Indeed, in practical terms Grote proposed a Cartesian bifurcation with regard to the moral sciences.

[59] Grote 1865: 157. See also Grote 1865: 167, 205; cf. Maurice 1862: 672 and Norton Wise 1989–90: II, 405–7.
[60] In his *Logic of Chance*, Venn paid tribute to Grote's "admirable and suggestive" *Exploratio* (Venn 1866: 171). For a letter from Venn to J. B. Mayor describing Grote's role in the composition of this book, see Gibbins 1988: 453. Venn also praised Grote's role in the Grote Club in an unpublished "Autobiographical Sketch" (Venn ca. 1902).
[61] Grote 1865: 194–5.
[62] Grote 1865: 198, 200. Compare Maurice's discussion of Kant in Maurice 1862: 630.
[63] Grote 1865: 153, emphasis in original.

My feeling about the whole 'Philosophy of the Human Mind' is this: … that it will have to divide itself, for utility and productiveness, into two lines of thought … it seems to me that the way is singularly open and inviting now for a good physio-psychology…. Philosophy … is something of an entirely different nature, and leads to entirely different fields of speculation…. A real philosophy without "notionalism," and a real, honest, thorough, study of nature without the feeling that we are to find our philosophy and morality, more than very subordinately, *there* (add emphasis) – these are the two things which I should like to see co-existing … these things seem to *belong* (add emphasis) the one to the other; the warfare carried on between the partizans of one and another seems quite uncalled for, and unreasonable.[64]

But this call for cohabitation and peaceful coexistence, though extended to the disciples of Mill, was by no means intended to include the followers of Hamilton and Mansel. In fact, Grote's strategy of reconciling the "physio-psychology" of Mill with his own "higher philosophy" was equally a means of refuting the common sense philosophy of Hamilton and Mansel. In his *Exploratio*, Grote's procedure was to discuss a series of books that formed "a sort of scale, spectrum, or gamut, of which Professor Ferrier represents the extreme philosophical end, and Professor Bain the extreme physiological or physical" (Alexander Bain, as we shall see, was an associationist psychologist closely allied to Mill).[65] Such a spectrum of philosophical opinions allowed Grote to develop his vision of a bifurcated moral science, in which phenomenalist studies of the mind like Bain's were encouraged and yet subordinated to the kind of philosophical inquiry into self-consciousness that Grote found in Ferrier. But such a reconciliation of the extreme ends of his spectrum served to undermine Mansel's claim that common sense philosophy provided a workable middle ground between Lockean sensualism and German rationalism.[66]

Grote's Anglican accommodation of the phenomenalism of Mill and Bain was grounded on his insistence that the facts of consciousness were of two fundamentally different kinds. He articulated this position in direct opposition to the conviction of Hamilton and Mansel that the whole of metaphysics consisted of an examination of the "facts of consciousness" from two distinct points of view. In his *Metaphysics*, Mansel quoted from

---

[64] Grote 1865: ix–xiii, emphasis in original. By "physio-psychology" Grote meant, primarily, the work of authorities such as Bain, Carpenter, and Spencer, and not the German work by, say, Wundt, which would not become influential in England before the early 1870s.

[65] Grote 1865: xxvi–xxvii.

[66] See Mansel 1875: 7–11. Initially a disciple of Hamilton, J. F. Ferrier (1808–64) became one of the first of the new generation of British idealists who took their metaphysics directly from the German sources (and were highly critical of Coleridge's secondhand version of idealism). His most advanced philosophical statement is contained in his 1854 *Institutes of Metaphysics*, from which work Marshall took what he called "Ferrier's proposition one."

Hamilton: "*We know*; and *we know that we know*: – these propositions, *logically* distinct, are *really* identical; each implies the other."[67] Grote's entire
philosophical endeavor can be seen as an attempt to refute this statement.
According to Grote, the "universe consists of phænomenon of matter,
thought of by mind, which thinks also of much besides." A phenomenalist
logic, of which J. S. Mill had provided an exemplary example, addressed
the universe, that is, the phenomena of matter as thought by mind. A phenomenalist psychology, of which Bain was the leading exponent, could
explain much about the mind in terms of the phenomena of matter: "from
the side of the universe, physiologists may make something of sensation
as a part of *life*." But neither phenomenalist logic nor phenomenalist psychology could speak of self-consciousness, for " 'I' is not a phænomenon of
the universe."[68] In other words, knowing something, and knowing that we
know, are far from identical; rather, they are instances of two quite different
kinds of knowledge: phenomenalist and "real." From Grote's perspective,
then, Hamilton and Mansel began from the conflation of consciousness
with self-consciousness, and from such a cardinal error followed an inevitable conflation of philosophy and phenomenalism, of self-conscious "I"
and those phenomena of the self that formed a part of the universe. Such a
conflation was, in Grote's eyes, "the master-confusion, the 'temporis partus
maximus' of mis-psychology."[69]

What was the position of Mill in this dispute between Anglican philosophers? Mill tells us in his *Autobiography* that he had long intended to engage
in "a hand-to-hand fight" with the British school of intuitionism. He adds,
however, that his resolve to attack Hamilton, whom he took to be its leading representative, was strengthened when he found how Mansel had made
Hamilton's "peculiar doctrines" the "justification of a view of religion which
I hold to be profoundly immoral – that it is our duty to bow down in worship before a Being whose moral attributes are affirmed to be unknowable
by us."[70] In the *Examination*, Mill therefore inserted a chapter specifically
attacking Mansel's religious doctrine, which was there described as "simply
the most morally pernicious doctrine now current," the debate over which
was "beyond all others ... the decisive one between moral good and evil in the
Christian world."[71] From one point of view, Mill's chapter on Mansel (which

---

[67] Mansel 1875: 25–6, emphasis in original. See also J. S. Mill's discussion of Hamilton's ren-
      dering of "self-consciousness" as "consciousness" in *Mill CW*, 9: 110–11.
[68] Grote 1865: 133.
[69] Grote 1865: 125; for an interesting comparison of Hamilton and Mill in this light, see
      Grote's footnote on p. 87 and also pp. 132–3.
[70] *Mill CW*, 1: 270.
[71] *Mill CW*, 9: 90.

Bain later described as a "considerable digression")[72] was superfluous; for as Mill argued, Mansel's "conclusion does not follow from a true theory of the human faculties."[73] In other words, Mill's refutation of Hamilton's philosophy in his book as a whole was at once also a refutation of Mansel's religious doctrine. Mill's chapter, therefore, was dedicated to demonstrating the flaw in Mansel's specific argument that God could not be an object of knowledge. This Mill achieved effortlessly. First, he pointed out that, to make his argument work, Mansel had to define the "Absolute" as that which has both all and no attributes. Second, he simply pointed out that the unknowableness of such an Absolute was irrelevant, given that what was actually at stake was the knowableness of a God who had the attribute of goodness. Mansel's whole argument, Mill explained, was simply "one long *ignoratio elenchi*."[74]

Is it any wonder that Maurice enthused over Mill's "noble language" in this chapter? For not only had Mill demolished Mansel's argument, he had done so explicitly in the cause of a moral Christianity. In this part of the *Examination*, Mill effectively lent his philosophical pen to the cause of that liberal Anglicanism which was at just that time engaged in a struggle to associate God, not with sin and suffering, but with universal fellowship and social progress.[75] What did other liberal Anglicans make of Mill's book? In his *Exploratio*, Grote concerned himself exclusively with Mill's *System of Logic*, and indeed he had not yet read Mill's book on Hamilton when his own went to press.[76] For reactions to the *Examination*, then, we have to turn to Hort, who constitutes an important witness for our purposes. Hort had stood as a candidate for election to the Knightbridge Chair in 1866, examined for the tripos several times in the following few years (as well as in 1853), and, before his appointment as a college lecturer in theology by Emmanuel College in 1871, was widely regarded as Maurice's natural successor to the Knightbridge Chair.[77] Hort thus provides us with an inside

---

[72] Bain 1882: 122. Bain tells us that Mill in private called Mansel's *Limits of Religious Thought* a "loathsome" book.

[73] *Mill CW*, 9: 90.

[74] *Mill CW*, 9: 97. Mill wrote of Mansel's definition of the "Absolute," "Is the inconceivableness of this impossible fiction any argument against the possibility of conceiving God, who is neither supposed to have no attributes nor to have all attributes, but to have good attributes?" (p. 96). Note also his comment: "One may well agree with Mr. Mansel that this farrago of contradictory attributes cannot be conceived: but what shall we say of his equally positive averment that it must be believed?" (p. 95).

[75] As Keynes observes, "Mill's *Essays on Religion*, which gave his final opinions, were not published until 1874" (Keynes 1925: 7, n. 2); on these essays see Bain 1882: 133–40, Capaldi 2004: 339–50, Carr 1962, and especially Millar 1998.

[76] See Grote 1865: xxx.

[77] Hort had in fact taken the tripos in 1851, and his letters at this time provide an interesting student's eye view of the earliest years of the tripos (see Hort 1896: I, 170–80). He notes

glimpse into the reception of Mill's *Examination* within the liberal Anglican world of the Cambridge moral sciences. In July of 1865 Hort wrote to his friend Westcott that he had nearly finished Mill's "book on Hamilton, which is for the most part very successful; perhaps I liked it the better for recognizing some favourite thoughts of my own; of course it sees but one side of philosophy, but as against the Scottish position, it seems to me on nearly all points unanswerable."[78] In other words, Hort responded to the *Examination* along the same lines that Grote had responded to Mill's earlier *Logic*, regarding it as a book that, while it presented but a part of philosophy, nevertheless dealt with that part well and, in so doing, successfully refuted the arguments of Mansel and the "Scottish school."

From Hort's point of view, Mill's *Examination* was entirely devoid of what Grote called the "higher philosophy." A close inspection of Mill's arguments, however, revealed that his phenomenalist psychology left unlocked a gate that might be opened by those who wished to develop some form of "higher philosophy" in conjunction with phenomenalist mental science; for in his *Examination*, Mill had been forced to concede that he was unable to provide a phenomenalist account of our idea of the self. As we shall see in the following section, it was just this point in Mill's book that provided Marshall's starting point as a moral philosopher. The question that confronted him was, effectively, given Mill's confession of defeat on this crucial point, should the mental philosopher turn for aid to the intuitionism of Hamilton and Mansel or to the idealism of Grote and Maurice? What we shall discover is that, after an initial period of uncertainty, Marshall opted unambiguously for the second of these two options. In other words, Marshall came to the conclusion that the way forward was to combine the phenomenalist psychology advocated by Mill with some postulate of self-consciousness. This was, of course, the position of Grote's *Exploratio*, and as such it was a position that entailed the rejection of Mansel's philosophy.

ALFRED MARSHALL'S EARLIEST PHILOSOPHICAL WRITINGS

Between 1867 and 1869 Marshall composed four philosophical papers, all apparently for presentation to the Grote Club. The second and third of these papers, which have been dated to 1868, were evidently read to the club at

---

of Monday afternoon's exam, for example, "Pryme's *Political Economy*, of which I thought myself lucky to do half, as I had spent (irrespective of a chapter or two in the summer) just half an hour upon it."

[78] Hort 1896: II, 38.

two successive weekly meetings and were explicitly presented as forming two parts of a single project in psychology.[79] These papers were entitled "Ferrier's Proposition One" and "Ye Machine." The fourth paper, which has been dated to 1869 and is entitled "The Duty of the Logician," is not part of this project (it concerns the axioms of geometry). Marshall's first paper, "The Law of Parcimony," would seem to have been composed in 1867. This first paper can be seen as a first step in Marshall's attempt to arrive at what, in a note added to the second paper, he described as "a general theory of psychology, which I have [a] growing tendency to believe, is capable of being developed into the true one."[80] The content of this general theory of psychology will be discussed in the following chapter. Our present objective is simply to see how in his first two papers Marshall navigated and positioned himself with respect to the philosophical issues that were at stake in the "great controversy" stirred up by Mansel's Bampton Lectures.

At the heart of Marshall's first Grote Club paper, "The Law of Parcimony," is a criticism of Mill's position in chapter XII of his *Examination*. In this chapter Mill had attempted to provide an account of how our conception of the self is constructed by means of inference from and the development of mental associations. Such an account followed from the arguments of the preceding chapter, where Mill had looked to the laws of association to account for our belief in an external world. In both cases Mill's intention was to reach a point where he could appeal to the law of parsimony in order to reject Hamilton's claims that our belief in both an "Ego" and a "non-Ego" (i.e., mind and matter) was founded on an intuition revealed by "the original datum of consciousness." As Mill had pointed out in chapter XI, the "first of the laws laid down by [Hamilton] for the interpretation of Consciousness, the law (as he terms it) of Parcimony, forbids to suppose an original principle of our nature in order to account for phænomena which admit of possible explanation from known causes." Thus, if the known causes of mental association could be shown to account for our belief in mind and in matter, Hamilton's

---

[79] For the dating of Marshall's early philosophical papers, see Raffaelli's introduction to *EPW*. That the second and third papers were read on successive Fridays is indicated by Marshall's comments in "Note on the Preceding," in which he refers to both the paper he had read "last week" defending Ferrier's first proposition and the paper that "I propose to read this evening" (*EPW*, 67).

[80] *EPW*, 67. The first paper is written in a more hesitant and exploratory style than the following two papers. The main conclusions of this first paper are incorporated and expanded in the second paper. But while the second paper makes several references to the third, it contains only the barest of explicit allusions to the first. Thus it seems clear that a not insignificant period separated the first paper from the next two.

intuitionist explanations of these beliefs must be rejected.[81] But Mill ran into trouble in attempting to develop a phenomenalist account of our belief in mind. In "The Law of Parcimony," Marshall can be seen engaging with Mill at just the point where Mill himself had been forced to conclude that, with regard to his analysis of mind, he had arrived at an "inexplicable fact." In order to establish the immediate context of this first stage of Marshall's psychological thinking, then, we need to be clear as to why Mill thought that his argument about belief in matter had run aground when applied to the mind.

Mill's model of belief was founded on associationist psychology. In his chapter on belief in an external world, he argued that in our experience various impressions of the world are associated with one another. Once any particular association has been repeated a number of times, these impressions are remembered together and come to be expected together. The long experience of the fulfillment of such an expectation, not only in us but in other people too, provides for Mill the ground on which we infer the existence of an external world. In turning to the nature of our belief in mind, Mill began by applying the same reasoning to sensations. Sensations, he argued, are first associated and then expected together; and the continued conformity of this expectation with experience leads to a belief in something, namely, mind, that is permanent and distinct from the mere flux of sensations. But as Marshall explained in his first paper, Mill then turned to memory itself, where "he confesses that, on his supposition, we are obliged to accept the paradox that 'something which *ex hypothesi* is but a series of feelings can be aware of itself as a series.'"[82] Mill's problem with memory (and indeed also with expectation) was that, unlike simple sensation, a memory refers backward to an earlier experience of ours. Hence the series that is supposed to explain the generation of an idea of self already presupposes a notion of self. As the twentieth-century philosopher Alan Ryan has put it, to "construct *my* mind, I must employ only *my* thoughts, *my* memories, *my* expectations. But to suppose that this can be done already implies that we have some criteria for identifying the person who is the owner of the appropriate thoughts."[83] As Marshall observed, Mill was "very candid" about his inability to explain the fact that (in Mill's words) "something which has ceased, or is not yet in existence, can still be, in a manner, present." But where did this leave the debate? By "far the wisest thing we can do," Mill rather lamely concluded, is "to accept the inexplicable fact without

[81] *Mill CW*, 9: 182.
[82] *EPW*, 55; see also *Mill CW*, 9: 194.
[83] Ryan 1970: 99.

any theory of how it takes place."[84] This was not, however, a course of action that commended itself to Marshall.

Quite where Mill believed that his argument in chapter XII had left him is perhaps an open question. In Ryan's view, Mill demonstrated that "in the case of the belief in our own identity he is not such an uncompromising enemy of intuition."[85] To Bain, writing in 1882, Mill's position "makes him appear, after all, to be a transcendentalist."[86] Marshall, by contrast, in both of his first two Grote Club papers presented Mill as arguing that in his discussion of our belief in matter he had won half of the battle against the intuitionist position and that having made such a start he was on course to a complete victory. Such an argument Marshall found unacceptable. "I object," he explained in "The Law of Parcimony," to Mill's "implied assumption that the phenomena to be accounted for are, so to speak, homogenous; that when, for instance, he has been able to account for our belief in the existence of other 'series of sensations' he has overcome a finite portion of the whole difficulty, and that he may fairly reason from analogy that if he could only apply his method more thoroughly he would be able to solve this difficulty also."[87] The same point was repeated in Marshall's second paper, "Ferrier's Proposition One", in language that clarifies what was at stake in Marshall's discussion of the law of parsimony:

[Mill] applies to the law of parcimony for authority to abolish any principle which can be resolved into more simple principles, and finally he has to admit that there are difficulties which he has not overcome; but [he] seems to think that as he has overcome some objections his theory is worth something. I say it is worth nothing as a theory because the difficulties which he has not overcome are not of the same kind as those which he has.[88]

Marshall's discussion in "The Law of Parcimony" was intended to draw limits to the application in psychology of the principle of that name. In this first paper he observed that the law of parsimony had recently been used with great success by Darwin, but explained that the "phenomena with which Darwin is concerned are very homogenous." A difference in method must

---

[84] *EPW*, 55; *Mill CW*, 9: 194.
[85] Ryan 1970: 90. Ryan also argues, however, that Mill's discussion of personal identity was "one of his greatest failures" and that this failure calls into question the entire foundation of "the metaphysics on which his system of ideas rests" (Ryan 1970: xix–xx).
[86] Bain 1882: 121.
[87] *EPW*, 55. Marshall adds, "In short, [Mill] talks of his difficulty exactly in the same manner as Darwin does of that due to the extremely complex adaptation of the component parts of the eye."
[88] *EPW*, 66.

be insisted on in psychology – and this because mental phenomena are not homogeneous. For example, between "the idea of a sensation and the idea of similarity between sensations there is no relation."[89] But the "important case which seems to me to be *fons errorum* in very many others" was "the question of self-consciousness."[90] Mill's fundamental mistake, then, was to have treated self-consciousness as if it could be explained as simply a complex association of simpler mental phenomena; he had mistaken a difference in kind for a difference in degree. Having dealt with Mill, in the concluding section of this first paper Marshall turned his guns on Mill's ally, Bain, who had committed the same error in attempting to establish physical correlates of mental phenomena. In all such attempts, Marshall observed, Bain "ignores or rather denies the presence of the element of self-consciousness. To me it seems all important, because in all its various stages of clearness it is quite *sui generis*, is totally devoid of analogy in any physical action."[91] In other words, a physicalist evolutionary account of the development of the brain and nervous system could not facilitate the construction of an account of the evolution of all aspects of the mind.

Overall, this first paper of 1867 provides a possible key to Keynes's account of Marshall's youthful crisis of mental development. It will be recalled that Keynes had suggested that Mill's *Examination* led Marshall to question "Mansel's defense of orthodoxy." What we have discovered is that Marshall in fact defended a core aspect of Hamilton's (and therefore Mansel's) psychology against Mill's attacks. Indeed, in the last sentences of his paper, Marshall illustrated a sympathetic attitude toward Mansel's *Metaphysics*. Against Bain's emphasis on physical correlates of mental phenomena, Marshall suggested that an evolutionary psychology that did not transgress the limits of the law of parsimony might well begin from the classification by Mansel of those mental powers "which alone are consistent with self-consciousness."[92] This sympathy toward the psychology of Hamilton and Mansel does not, of course, necessarily imply that Marshall was also sympathetic to Mansel's "defense of orthodoxy." If we accept Keynes's basic contention that Marshall was at this time struggling with religious doubts, what is suggested by this first paper is rather that line of thought, pointed to by Leslie Stephen, that rejects Mill's attack on Mansel and leads from Mansel's arguments via Spencer to Huxley's agnosticism. And, indeed, it is

[89] *EPW*, 53.
[90] *EPW*, 54.
[91] *EPW*, 55–6.
[92] *EPW*, 56. See Mansel 1875: 144–6 and pp. 26, 45.

perhaps not insignificant that in this first paper Marshall referred approvingly to Spencer's criticisms of Mill's empiricism.[93] But if this was the direction in which Marshall was leaning in what was apparently the first year of his mental crisis, his subsequent psychological thinking led him to make a radical change of track.

Marshall's second Grote Club paper, "Ferrier's Proposition One," was introduced as a discussion of "Ferrier's first proposition, viz. that 'along with whatever any intelligence knows, it must, as the ground or condition of its knowledge, have some cognizance of itself.' This proposition I shall endeavour to defend against its great antagonist Bain."[94] In fact, in this second paper Marshall was equally concerned to praise Bain's attempt to show the "successive steps by which the subject–object cognition is developed."[95] Thus near the start of the paper Marshall announced with regard to J. F. Ferrier and Bain, "With each of them I agree in what they affirm, but not in what they deny. And it seems to me that in this as in so many other cases the strength of the position of each lies in the fact that he has something to say which his antagonist denies and which is true."[96] Thus from the start Marshall in this paper indicated that he had absorbed what might be called the kernel of the Coleridgean philosophical method. In arguing that the two extreme positions represented by Bain and Ferrier were to be reconciled by accepting the affirmations but not the denials of each party, Marshall was, of course, employing the method habitually used by such Cambridge liberal Anglicans as Maurice, Grote, and Hort ("Middle ways have less attraction to me than the attempt to combine extremes", Hort once wrote).[97] Furthermore, in selecting Bain and Ferrier as the representatives of the two positions to be reconciled, Marshall was following the lead of Grote, who, as we have seen, discussed in his *Exploratio* a scale of opinions "of which Professor Ferrier represents the extreme philosophical end, and Professor Bain the extreme physiological or physical."

The reconciliation of the respective contentions of Ferrier and Bain was achieved by means of a distinction that, in this second paper, Marshall introduced between "the subjective and the objective sides of the Ego." Such a distinction turns on the claim that there are two separate elements

[93] *EPW*, 55. A similar reference to Spencer's criticism of Mill's empiricism is also found in "Ferrier's Proposition One" (*EPW*, 64).
[94] *EPW*, 68.
[95] *EPW*, 59.
[96] *EPW*, 59–60.
[97] Hort 1896: II, 92.

contained within all cognitions, one "variable" and the other "permanent."⁹⁸ Let us deal first with what is meant by that permanent element of cognition from which Marshall derives the idea of a subjective side of the self. Ferrier had argued in his first proposition that (in Marshall's words) "in *every* cognition there is a certain reference to the subject which refuses to be solved by any analysis."⁹⁹ Agreeing with Ferrier, Marshall now identifies this irreducible reference to the subject with what he describes as the "permanent element" of consciousness. This permanent element, he insists, stands as the ground of all mental phenomena (including our phenomenal idea of the self). It is, in fact, precisely that self-consciousness which, in the first Grote Club paper, Marshall had declared to be "totally devoid of analogy in any physical action." This self-consciousness, Marshall now explains, is the "one thing which is capable of changing mechanical phenomena into mental phenomena."¹⁰⁰ In other words, without this permanent and irreducibly spiritual element of consciousness, the physiological processes of the nervous system can never generate any of the elements of that which we call "mind."

Marshall derives his definition of the "variable element" of consciousness by pointing out that, when he talks of self-consciousness, Bain means something other than the "permanent element" of cognition. According to Marshall, Bain takes self-consciousness to signify taking cognizance "of our own mind as phenomena." What Bain intends by this, Marshall explains, is "the objective sides of states of Internal Sense," which is to say "the variable element of certain cognitions, namely those that are introspective." Bain's definition, Marshall insists, takes no account of the permanent element of such introspective cognitions; it consists of no more than our consciousness of the difference and agreement of mental states *as phenomena*. For Marshall, in contrast to Bain, self-consciousness is "the consciousness of the Self in which those changes and correspondences" in mental phenomena take place. On this consciousness of a permanent self, Bain is completely silent.¹⁰¹ Yet Bain's notion of the variable element of cognitions is not empty, and what Bain has to say about the phenomenal self is valid (Ferrier, for his part, was

⁹⁸ *EPW*, 63.
⁹⁹ *EPW*, 59, emphasis in original.
¹⁰⁰ *EPW*, 65 (see also the comments on Mill's discussion of memories and expectations on p. 66). In this way Marshall in this second paper takes his earlier criticisms of Mill a step further. Self-consciousness not only is the foundation of our idea of the self, but is also the foundation of all our mental ideas, including that of matter.
¹⁰¹ *EPW*, 62–3. Marshall tells us that what Bain means by self-consciousness is exactly what Locke meant by "reflection" (see book 2, chapter 1 of Locke's *Essay Concerning Human Understanding*).

charged with overlooking this variable element of the self). Marshall suggests (and this suggestion will be developed in detail in his third paper, "Ye Machine") that Bain was correct to search for physiological correlates of the variable element of consciousness. Furthermore, he states that "the human mind does go through some education" with regard to its knowledge of the phenomenal self. Indeed, Marshall suggests that such education occurs not only in the individual, but also "in the race." But while Bain's account of the phenomenal self was limited to the education of the individual, nevertheless "as far as it goes," as an explanation of the variable element of consciousness it is "very near the truth."[102]

What had become of Marshall's earlier hope that Mansel's *Metaphysics* could supply the classificatory framework for an evolutionary psychology? In his second paper Marshall made it clear that with regard to the contention that all cognition contains an irreducible reference to the self, both Hamilton and Mansel stood on the same ground as did Ferrier. Yet he was at pains to emphasize that "the charge of having neglected to examine the stages by which the objective idea of self has grown into its present state of clearness and fullness … presses more heavily on [Hamilton] than on Ferrier. But even more strongly does the charge press against Mansel."[103] Evidently, Mansel's classification of mental powers, which had not so long ago appeared so promising, had proved to be, on closer inspection, a disappointment. Not only was Mansel now charged with failing to recognize gradations in the variable perception of the permanent self, but his reasoning was declared no less circular than that of Mill: "Mansel's contribution to the question of the classification of the various orders of Intelligence mainly consists in giving as a condition for a state of self-consciousness one which means nothing unless by implying the previous existence of a state of a self-consciousness."[104] Thus the earlier sympathy toward Mansel's *Metaphysics* had now given way to the conclusion that "there is much confusion in what [Mansel] says," and "though what he gives is chiefly what Bain shirks, he seems to me not to have as clear ideas of what he means as Bain has."[105] In fact, Marshall's underlying position in this second paper constituted far more than a mere dissatisfaction with Mansel's reasoning.

---

[102] *EPW*, 65, 61.
[103] *EPW*, 61; see also Mansel 1875: 41–7.
[104] *EPW*, 61–2. Note that Marshall utilizes the conclusions of "Ye Machine" to expose a flaw in one part of Mansel's classification.
[105] *EPW*, 61, 62.

Marshall concluded his second paper by contrasting, on the one hand, the positions of Mill and Bain and, on the other, those of "the Scotch school." (Ferrier, Hamilton, and Mansel are all – somewhat loosely – lumped together here as representatives of the common sense school of Scottish philosophy.) The problem with the "Scottish school," Marshall pronounced, was that "they were so confident that the subjective idea of the Ego was ultimate and beyond the power of analysis, that they made no attempts and paid no attention to the attempts of others to subject to a scientific analysis the objective idea of the Ego."[106] Mill and Bain were blamed in their turn "for not recognizing the distinction between the subjective and the objective sides of the Ego," and for thereby failing to recognize that no amount of analysis of the latter could ever derive the former. "But in exactly the same manner, on the other hand, do I blame the Scotch school for not recognizing the distinction between the two." This, of course, was precisely Grote's position. And as Grote had been acutely aware, this was a position that in the very attempt to reconcile Mill's phenomenalism with a "higher philosophy" founded on self-consciousness, necessarily denied the basic metaphysical ground of the philosophy of Hamilton and Mansel.

If a phenomenalist form of psychology could be reconciled with Ferrier's first proposition, such reconciliation itself arose from a rejection of Hamilton and Mansel's core metaphysical doctrines. As we have seen, Hamilton and Mansel insisted that knowing an object and knowing oneself knowing that object meant the same thing. Furthermore, the culmination of Mansel's study of the facts of consciousness from the point of view of psychology was the conclusion that the "function of thought is in all cases the same." In distinguishing between permanent and variable elements of consciousness – a distinction that formed the very ground of his attempt to reconcile intuitionism and phenomenalism – Marshall was insisting on a fundamental difference between two functions of thought. Indeed, in drawing such a distinction in terms of self-consciousness and a form of reflective introspection of phenomenal mental states, Marshall was constructing a form of mental dualism that distinctly echoed Coleridge's seminal distinction between reason and understanding. In short, in attempting to reconcile phenomenalist and intuitionist accounts of the mind, as he did in his second Grote Club paper, Marshall was necessarily rejecting the very foundations of the metaphysical psychology that Mansel had developed in his *Metaphysics*.

---

[106] *EPW*, 66–7.

What, if anything, does the turn from Mansel to Grote illustrated by this second paper tell us about the course that Marshall's religious doubts had now taken? Keynes, it will be recalled, quoted Marshall as having told him that around 1867 he had become deeply interested "in the philosophical foundation of knowledge, especially in relation to theology." The rise of such an interest might perhaps have been sparked by an encounter with Mansel's "theological relativism," but by around 1868 Marshall had arrived at a psychological theory of the mind that posited self-consciousness and phenomenal understanding as different kinds of thought. Such a position was incompatible with Mansel's psychological argument that the Coleridgean claim to know God through reason (as opposed to understanding) was untenable because the "function of thought is in all cases the same." Clearly, then, Marshall's insistence on a distinction between self-consciousness and phenomenal understanding points to a quite different path than that taken by Spencer and Huxley when they converted Mansel's theological argument into what Stephen called "the first principles of Agnosticism." Thus, if Marshall was indeed beset by religious doubts throughout this period, the terms in which he questioned the grounds of his Christian faith changed within the space of a year or so; for by around 1868 the framework of Marshall's philosophical thought was incompatible with that of Hamilton and Mansel, and fully in accord with that of Grote. But if Marshall's philosophical framework was compatible with liberal Anglican thought, the question then becomes at what point, if any, Marshall would have objected to the liberal Anglican attempt to arrive at knowledge of God through the employment of self-conscious reason.

Let us return to Grote's *Exploratio* and see how Grote moved from an initial postulate of self-consciousness to the claim that God was knowable. Such a justification of theological knowledge began with an acceptance of Ferrier's argument that self-consciousness is a part of all cognition. According to (one of) Grote's interpretations of Ferrier's proposition that, in the act of knowing phenomena, we also know ourselves knowing, "*we* are here ... in two positions; in the lower, things appear to us; in the higher, we watch the process." Here is the essence of Grote's conception of the relationship between real and phenomenal logics. The "complete or higher knowledge" provided by real logic consists of "the observation and criticism of the way in which things appear (are phenomena) to *us*."[107] Here is self-consciousness at work, reflecting on phenomenalism at work; or, in Marshall's terms, and as applied to phenomenalist psychology, we might say that here

---

[107] Grote 1865: 79, emphasis in original.

is the subjective self in a state of self-conscious awareness concerning the development of the objective self. So far, however, Grote is saying no more than is already stated in Ferrier's first proposition, and, indeed, Grote was well aware of this:

> Mr Ferrier hardly sufficiently explains whether he means to pass from the notion of ourselves as knowing, or from knowledge being "knowledge that we know," which of itself, I think, is not very important, to the notion of ourselves, or part of our selves, known in the object, which is the important one. It is this which really leads on, in the chain of thought, to the notion of knowledge being the meeting, through the intervention of phenomenal matter and the conversion of it into intellectual objects, with the thoughts, proceeding in the opposite direction, of mind or a mind like our own, however wider and vaster.[108]

In short, and as Grote here makes clear, theologically speaking, Ferrier's first proposition is not particularly exciting. It is a necessary but not a sufficient step toward knowledge of God. For Grote, self-consciousness allows for the *further* discovery that, at the root of reality, we meet a divine self-consciousness which is the ground of that reality. For Grote, the continuous correction of our "informed ideas" through the creation of "informed sensation" generates, on the one hand, the advance of phenomenal knowledge and, on the other, an advance in our knowledge of both our own mind and the mind of God. The observation of ourselves knowing reveals that just as phenomenal knowledge generates order out of chaos in our understanding of the "non-ego" that the mind advances into, so that "non-ego" itself is ordered only because it has been given shape by the mind of God.[109] This is a coherent, if subtle, theological argument that, as Grote shows goes well beyond the initial postulate of self-consciousness.

What Marshall made of such theological arguments, which he would have encountered in both Grote's *Exploratio* and in conversations with Maurice, we have no way of knowing. We know for certain that Marshall accepted the initial postulates of such an argument, because they are given in his distinction between the objective and the subjective ideas of the self. But while he demonstrated the irreducibility of self-consciousness to phenomenalist analysis, Marshall's Grote Club papers provide no indication of what his thoughts might have been as to the possibility that self-consciousness could disclose the existence of God. Of course, it is open to us to infer, given Keynes's insistence that "after a quick struggle religious beliefs dropped away," that by around 1868 or 1869 Marshall had come to

[108] Grote 1865: 67–8.
[109] Grote 1865: 87–91.

the conclusion that self-consciousness did not disclose what Coleridge, Maurice, and Grote believed that it did. But in light of the paucity of contemporary evidence on this point, it seems safer not to speculate on the precise state of Marshall's theological beliefs before around 1872, at which point it is possible to pick up the thread of Marshall's thoughts concerning theology and religious faith.

In 1872 Marshall discovered Hegel's *Philosophy of History*. His notes on this book, as well as the use that he made of Hegel's thought in his historical writing of this period, point clearly to the way in which Marshall would transform the liberal Anglican philosophical framework that he had inherited from Grote into a metaphysical framework that one might perhaps describe as "agnostic" (although the antimetaphysical associations of such a term render it problematic as a label for Marshall's mature metaphysical faith). For the Cambridge Coleridgeans, the point about Ferrier's first proposition was that it established, against the arguments of Hamilton and Mansel, the independent reality of that self-consciousness that would now serve as a means of coming to know God. What Marshall would find in Hegel's thought, however, was a means of transforming the status of such self-consciousness from a theological tool to a subject of evolutionary development, such evolution itself generating the variety of theological beliefs that constituted the religious history of the world. Again, whether such a metaphysical position really amounted to a nonreligious vision of life is a moot point; yet there can be little question that this position allowed Marshall to frame a definitive solution in his search for the grounds of theological knowledge. But this is to get ahead of ourselves. In the next two chapters, we must first examine the physical and mechanical side of Marshall's psychological project and then turn to his studies in political economy between 1868 and 1872. In doing so, we have little choice but to concede that the available evidence does not enable us to establish any clear-cut conclusions as to the state of Marshall's religious beliefs in the period in which he engaged in these studies.

FOUR

The Way of All Flesh

INTRODUCTION

On a Friday evening in the late 1860s, the Grote Club assembled as usual in the college rooms of one of its members. The week before, this discussion group of Cambridge moral scientists had listened to Marshall's defense of Ferrier's first proposition. This week they were to hear the second half of his psychological project – a paper entitled "Ye Machine." The members of the Grote Club, or at least those who had been in attendance at the earlier meeting, had some idea of what to expect from the evening's paper. As we have seen, in "Ferrier's Proposition One" Marshall had expressed approval of Bain's attempt to establish physical correlates of mental phenomena. He had also insisted that self-consciousness had no physical analogy and argued that, in the absence of self-consciousness, no changes in the body could generate mental phenomena. But the position outlined in this previous paper suggested that much of our mental life was nevertheless explicable in terms of changes in the state of the brain. The business of this Friday's paper, "Ye Machine," was to outline a model of the operation of the physical correlates of mental phenomena.

Marshall's model is at first sight rather odd. He begins "Ye Machine" by postulating the existence of a machine capable of receiving impressions from the outside world, and the main part of the paper is devoted to building up an account of the various parts of the machine that enable it to deliberate on its actions in the world. The machine works by forming ideas of impressions and then associating various ideas; it in fact embodies Marshall's version of the associationist psychology of Mill and Bain. In "Ferrier's Proposition One," Marshall had stated that all the development "of the law or rather of the faculty of association," through which Bain had accounted for the education of the phenomenal self, is "perfectly explicable {as we shall shew} by the process of mere mechanism."[1] Hence one of the purposes of "Ye Machine" was to show that Bain's associationist psychology could indeed be reduced to a purely mechanical account of the relationship between impressions, ideas, and actions. But the way that Marshall proceeds to do so is curious. At the start of "Ferrier's Proposition One," he had announced his "wish to investigate what operations can, and what cannot, be performed by pure mechanism – mechanism, that is, such as is the subject of the daily occupation of the practical Engineer."[2] "Ye Machine," then, is essentially a hypothetical exercise in practical engineering, designed to demonstrate the range, and also to discover the limits, of mechanical cerebration.

The present chapter is devoted to a close reading of "Ye Machine." Over the course of this exegesis, we shall discuss the contexts that informed Marshall's mechanical rendering of Bain's associationist psychology and relate the various stages in his argument to their sources in a wider contemporary literature. In so examining "Ye Machine," we shall come to see how, sometime around 1868, Marshall was able to establish a working dualistic model of human character, such that a wide variety of mental and emotional states and operations came to be regarded as the mental reflections of underlying physical processes; it was a model, however, that looked to self-consciousness to account for a significant number of distinctly human activities. Such a dualistic division between body and mind had far-reaching consequences for Marshall's social thought. In the following chapter, we shall see how it provided him with a crucial interpretative tool in his readings in the history of political economy. More germane to our present concerns is the way in which this dualistic model informed Marshall's early distinction between "ordinary" students, who required external motivation, and "true men of learning," who did not.[3] The "ordinary" students of Chapter Two, we shall find, are engaged primarily in developing mechanical connections in their brains, while the creative research of "true men of learning" is an activity

[1] *EPW*, 63. Shortly after making this claim, Marshall had declared that self-consciousness was "the one thing which is capable of changing mechanical phenomena into mental phenomena." The business of "Ferrier's Proposition One" was, after all, to argue that self-consciousness was a definitive feature of the mind. But given "this one postulate" of self-consciousness, Marshall had announced in this earlier paper, "everything else is accountable for by the evolution of purely mechanical agencies" (*EPW*, 64–5).

[2] *EPW*, 60. Although my interpretation of "Ye Machine" diverges from that of Raffaelli on a few points (most importantly in emphasizing the relationship between this paper and the defense of self-consciousness in "Ferrier's Proposition One"), the following discussion is intended to complement – and is very much indebted to – Raffaelli's groundbreaking work. See in general Raffaelli's introduction to *EPW*, Raffaelli 1991, 2003, and his various entries in *ECAM*.

[3] See pp. 82–3 above.

primarily of the self-conscious mind. In other words, Marshall's dualistic model of human character provided the philosophical grounds of his early views on a liberal education.

Taken together, the two papers, "Ferrier's Proposition One" and "Ye Machine," provide us with further clues to the possible origins and partial resolution of Marshall's early mental crisis. The model of body and mind that Marshall set down in these papers allows for an explanation of not only the physical and mental but also the spiritual difficulties Marshall seems to have experienced at this time. Specifically, it will be suggested later in this chapter that the crisis in Marshall's mental development may well have had its origins in a physical collapse brought on by overwork. Such a breakdown in health, it will be further suggested, gave rise to a questioning of the meaning of his studies to date and a subsequent determination by the young Marshall to establish to his own satisfaction that he was more than simply a "thinking machine." Such a narrative, of course, cannot be proved. Nevertheless, it is clear that Marshall's dualistic model of the mind provided him with a means of thinking through his own mental crisis. Crucially, the model allowed him to conclude that if the proximate cause of his breakdown was indeed an excess of mechanical cerebration leading to a state of mental and emotional exhaustion, this loss of vitality may well have reflected a deeper, spiritual malaise. In this way, perhaps, Marshall came to associate a period of physical exhaustion and intense emotional stress with a religious crisis regarding the foundations of theological knowledge. "Ferrier's Proposition One" and "Ye Machine" did not in themselves provide a solution to such religious doubts, but they did provide a framework for understanding the experience of such doubts and pointed toward the path along which Marshall's thinking must move if he was to resolve them.

NOTE ON THE PROCEEDINGS

Before presenting "Ye Machine" to the members of the Grote Club, Marshall delivered a brief clarification of his paper in the preceding week. Referring to the discussion that had followed his reading of "Ferrier's Proposition One," he explained that "in assuming self-consciousness I was not understood to assume as much as I intended to assume."[4] Marshall now reiterated his earlier position that self-consciousness stood as the gateway leading from physical to mental phenomena. "My eye supplies me with the affection," he explained with regard to vision, and "my self-consciousness

---

[4] *EPW*, 68.

turns the affection into a conscious affection or feeling, and by the aid of memory enables me to perceive differences between feelings."[5] Marshall is here postulating a three-way division between the physical instruments of consciousness (i.e., the body), the mental phenomena of consciousness, and self-consciousness. This three-way division supports a rigid dualism between body and mind. At the same time, however, it divides the realm of the mind into two parts, one of which – consciousness of phenomena – is distinct from, yet nevertheless correlated with, events in the body. To use another of Marshall's examples in this note, an "increase in potential energy" within the body constitutes the physical basis of a conscious feeling of pleasure; without self-consciousness such a change in the body makes no impression on a conscious mind, but given self-consciousness, conscious pleasure is no more than a reflection of the fact that the potential energy of the body has increased. "My psychological facts are independent of my physical facts," Marshall explained, "although in any hypothesis or theory by which I attempt to connect my psychological facts I shall be indebted at every step to my corresponding physical theories."[6]

Two aspects of "Ye Machine" can seem particularly puzzling. One is an implication of the fact that in providing a model of the physical basis of consciousness, Marshall assumes away self-consciousness. Marshall describes a machine devoid of self-consciousness that nevertheless associates (the mechanical equivalent of) ideas. But given his philosophy of mind as a whole, the absence of self-consciousness entails that these ideas are not conscious ideas.[7] It is not immediately obvious, however, just what a "non-conscious idea" might be. The key point to grasp here is that Marshall sees mental phenomena as epiphenomena – reflections, that is, of underlying physical interactions. Self-consciousness is merely a precondition of the consciousness of these phenomena; it does not shape or determine this consciousness. In other words, the explanation of the phenomena of consciousness is to be found in the physical realm (self-consciousness is another story, as is the explanation of the nature – as opposed to the behavior – of mental phenomena). Marshall's mechanical ideas are thus the

---

[5] *EPW*, 69.

[6] *EPW*, 70.

[7] In "Ye Machine," Marshall places one or two accents over the middle letter of his key terms to indicate that he is speaking of the machine, as well as to indicate whether he means the first or the second circuit of the machine (see *EPW*, 39, n. 5). I have not reproduced these accents because in isolated quotes they complicate rather than illuminate. It is, however, important to appreciate that Marshall went out of his way to indicate the difference between, for example, a conscious sensation and a nonconscious or mechanical "sensâtion."

physical determinants of what would be conscious ideas if his machine were endowed with self-consciousness. But even if we put aside for a moment any remaining puzzlement concerning the nature of nonconscious ideas, we are still left wondering why he decided that such ideas could be associated by a *machine*. For a twenty-first-century audience, at least, Marshall's third Grote Club paper requires some further preliminary discussion.

We can begin by noting that by the mid–nineteenth century, recent developments in the physiological study of the nervous system appeared to point toward a physical explanation of one of the most distinctive elements of J. S. Mill's mental philosophy. In his *System of Logic*, Mill argued that both children and animals reason or infer from experience.[8] Such an imputation of rationality to infants and even brutes followed from Mill's conviction that humans habitually make inferences without being conscious of the fact. For example, in his famous defense of Berkeley's theory of vision (1842), he argued that although "the distance of an object from us is really a matter of judgment and inference, we cannot help fancying that we see it directly with our eyes." Such a mistake, he explained, was but an instance of a more general error "whereby a process of reasoning, which from habit is very rapidly performed, resembles, so closely as to be mistaken for, an act of intuition."[9] And that, of course, was the real point of his strident defense of Berkeley; for Mill's standard argument against the intuitionist philosophy was to demonstrate that beliefs supposedly founded on intuitions could in fact be explained in terms of a process of association and inference that was habitual, rapid, and so occurred below the threshold of consciousness. But by the late 1850s, as Mill himself appears to have recognized, the foundations had been laid for the physiological explanation of just such unconscious processes of reasoning.

In his 1859 review of Bain's psychology in the *Edinburgh Review*, Mill distinguished between motions of the body in which the brain cooperates and motions of the body that are "automatic and mechanical."[10] Mill was here simply following the first part of Bain's *The Senses and the Intellect* (1855), in which a physiological sketch of the brain and the nerves served,

---

[8]   See *Mill CW*, 7: 188. Ryan argues that Mill here fails to distinguish between "mere expectation and rational expectation." Inference, Ryan insists, is "essentially a process of justifying expectation rationally" (see Ryan 1970: 29). Marshall, of course, preferred to speak in terms of self-consciousness rather than rationality, but it could perhaps be said that his entire dualistic psychological project emerged out of precisely this distinction. See in particular Marshall's discussion of Bain's account of belief in external reality in "Ferrier's Proposition One" (*EPW*, 64–5).

[9]   *Mill CW*, 11: 249.

[10] *Mill CW*, 11: 352–3.

as Bain put it, to "draw a broad line" between body and mind. Physiologists had now ascertained, Bain had explained, that there were two types of nerves: "out-carrying nerves," or "*motor* nerves," and "in-carrying nerves," or "*sentient* nerves." In the spinal cord are to be found a number of "nerve centres," that is, "locations of complete circles of nervous action, instances of communication between in-carrying and out-carrying nerves." Thus the spinal cord and the medulla oblongata constitute "power-originating portions of the nervous system." Yet while the "actions maintained by the cord and the medulla oblongata resemble many of the true mental actions," they do not "require feeling as an indispensable condition of their performance" and, so insisted Bain, are properly excluded from the province of mind. Those physical actions, Bain explained, that "seem to be mental and are not … are termed *automatic*, or self-moved actions, and also *reflex* actions."[11] As Mill commented in his review, such discoveries of physiology had been "brought to light only within the present generation."[12] Yet such discoveries clearly pointed to a physiological explanation of those processes of rapid and habitual reasoning that Mill habitually invoked to account for supposedly intuitive beliefs.

The mid-Victorian physiological authority on "involuntary" action was William Carpenter of University College London. For Carpenter the physiological theory of reflex action provided a complete account of the behavior of lower animals such as insects. As he put it in his 1875 essay "On the Doctrine of Human Automatism" (an essay that Marshall placed in his collection of bound periodical articles), the "essential characteristic" of insects is "Instinct," which he defined in terms of "the working-out of results by an *automatic* mechanism." Carpenter labeled this mechanism "*original* or *primary* automatism." A particular combination of these primary automatisms could explain the behavior of any one particular insect, without recourse to some kind of insect consciousness. In higher animals such as humans, Carpenter went on to argue, habitual or routine behaviors provided an analogous form of automatic behavior. The habitual performance of a standard action was said by Carpenter to result in the formation of a "*secondary* automatism."[13] Such a "secondary automatism" allowed for the mechanical performance of an action that, although initially learned by means of

---

[11] Bain 1977: 40–7, emphasis in original.

[12] *Mill CW*, 11: 353–4.

[13] Carpenter 1875: 405–7 [BV, ML], emphasis in original. Carpenter's article commences with a useful summary of the history of recent physiological work on the nervous system. On Carpenter's model of the nervous system, see Raffaelli's introduction to *EPW* and Haley 1978: 36–40.

conscious volition, had nevertheless now become habitual and therefore could be performed by nervous circuits without recourse to conscious direction. For example, as Carpenter observed in a different essay, "it is no uncommon experience in telegraph offices, for transmitters of messages, when they have been for some time in the service, to work the instruments without conscious thought of what they are doing."[14] Or as he explained in his 1875 paper, the act of walking, while originally "learned by experience under the guidance of sense-impressions" comes to be "completely automatic":

Thus have I seen John S. Mill making his way along Cheapside at its fullest afternoon tide, threading his way among the foot-passengers with which its narrow pavement was crowded, and neither jostling his fellows nor coming into collision with lamp-posts; and have been assured by him that his mind was then continuously engaged upon his System of Logic (most of which was thought-out in his daily walks between the India office and his residence at Kensington), and that he had so little consciousness of what was taking place around him, as not to recognize his nearest friends among the people he met, until his attention had been recalled to their presence.[15]

Let us for a moment imagine Carpenter hailing Mill from the other side of the street. His attention having been drawn from his ratiocinations to his immediate environment, Mill looks around and now, as it were for the first time, sees his surroundings. Yet according to his own account of the theory of vision, all that his sense of sight informs him of are "light and colours, and a certain arrangement of coloured lines and points."[16] Owing to unconscious and rapid inferences made from data supplied by his visual organs, however, his visual experience appears to reveal a multitude of people at various distances from him and from one another, one of whom he recognizes as the physiologist William Carpenter. In other words, not only the unconscious act of walking, but also the unconscious act of inferring the spatial arrangement of pedestrians on Cheapside, and even of identifying a familiar face, constitute reflex actions performed by means of the "ganglionic centres of the organs of special sense"; all such actions, in other words,

---

[14] Quoted in Morus 2000: 473.

[15] Carpenter 1875: 407 [BV, ML]). For an example of contemporary criticism of Carpenter's theory of attention from the point of view of the "automaton hypothesis," see Lingard 1877. On the centrality of attention to psychology in this period, see Daston 1978. For the relationship between the psychological theory of attention and developments in modern art, see Crary 1999. And for a discussion of the role of "attention" in "Ye Machine" in relation to subsequent British psychology, see my "Marshall and Psychology" in *ECAM*.

[16] *Mill CW*, 11: 248.

can be explained in terms of the performance of some combination of "secondary automatisms." But if such unconscious habitual reasoning processes are performed by physiological automatisms, analogous to instincts, what reason is there to suppose that conscious reasoning is not also an automatic physical phenomenon? And if consciousness is thereby proclaimed to be no more than an epiphenomenon, what reason could be given for denying that even occasional so-called voluntary mental activity is not simply a form of mechanical physical behavior? After all, in his *System of Logic*, Mill had drawn no distinction in kind between the reasoning of brutes, habitual unconscious inferences, and the conscious inferences of the moral philosopher.

In his *Methods of Ethics* (1874), Henry Sidgwick would frame such questions in relation to the scientific demand that all natural phenomena be explained in terms of the determination of any one state of affairs by the state immediately preceding. Such a causal approach to the explanation of natural phenomena, he noted, had of late swept away all other modes of explanation and conquered all realms of speculation bar one – the still "mysterious citadel of Will." Sidgwick himself held out against this last assault on a libertarian faith in the freedom of the will on the ground that introspection revealed an "immediate affirmation of consciousness in the moment of deliberate action." Nevertheless, he felt obliged to concede that "no clear line can be drawn" between actions "which are conscious and voluntary" and those that are unconscious and physically determined. What is more, "actions which we habitually perform continually pass from the conscious class into the – wholly or partly – unconscious; and the further we investigate, the more the conclusion is forced upon us, that there is no kind of action originated by conscious volition which cannot also, under certain circumstances, be originated unconsciously." Indeed, our own conviction that we are free agents notwithstanding, "we always explain the voluntary action of all men except ourselves on the principle of causation by character and circumstances."[17] From the point of view of William Carpenter, then, watching Mill walk down Cheapside thinking about his *System of Logic*, no clear line of demarcation would be apparent between Mill's cerebral and his other bodily activities. With the possible exception of Mill himself, who was to say that Mill had not only walked down Cheapside automatically, but had also composed his entire *System of Logic* mechanically?

By 1874 Marshall's close friend from the Grote Club, W. K. Clifford, had joined Thomas Huxley in proclaiming that humans were simply automata

[17] Sidgwick 1890: 63–7.

who happened to be conscious (such consciousness playing no causal role in the mechanical activity of the nervous system). Indeed, the 1875 paper by Carpenter quoted earlier was explicitly composed to counter what the London physiologist saw as Huxley and Clifford's physiological determinism. At first sight it might appear that Marshall in 1868 had already arrived at a similar position; for the crucial step that Marshall made in "Ye Machine" was to attempt a mechanical (i.e., physical) explanation of voluntary action. Such a step involved obliterating the barrier that Bain, in *The Senses and the Intellect*, had drawn between "automatic" and "true mental actions"; or to put the matter another way, it involved the reduction of the whole associationist psychology to a physiological basis. Yet Marshall's psychological project as a whole, while almost certainly an inspiration for Clifford's development of the "automaton hypothesis," did not itself embody any implication that free will was a mere illusion. The crucial difference between Marshall's position in 1868 and Clifford's in 1874 was that Marshall insisted that the mind was something more than just the (mechanical) faculty of association. Marshall's mechanical treatment of voluntary mental behavior was explicitly not an account of *self-conscious* voluntary behavior (however paradoxical that might sound). As we have seen, the prefatory note to "Ye Machine" insisted that only self-consciousness could transform the physical basis of mental behavior into a properly mental phenomenon. In Marshall's "general theory of psychology," then, the psychological fact of free will, resting as it did on a nonreducible self-consciousness, was independent of any mechanical basis of volition.

Marshall's early model of the mind would seem to have led him to Kant's moral philosophy. When Marshall "was still in his metaphysical stage," Keynes tells us, "a desire to read Kant in the original led him to Germany."[18] As we saw in the preceding chapter, Kant's *Critique of Pure Reason* loomed large in the background of the disputes arising out of Mansel's Bampton Lectures. Nevertheless, none of the first three Grote Club papers suggest that Marshall had yet studied this book. The psychological theory outlined in the second and third papers, however, brought Marshall to a position very close to that dualism of the will that stood at the basis of Kant's ethical theories. Sidgwick, in his *Methods of Ethics*, observed that according to Kant "the natural determination of the Will is by motives of pleasure and pain," but "when our action is truly rational, a higher law of causation comes into play."[19] Marshall also came to believe something like this. For

---

[18] Keynes 1925: 10.
[19] Sidgwick 1890: 51–2. Sidgwick, we might note, was here explaining Kant's position in order to signal his dissent from it.

Marshall, ordinary volition is determined by physical processes in the body, but self-consciousness allows for a truly free will. In other words, Marshall independently arrived at a form of mental dualism with a deep affinity to Kant's contrast between a free noumenal self that stands outside of time, space, and causation and an empirical or phenomenal self that exists in the world of sensation. Hence there is reason to suspect that it was not epistemological considerations relating to the grounds of theological (or other) knowledge that led Marshall to Germany to study Kant, but rather a recognition, which perhaps arose during discussions with Sidgwick at the Grote Club, that his dualistic model of the mind lent itself to a Kantian approach to moral philosophy.[20]

If the philosophical background of Marshall's third paper is now clear, this is not the case with regard to his choice to make a machine his model of the physical basis of mental phenomena. As we have seen, Carpenter also employed mechanical analogies. But Marshall went much farther than Carpenter: where Carpenter described the "nervous circle" composed of a sensory nerve, the nerve center to which it proceeds, and the motor nerve passing from that center to the muscles, as "furnishing the mechanism" of reflex actions,[21] Marshall in "Ye Machine" accounted for mental behavior in terms of the whirring of rotating wheels and the tightening of connecting bands. Thus we must look to additional factors in order to understand why Marshall decided to translate the operations of the brain and nervous system into an extended analogy drawn from the work of the practical engineer.

Our first step must be to recognize the fact that the second wrangler of 1865 had been habituated to thinking of reality in terms of mechanism. Whewell's midcentury reforms had given rise to a mathematical tripos that emphasized physical realities such as pulleys and machines over mathematical symbols.[22] Indeed, at the heart of the tripos stood mechanics, the science

---

[20] It does not seem to be a coincidence that the only work by Kant that has survived in Marshall's library is an 1869 edition of *The Metaphysics of Ethics*. Kant's identification of moral agency with human rationality and autonomy must have played some role in leading Marshall to that firm identification of self-consciousness with moral freedom that is the hallmark of his adaptation of Hegel's philosophy of history.

[21] Carpenter 1875: 399.

[22] On Whewell's midcentury reforms. See pp. 60–1 above. The tripos from which Marshall graduated in 1865 was, according to Andrew Warwick, concerned primarily with "the application of analysis to well formulated problems in geometry and dynamics" (Warwick 1998: 359). Smith asserts that Whewell's tripos contained a "metaphysical bias" but concedes the underlying similarity to the mechanical mathematics taught in Scotland (Smith 1998: 193–7). The nature of the mathematics studied in the Cambridge Mathematical

of both artificial and natural machines.[23] The fruit of such a mental training is illustrated by Marshall's recollection, many years later, that in "the years of my apprenticeship to economic studies, between 1867 and 1875, I endeavoured to learn enough of the methods of operation of the greater part of the leading industries of the country, to be able to reconstruct mentally the vital parts of the chief machines used in each."[24] Such an endeavor, however, was preceded by an attempt to construct mentally the working parts of a thinking machine.

But at just the point that Marshall was composing "Ye Machine," the Mathematical Tripos was again reformed. These new reforms reflected the growing influence within Cambridge of such Scottish energy scientists as W. Thomson, P. G. Tait, and J. C. Maxwell. In midcentury Whewell had deemed thermodynamics a "progressive science," and therefore unfit for undergraduate studies. The 1868 reformers, however, claimed that in Thomson and Tait's 1867 *Treatise on Natural Philosophy* the science of thermodynamics had been established as a "permanent science." *Treatise* was the culmination of a half-century-long transformation of the science of mechanics into a science of work or energy exchange. As historians of science like M. Norton Wise and Crosbie Smith have pointed out, the kernel of Thomson and Tait's *Treatise* consisted of the transformation of Newton's second law of mechanics, the principle of equal actions and reactions, into a law of energy exchange. In this thermodynamic rendering of mechanics, "work" was defined as change in energy, and "statics" now referred to those situations in which the work that would be done by all the forces acting in a system, if it changed configuration, would sum to zero (statics thus becoming but a special case of dynamics).[25] While Marshall had stopped coaching for the Mathematical Tripos by 1868, it is evident from a number of his statements that he absorbed the core lessons of Thomson and Tait's *Treatise*.[26] In fact, in one of his letters to the *Cambridge Gazette* in 1868 we

Tripos has by now received a significant amount of scholarly attention; see, e.g., Richards 1988, Warrick 1994, and Weintraub 2002.

[23] As Thomson and Tait put it, "We use the word 'mechanics' in its true classical sense, the science of machines, the sense in which Newton himself used it" (Thomson and Tait 1879: I, 250n).

[24] Pigou 1925: 358. See also Marshall's testimony in Groenewegen 1996: 33–45. A. C. Pigou reported that Marshall "told me once that, had he been planted in a desert island, he thought he could have re-designed the great majority of important machines currently in use – other than electrical machines" (Pigou 1935: 12); electromagnetism, we might note, was included as a subject in the Mathematical Tripos only after the reforms of 1868.

[25] See Smith 1998, Thomson and Tait 1879: I, 247–74, and Norton Wise 1989–90.

[26] For example, the statement in the *Principles* that "Statics is really but a branch of Dynamics" (*Principles*, I: 366, n. 2) articulates the fundamental lesson of Thomson and Tait's *Treatise*.

find him hoping that even students who aspire to classical honors might, by means of Marshall's proposed mid-university honors in applied science, come to understand that "connecting link between the Physical Sciences," the "Principle of the Conservation of Energy."[27] Physiology, of course, was a physical science, and it is evident from "Ye Machine" itself that Marshall's thinking machine was conceived as a thermodynamic engine.

The engine described in "Ye Machine" performs work by way of both external and internal activities. In addition to the mechanical processes of deliberation, internal work involved, for example, adding "fresh water to the boiler" or adding more coals to its furnace or bringing "more steam into play, so as to increase either the store of energy or the *visviva* of the Machine."[28] (Such actions, we may note, Marshall classified as "pleasurable" – in physical terms – thus instantiating the brief allusion in his prefatory note to a physical theory of pleasure as an increase in potential energy.) In other words, Marshall's machine as a whole converts the potential energy contained in the coal that it feeds into its boiler into the muscular and nervous energy required both to act bodily in the world and to deliberate mentally before the performance of such actions.

If Marshall's wholesale adoption of a thermodynamic analogy of the mind was unprecedented, he was nevertheless merely developing what had become a convention in physiology. Since midcentury Bain and Spencer had looked to the principle of energy conservation as a heuristic guide in their psychological theories, and when in his 1875 essay Carpenter declared that "the doctrine of the conservation of energy holds good in the animal body as completely as it does in the universe around," he was merely reiterating a physiological commonplace.[29] Furthermore, by the late 1860s a two-way metaphor commonly employed among Victorians represented the nervous system as the "telegraphic network of the body" and the telegraph network of the nation as the "nervous system of the body politic." Nevertheless, it is important to observe here that Marshall appears to have accepted Bain's insistence that there was a crucial distinction between

---

Warwick (1994: 69) notes that it was not until around 1875 that the most famous coaches such as Routh had mastered the skills required for teaching thermodynamics within the Mathematics Tripos (Warwick 1994: 69). It is also clear that in 1873 Cambridge dons were typically unfamiliar with even the most basic principles of the new science (see Smith 1998: 171).

[27] *CAM*, I: 3.

[28] *EPW*, 75. Marshall began his paper by stating that the reception of impressions from the outer world can lead to changes in both the "statical and dynamical" relations of a machine's internal parts (*EPW*, 72).

[29] Carpenter 1875: 398.

electrical and nervous circuits. According to Bain, the latter were distinctive in that an initial stimulus could be propagated "with increase by the consumption of its own material. ... The [nerve] fibres are made to sustain the force at the cost of their own substance."[30] If Bain's point was conceded, the nervous system could not be analyzed as a closed system of energy exchange, and on this ground Bain rejected an emerging movement within psycho-physiology that attempted to measure psychological processes. This would appear to explain why Marshall did not attempt to construct – or even allude to the possibility of constructing – a quantitative mechanical model of the nervous system.[31]

There is also a more local context for Marshall's attempt to outline the nature and the limitations of a mechanical mind. As Warwick has observed, the Cambridge Mathematical Tripos evoked in both students and visitors a vision of the "industrialization of the learning process."[32] While Whewell had set students to cultivate their higher mental faculties through the study of machines, ambitious Cambridge undergraduates increasingly adopted a language that identified their own reasoning powers with those of a machine. Such language suggests a further, more personal dimension to Marshall's construction of a mechanical model of the mind but three years after graduation. Throughout his life Marshall would frequently employ mechanical metaphors for mathematical thought, writing, for example, of the "cog-wheels of ... mathematical machinery."[33] If reminiscent of "Ye Machine," such language was probably first used by Marshall as an undergraduate. Emerson, visiting Cambridge in the late 1840s, observed that the English "train a scholar as they train an engineer." Cambridge undergraduates, however, understood themselves to be steam engines rather than apprentice engineers. In his midcentury account of undergraduate life, the American Charles Bristed described how students preparing for examination were said to be "getting up steam," while the highly trained wrangler could solve mathematical problems with the "regularity and velocity of a

---

[30] Bain 1977: 59.
[31] This seems to provide an important clue to the underlying differences in the mechanical approaches to the mind adopted by Jevons and Marshall, differences that in turn cast light on the development of a quantitative theory of marginal utility by Jevons and Marshall's evident mistrust and suspicion in the early 1870s with regard to such a proposed psychological ground of a mathematical political economy. On Jevons and psycho-physiology, see Maas 2005 and White 1994.
[32] Warwick 1998: 300.
[33] *CAM*, II: 307.

machine."[34] After his breakdown, Galton complained that a "mill seemed to be working inside my head" and reflected that he had "tried to make a steam-engine perform more work than it was constructed for, by tampering with the safety valve and thereby straining its mechanism."[35] Such examples could readily be multiplied, and provide an explanation for Marshall's use of mechanical analogies for mental work only a few years after his graduation. The further investigation of this more local – not to say personal – dimension of "Ye machine" is best postponed, however, until we have worked our way through the earlier parts of the paper delivered to the Grote Club on a Friday evening in Cambridge.

MECHANICAL CEREBELLUM

Marshall began "Ye Machine" by positing the existence of a hypothetical machine that could receive input from the outer world. He described the inner composition of the "brain" of his machine as containing "an indefinite number of wheels of various sizes, in various positions." These wheels were the mechanical equivalent of ideas, which were formed in response to the reception of the mechanical equivalent of sensations. Marshall then proceeded to establish mechanical analogies for the two basic principles of Bain's associationist psychology. When any two wheels are moving together, "the Machine itself connects them by a light band"; such a connection provides the mechanical equivalent of what traditional associationist psychology defined as the association of ideas through contiguity. Just as repetition of the experience of two ideas together strengthens the mental association between them, so such repetition is held to tighten the connecting band between the two wheels. The turning of one wheel can also set in motion a different but similarly placed wheel; this provides the mechanical equivalent of association by similarity. The "brain" of the machine evolves as new sensations from the external world generate new wheels, the mechanical equivalent of the ideas of these new sensations. But these new wheels then become associated with other wheels and, in so doing, increase the multitude of circuits in the brain of the machine. A circuit can lead from an idea of sensation to an idea of action in the world, and from ideas of action

---

[34] Bristed 1852: I, 319, quoted in Warwick 1998: 300–1. Bristed regarded the Cambridge tripos experience as characteristic of a country "where the division of mental labour, like that of mechanical labour, is carried out to a degree which must be witnessed and experienced to be conceived."

[35] Quoted in Warwick 1998: 301.

are born physical – environment-altering – actions in the "body" of the machine.

Marshall placed his machine within the evolutionary order. He posited that it could distinguish between "pleasurable" and "painful" sensations and ideas. This allowed him, first of all, to establish a mechanical definition of "volition." An external stimulus may set in motion more than one "train of ideas," and there will be occasions when the resultant ideas of action are in conflict. The machine resolves this "internal strife" by "deliberation," and such a resolution Marshall regarded as "rudimentary volition." Yet such volition is no more than the determination of deliberation according to the relative strengths of the connections between ideas and pleasures.[36] There will be times, however, when no train of ideas can lead to any idea of pleasure-producing action, and in such cases the elicited wheel corresponding to an idea of pleasure continues to revolve until, by chance, it sets in motion a wheel corresponding to some idea of action. The resulting actions are by definition random. Nevertheless, occasionally such an action may so alter the external world as to allow for the performance of a pleasure-producing action that was hitherto not possible. This new circuit, once hit upon, is liable to be repeated. Marshall called this a "contrivance" and the "germs of *instinct*."[37] Furthermore, the machine might build others like itself, thus giving rise to "hereditary and accumulated instincts." Owing to accidental circumstances the descendents, however, would vary slightly, and those most suited to their environment would survive longer: "The principle of natural selection, which involves only purely mechanical agencies, would thus be in full operation."[38]

Although this mechanical account of both volition and instinct might seem a long way from Bain's associationist psychology, hints of all the features of Marshall's mechanical model of the mind as so far set down can be identified in Mill's 1859 review of Bain's work. As we have already noted, in this review Mill distinguished between voluntary and "automatic and mechanical" motion, associating the former with cooperation in physiological processes by "the central organ of the nervous system, the brain." While holding with Bain that voluntary action was the distinguishing

---

[36] See *EPW*, 75–6. Marshall proceeds to establish a "higher form of deliberation and volition" in terms of conflicting "desires" (a particular connection of one set of motions with another). But this does not in any way make his account of "volition" less automatic.

[37] *EPW*, 72–7, emphasis in original.

[38] *EPW*, 76–7. Marshall did not, however, discuss this principle any further because, as he put it, reproduction of machine by machine throws "great additional difficulties in the way of any attempt to form a representation in thought, however vague, of the machine." On Marshall's "contrivances," see Raffaelli 1991: 41–2.

characteristic of mental as opposed to automatic physical behavior, Mill also followed Bain in emphasizing what he described as "the *connexion* between the functions of the nervous system and the phenomena of the mind."[39] Mill further followed Bain in identifying the brain as the necessary physical agent of any mental activity. In a passage from this review, which Marshall copied out into his loose-leaf notebook in the late 1860's, Mill explained that whether "organisation alone could produce life and thought, we probably shall never certainly know, unless we could repeat Frankenstein's experiment; but that our mental operations have material conditions can be denied by no one who acknowledges, what all now admit, that the mind employs the brain as its material organ."[40] Despite insisting on the ultimate independence of mental from physical science, both Bain and Mill came dangerously close to transforming psychology into a study of the "material conditions" of our mental operations.

In his 1859 review, Mill hailed Bain's physiological account of volition as a "capital improvement" in associationist psychology. Bain, according to Mill, held that the brain is "a self-acting instrument." Under "the organic stimulus of nutrition," he explained, this instrument produces "a rush of bodily activity." Such spontaneous activity, he went on to explain, can be witnessed in "the random motions which we see constantly made without apparent end or purpose by infants." Now, Mill continued, of the "numerous motions given forth indiscriminately by the spontaneous energy of the nervous centre, some are accidentally hit on, which are found to be followed by a pleasure, or by the relief of pain." Here, Mill concluded, is "the ultimate basis of voluntary action."[41] But here too is the origin of the randomly spinning wheels of Ye Machine, which occasionally hit upon some chance "contrivance" that is henceforth adopted by the machine and, when passed on to its mechanical offspring, becomes a mechanical instinct. Indeed, we can see how easy it was for Marshall to extend Bain's account of the education of the individual to an evolutionary account of the education of the "race." But even more important than this account of the evolution of the race in terms of mechanical agencies is the basic fact that, however much

---

[39] *Mill CW*, 11: 348, emphasis added.

[40] *Mill CW*, 11: 348; and M 4/1, f. 231.

[41] See *Mill CW*, 11: 354–9. For Mill, Bain's physiological explanation of volition was of "capital" importance because it allowed for the explanation of an active, or spontaneous, element within the mind. The traditional associationist model of the mind was purely passive, with the association of ideas treated as a process initiated by the external imprint of a sensation. Coleridge, Mill observed, while at one time an advocate of associationist psychology, had become alienated from the theory precisely because it could not account for the mind's activity.

Mill and Bain distinguished between physical and mental phenomena, they saw their shared explanation of volition as founded on a physiological account of nervous energy. In the first sections of "Ye Machine" then, we see that Marshall's mechanical psychology was not a subversion of but rather a development from that midcentury version of the associationist psychology developed by Bain and celebrated by Mill.[42]

MECHANICAL CEREBRUM

The model of the mind outlined in the preceding section and set down in the first few folios of "Ye Machine" is a model of a lowly brute intelligence.[43] The mind of such a brute, it might be noted, may be relatively sophisticated. Indeed, by means of the repetition of actions that alter the external world each time in the same fashion, such a mind can come to form very basic "expectations" – that is, an idea that a particular sensation will result from the performance of a particular action.[44] Nevertheless, having outlined the workings of this basic brain, Marshall immediately noted that his machine as described so far would be unable "to anticipate, in any sense, or represent to itself beforehand the consequences of its actions so as to readjust them to the circumstances."[45] To enable his machine to do this, he now added a second-level circuit to the "brain" of the machine; in the physiological terms of the paper, he added a mechanical "cerebrum" to the already described "cerebellum." This second circuit, also consisting of wheels and bands, is activated when the machine's "deliberations" lead nowhere and, there being no wheel set in motion that leads to behavior that might realize its desires

---

[42] In his study of Jevons, Maas 2005 suggests that Mill's 1836 essay on method was founded on an associationist psychology that was undermined by developments after midcentury in physiology. Yet while Jevons rejected both associationist psychology and Mill's methodology in political economy, it is clear that Mill himself, as well as Marshall, saw recent physiological work as complementing rather than undermining associationist psychology. The important point, perhaps, was whether or not the new versions of physiology were seen as aiding the measurement of psychological states.

[43] An interest in the comparative mental faculties of animals and humans is evidenced in Marshall's notebook of this period. Under the heading "Man and Beast" in his loose-leaf note book (M 4/1, f. 27), we find a list of similarities (e.g., both "can deliberate and will") and differences (e.g., brutes "cannot reason by consequences" and "have memory but want of induction").

[44] Of course, and as Marshall had insisted in "Ferrier's Proposition One," from such "anticipation" of a certain event by a machine, "no belief in an external world could result. The one thing needed [for this belief] is the permanent element of a conscious self" (*EPW*, 65).

[45] *EPW*, 77.

(i.e., it has no idea how to gratify its wants), its first circuit grinds to a standstill. Previously the outcome of such a situation was the spinning of a random wheel that, with luck, hit upon a contrivance. Now, however, the standstill activates the second circuit, the wheels of which replicate the wheels of the lower circuit, with the associations between wheels in the upper level now allowing for any lower-level idea of action to be followed out, as it were, in the imagination, with the machine picturing to itself the consequences of various possible actions. "In this way," concluded Marshall, "the Machine will have gone through, whether rightly or wrongly, what I shall call a chain of *reasoning* with regard to the effects of any actions."[46] The implication is that in humans (and perhaps also the more developed animals), adaptation brought about by reasoned forethought supplements, and to some degree replaces, adaptation through random variation.

This two-level aspect of the machine, which endowed it with powers of anticipation and reasoning, was modeled on a key feature of the calculating engines that Charles Babbage had attempted to construct. In 1822 Babbage launched his project of constructing a "Difference Engine" that would replace the work of addition and subtraction by human "computers" in the composition of mathematical tables. After this project collapsed in 1834, Babbage began work on an even more ambitious project, the "Analytical Engine." The latter project has been primarily responsible for the excitement generated by Babbage's designs in our present digital age. As one recent commentator explained, while the difference engines were "designed to compute tables of numbers according to the method of finite differences," the analytical engines were designed as "versatile, programmable automatic calculators" that can be seen as "precursors of the modern digital computer."[47] In designing the analytical engine, Babbage not only vastly increased the memory capacity of his machine but also, and more importantly, contrived to enable his machine to change the basis of its calculations. As Babbage explained his intentions for the analytical engine in his autobiography, "Nothing but teaching the Engine to foresee and then to act upon that foresight could ever lead me to the object I desired."[48] As we shall see later, internal evidence demonstrates that Marshall had read Babbage's autobiography and so absorbed these ideas, and, of course, such a capacity to form and then

---

[46] *EPW*, 78, 79, emphasis in original.
[47] Hyman 1982: 123–35; see also Babbage 1864: 53–74. For useful commentary on Babbage's project, see Schaffer 1994, 1996 and also Norton Wise 1989–90: II, 410–24. The date of Babbage's patent on his calculating engine is recorded in Marshall's Red Book (M 7/5: f. 8).
[48] Babbage 1864: 114; see also pp. 59–63, 114–16).

act on anticipations of the future was precisely what Marshall's second-level circuitry provided for his hypothetical machine.

Marshall's friend from his Grote Club days, W. K. Clifford, observed that the key innovation embodied in the analytical engine in fact had its origin in the difference engine. As he pointed out in an unpublished talk of 1872, Babbage had contrived to design machines of necessarily finite parts that could nevertheless engage in potentially infinite calculations. The key contrivance embodied in the difference engine that made such a performance possible was a connection between higher-figure wheels and lower wheels of column differences. For example, Clifford explained, a connection between, say, the ninth-figure wheel and the difference wheel would cause the difference wheel to turn once the number one hundred million was arrived at. In Clifford's example, "after the machine has gone on adding *ones* for a hundred million times it will suddenly begin to add *twos*." Thus, Clifford proclaimed, Babbage's difference engine "possesses the power of changing its law at a prearranged time."[49]

A vastly improved version of this contrivance, which Clifford described as the engine "eating its tail," was embodied by Babbage in the design of the analytical engine. In Babbage's initial design, the new engine was to consist of two main units: a store and a mill. In the store were held the numbers derived from the mill, while in the mill – using numbers brought from the store – were carried out the various numerical operations such as addition and subtraction.[50] This division of calculating labor meant that the results of calculations in the mill could be placed into the store and at a later moment fed back into the beginning of new calculations.

Writing in his old age, Marshall would describe Babbage's "Differential Machine" as "probably the most marvelous mechanism ever devised."[51] Such admiration was no doubt born in the late 1860s, when both he and Clifford were studying Babbage's designs for his engines. As we shall see in Chapter Six, Clifford saw in the ability of Babbage's engines to "eat their own

[49] Clifford's unpublished manuscript notes on Babbage (Clifford ca. 1872; now in the Babbage Collection at the Cambridge University Library) provide the most important source for ascertaining the context in which Marshall read Babbage (see also the further discussion of Clifford's reading of Babbage's work in Chapter Six of this book). Note that Hyman also observes that the ability of Babbage's analytical engine to "eat its own tail" was "already embodied in the old Difference Engine – and can even today be seen in the actual cogwheels of the extant portion of the Engine" (Hyman 1982: 166).

[50] Hyman notes that Babbage was here making an analogy with cotton mills: "Numbers were held in store, like materials in the storehouse, until they were required for processing in the mill or dispatched to the customer" (Hyman 1982: 164–73).

[51] Marshall 1919: 377n.

tails" a profound evolutionary lesson. But for Marshall as well as Clifford, it
would seem that precisely this aspect of Babbage's designs served to bridge
the apparent difference in kind between involuntary and voluntary actions.
After all, a voluntary action is nothing if not the changing of a law of operation. The lesson that Marshall drew from Babbage's engines was that the
same kind of wheels and connecting bands that can perform routine calculating labor can, by means of a mechanism that allows feedback within
a routine, also perform meta-operations that switch the nature of these
routine operations. Marshall's two-level machine, that is to say, is designed
so that trains of reasoning in the first circuit may initiate activity in the
second circuit, with the results of the deliberations carried on in the second
circuit fed back into, and thereby switching the direction of, the trains of
reason in the first circuit. Such a design embodies a version of the feedback
mechanism that Babbage built into all of his calculating engines.[52] The analogy is clear, and it is therefore no accident that immediately after Marshall
examined the operations of the higher-level circuit he proposed illustrating
the nature of his machine by investigating "the very simple case of a chess
automaton" of the kind "proposed by Babbage" in his autobiography.[53]

When a man is playing chess, just as when he is doing anything else, his character
is displayed in the way in which he grasps at immediate advantages or, on the other
hand, tries to look further. But it will depend on his power whether he can do so or
not. If the wheels of the machine be sufficiently numerous, it must of course have
infinite power. And if its character is such that distance does not tell at all (i.e. if the
tightenings ... take place in an infinitely short space of time), its desire to win the
game would always prevail over every other desire; and it would always win, if it
were possible to do so under the given circumstances.[54]

There is a curious – because inverted – echo of Babbage in this passage.
In his autobiography (which discusses the "chess automaton" that Marshall
here refers to), Babbage explained how he had contrived to build a machine
of only finite parts that could engage in potentially infinite calculations, by

[52] See Cook 2005 and my entry "Marshall and Babbage" in *ECAM*. Groenewegen notes
the few explicit references to Babbage in "Ye Machine," but does not comment on them
(Groenewegen 1995: 20). Raffaelli goes considerably further, but does not state the precise
relationship (see Raffaelli 2003: 25–6). Mirowski proposes an opposing reading of the passage of "Ye Machine" discussed above and explicitly rejects any connection of Marshall's
paper to Babbage (Mirowski 2002: 41–2).
[53] *EPW*, 89; see Babbage 1864: 465–91. For an account of Babbage's musings on an engine
playing chess in the context of the interest generated in England by von Kemplen's infamous "chess automaton," see Schaffer 1996.
[54] *EPW*, 81. For a useful discussion of other aspects of this passage; see Raffaelli 1991:
29–30).

means of a solution that translated from the "infinity of space, which was required by the conditions of the problem, into the infinity of time."[55] In describing an ideal chess player in which the spatial connections between wheels are traversed by bands that are tightened in "an infinitely short space of time," Marshall can be seen to have reversed the direction of Babbage's own translation of space into time.

Marshall's inversion of Babbage's words reflects the different purposes of their respective projects. Babbage faced a practical engineering problem. By contrast, Marshall was concerned with forming an analogy drawn from the mechanisms of practical engineering in order to construct a hypothetical and mechanical rendering of associationist psychology. While in the workshop it was possible to connect only a finite number of wheels, within the human body problems of space were understood to be unimportant. As Clifford wrote with regard to human voluntary action, within the human nervous system there "seems *plenty of room* for the requisite mechanism on the physical side."[56] Thus Marshall was able to posit what was in practice an infinity of space and furthermore to reverse the conditions of Babbage's practical problem in order to arrive at a theoretical limit to the possible development of a mechanical intelligence – a machine with almost infinite wheels and instantaneous connections between such wheels. Again, in "Ye Machine," Marshall used the analogy of physical bands to describe the connections between the various wheels of the mechanical "brain." Such bands were, of course, an analogy for nerves, and if Helmholtz had recently demonstrated that nervous transmission was not instantaneous, nevertheless, for the purposes of his thought experiment Marshall could still regard such human "bands" as tightening "in an infinitely short space of time."[57]

The description of a machine with infinite wheels is in fact the terminus of this section of "Ye Machine"; for Marshall has now reached the limits of his account of what mechanism can do. In "Ferrier's Proposition One," Marshall had insisted that intelligent mental action could be resolved into self-consciousness and mechanical association. In "Ye Machine," he proceeded to analyze the evolution of the mechanical agencies of the human mind. From the lower-level brutes, equipped with but one mental level of circuitry (a mechanical "cerebellum"), Marshall moved to the kind of higher intelligence found in humans (and perhaps the higher animals) by

---

[55] Babbage 1864: 123–9. But see the discussion on p. 138 above about how the germ of this solution already existed within the original difference engine.
[56] Clifford 1879: II, 156, emphasis added.
[57] On the standard view of nervous transmission as instantaneous, see Morus 2000: 456–8.

the addition of a second level of circuitry (a mechanical "cerebrum"). The interaction of the two circuits, modeled as it was on Babbage's analytical engine, allowed for a kind of programming loop in the mechanical deliberations of the machine. Such a feedback mechanism provided a mechanical equivalent of imaginative deliberation. Finally, Marshall looked to the most developed form such a machine could take, in which the number of "wheels" and "bands" has no limit. Immediately following this discussion of "Babbage's chess player," however, Marshall observed that whereas his machine can engage in several trains of thought at the same time, humans can follow but one. The ideal form of the machine, in other words, represents an evolution of mechanical intelligence beyond the point that has yet been achieved by human beings. Nevertheless, if such an ideal machine could always play a winning hand of chess, there remained much human activity that it could not do. By implication, any possible human action that cannot be performed by such an ideal machine must be understood as a manifestation of self-consciousness as opposed to mechanical agency.[58]

A LIBERAL EDUCATION

Following his account of an ideal thinking machine, Marshall announced that to test the abilities of his machine, he would "now proceed to instruct my Machine in the leading branches of a liberal Education."[59] Such a procedure in effect allowed him to test aspects of Mill's phenomenalist philosophy and thereby to point to those mental operations that were predicated on self-consciousness. Language presented no problem to the machine, as by the initially arbitrary construction of signs "any one group of sensations can be represented by one Machine to another."[60] Words, then, are for Marshall simply publicly observable tokens of private mental phenomena, and their employment and interpretation are determined by the activities of the body rather than the self-conscious mind. "In Mechanics," Marshall continues, much "progress would be made. Indeed all the Laws of Nature on which Statics and Dynamics depend would be speedily apprehended."[61] But basic arithmetic and geometry presented stumbling blocks; in the former, for example, the machine could do no more than obtain "in a *rough* manner the whole of the multiplication table."[62] The problem was "the absolute want

---

[58]   See Raffaelli's entry on "Ye Machine" in *ECAM*.
[59]   *EPW*, 82; see also pp. 83–94.
[60]   *EPW*, 83.
[61]   *EPW*, 91.
[62]   *EPW*, 84, emphasis in original.

of any idea which will in any manner correspond to Equality." Marshall did
claim that as a result of a special case of an association of similarity, the
ideas of equal things might become associated, but "there would be nothing
more than an association – nothing *sui generis*. And the association would
always be liable to be interfered with by other associations."[63] Furthermore,
Marshall confessed that he could not "see any means whatever by which the
Machine could acquire any power of dealing with abstract symbols such
as *a* where *a* may be any number."[64] Finally, the machine could not form
any idea of the deepest sources of human creativity: "Of the secret springs
of human action it could say nothing ... nothing corresponding to them
would have ever entered into the Machine and nothing corresponding to
them could ever come out of it."[65]

With this last point, Marshall had arrived back at his starting point in
"Ferrier's Proposition One." In that paper, Marshall had explained that
much of the speculations on the nature of "the human soul which are exhibited in the religious history of the world" could be related to the "fact that
self-consciousness was known to exist in man" but "was not proved to exist
in Brutes." Not only was Marshall's machine devoid of self-consciousness,
it could not be expected to discover the existence of "what people call the
human soul."[66] There is an echo here of Coleridge's distinction between
the fancy and the primary imagination. Coleridge described the former as
"a mode of Memory emancipated from the order of time and space," which
must "receive all its materials ready made from the law of association." The
primary imagination, by contrast, Coleridge described as "a reception in
the finite mind of the eternal act of creation in the infinite I AM."[67] As with
Coleridge's "fancy," Marshall's machine receives its material from sensation and operates according to mechanical rules of association. But the
imagination that arose in self-consciousness, and that penetrated through
the physical layers of human character to the very essence of human self-
consciousness, is a human faculty utterly distinct from any mechanical
power. Passing over the delicate question of whether Marshall at this point
believed that human self-consciousness could perceive its own origins in
an infinite assertion of divine self-consciousness, the point to note is that
Marshall's machine cannot grasp the existence of that "I" which, as Grote
had put it, "is not a phænomenon of the universe." Yet Marshall's psycholog-

[63] *EPW*, 88–9.
[64] *EPW*, 87.
[65] *EPW*, 99–100.
[66] *EPW*, 57.
[67] Coleridge 1983: 304–5.

ical project as a whole demonstrates that he himself was firmly convinced of the existence of such an "I." From this perspective, then, Marshall's second and third Grote Club papers can be seen as a demonstration that if many aspects of thought were but reflections of complicated bodily activities, nevertheless human beings were more than mere automata.

Marshall's psychological project of the late 1860s can in fact be read as providing a partial philosophical solution to his mental crisis of these years. The three Grote Club papers examined do not provide evidence for any resolution of a crisis of religious faith (although they certainly point to the direction that Marshall's thinking in these years must have taken). These papers, however, do demonstrate that by the late 1860s Marshall had adopted a romantic conception of the self. Though he may still have harbored theological uncertainties in 1869, Marshall had nevertheless already arrived at a conviction that in addition to being a reasoning machine, he was also a self-conscious and autonomous agent. Like Mill before him, Marshall in this period can be seen to have discovered that there was more to his mind than merely the ability, as Mill had put it, to work "mechanically, by the mere force of habit." Of course, and as we saw in the preceding chapter, Marshall's adoption of romanticism arose by way of his conclusion that Mill's mental philosophy afforded but a partial glimpse of the truth regarding the nature of the mind. But such explicit differences with Mill notwithstanding, it is interesting that for both Mill and Marshall a conviction that romanticism provided important insights into the human condition was bound up with a reaction against the strenuous and unrelenting analytical education that had hitherto provided their standard mental diet. Indeed, in Marshall's case there is reason to suspect that the "crisis in his mental development" was sparked off not by a spontaneous and "sudden rise" of theological doubt, as Keynes suggested, but by a breakdown in his health caused by excessive mental labor.

Unlike those of Fawcett, Galton, and many other ambitious Cambridge students, Marshall's nerves held steady during his undergraduate training. But upon returning to Cambridge in 1867 and turning his attention to philosophy, Marshall apparently suffered some kind of physical breakdown. "My zeal for economics would never have got me out of bed at five o'clock in the morning, to make my own coffee and work for three hours before breakfast and pupils in mathematics," he explained in a letter of 1900 to James Ward, "but philosophy did that, till I became ill and my right foot swelled to double its normal size."[68] Such an experience seems to inform

---

[68] Pigou 1925: 418.

the statement in the *Principles of Economics* that although in intellectual work "the pleasures of excitement, after they have once set in, often go on increasing till progress is stopped of necessity or by prudence," nevertheless everyone "in health has a certain store of energy on which he can draw, but which can only be replaced by rest; so that if his expenditure exceed his income for long, his health becomes bankrupt."[69] In fact, one of the books that Marshall devoted his time to reading in the 1860s offered an explanation of his condition. "Nervous fatigue and exhaustion," Bain declared in *The Senses and the Intellect*, "is produced by excessive expenditure in one or other of the forms of nervous exercise; by emotions, by over-much thought, or by too long continued activity of either body or mind." Such nervous fatigue Bain described as a state of "ennui" and associated with a decline of "vital energy" and "spontaneous activity."[70] Translated into the terms of "Ye Machine," Marshall's excessive study of philosophy could be said to have given rise to a general decrease in "the *vis viva*" of his body, a slowing down of the rotation of the "wheels" of his brain, and perhaps even to a loosening of the "bands" connecting those wheels. Whether such a running down of the mechanism of the nervous system would lead to a swelling of a mechanical foot in the "body" of this "machine" is a question that perhaps Marshall alone could have answered.

If this physical breakdown did indeed mark the beginning of the crisis in Marshall's mental development, such a crisis soon came to encompass a spiritual dimension. And if theological doubts remained after 1868, by then Marshall had at least established to his satisfaction that if much of his thought was the product of a mechanical brain, this material organ was nevertheless in the service of a spiritual entity. It seems likely, then, that from such a dualist perspective Marshall came to understand his own mental crisis as having an ultimately spiritual cause. A lack of physical vitality could certainly be explained in physical terms, but if the ultimate source of "spontaneous activity" was not physical but spiritual energy, the problem might be diagnosed in terms of a failing of spiritual vitality as readily as a dearth of fuel or a clogging of mechanical circuitry. Indeed, it seems clear that Marshall came to believe that even mechanical strength of character

---

[69] *Principles*, I: 142.
[70] Bain 1977: 123–4, 83. In his short book on J. S. Mill, Bain took issue with Mill's autobiographical account of his mental crisis of 1826–7. Mill had described his crisis in "purely spiritual or mental terms," Bain complained, "the physical counterpart being wholly omitted." In fact, Bain confidently asserted, "the dejection so feelingly depicted was due to physical causes." Indeed, "that the chief of these causes was over-working the brain, may I think be certified beyond all reasonable doubt" (Bain 1882: 37–8).

has an ultimately spiritual source. Such, at any rate, was the lesson of the discussion of "vigour" that he later set out in his *Principles of Economics*. At one point in this volume, Marshall identified "physical vigour" with "muscular strength, a good constitution and energetic habits."[71] Yet such characteristics alone do not make a "manly character." For vigor itself (as opposed to physical vigor) is "moral rather than physical." Vigor was for Marshall the "strength of the man himself," his "resolution," and his "self-mastery." Vigor did indeed depend "upon the physical conditions of nervous strength"; but while "the power of sustaining great muscular exertion seems to rest on constitutional strength and other physical conditions, yet even it depends upon force of will, and strength of character." Thus, while a mental crisis might be explained as no more than a bad state of "nerves," it could also be interpreted as pointing to a deeper problem, its source lying in the realm of self-consciousness as opposed to nervous machinery. This distinction between physical and spiritual vigor was but a variation on the distinction between mechanical nervous activity and self-consciousness that Marshall had established in his early psychological project.

It is therefore of more than passing interest to find in the *Principles* that vigor "shows itself in great deeds, in great thoughts and in the capacity for true religious feeling."[72] Marshall's physical collapse, it seems clear, was soon followed by a crisis of religious feeling (or perhaps, rather, a profound awareness of the lack of it). In light of the psychological theory that he developed over this period, it is hard not to suspect that he came to believe that his physical and spiritual crises were but two sides of the same dualistic coin. Like Mill before him, Marshall appears to have discovered that long weary years of mechanical drill and analytical toil had contributed to a feeling of an emotional and intellectual void within. Indeed, it does not seem unreasonable to suggest that, like Mill, Marshall began to reflect on the value of his education to date. If this was so, such reflections did not lead to a rejection of the value of mechanical drill, but they did lead to an appreciation of the limits of the kind of mental gymnastics required of the successful Cambridge wrangler. Marshall continued to believe that a Cambridge

[71] *Principles*, I: 193. Compare Marshall's use of the term "energy" with Fawcett's (on which see Collini 1991: 170–96). Compare also Marshall's recollections in a letter of 1908: "Every rowing man knows that character is as important as physique: the Johnian freshman of my year who, judged by physique, was easily first, turned out to be *absolutely* useless. After a while the captain of the sixth boat would not look at him; and mere 'weeds' full of good pluck made it to the first boat" (letter to William Bateson in 1908, emphasis in original; quoted in Groenewegen 1995: 483).

[72] *Principles*, I: 194.

mathematical education was very valuable. Indeed, as the quotations from the *Principles* given earlier suggest, he was convinced that the mental circuitry that such an education developed was necessary – if insufficient – for great thoughts, deeds, and feelings. Nevertheless, there was more in heaven and earth than dreamt of in a mechanical philosophy, and more to a Cambridge wrangler than simply the cog wheels of his mind. It was about this time that Marshall began to spend his summer vacations walking in the Alps. Once in the mountains, Mary Paley tells us, he "would walk with knapsack on his back for two or three hours. He would then sit down, sometimes on a glacier, and have a long pull at some book – Goethe or Hegel or Kant or Herbert Spencer – and then walk on to his next halting-place for the night."[73] Such mountain excursions were no doubt taken up in the wake of Marshall's breakdown in physical health and were intended to provide a physical balance to a term-time regime of strenuous mental exertion. But if mental exhaustion could be cured through mountain walks, mental crisis required a philosophical tonic. As his mountain reading indicates, Marshall found this remedy primarily in German philosophy.

MORAL CHARACTER

In the last part of "Ye Machine," Marshall announced that "I have said, I think enough, about [the machine's] intellectual education. I now come to describe it as a moral being." The machine, as we have seen, experienced various states as pleasurable and painful, and wherever possible acted to lessen feelings of pain and increase feelings of pleasure. So construed, such a mechanical agent was not too dissimilar to the "economic man" of midcentury political economy (who, as we saw in Chapter One, was driven by a desire for the pleasures of wealth and luxury and an aversion to the pains of labor). Such similarity followed, of course, from the fact that J. S. Mill had derived the characteristics of this abstract economic agent from associationist psychology. But in this last section of "Ye Machine" Marshall declared that as a *moral* being the "fundamental principle" of his machine "would be that of Sympathy." Mechanical sympathy arose when a machine experienced pain on registering the pain of another machine. Such a feeling of sympathy might lead the machine, if it could, to act so as to reduce the pain of its fellow machine, the successful outcome of such an action giving pleasure to the recipient as well as the receiver. Different machines, Marshall explained, would have different moral characters. A strong

---

[73] Quoted in Keynes 1925: 13.

mechanical moral character would tend to sacrifice direct pleasure for the indirect pleasure of helping a fellow machine.[74] Thus Marshall's machine may have been a pleasure-seeking automata, but it nevertheless contained a moral nature. The machine, in other words, contained within its emotional and intellectual makeup both components of character that, as we saw in Chapter One, Buckle influentially (if quite erroneously) stated to have informed Adam Smith's two great works, the *Wealth of Nations* and the *Theory of Moral Sentiments*.

Yet the machine could not straddle the divide that we saw Marshall making in 1868 or 1869 between "ordinary" students and "true men of learning." A machine that sought to avoid pain and increase pleasure could derive pleasure from observing the pleasure of another machine, even to the extent that it would sacrifice its own fuel for the sake of sympathetic pleasure. But such a sympathetic machine could not arrive at an entirely "non-self-regarding frame of mind." It could not transcend its own nature by the kind of enthusiastic devotion to a higher cause that was for Sidgwick the cardinal doctrine of Jesus of Nazareth, for Mill the basis of a religion of humanity, and for Marshall the primary characteristic of those "true men of learning" who were "wedded heart and soul" to their studies. A machine, in short, could not entirely forget its own desires; for the act of such transcendence of self-regarding states of mind is at once also the discovery of a higher self, an "I," of which the machine has not, and can never have, the slightest conception. Just as with intellectual education, so too with moral character Marshall drew limits to mechanism and looked to self-consciousness to explain those higher psychological states that arose beyond those limits. We now see that the contrast between ordinary students and true scholars, which in Chapter Two was identified as the framework behind Marshall's early thinking about university reform, was grounded on a distinction between mechanism and self-consciousness. Or to make the same point in more general terms, it is possible to detect in Marshall's earliest thinking as a moral scientist a conviction that the limits of political economy are coterminous with the limits of mechanical thinking, and that where self-consciousness takes over from mechanism, the political economist must halt and look to the Coleridgean philosopher to provide explanations of motivations, character, and action.

Such conclusions allow us to relate Marshall's early thought to the wider framework that informed the moral universe of educated mid-Victorians.

---

[74] *EPW*, 100–1. Note that Marshall called attention "to the power of Natural Selection in preserving those races in which the principle of sympathy was most powerful."

In the first chapter of this book, we took note of Collini's argument that in this period both liberals and romantics shared a common dichotomy between selfish and altruistic actions. Thus, for Collini, Buckle was speaking in the "voice of the mid-nineteenth-century" when he distinguished between Smith's two volumes on the basis of a division in human nature between selfish and sympathetic actions. But as should now be clear, "sympathy" and "altruism" were not always the synonymous terms that Collini seems to suggest. For Marshall, at least, these two moral qualities were different in kind, the former being a mechanical characteristic, the latter an attribute only of self-consciousness. Such a distinction corresponded to Marshall's philosophical interpretation of the romantic and the academic liberal ideals of manly character. The Victorian ideal of manly character derived in the first instance from a romantic tradition descending from Coleridge, Arnold, and Maurice. To cultivate a manly character was, for these romantic moralists, to strive to overcome an initial state of childish self-absorption. In this Coleridgean tradition, "manly" did not mean "masculine" so much as "humane"; its opposite was not "effeminate" but "beastly."[75] By midcentury, however, academic radicals such as Fawcett and Stephen had come to identify a manly character with an athletic masculinity in thought and feeling as well as physical activity; such a manly character had conquered "cowardly," "effeminate," and "sentimental" ways of thought and action.[76] For both liberals and romantics, then, a manly character allowed one to overcome a natural selfishness, but such self-transcendence produced different outcomes. These different outcomes, and indeed these different ideals of character as a whole, were related by Marshall to distinct spheres of the mind. In the terms of Marshall's mental dualism, academic liberals like Fawcett and Stephen mechanically exercised a sympathetic (but not sentimental) feeling toward the working classes, while more romantically minded Cambridge fellows self-consciously cultivated an enthusiasm for altruistic self-sacrifice on behalf of society. Marshall himself embraced both of these paths to goodness, but differentiated between them in terms of their ultimate source, holding that altruism was a higher good than mere sympathy.

Marshall reconciled liberal Anglican and academic liberal ideals of moral character with the same philosophical framework with which he reconciled romantic and associationist psychologies. The manly moral character

[75] See Collini 1991: 186–7, Hilton 1989, and Newsome 1961: 195–206. The most famous expression of the ethos of Christian manliness is to be found in Thomas Hughes's classic, *Tom Brown's Schooldays* (1857). As Hughes's book illustrates, in the romantic tradition the boy became a man when he had overcome his self-absorbed boyhood nature.
[76] Collini 1991: 187.

valued by Fawcett and Stephen became an attribute related to the physical body, while that valued by Coleridge and Maurice was related to the self-conscious mind. We have seen how in the *Principles* Marshall would posit nervous strength as a necessary condition of spiritual vitality, but insist not only that such moral strength of character was different in kind from mere physical vigor, but that spiritual energy provided the ultimate source of physical energy. We may suspect that a similar relationship was conceived with regard to mechanical sympathy and self-conscious altruism; for in general terms Marshall pictured the physical as leading toward the mental, which was separated from it by a gap that could not be bridged by the body, yet in some way could be bridged by the spirit. For example, in one of his letters of 1868 to the *Cambridge University Gazette*, Marshall argued that, because it promoted thoroughness, the Mathematical Tripos achieved "what art can do to create genius."[77] Mechanical art could indeed do *something*, but the gap between a thoroughly organized mechanical mind and the spirit of genius could be overcome only by self-consciousness. In the same way, we may assume, only self-consciousness could lead from even the most finely tuned mechanical sympathy to the kind of altruistic spirit of self-sacrifice characteristic of true scholars, men of action, and religious seers. As Marshall would insist in the *Principles*, it was not "physical vigour," but that spiritual or moral force manifested in "vigour itself," that was "the source of all progress."[78]

[77] *CAM*, I: 4.
[78] *Principles*, I: 194.

FIVE

Political Economy

INTRODUCTION

In later life, Marshall recalled that "I always said till about 1871 that my home was in Mental Science." Nevertheless, in 1868 he was asked to give lectures on political economy to students at St John's College. "I consented," he reminisced, although "I should have preferred philosophy."[1] Within a year or so, Marshall was not only providing intercollegiate lectures on political economy, but also conducting his own independent research in the subject. Both activities inevitably entailed, first and foremost, a close engagement with the text of J. S. Mill's *Principles of Political Economy*. By 1873, as we shall see in subsequent chapters, Marshall was embarked on a revision of the philosophical framework that informed the organization of Mill's *Principles* as a whole. Between around 1869 and 1871, however, his work in political economy was limited to exercises in the interpretation, revision, and improvement of Mill's method, terminology, and doctrines. It is with this initial engagement that the present chapter is concerned, and the core argument developed here is that this early work was informed by Marshall's dualist mental philosophy. Before turning to Marshall's earliest economic writings, however, we should acquaint ourselves with certain aspects of Mill's economic legacy. In the following section, we will examine the organization of the "bible of mid-century political economy," Mill's *Principles*, to provide a context for Marshall's early reformulation of political economy as

[1] Pigou 1925: 418–19. Only around 1872 did Marshall come to the conclusion that "the time had come at which I must decide whether to give myself to psychology or economics." This date would seem to suggest that Marshall's decision was made during the period of his engagement with Hegel's *Philosophy of History*, and indeed he would inform Keynes that his encounter with Hegel's book was instrumental in "finally determining the course of his life" (Keynes 1925: 11, n. 1).

recounted in the rest of this book. We will then turn to the controversy over wages that erupted in 1869, which brought into prominence those particular elements of Mill's economic thought whose interpretation by Marshall provides the main theme of this chapter.

JOHN STUART MILL'S *PRINCIPLES OF POLITICAL ECONOMY*

In the preface to his *Principles*, Mill declared that the "design" of his work was "different from that of any treatise on Political Economy which has been produced in England since the work of Adam Smith." Behind such a claim stood a distinction between the pure science of political economy and the practical application of its doctrines. This distinction itself rested on the austere definition of political economy that Mill had established in his 1836 essay on method. In this essay, Mill had defined the method of political economy as the deduction of hypothetical lawlike tendencies from axiomatic postulates such as the primacy of self-interested motivations in driving wealth-begetting activity. The validity of such postulates was established independently by the natural scientist and the psychologist, and accepted a priori by the political economist. The hypothetical lawlike tendencies deduced from these psychological and physical premises were identified by Mill with the standard doctrines concerning production and distribution set down by Smith and improved by Ricardo. But while Mill saw Ricardo as concerning himself solely with the improvement of doctrine, he saw Smith as mixing theory and practice and, in doing so, intertwining the doctrines of political economy with many other branches of social philosophy. Hence, in taking the *Wealth of Nations* as his model, Mill was pointing to a twofold objective for his *Principles*. First, he proposed combining Adam Smith's "practical mode of treating his subject with the increased knowledge since acquired of its theory," which was to say that his formulation of economic theory would be indebted primarily, if not exclusively, to Ricardo. But in addition, he also proposed that he "exhibit the economical phenomena of society in the relation in which they stand to the best social ideas of the present time," as Adam Smith had done "in reference to the philosophy of his century."[2]

An illuminating perspective on Mill's prefatory remarks can be gained if we turn our attention back to his awakening from mental crisis in 1827. In his *Autobiography*, it will be recalled from Chapter Three, Mill had declared that at that moment the influences of "the reaction of the nineteenth century against the eighteenth, were now streaming in upon me." Recovery

[2]   *Mill CW*, 2: xcii; cf. Mill *CW*, 1: 243–5.

from mental crisis, then, had (at least in hindsight) involved the washing away, in a romantic tide of aesthetic feelings and moral sentiments, elements of what Mill took to be the eighteenth-century mechanical philosophy imbibed from his father. It would take Mill at least a decade to work though this internal commingling of the thought of two centuries, and the result, as we saw in Chapter Two, would be a social creed that rejected intuitionism and idealism but embraced the notion of aesthetic and sympathetic moral feelings as states of mind higher than mere self-interest. But while this revitalized form of utilitarianism became for Mill synonymous with the social philosophy of the nineteenth century, he nevertheless remained committed to a mechanical and a priori method in political economy. In other words, in political economy Mill remained an adherent of what he took to be the method and doctrines of that eighteenth-century science founded by Adam Smith (although, in fact, Mill's methodology owed far more to Dugald Stewart than to Smith).[3] In the preface to his *Principles*, then, we find the clearest expression of the ultimate outcome of Mill's youthful mental crisis. The initial turbulence produced as the seas of thought of a new century washed over the dry rocks of the old had now given way to a distilled mixture of nineteenth-century social philosophy and eighteenth-century political economy.

It is this particular juxtaposition and combination of eighteenth- and nineteenth-century thought that stands behind Mill's arrangement of the subject matter of political economy. Mill was quite clear about the fact that Ricardo and others had greatly improved Smith's formulation of the science of political economy, but he believed that in so doing they had corrected the doctrines rather than transformed the basic substance or method of the science. In supplementing Ricardian doctrine with some recent economic speculations, Mill therefore considered himself to be doing no more than bringing to even greater perfection a science whose mechanistic doctrines had been firmly established by Adam Smith. Mill in fact claimed little originality for the theoretical side of his treatise (as is well known, in a letter of 1848 he expressed doubt as to whether his *Principles* contained a single opinion on pure political economy that was not a corollary of Ricardo's doctrines).[4] This was not the case, however, with regard to the social philosophy applied in his *Principles*, which was very much of his own making. Taken as a whole, then, Mill's *Principles* juxtaposed economic doctrines founded on the principle that economic agents acted according to self-interest with a social

[3]   See pp. 19–30 above.
[4]   *Mill CW*, 13: 731.

philosophy that looked to the moral improvement of human nature, and even held out the possibility that sympathy might at some future date come to replace self-interest as the primary motivation for economic activities. It was to the particular ruling balance between self-interest and sympathy that Mill the social philosopher looked when discussing the social arrangements that determined how wealth was distributed. But it was to self-interest that Mill the political economist looked when outlining both the laws of production and the necessary consequences of any particular social arrangement for distribution. This juxtaposition of economic doctrine and social philosophy, of assumed self-interest and the potential to act sympathetically, allowed Mill to attempt, as De Marchi has put it, "to reiterate stern necessities, while avoiding the Scylla of 'hardheartedness.'"[5]

Let us follow through a key example of Mill's transition from scientific doctrine to social philosophy and moralizing conclusion. In the second book of the *Principles*, he examines the laws of distribution as they operate in a modern commercial society, in which the agents of production are owned by the three classes of landlords, capitalists, and workers. The capitalist, Mill tells us, advances all the expenses of production, including the entire remuneration of the laborer, and receives all the produce. The profit of the capitalist therefore consists of the excess of the produce over these advances.[6] Wages in turn depend "upon the demand and supply of labour; or as it is often expressed, on the proportion between population and capital."[7] Here is a clear statement of the wages-fund theory. And it is evident that, according to this doctrine, if all of the working population is employed and there is a surplus of that part of capital that constitutes the wages fund, wages must rise; alternatively, if the supply of labor is in excess of that part of the wages fund, wages will fall.[8] Now, Mill also took over from Ricardo the doctrine that, as society progresses, profits tend to fall and, consequently, the rate of capital accumulation tends to decline. Taken together, these doctrines of political economy, formulated as natural laws of capitalist society, provide the ground on which Mill proceeds to preach the lesson of the practical social philosopher. According to the inexorable mechanical laws of cause and effect, he now declares, if those in the ranks of the working class are driven only by "blind instinct" and multiply like animals, then wages will be driven down to such a level that the growth of population

---

[5]   De Marchi 1974: 136. De Marchi's seminal article remains the starting point for any discussion of Mill's intentions in his *Principles*.

[6]   *Mill CW*, 2: 411–12; cf. Mill's early essay "On Profits, and Interest" (*Mill CW*, 4: 290–308).

[7]   *Mill CW*, 2: 337.

[8]   Cf. Mill *CW*, 5: 643.

will be checked by starvation and disease. But there is a ground for hope: "the conduct of human creatures is more or less influenced by foresight of consequences, and by impulses superior to mere animal instincts; and they do not, therefore, propagate like swine." The practical lesson, then, in which moral imperative fuses with causal analysis, is that to the extent that those of the working class "rise above the condition of the beasts," to that extent will they rise out of poverty.[9]

Mill's contrast between natural laws and human will laid the grounds for what in Chapter One was described as the midcentury moralizing of political economy. His fusion of eighteenth- and nineteenth-century thought finds its most concise expression in three sentences of the second book of his *Principles*: "Poverty, like most social evils, exists because men follow their brute instincts without due consideration. But society is possible, precisely because man is not necessarily a brute. Civilization in every one of its aspects is a struggle against the animal instincts."[10] Mill's formulation of economic doctrines thus provided the social philosopher with a vision of the disciplining of mankind's animal nature by the natural processes of economic cause and effect. The political economist in turn recognized that such moral improvement might, eventually, lead to a transformation of the social arrangements of society such that capitalistic relations between the different productive classes would give way to a socialistic society characterized by cooperation.[11] It was thus possible to draw two distinct moral lessons from Mill's *Principles*. On the one hand, there was a warning to the present age, a stern reminder that between civilization and barbarism stood only self-control, strength of character, and abstinence from immediate sensual gratifications. This was the primary moral lesson that academic liberals like Fawcett and Stephen imbibed from Mill's *Principles*. On the other hand, however, it was possible to find in Mill's volume the promise of a reward for increased moral virtue – a vision of a more tranquil and classless future, in which the "trampling, crushing, elbowing, and treading on each other's heels" of contemporary social existence will have given way to a life of economic cooperation and cultural improvement passed amid the greenery and fresh air of urban parks and unspoiled countryside, all as a result of the growth of moral discipline and sympathetic feelings.[12] In Chapter Seven we shall find Marshall in 1873 sketching a revised version of such a liberal vision of the future.

---

[9] *Mill CW*, 2: 157.
[10] *Mill CW*, 2: 367.
[11] On this last point, see Riley 1998: 294.
[12] *Mill CW*, 3: 754.

Before we commence our study of Marshall's early reading, interpretation, and revision of Mill's ideas, it is useful to look at how he would present these ideas at the end of his intellectual apprenticeship. To do so, let us turn to Marshall's 1876 essay in the *Fortnightly Review*, "Mr Mill's Theory of Value." "It was known, even before the publication of his *Autobiography*," Marshall wrote, "that Mill regarded, as perhaps the chief of the services which he had rendered to economics, his work in breaking up and rearranging its chief problems; and though experience may have shown that in some details his arrangement is not wholly successful, we are bound to take account of the important truth which the general plan of his arrangement embodies."[13] Mill's "plan," Marshall reminded the readers of the *Fortnightly*, "was in separate books, first to treat of the nature of human efforts, and the laws of the production of wealth generally; secondly, the distribution of wealth; and thirdly, to devote a book exclusively to 'the machinery of exchange.'"[14] Marshall insisted that in his *Principles* Mill had more than adequately explained the reasoning behind this organization. But to underscore his point, he quoted at length from a passage in Mill's recently published *Autobiography*. Here Mill explained that the distinctive tone of his *Principles* had "consisted chiefly in making the proper distinction between the laws of the Production of Wealth, which are real laws of nature, dependent on the properties of objects, and the modes of its Distribution, which, subject to certain conditions, depend on human will."[15] In light of this fundamental distinction between natural necessity and human will, Marshall offered the following synopsis of Mill's tripartite division of political economy:

(i) Natural laws determine the total stock of the material wealth of material sources of enjoyment, which will at any stage of progress be produced at the total cost of given human efforts and sacrifices: (ii) the "human will" and "particular social arrangements" determine the scheme according to which remuneration shall be distributed out of this total sum to each class of efforts and sacrifices: (iii) this distribution is effected by the instrumentality of a "machinery of exchange," the greater part of which would be put in requisition under almost any social arrangements that are likely to exist in the civilized world. The science of this machinery is the proper province of "pure" or "abstract" economic investigations.[16]

---

[13] *MTV*, 122. Marshall did, in fact, copy a few key passages from the preliminary remarks of Mill's *Principles* in his advanced lectures notes of around 1871 (M 4/19, f. 85).

[14] *MTV*, 122.

[15] *MTV*, 124 (and *Mill CW*, 1: 255). In his *Principles*, it should be stressed, Mill had been careful to insist that, once such social arrangements had been determined, the consequences of such rules "have as much the character of physical laws, as the laws of production" (*Mill CW*, 2: 200).

[16] *MTV*, 125.

Once we fully understand both Marshall's 1876 interpretation of, and his verdict on, Mill's organization of his *Principles*, we will to all intents have concluded our study of Marshall's early economic thought. In the course of our circuitous journey toward this goal, however, we will need to avoid some potential pitfalls, perhaps the most hazardous of which is what at first sight appears to be the "Humpty-Dumpty" method of interpretation that Marshall brought to bear on the classic texts in the history of political economy. Marshall's verdict regarding Mill's *Principles* was passed on a volume that for the past eight years he had subjected to an intense scrutiny, thereby generating a series of apparently idiosyncratic interpretations of Mill's meaning. In the synopsis just quoted, for example, the identification of costs of production with "human efforts and sacrifices" is a distinctly Marshallian interpretation of what Mill had in mind concerning the natural laws of material wealth; and much the same could also be said for the identification of the "pure" science of economics with the province of the machinery of exchange. Thus we are liable to run into trouble if we attempt to grasp the meaning behind Marshall's mixed verdict on Mill's tripartite division of subject matter before we have pinned down how he came to interpret some of the basic terms and doctrines that Mill placed within his three general divisions. To establish Marshall's method of interpreting Mill's terms, and also to examine his early attempt to reformulate and advance Mill's theory of value, are the tasks of the present chapter. Yet it is important first to establish the context in which Marshall initially read Mill's *Principles*.

THE WAGES QUESTION

The "wages question," Marshall would write in the long historical essay that he composed around 1873, is "*the* question of modern P[olitical] E[conomy]."[17] The wages question for Mill, as we have seen, provided a hinge on which political economy turned into social moralizing. But at just that moment that Marshall was first coming to grips with Mill's *Principles*, the nature of the wages question was transformed. In 1867, in the wake of the appointment of a royal commission on labor relations, issues relating to trade unions were pushed to the forefront of public discussion. The subsequent debate generated intense criticism of the doctrinal orthodoxy set forth in Mill's *Principles*; for such orthodoxy appeared to support the position that wages were fixed by a natural law that could not be modified

---

[17] *EHC*, M 3/1, f. 37, emphasis in original.

by trade union activity. As we have seen, Mill stated unambiguously in his *Principles* that wages were determined by the ratio of the working population to the wages fund, that is, the stock of capital that was advanced by the capitalist in the form of wages. Trade union activity in the form of a strike, therefore, might indeed interrupt the instrumental machinery of exchange in the labor market but could not hope to influence the underlying causal determination of the wage rate. Of particular importance in the criticism now directed at Mill's position was W. T. Thornton's *On Labour* (1869), which Mill reviewed in the *Fortnightly Review*.[18] Responding to Thornton's attacks on the received account of wages, Mill declared that the "doctrine hitherto taught by all or most economists (including myself), which denied it to be possible that trade combinations can raise wages … is deprived of its scientific foundation, and must be thrown aside."[19] Mill's "recantation," as it came to be known, had potentially corrosive implications for that part of the tripartite division of subject matter in his *Principles* in which the instrumentality of the "machinery of exchange" had been clearly separated from the causal laws of production and distribution. Thus, at a very early moment in Marshall's economic studies, the "wages question" began to be perceived as a troubling theoretical issue within political economy.

Because a trade union strike was understood as operating on the level of the labor market (i.e., a temporary withholding of supply), it was generally assumed that it could have no real effect on the distribution of wealth. A crucial part of Thornton's strategy, however, was to challenge the orthodox theory of wages on the level of supply and demand theory. Thus he mounted an attack on the general idea that the "price of all things, labour included, depends upon the proportion between supply and demand."[20] In his opinion, no consistent and satisfactory definitions of supply, price, and (particularly) demand had been offered by political economists, and by numerous discussions of possible market situations he attempted to demonstrate that the actual price in a market need not be one equating supply and demand. In his review of Thornton, Mill conceded that on occasion the law of supply and demand indeed might be consistent with two different

---

[18] "Thornton on Labour and Its Claims," reprinted in *Mill CW*, 5: 631–68. For Thornton's friendship with Mill, which may have a bearing on why Mill chose this review to revise his position on trade unions, see Donoghue 2004.

[19] *Mill CW*, 5: 646.

[20] Thornton 1870: 43. Thornton had already published some of his key arguments in the *Fortnightly Review* (see especially Thornton 1866). For Marshall's comments on Thornton's book as a whole (evidently intended for students) see *EEW*, II: 262–3. For a discussion of Thornton's arguments in relation to both Mill and Marshall, see Bharadwaj 1989: 137–40.

prices. He denied, however, that this called for anything more than a minor correction of the existing theory of supply and demand; for in such cases it was necessary only to invoke a "supplementary law, which determines the effect, between the limits within which the principal law leaves it free."[21] Nevertheless, Mill went on to make the crucial concession that labor, as a commodity, belonged to one of the "excepted cases" where more than one price may satisfy the law of supply and demand. Behind such a feature of the labor market, he went on to explain, was the fact that the conventional distinction between circulating capital (i.e., capital that "fulfils the whole of its office in the production in which it is engaged, by a single use" and that included the wages fund)[22] and the income of the capitalist – a distinction found "in every systematic treatise on political economy, my own certainly includes" – was "wholly imaginary." Hence the "real limit" of any rise in wages "is the practical consideration" by the capitalist of "how much would ruin him, or drive him to abandon the business: not the inexorable limits of the wages-fund." Such a conclusion, however, suggested that willful behavior at the supposedly purely instrumental level of the market (such as a trade union strike) could play a causal role in the determination of wages.

Thornton's criticisms and Mill's "recantation" thus introduced a whole new element into the "wages question." For Mill in his *Principles*, the theory of wages provided a link between material interest and moral prudence, and hence mediated between political economy and social philosophy. After Mill's review of Thornton, however, the wages question was increasingly seen as a theoretical problem within political economy itself.[23] Behind this theoretical development stands the fact that only in the decades after

---

[21] *Mill CW*, 5: 637.

[22] *Mill CW*, 1: 91. Note that in his advanced lecture notes Marshall discusses the distinction, made by W. L. Sargant in his *Recent Political Economy* (1867), between income employed as "Self-Maintenance" and income employed as capital. On the basis of this distinction, Marshall observes, Sargant had shown that "Fawcett is wrong in saying that wages must come out of capital ... they may be drawn from nearly the whole of the effects of past labour." He adds that Sargant "wrote in 67 and anticipated not only in substance but also in form what Mill says in his review of Thornton" (M 4/19, f. 58; see also Sargant 1867: 45).

[23] By 1879 Sidgwick could describe the wages-fund doctrine as the most divisive and the most "burning question in the present state of Economics" (Sidgwick 1879: 401 [BV, ML]). But Sidgwick was here writing a decade after Mill's recantation, by which date it had become clear that the continuing controversy over the theory of wages was intimately bound up with a perceived crisis in the more general authority of political economy. Sidgwick's words could not have been written earlier in the decade, and the fact that in the early 1870s Marshall became increasingly convinced of the significance of Mill's recantation, and of the need to revise and ultimately to reformulate economic doctrines accordingly, is a mark of his precocity.

midcentury did the trade union movement begin to assume something like its modern form. Political economists such as Ricardo, and following in his footsteps J. S. Mill, had constructed an account of the natural value of wages with little or no thought as to the significance of trade union activity. An exception had been Henry Fawcett, who, in his 1860 essay "Strikes," argued that trade unions could not alter the natural wage rate, but could prolong the period in which market wages remained above the natural rate and could hasten the rise of market wages when they were below the natural rate.[24] Mill's position in his 1869 review is not free of ambiguity, but he seems to have followed Fawcett's analysis in his recantation, suggesting that trade unions could influence the market wage but insisting that the orthodox theory applied only to the natural rate of wages. Hence Mill seems to have believed that his recantation left the Ricardian theory untouched. Certainly, in the 1871 edition of his *Principles*, he did not see fit to alter the statement that no "remedies for low wages have the smallest chance of being efficacious, which do not operate on and through the minds and habits of the people."[25] But it was far from clear whether the theoretical fallout from Mill's recantation could be so easily contained. As we shall now see, for one student of political economy in this period at least, the whole episode not only highlighted the imprecision with which the orthodox theory had hitherto been expressed, but furthermore called attention to its inadequate treatment of the relationship between market and natural values .

ADVANCED POLITICAL ECONOMY

It could be said that Mill's 1869 recantation laid the grounds for Marshall's first research program in political economy. The sense of the need for research must have been heightened by Mill's comments in the preface to the 1871 edition of his *Principles*. Mill here alluded to his recent exchange with Thornton, but only to conclude that, in his opinion, the results of such discussions of supply and demand theory and the law of wages were "not yet ripe for incorporation in a general treatise on Political Economy." One is reminded of Mill's somewhat lame conclusion to his attempt to provide a purely phenomenological account of our idea of the self in his *Examination*. As we saw in Chapter Three, his conclusion that "by far the wisest" course of action was to accept an "inexplicable fact without any theory of how it

---

[24] See Fawcett 1860. Fawcett's article led Mill to modify his discussion of trade unions from the third edition of his *Principles* onward (Schwartz 1972: 86–8).

[25] See *Mill CW*, 2: 366.

takes place" had not been accepted by Marshall in 1867. Four years later this
now more confident Cambridge moral scientist was hardly likely to be any
more patient when it came to Mill's refusal to reflect further on issues that
Marshall could already see to be of great potential significance in political economy. But it is clear that before 1871 Marshall had already come
to the conclusion that the fundamental propositions of political economy
concerning not only the doctrine of the wages fund, but also the theory of
value, were in need of restatement. Such concerns fed into, and no doubt
also stimulated, a further suspicion that Mill's methodological formulation
was too restrictive and as such was not up to dealing with the demands now
placed on it. In short, from 1869 onward Marshall seems to have become
increasingly aware that political economy offered a research project in the
waiting.

Many of Marshall's early manuscripts bear witness to his unease with
what he took to be a widespread tendency in the literature to employ loose
modes of argumentation and imprecise terminology. In part, this concern
can be related directly to the seriousness with which he took Thornton's
criticism that political economists had failed to define satisfactorily the
terms of supply and demand theory. In his voluminous notes on Smith's
Wealth of Nations, for example, we find him complaining that the "great
fault" with Smith's discussion of taxes on wages "is that there is no definite
meaning attachable to 'demand.' We want 'demand at a price.'"[26] Yet it is
evident that Marshall early on came to see Thornton's criticisms as indicative of a more general problem in the literature. In his notes on the *Wealth of
Nations*, for example, we find Marshall complaining that a tacit assumption
"should have been stated distinctly" or that certain phrases employed by
Smith "have no definite meaning."[27] Such general dissatisfaction was surely
related to Marshall's need, as a neophyte lecturer, to provide his students
with standard definitions and workable doctrinal formulas. But it is also
evident that an attempt to establish systematic terminology and rigorous
demonstration comprised the primary method of his earliest research project in political economy.

---

[26] M 4/5, f. 16. Cf. Marshall's comments on Ricardo's discussion of supply and demand in
       EEW, II: 260.
[27] M 4/4, f. 9 and M 4/3, f. 16. At another point Marshall comments that while Smith "is
       supposed to hold inaccurate opinions" with regard to taxes on profits, it "would be more
       true to say that they were not absolutely clear" (M 4/5, f.15). See also his copy of Nassau
       Senior's *Political Economy* (1850), where we find marked the discussion of imprecision
       and ambiguity in "the established nomenclature," and also Ricardo's confusion of the terms
       "amount" and "proportion" (Senior 1863: 133, 143 [ML]).

One of the first steps that Marshall took in his early research project, therefore, was to attempt to reformulate the traditional doctrines of political economy in language that was clear, exact, and precise. Thus, as Marshall later recalled, in his early study of political economy he "translated Mill's version of Ricardo's or Smith's doctrines into mathematics."[28] The earliest of such "translations" are no doubt those in Marshall's copy of Mill's *Principles*, where on a few blank leaves he transposed into graphical form Mill's discussion of the effect of an improvement in the arts of production.[29] Such exercises were soon transplanted from marginalia to manuscript, and the resulting short set of notes entitled "Improvements in the Art of Production, Labour and Capital being Stationary" can be read in Whitaker's edition of Marshall's *Early Economic Writings*.[30]

By 1870 Marshall was evidently employing some form of diagrammatical analysis of value in his advanced lectures.[31] Now, to the extent that the diagrams that Marshall drew in Mill's *Principles* represent the output of a unit of a given factor on the horizontal axis and factor rewards on the vertical, it could be said that they prefigure the graphical representation of supply and demand in the essay "On Value" (ca. 1871) and probably – although we have no way of knowing – also of the treatment of value in the lectures of 1870. Indeed, according to a later manuscript, entitled "Approximate History of Curves," this short graphical formulation of classical rent theory in 1869 "decided me to adopt curves as an engine."[32] As can be seen in an early diagram from "On Value," shown later in the chapter, Marshall measured the quantity of a commodity traded on the horizontal axis of a coordinate diagram and the price of that commodity on the vertical axis. Nevertheless, there is a conceptual gap between the early graphical descriptions of simple changes in real factor rewards (wages are corn wages) and the working machinery of price analysis set out in "On Value." This conceptual gap provides a hint that we should not be misled into thinking that "On Value" was derived by means of a direct diagrammatical translation of Mill's account of value. As we shall discover, Marshall's early reformulation

---

[28] Pigou 1925: 416.
[29] See Marshall's copy of Mill (1865: 433–7 [UL]). In Marshall's edition of the *Principles*, blank pages were interleaved with printed ones; thus Marshall had a space in which to make notes and to "translate" Mill into mathematics. Groenewegen 1995 reproduces some of these diagrams and, in his "Interpreter of the Classics" (*ECAM*, 121), provides a summary statement of the general pattern of Marshall's annotations in Mill's *Principles*.
[30] *EEW*, I: 231–9.
[31] See Foxwell's letter to J. M. Keynes of 1910 in *EEW*, I: 45, n. 26, and also Cunynghame 1904: 9.
[32] *EEW*, I: 41, n. 12.

of value theory was not conducted simply on the level of terminology; it also incorporated advances on Mill's actual ideas. Hence, it could be said that "On Value" is not so much a mathematical translation as a diagrammatical interpretation of Mill's theory of value.[33]

Interpretation for Marshall was by no means a simple mechanical procedure. At the heart of the 1876 essay on Mill's theory of value stood the claim that the main problems in Mill's account of value were to be attributed to the "imperfect presentation of clear thought" rather than to the "perfect presentation of confused thought."[34] The general distinction delineated here between thought and its expression was grounded in Marshall's early philosophical studies. While Marshall's distinction between thought and words might remind us of Coleridge's distinction between opinions founded on understanding and the truths grasped by reason, it should certainly call to mind the related mental dualism that informed Marshall's psychological distinction between the mechanics of deliberation and the reflections of self-consciousness. In Marshall's early psychological project, creative scientific thought is associated with the sphere of self-consciousness, while in "Ye Machine," language is described explicitly as a mechanical business. From this perspective, the grounds of Marshall's careful separation of thought and words in his reading of the history of political economy, and also the priority he gave to the former, become immediately intelligible. Between 1869 and 1871 Marshall, still committed to mental philosophy, set about interpreting the various core doctrines of political economy. Such acts of interpretation consistently entailed fairly radical reformulations on the level of terminology, but on the level of ideas Marshall was convinced that his own thought was continuous with that of his predecessors.

The following discussion will show how Marshall came to the conclusion that one could discern three basic types of relationship between words and thought in the history of political economy. First, it was by no means unprecedented for both thought and expression to be on the wrong track entirely. Second, and as had often been the case with Mill, clear ideas might have been betrayed by an ill-chosen mode of expression.[35] Third, clarity of

---

[33] On Marshall's distinction between mathematical and diagrammatical curves, see *EEW*, I: 156. Compare the distinction between "graphical" and "geometrical curves" in the preface and chapter 12 of Cunynghame 1904.

[34] See *MTV*, 126–7.

[35] The following annotation in Marshall's copy of Jevons's *Theory of Political Economy* is representative: "Mill's language is horribly slipshod but there is nothing stated in this account which Mill does not state in some form or other at some part of his account" (Jevons 1871: 102 [ML]). The annotation is written beside Jevons's statement "The theory of value, as

prose might reveal imperfections at the level of thought (e.g., Smith's writing illustrates that he "had not *clear ideas* of 'supply & demand as regulating price'").[36] In addition to these three basic types of relationship, we shall find that Marshall also posited a fourth kind of relationship not necessarily typical of the history of political economy, but rather useful as a means of advancing economic thought in the present; for while any one author might not have had clear ideas on a particular topic, it was not unlikely that he had been groping his way toward the truth and that his words reflected some partial aspect of this truth. Furthermore, in cases where two authorities disagreed, it was quite possible that both had been seeking different aspects of the same truth. Hence there arose the possibility of employing a Coleridgean method in political economy, such that the reconciliation of opposing and partial opinions might lead to the discovery of a deeper truth that both sides of a dispute had glimpsed only partially.

If the ground of Marshall's distinction between thought and expression lay in mental philosophy, his conviction of its relevance to political economy emerged by way of his early study of the history of economic doctrines. Marshall's first steps toward mastery of the wider canon of political economy began with his attempt to establish the theoretical steps that led from Smith's *Wealth of Nations* to Mill's *Principles*. His extensive notes on Smith's treatise, which in terms of sheer volume far exceed his notes on any other author or text, contain not only synopses but also numerous criticisms of Smith's arguments. Such criticisms served to confirm Mill's statement in the preface of his *Principles* that the *Wealth of Nations* was "in many parts obsolete, and in all, imperfect."[37] Marshall used McCulloch's edition of Smith's work, and his own discussions of Smith's text were, at least in the first instance, directed by McCulloch's Ricardian corrections of what he took to be the various fallacious positions advanced by Smith. But Marshall's commentary also contains numerous direct references to, and quotations from, various discussions of Smith's arguments in David Ricardo's *Principles of Political Economy* (1817). Thus, if the study of Mill's *Principles* had directed Marshall back to the Ricardian doctrines that provided the backbone of Mill's science, so too his critical engagement with Smith directed Marshall forward to the correction and improvement of Smith's doctrines by Ricardo. Hence Marshall arrived at a canon comprising Smith, Ricardo, and Mill.

---

expounded by Mr. Mill, fails to reach the root of the matter, and show how the amount of demand or supply is caused to vary."

[36] M 4/5, f.17, emphasis added.

[37] *Mill CW*, 2: xcii.

Marshall's next step in establishing a usable history of political economy was recalled by him in a letter of 1892. In "the early seventies," he wrote, "when I was in my full fresh enthusiasm for the historical study of economics, I set myself to trace the genesis of Adam Smith's doctrines."[38] Having made a careful study of Smith's chapter on rent in the first book of the *Wealth of Nations*, Marshall turned to Turgot's *Réflexions sur la formation et la distribution des richesses* (1774).[39] The comparison of Turgot's work with Smith's chapter on rent, and then the comparison of both Turgot and Smith with the exposition of doctrine by Ricardo, led Marshall to draw two general lessons concerning the nature of progress in economic thought. First, in certain cases progress had involved the correction of erroneous doctrine. Smith's theory of rent had been marred by a Physiocratic emphasis on "the superior productivity of agricultural labour";[40] it was left to Ricardo to show that land constituted a monopoly and that its value was calculated at the margin of productivity. Second, scientific progress had also arisen by way of the gradual explication of initially implicit assumptions. Marshall interpreted Turgot in his *Réflexions*, for example, as assuming "that every one is at starvation['s] door except landowners & capitalists." Such an assumption, Marshall argued, was "implied rather than expressed" (and indeed Turgot "does not know clearly what he is assuming"). But where Turgot had simply asserted that the "competition of other artisans limits the means of each artisan to his own subsistence," Adam Smith had explained that the reason for this was that, "like all other animals," men "naturally multiply in proportion to the means of their subsistence."[41] In other words, the "definite step made in advance of Turgot by Adam Smith was the *explicit* recognition of the population principle."[42] Yet Smith's formulation of this principle was

---

[38] Pigou 1925: 379. Marshall seems to have been led to study the Physiocrats by McCulloch's emphasis on Smith's debt to their writings. (Dugald Stewart had made the same point, but Marshall seems to have been unfamiliar with Stewart's economic writings.)

[39] The chronology can be established because Marshall has cross-referenced these notes. The reference to the notes on Turgot is written at the top of the notes concerning Smith on rent, while the corresponding reference to Smith is found embedded within the text of the notes on Turgot. Both references are omitted from Whitaker's transcription of the notes concerning Smith on rent and the last two folios of the notes on Turgot (*EEW*, II: 252, 253), and Whitaker does not note that the two sets of notes come from the same folder in the Marshall archive.

[40] M 4/19, f. 64. This quotation is from a sentence in the section on method in the advanced notes, which refers to Smith's chapter on rent. Cf. McCulloch's comments in his introduction to Smith's *Wealth of Nations* (Smith 1871: xliv–xlv [UL]).

[41] M 4/15, ff. 46, 36; and see *WN*, 162 (I. xi. b. 1).

[42] M 4/15, f. 45, emphasis added. Note that Whitaker (*EEW*, II: 252–3) reads "and" instead of "by" in this sentence, thus changing the meaning of the passage (and so finding a need

vague, and this because his thoughts were not fully clear: the "distinction between Adam Smith & Ricardo is that Ricardo knew clearly what he was assuming: & Smith did not."[43] Ricardo had thus clarified as well as corrected earlier economic thought.

We have here concrete examples of two of the three forms of criticism that Marshall came to employ in his interpretation of the canonical texts of the history of political economy. In both cases interpretation is born out of an identification of the relationship between thought and words, and in both cases proceeds from perceived inadequacies on the level of expression. But problematic expression could point toward different evaluations of the thought that had stood behind those words. In one scenario, thought was on the wrong track entirely. This was the case with the thinking of the Physiocrats and, to a lesser extent, that of Smith, with regard to the theory of rent. But another option was that confusion on the level of words reflected the fact that thought was groping toward the truth but had not as yet arrived at a fully developed conception of its object. Such had been the case when Turgot had vaguely grasped that population pressure might be the cause of a downward pressure on wages, and to a lesser degree the same was the case with regard to Smith's thought on the population principle. But a further scenario is also possible: past thought might be true but the mode of its expression could leave something to be desired. This last was in fact the way that Marshall came to interpret his canonical texts on the fundamental question of the definition of value.

In his 1876 essay on Mill's theory of value, Marshall insisted that both Smith and Mill had known that value was a measure of subjective cost. Smith, indeed, was hailed as having initiated a new scientific era by conquering that point of view from which a commodity could be "regarded as the embodiment of measurable efforts and sacrifices."[44] Behind this statement it is possible to detect the statement in the *Wealth of Nations*, quoted approvingly by Ricardo and carefully copied out by Marshall in his advanced lecture notes of around 1871, that the "the real price of every thing, what every thing really costs to the man who wants to acquire it, is the toil and

---

to insert an editorial clarification). His version reads: "The definite step made [by the Ricardians] in advance of Turgot and Adam Smith was the recognition of the population principle."

[43] M 4/15, ff. 45–6. See also in this folder Marshall's introductory lecture notes on the Physiocrats, in which he states, "The physiocratic theory would be roughly true if all but Proprietors were actually at starvation limit. ... Physiocrats had not thought theory out. A Smith had but fragmentarily."

[44] *MTV*, 126.

trouble of acquiring it."[45] Labor, in such a reading, is a measure of subjective valuation as opposed to a physical activity that, in the process of production, transfers an energy-like substance called "value" into a material object. In the 1876 essay, a similar sentence by Mill is quoted twice: "What the production of a thing costs *to its producers*, or its series of producers, is the labour expended in producing it."[46] For Marshall this sentence demonstrated that Mill had known that value was a measure of effort and not a manifestation of that effort itself. That his meaning had been widely misinterpreted Marshall blamed on Mill's carelessness of expression. Specifically, Marshall insisted, Mill had on occasion employed the term "costs of production" when what he actually meant would often have been more happily expressed by the term "expenses of production."[47] Marshall's point was that the former term should have been employed when what Mill meant was the subjective measure of efforts, so that the latter term could refer unambiguously to those material resources or energies used up in the process of production. Such an argument, however, rested on the not entirely self-evident claim that when Mill had written of costs of production he had at different moments meant quite different things.

Interpretation, as Marshall emphasized in his 1876 essay, was a tricky business, calling for both charity and close attention to context.[48] More to the point, perhaps, correct interpretation for Marshall evidently rested on prior knowledge and clarity, on the part of the interpreter, on the level of both ideas and of words. That is to say, in order to understand why Marshall interpreted Smith and Mill as really knowing that costs and therefore value are subjective, we need first of all to understand why Marshall himself already believed the subjective definition of value to be the true one. We can start to answer this question by turning to a fairly large bundle of lecture notes that appear to be the first part of the notes Marshall used in his advanced lecture classes.[49] These notes were no doubt composed piecemeal over a number of

---

[45] M 4/19, f. 29; Ricardo 2004: 6; and *WN*, 47 (I. V. 2).

[46] *MTV*, 122, 127, emphasis added; and see *Mill CW*, 3: 477.

[47] See *MTV*, 126–7.

[48] *MTV*, 121. That the approach to the various interpretations (and misinterpretations) of Ricardian doctrine taken by Marshall was not altogether dissimilar to that of J. S. Mill is suggested by comparing the discussion in the main text with De Marchi 1974: 140–3.

[49] By the early 1870s, Marshall was giving two separate classes in political economy, for ordinary and advanced students. In his ordinary classes, he followed the procedure of other Cambridge moral scientists such as John Venn and worked through Mill's *Principles*. But in his advanced classes, he tackled a range of issues that arose out of his critical reading of the wider literature of political economy. Identification of these notes is aided by a letter of 1879 to H. S. Foxwell (*CAM*, I: 120), in which Marshall reminded his former student of

years, but in the main seem to have been written no later than 1871. The notes contain a variety of material, but for our purposes three main sections may be singled out. Marshall begins these notes with a discussion of the definition of political economy, turns to a discussion of induction and deduction, and then moves on to a historical and critical treatment of three key terms: "productive labor," "value," and "capital." The purpose of each of the three sections was to provide Marshall with the grounds not only for correctly interpreting Mill's definition of value, but also for revising his methodological position and advancing beyond Mill's formulation of the theory of value in general and his account of the determination of wages in particular.

The first folio of the advanced lecture notes is headed "'Definitions of P[olitical] E[conomy].'" Having quoted from Whewell, Kant, and Mill, Marshall begins his discussion by declaring that political economy "cannot conveniently be narrowed to catallactics" (i.e., the science of exchanges), because this would exclude vital aspects of economic life such as "personal faculties" and "business connections."[50] Political economy, he then insists, must include the discussion not only of "natural wealth," but also of other valuable forms of wealth such as "mental capital" and "organizational capital," as well as "allusions to other sources of enjoyment." This broad conception of political economy ensured that the science retained an intimate connection to social philosophy. Indeed, Marshall insists that, alongside its other objectives, political economy "must consider how far the possession of a certain amount of wealth & of a certain amount of leisure are necessary conditions for the development of man[']s higher faculties."[51] Now, here we encounter the very heart of Marshall's early economic thought, or at least precisely that aspect of his early economic thought that was primarily responsible for the uniqueness of his subsequent work in relation to both his contemporaries and his predecessors. To begin with, the rejection of catallactics as too narrow constituted a rejection of a tradition dating back to Richard Whately and embraced by Henry Dunning Macleod, the latter arguing that any exchange constituted a reciprocal demand and that demand was therefore the origin of value. But at the same time, the

how, in the early 1870s in Cambridge, he would commence his advanced lecture classes with a long discussion of method.

[50] M 4/19, f. 1; cf. Mill *CW*, 3: 455. Marshall commences his notes with the instruction to quote from the section "Of the Language of Science" in Whewell's *Novum Organon Renovatum*. Whewell here laid down the Baconian aphorism "In framing scientific terms, the appropriation of old words is preferable to the invention of new ones" (Whewell 1858: 278). The content of these notes suggest that Marshall also had one eye firmly fixed on the first lecture of Whewell 1862.

[51] M 4/19, ff. 1–4.

insistence that wealth was not exclusively material constituted a decisive rejection of the orthodox tradition, the history of which Marshall had by this point become thoroughly acquainted with. In fact, Marshall's rejection of the orthodox definition of wealth was closely bound up with his insistence that value was a subjective and not an objective measure of effort. To clarify why this was so, however, it is useful to turn to a later section of these advanced lecture notes, where Marshall engages in a historical account of the terms "productive" and "unproductive labour."

This historical survey leads Marshall to reject the distinction between productive and unproductive labor. Behind his survey one may detect McCulloch's "Introductory Discourse" to his edition of the *Wealth of Nations*, in which great emphasis had been placed on Smith's advance over the Physiocratic doctrine that nature alone is the source of all value. This dogma, McCulloch explained, had led the Physiocrats to suppose "wealth to consist of matter." Adam Smith, however, had grasped the fundamental truth that it was only through labor that a utility is fixed or realized within matter. Thus, McCulloch concluded, Smith had arrived at the true doctrine that "labour is the only source of wealth."[52] But while switching perspectives from nature to labor as the source of value, Smith was generally held to have retained the principle that value was embodied only in material objects. Hence there arose that seemingly interminable early-nineteenth-century debate over the precise definitions of productive and unproductive labor, in which the former was held to fix or realize a utility in a material object and the latter to add nothing to the value of the subject on which it was bestowed.[53] By way of his historical discussion of productive and unproductive labor, however, Marshall arrives at the conclusion that the conventional denigration of supposedly unproductive labor and immaterial services "is just as arbitrary" as the Physiocratic condemnation of manufacturing as "sterile" and the Mercantilist disregard for nonmonetary forms of wealth.[54] This rejection of the distinction between productive and unproductive labor is, of course, bound up with his earlier insistence that wealth is not confined to material commodities. Once a materialistic definition of wealth has been rejected, the distinction between labor that produces material objects and labor that does not loses its significance.

Marshall's revisionist definitions of wealth and labor were the natural correlates of a subjective definition of value; for in rejecting the identification of

---

[52] See McCulloch's comments in Smith (1871: xl–xliii [UL]).
[53] For the relevant passage of Smith and commentary by both McCulloch and Macleod, see M 4/19, ff. 22–3, 61–2.
[54] M 4/19, f. 27.

wealth with material objects, Marshall was also rejecting the idea that value
was in some way embodied by productive labor within a material commodity. As we shall see when we turn to the text of "On Value," the starting
point of Marshall's approach to value was the conviction that the utility that
constituted the value of a commodity to an individual was located in the
buyer or seller of the commodity, and not in that commodity itself. (Hence,
while rejecting out of hand the notion that political economy could be narrowed down to the science of exchange, Marshall nevertheless relied on the
notion of exchange as the starting point for his reflections on the theory of
value.) It is particularly important to note that, in these advanced lecture
notes, Marshall's nonmaterial definition of wealth and subjective definition
of value went hand in hand with a subjective approach to the meaning of
the term "capital." This is significant because, as we shall see in the later
discussion of the essay "On Wages," Marshall came to the conclusion that
the underlying flaw in the wages-fund doctrine was that, in the short term
at least, the nature of any item of capital was determined by the subjective
decisions of individual capitalists.

In his historical survey of the term "capital," Marshall pays particular
attention to the distinction between "fixed" and "circulating capital." He
quotes Adam Smith's distinction between these terms and takes note of
Smith's statement that fixed capital includes those "useful abilities" that are
acquired during a person's education and that always cost "a real expense
which is a capital fixed & realised as it were in his person."[55] Marshall then
approvingly quotes Macleod, who points out that Smith's statement under-
mines the general supposition that, because of his position on productive
labor, Smith confines wealth to material objects.[56] Here, of course, we find
one of Marshall's grounds for believing that his subjective theory of value
and his rejection of a material definition of wealth were true to what Adam
Smith had really meant. Marshall goes on to quote Macleod's argument that
the "same article may be *floating* Capital in the hands of one man, & *fixed*
Capital in the hands of the next possessor" and that it is therefore "improper
to apply the terms either of floating or of fixed capital to any object whatever
be its nature unless we know the intention of its owner in using it."[57] As we
shall see, Macleod's subjective definition of capital provided Marshall with
his primary tool for interpreting Mill's 1869 recantation of the wages-fund
doctrine.

[55] M 4/19, ff. 60–1; and see *WN*, 282 (II. i. 17).
[56] M 4/19, ff. 61–2; and see Macleod 1863: 360 ("Capital").
[57] M 4/19, f. 63 and M 4/19, f. 71; both quotations are from Macleod 1863: 361 ("Capital").

It is clear that the wages question colored all of Marshall's earliest economic thinking. We may wonder, then, whether Marshall's subjective definition of value arose only in the wake of an initial conclusion that the meaning of the term "capital" was subjective – this initial conclusion giving rise to a subsequent derivation of subjective or at least nonmaterial definitions of wealth, labor, and value. Such a conjecture is compatible with our survey of Marshall's early economics writings and is supported by what we know of the context that informed these writings. As such, it perhaps has more to recommend it than the standard discussions of "influence" that are concerned with correlating the particular treatments of value constructed by Marshall and one or more of his contemporaries. Nevertheless, we cannot discount the possibility that Marshall was here influenced by Jevons's 1871 *Theory of Political Economy*.[58] Marshall did indeed employ a graphical analysis of value in his lectures of 1870, but we do not know the extent to which such analysis was the same as that which has come down to us in the essay "On Value," and it is therefore not impossible that reading Jevons influenced Marshall's thought. What evidence we have, however, suggests that Marshall's own thought was already fairly developed by the time he read Jevons's book.[59]

By the same token, we cannot reject out of hand the possibility that Marshall was reacting against Karl Marx's *Das Kapital* (1867), which he

[58] Marshall reviewed the *Theory of Political Economy* in 1872 in the *Academy* (reprinted in Pigou 1925: 93–100). An unsigned note on Jevons's work, also by Marshall, appeared in the *Academy* in 1874 (reproduced in Whitaker 1994). Jevons is hardly mentioned in Marshall's early notes. One exception occurs in his notes on Turgot's account of exchange. Turgot, according to these notes, argues that buyers and sellers "do not look only at the particular bargain before them but they look around them to see how the matter stands with other buyers & sellers." Marshall criticizes this account for failing to include "cost of production." There follows the remark, subsequently crossed through yet still quite legible, "He is very like Jevons" (M 4/15; f. 46; see also ff. 38–40). Michael White has pointed out to me (in private correspondence) that Marshall's initial treatment of capital, as discussed in the main text, has marked similarities with that of Jevons in *Theory of Political Economy*. As White suggests, these similarities may well reflect the fact that both men were influenced by Macleod in this aspect of their economic thought.

[59] That Marshall's ideas were fairly developed by the time he read Jevons's book is suggested by a marginal annotation that has been written next to Jevons's assertion that "value depends entirely on utility." Marshall writes: "Prospective utility cannot be determined by enquiring how great a want a man will have of a thing. We must also enquire how great difficulty he expects to have in obtaining it; thus labour is *a* cause of value" (Jevons 1871: 2 [ML]). This comment, it should be noted, repeats the marginal summary that, in his copy of Mill's *Principles*, Marshall had made at the head of the chapter "Of Demand and Supply, in their Relation to Value": "Two kinds of value Utility & difficulty of attainment" (Mill 1865: 268 [UL]). For Marshall's references to Jevons after he had read *Theory of Political Economy*, see White 1990.

seems to have purchased on his 1868 visit to Germany.[60] In his first chapter, Marx had followed Adam Smith in assuming that "use value" inheres within a material object and from there had proceeded to construct a dialectical demonstration of the "peculiarities" of the exchange form of value, in which a quantity of social labor is supposedly expressed in terms of the qualitative use value of a privately produced material body.[61] In the first sentences of Marshall's "On Value," Smith is taken to task for stating that "value in use" inheres within a commodity, and by means of this simple criticism, Marshall effectively short-circuited Marx's entire dialectical analysis of capitalist value.[62] Yet (as we shall see in the following chapter) while Marshall in these years was certainly disconcerted by Ferdinand Lassalle's rendering of the orthodox Ricardian theory of wages and was also aware of Lassalle's role in the modern socialist movement that he encountered in Germany, there is no indication that at this time he saw the torturous logic of the first chapter of *Kapital* as either a significant theoretical challenge to orthodoxy or a practical danger that warranted refutation.

We may also approach this central aspect of Marshall's early economic thinking from a different point of view. In 1871 Marshall's thinking on the relationship between education and society underwent a crucial shift. As we shall explore in detail in Chapter Seven, while continuing to regard self-consciousness as the precondition of creative scientific research, Marshall now came to see that a large part of teaching and learning involved only routine mechanical activity. At the same time, he increasingly came to consider education, as *the* key to increased productivity. Hence the political economist had no choice but to bring the business of education within his field of vision. But a definition of wealth as purely material necessarily excluded both teaching and research from the sphere of productive labor. By the same token, to define political economy as catallactics excluded from consideration the production of "mental capital," as well as the relationship between wealth and the development of the "higher faculties." A revision of Marshall's initial romantic separation of the spheres of commerce and

[60] In a letter of 1889 Marshall would declare that he had read *Kapital* in 1870 and found Marx's theory of value to be "a series of *petitiones principii*" (see *EEW*, I: 52). If the date of 1870 is correct, this would suggest that Marshall purchased *Das Kapital* on his first visit to Germany, rather than on his return in the winter of 1871-2.

[61] Marx 1954: 62, 64.

[62] In Marshall's copy of Marx's *Kapital* we find a "NO" written beside the following sentence: "Der Tauschwert erscheint zunächst als das quantitative Verhältnis, die Proportion, worin sich Gebrauchswerte einer Art gegen Gebrauchswerte anderer Art austauschen" ("Exchange value, at first sight, presents itself as a quantitative relation, as the proportion in which values in use of one sort are exchanged for those of another sort") (Marx 1867: 2 [UL]).

culture therefore demanded precisely the kind of subjective interpretation of key terms that, as we have seen, had been suggested by Macleod's observation that Smith regarded education as forming "fixed capital." We can see the same connection between his changing views on education and his revision of key terms at the point in his advanced lecture notes at which Marshall criticizes the "arbitrary" nature of mercantilist, Physiocrat, and modern distinctions between different kinds of wealth. Marshall here offers the comment: "And just as from a precise definition of money as wealth the mercantilists got to deny that people need look after any other kind of wealth or might even sacrifice national bullion to it, so now people say such a course (eg of national education) would make men but be ruinous to the national wealth."[63] Such contemporary errors were founded on a failure to recognize that "mental capital" formed a part of "natural wealth" and that the business of education was at least as productive as any other. I would suggest that a rethinking of the economics of education played a pivotal role in motivating Marshall to redefine such key economic terms as "capital," "wealth," "labor," and also "value"; the connection, of course, is likely to have worked both ways, with Marshall's revisionist definitions of such terms as "wealth" and "capital" further undermining his initial separation of the spheres of university and economy.

Marshall's subjective definitions of the key terms of political economy were not in themselves sufficient to resolve the problems that he perceived to have been exposed by Mill's recantation; for Marshall not only held that Mill's faulty expressions had betrayed his clear ideas, but also held that certain of Mill's ideas were in need of further development. The key advance in political economy that Marshall considered himself to be making in these early years was the development of what has been called "period analysis." This was an advance on the level not of definitions but of ideas, or as Marshall puts it in his advanced lecture notes, of "fundamental propositions." Period analysis, we may observe, has by now become the hallmark of Marshallian value theory and, indeed, for many the hallmark of Marshallian economics *tout court*. But while his seminal statement of period analysis is indeed found in "On Value," it should not be forgotten that for Marshall at this time the main value of this theoretical development was that it appeared to provide a means of restating the orthodox theory of wages. Yet as we will see, Marshall's entire early research project ran into the sand as it became clear to him that the resultant restatement of orthodox wage theory by means of period analysis was unsatisfactory. Hence Marshall's early research project

---

[63] M 4/19, f. 27.

could be said to have failed in its primary ends and yet, in his diagrammatical theory of value, to have left him with a theoretical achievement that proved of enduring significance.

In his advanced lecture notes, Marshall moves from his initial treatment of definitions to historical surveys of key terms by way of a discussion of methodology. The general trajectory of the first part of the notes, from definition to methodology, suggests that Marshall had one eye on Mill's 1836 essay "On the Definition of Political Economy; and on the Method of Investigation Proper to It." To see the significance of this trajectory for Marshall's derivation of period analysis, we need to follow his unambiguous rejection of Mill's fundamental claim that, as a moral science, political economy could not employ the inductive methods of the physical sciences. Like every science, insists Marshall, political economy builds up from first principles, deduces consequences from these principles, and then, by examination of actual cases, tests these principles and corrects them accordingly. Hence political economy "is neither inductive nor deductive but always both & in turns prominently the one & prominently the other."[64] This formulation encompasses Mill's "method *a priori*" but places it within a wider framework, for Marshall does not here explicitly reject Mill's contention that the political economist must assume – as opposed to derive – first principles. Nevertheless, Marshall in these notes immediately went on to argue that, while political economy attempted to utilize only such principles on which consensus existed across the whole of the scientific world, it "cannot do this entirely," and as a matter of fact the "fundamental propositions" that "are most peculiarly its own are liable to be from time to time called in question."[65] There can be little doubt that when Marshall penned these sentences he believed the present moment to be just such a time and that the fundamental propositions that had been called into question were related to the received doctrines regarding value and wages.

---

[64] M 4/19, ff. 4–8; see also f. 95. Marshall adds that political economy "is called deductive or inductive according to the bent of peoples minds. I think it best to say it is both deductive & inductive & to call attention to the mutual interdependence of inductive & deductive processes."

[65] M 4/19, ff. 2–4. Note that Marshall was careful to set boundaries that protected political economy from the kind of disagreements he had with Mill and Bain concerning the ultimate nature of the mind. The investigations of the political economist, he insisted, must be carried on "only so far as can be done without entering on complicated discussions with regard to subjects not distinctly its own." On a more general level, what this meant was that political economy "avails itself only of such results of physical & mental sciences as are the common property of the world" and "avoids as far as possible the use of propositions, the truth of which is admitted only by a portion of the scientific world."

Marshall's historical surveys of the different definitions and theories of key terms amounted to an inductive and idealist method of establishing the "fundamental propositions" of political economy. "Productive labor," "value," and "capital" were three terms whose meaning would have to be firmly settled to make a restatement of the theory of wages possible. In each case Marshall's procedure was to move through a series of key quotations from various authorities, beginning with Smith's *Wealth of Nations* (at least in the discussions of value and capital), moving through the views of later political economists like McCulloch, Ricardo, and J. S. Mill, and culminating with more heterodox recent writings by such writers as F. Bastiat and H. D. Macleod. Such a practice embodied the opinion that he would later state explicitly in a letter of 1879 to Foxwell: "confusions about terms" can only be "satisfactorily dealt with … historically."[66] The immediate inspiration for this approach seems to have been Macleod, whose *Elements of Political Economy* (1858) and *Dictionary of Political Economy* (1863) figure prominently in Marshall's historical surveys of value and capital. In his *Dictionary*, Macleod had utilized this same historical method, which he explained in his article "Capital" as consisting of the attempt "to discover the origin of the term, and the meaning attributed to it by those who used it first, and then to follow the current of usage down to the present time." This method, Macleod explained, would allow for the elimination of any "accidental ideas" and the discovery of that one "fundamental idea, which alone it is permitted to generalize."[67] Marshall's employment of this method embodied a related, if not identical, methodology.

Macleod's notion of "fundamental ideas" was expressly derived from Whewell's *Novum Organon Renovatum*, as indeed was his general historical approach to scientific discovery. As noted in Chapter Three, Whewell presented his *Novum Organon* as a rival to Mill's *System of Logic*. For a relentless opponent of Millian economic orthodoxy like Macleod, Whewell's book provided a natural starting point for methodological reflection. Marshall's own adoption of Whewell's inductive methodology, however, was the natural consequence of his idealistic commitment to Ferrier's first proposition

---

[66] *CAM*, I: 117. The Marshalls (the book was written jointly by Alfred Marshall and his wife, Mary Paley Marshall) in fact planned a third volume to the *Economics of Industry*, which would provide a historical treatment of economic terminology.

[67] Macleod 1863: 324. Note that in his 1887 essay Foxwell, who must have attended these lectures, commended Macleod for having done "much to call attention to the internal contradictions in the received theory" (Foxwell 1887: 88). Macleod's role in calling attention to the inconsistencies and confusion in Mill's account of value is also mentioned in Marshall's 1876 essay on Mill's theory of value (*MTV*, 128). While the secondary literature on Macleod is slim, for an overview see White 2004.

and his related belief that truly creative thought was born from self-consciousness. Put another way, this manifestation of methodological divergence from Mill's 1836 essay was the corollary of Marshall's rejection of Mill's exclusively phenomenological account of the self. But if, as Grote had suggested, history provided the medium in which self-consciousness could reflect on the movement of phenomenological thought, self-consciousness could hope to achieve more than merely the elimination of "accidental ideas." Marshall had learned from Grote and Maurice that conflicting opinions provided self-consciousness with the material from which, by way of their reconciliation, deeper grounds of truth might be arrived at. To the extent that history revealed not only a clarification of doctrine but also unresolved disagreements, to that extent a Coleridgean method might provide a reconciliation that also constituted progress in political economy. In Marshall's historical survey of the definition of the term "value," the possibility of precisely such a Coleridgean advance is raised.

In his discussion of the definitions and treatments of value that had been employed in the history of economic thought, Marshall worked his way through various statements by Smith, Ricardo, and others. Reaching J. S. Mill, Marshall notes that Mill "adds nothing to the substance of the preceding, but expresses a few things more clearly." He then quotes from Mill's account of market or temporary value in his *Principles*: the market value of a commodity depends on demand and supply, the demand "varies with the value," and "the value always adjusts itself in such a manner that the demand is equal to the supply."[68] In a subsequent folio in this series of notes, Marshall turned to Macleod's *Dictionary* and summarized Macleod's account of value as consisting of two laws. The first of Macleod's laws is that the "relation between supply & demand is universally the only regulator of value." His second law is that, in "such cases as production can be increased without limit people learn to adjust the supply to the demand so that the value of the article will nearly agree with its cost of production."[69] At this point in the same folio, Marshall returns to Mill, whom he now declares to provide the best expression of the orthodox account ("McCulloch is

---

[68] M 4/19: f. 37 and see Mill *CW*, 3: 497.

[69] Macleod followed Whately in defining economics as the "science of exchanges," such that any exchange was a reciprocal demand, hence leading him to the conclusion that demand is the origin of value (White 2004: 314). In his discussion of value in this folio, Marshall did not engage with this aspect of Macleod's position, having concluded at the very start of his advanced lecture notes that political economy "cannot conveniently be narrowed to catallactics."

not so clear as Mill. Fawcett repeats Mill. Rogers is loose").[70] Marshall now observes that Mill's definition of the "permanent or natural value" of a commodity, in terms of cost of production, "does not apply in all cases." Hence "the advantage that McCleod obtains" over Mill is that his first law – that value is universally regulated by supply and demand – "is universally valid when explained by" his claim that supply adjusts so that value nearly agrees with cost of production. But Marshall also criticizes Macleod for maintaining in his second law that supply adjusts to demand: "It is equally true," as Mill had insisted, that "demand adapts itself to the supply." Having contrasted the two positions, Marshall concludes, "It seems possible to combine the advantages of the two methods."[71] As we shall now see, it was precisely such a Coleridgean attempt to reconcile two apparently opposing positions that gave rise to the period analysis set down in Marshall's early essay "On Value."

THE ESSAY "ON VALUE"

Marshall begins "On Value" with the following two sentences: "Adam Smith regarded the 'value in use' of any particular object as depending upon its utility. He thereby makes himself the judge of what is useful to other people and introduces unnecessary confusion."[72] In explicit opposition to Adam Smith (and implicit contrast with Karl Marx), Marshall proceeds to define "value in use" in relation to a person rather than a commodity: the "value in use of a thing to a person" is "the value of the things which must be given him in order that he may be induced to give it up." This is the pivot on which the essay as a whole turns; and this, of course, was a correction on the level of words and definitions that brought terminology into line with truths long thought (by Smith, among others). Having so defined "value in use," Marshall turned to the nature of money, which he defines, following Mill, as "command over commodities in general." This allows him to define a buyer and a seller in terms of whether they wish to give or receive a commodity in return for money. The amount of money that sellers must be given in order to induce them to part with a commodity, and that a buyer is willing to give

---

[70] M 4/19, f. 44. This folio, from Marshall's historical survey of accounts of the theory of value, was selected for publication by Whitaker (*EEW*, II: 261), but this particular sentence, which is the last on the folio, is omitted from his transcription.
[71] M 4/19, f. 44.
[72] *EEW*, I: 125. For a discussion of the more general nineteenth-century reception and criticism of Smith's conception of value in use, and hence the wider context of Marshall's comments, see White 2002: 665–9.

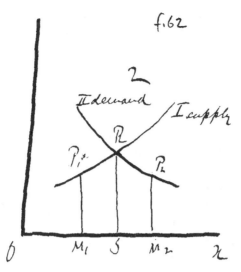

Figure from "On Value" (M 4/32; the annotation "f. 62" at the top right is a later folio reference added by an archivist). Reproduced by kind permission of the Faculty of Economics, University of Cambridge.

in order to obtain a commodity, "represents the value in use." Following these initial definitions, Marshall announces, "We are now in a position to give an accurate account of the terms demand and supply." In other words, once basic terminology has been rigorously defined, it becomes possible to proceed to the more difficult terms of supply and demand, which are in fact defined by way of a diagram.

In defining supply and demand, Marshall first of all insists that whenever these terms are used there "is always a reference tacit or explicit to a particular market at a particular time." He then declares that the "true meaning of demand and supply can best be seen by referring to a figure."[73] This figure, reproduced here, is the by now ubiquitous supply and demand curve, in which price is measured on the vertical axis, quantity on the horizontal. It should be noted that the employment of the graphical figure to show the "true meaning" of supply and demand means that while value in use is defined in relation to individual market traders, demand and supply are defined in terms of the market as a whole. Marshall assumes not only that it is possible to divide all market traders into two groups, buyers and sellers, but also that it is possible to arrange both groups in a single series

[73] *EEW*, I: 125–9.

such that the quantity of individual value in use can be seen to be continuously increasing (from the lowest negative value of the most eager seller to the highest positive value of the keenest buyer). Thus the derivation of the demand curve presupposes uniformity at the level of the market such that "whatever number of persons are willing to buy a commodity at any particular price, a number at least as great will be willing to buy it if the price falls."[74] Ultimately then, and this is the crucial step in Marshall's derivation of his basic supply and demand theory, two finite and discrete series of values in use of individual market traders are transposed into two continuous curves, with the effect that the theory of value becomes an investigation of market phenomena, as opposed to an analysis of individual desires. Thus Marshall can now conclude with an initial definition of (exchange) value: "At a point at which the curves cut one another there will be equilibrium, that is the amount bought will be such that the price at which it can just be brought into the market will be equal to the price at which that amount can be just got rid of."[75]

By the time he published his *Principles of Economics* in 1890, Marshall had adopted the marginal utility theory developed by W. S. Jevons, in which the desire of any one individual consumer falls at a diminishing rate with each additional unit of the commodity consumed. As such, he no longer treated the supply and demand curves as an expression of a series of market agents, ranked according to the measure of their individual values in use for a commodity. In Marshall's early theory of value, however, the concept of diminishing individual marginal utility plays no role.[76] The "marginal" element of demand in Marshall's early value theory has no relation to the final degree of satisfaction of an individual consumer, but is rather to be identified with the final individual buyer to purchase the commodity at any one particular market price. This is brought out clearly in the opening section of Marshall's early essay "On Money," which, as Whitaker observes, appears to refer to "On Value."[77] After stating that the "value of

[74] *EEW*, I: 145. Cf. Mill in his review of Thornton: "where buyers are counted by thousands, or hundreds, or even scores … it is the next thing to impossible that more of the commodity should not be asked for at every reduction in price" (Mill *CW*, 5: 637).

[75] *EEW*, I: 131.

[76] The publication of "On Value" thus confirmed Gerald Shove's conjecture in the *Economic Journal* of 1942 that "Marshall began with the objective demand and supply schedules, the phenomena of the market place, and worked backwards from them to their psychological basis, not (as was the case with Jevons) the other way about" (see Shove 1942: 307 and also *EEW*, I: 46). Here we perhaps detect a corollary from Marshall's agreement with Bain that it was not possible to quantify individual nervous behavior (see p. 132 above).

[77] *EEW*, I: 166, n. 1.

all commodities is determined by an equation of supply and demand," Marshall explains that we "here have the causes which determine prices expressed in terms of the desires of individuals"; for "the price at which any given amount can be sold" is such that for "the last induced to buy" the value in use of the commodity is at least as great as the value in use of the money that they must exchange for it. Equally, "this price must be such that even for those who are the last to be induced to sell and who would not have sold if the price had been lower the desire to retain it is certainly not greater than the desire to obtain that which they do obtain for it."[78] These market agents, who are "the last" to buy or sell, are thus what might be called the "marginal agents" in Marshall's diagrammatic formulation of the theory of value.

After defining a market, Marshall makes the following seminal observation: "The circumstances which determine the supply and demand of a commodity are widely different for different cases, the differences depending mainly on the length of the period of time to which the investigation applies."[79] Marshall proceeds to distinguish four classes of period, and so four different kinds of equilibrium value. The first class, which Marshall stated to be "very unimportant in itself," comprises very short periods in which prices are set according to precedent and goods are sold from existing stock (the supply curve thus being horizontal). In the second class, "the time is not long enough for fresh commodities to be produced in order to eke out the supply," but sellers "calculate the 'value in use' to themselves of the commodity by looking forward to what are likely to be the relations between supply and demand." This second class is the standard short-period class, in which value is determined in the first instance by subjective expectations as opposed to cost of production. In the third class, however, while the mode of production is fixed, "the periods are sufficiently long to enable the supply to be regulated so as to meet the demand." In this third class, "taking average results, the value in use to the sellers, the price at which they are willing to sell when any given amount of the commodity is sold in a given time, is the cost of production, including profits, at which this amount can be sold." In the fourth class, the periods are long enough to include changes in modes of production (but still short enough that changes in habits and skill are unimportant).[80] The crucial distinction is between the second and the third class; for although in both classes supply

[78] *EEW*, I: 165.
[79] *EEW*, I: 134.
[80] *EEW*, I: 135–9.

and demand may be adjusted in order to determine the equilibrium value, in the second class it is demand – or expectations of demand – that provides the dominant market force, while in the third period the key adjustments occur at the level of supply.

It is through this device of distinguishing between shorter and longer periods that Marshall was able "to combine the advantages" of the opposing accounts of the law of value of J. S. Mill, on the one hand, and of Macleod, on the other. In a letter of 1902 to J. B. Clark, Marshall recalled how in his younger days, "when I was very much exercised by McLeod's criticisms – now unjustly forgotten – of the unqualified statement that cost governs value," he had "started out on a theory of value in which I conceded to McLeod all that he asserted *for short periods*."[81] Actually, Marshall's theory of value was indebted to Macleod in a more general way. Mill's account of value invoked distinctions both between different classes of commodity and between "temporary" and "permanent" values; as Marshall had pointed out in his advanced lecture notes, Mill's main definition of value as determined by cost of production "does not apply in all cases." Marshall's starting point in his essay can be identified with Macleod's complaint that, by "the law of continuity, the true principles which govern value in the case of one commodity, must govern the value of *all* commodities, and the causes which influence it at one point of value must be the same which influence it at *all* points."[82] Marshall's first step in framing his restatement of Mill's theory was to adopt what, in his advanced lecture notes, he described as Macleod's first law of value, namely that the "relation between supply & demand is universally the only regulator of value." But within his general model of supply and demand, Marshall's distinction between short- and long-period equilibrium values allowed him to maintain that in the longer period Mill (and Ricardo before him) had been on the right track when they had pointed to cost of production as the key determinant of value. Thus, while both supply and demand play a role in the determination of both short- and long-period values, in the short period demand is the dominant factor, whereas in the long period the supply is regulated to meet the demand, and the value of a commodity comes to be governed, on average, by the costs of production.

The derivation of period analysis both parallels and goes beyond Marshall's earlier psychological distinction between objective and subjective ideas of the self. In both cases, Marshall's procedure was to formulate

---

[81] Pigou 1925: 414, emphasis in original.
[82] Macleod 1863: 54.

a clear division between two aspects of what had hitherto been treated as a somewhat amorphous and undifferentiated whole (the contents of introspective reflection and self-consciousness in the first case, short- and long-period values in the second) and, by doing so, to demonstrate that superficially contradictory statements concerning that whole were in reality correct treatments of but one part of that whole. In other words, we have now seen Marshall employing, in both psychology and political economy, the Coleridgean formula that in any dispute both parties are right in what they affirm but wrong in what they deny. However, the employment of this Coleridgean method with regard to political economy embodied a new component that would henceforth play a crucial role in Marshall's thinking; for where the psychological distinction between reflection and self-consciousness was simply a distinction in kind, the distinction between demand-driven and supply-led determination of value according to different periods rested on a distinction not in kind, but in time. That is to say, Marshall can be seen to have refined the Coleridgean method such that in the dispute over value each party was correct in what it asserted, but with regard to different temporal perspectives. In the following chapters, we shall see how the element of time would become, for Marshall, the ground on which – ultimately – the differences in kind between self-consciousness and physical mechanism were to be reconciled in a dialectical conception of social progress. Before turning to Marshall's discovery of history, however, we should examine what happened when Marshall attempted to apply his theory of value to the particular case of wages.

THE ESSAY "ON WAGES"

Armed with such a comprehensive, powerful, and rigorously defined reformulation of value theory, Marshall could now turn his full attention to the theoretical controversy over wages. In his early essay "On Wages," he attempted to utilize the period analysis derived in "On Value" in order to clarify the workings of the labor market. Marshall's basic intention, which must have stood behind his development of period analysis in "On Value," was to use the distinction between periods in order to reconcile the orthodox account of natural wages and the concessions that Mill made to Thornton's criticisms in his 1869 article. Yet as Whitaker observes, "On Wages" lacks the polish of "On Value" and indeed appears to be but an early draft. Although it is, of course, possible, Whitaker adds, that a more polished version was composed but has since been lost, in light of our knowledge of the subsequent development of Marshall's thought it seems more likely that he simply abandoned the approach to wages developed in this essay.[83]

At the heart of the essay "On Wages" stands the third class of equilibrium, by means of which Marshall attempted to formulate the labor market as described by Mill in his recantation. In this period the supply of labor could be treated without reference to population growth. Marshall's main concern here was to show that the number of workers "which can 'be supplied at a certain price (i.e. wages)' does not depend on the cost of production [of the workers] in the same direct and immediate way as it does for slaves or other chattels."[84] Setting aside issues such as migration, the special advantages of any particular trade, and differences in knowledge of the state of the market, Marshall's claim was that the wages in any particular employment represent the cost of the preparation required for entering that employment. In other words, and in contrast to Lassalle and other modern German socialists, Marshall insisted that the cost of production of labor could not be identified with the costs of subsistence, but rather included also the cost of the education of labor (which, of course, in the case of unskilled labor was zero). The kind of education in question, it is important to note, was explicitly stated to be a technical as opposed to a liberal education. But if he still regarded the value of a liberal education as beyond the scope of economic analysis, he now posited the value of a technical education as a crucial factor in the determination of wage rates. As I shall suggest later in this section and argue in detail in Chapter Seven, a pivotal step in Marshall's subsequent economic thought occurred when he removed this distinction between technical and liberal forms of education.

The crucial factor in this third class, however, was not the supply of labor but rather the demand for it. Marshall's treatment of labor demand in this third period rested on Macleod's argument, discussed earlier, that it is "improper to apply the terms either of floating or of fixed capital to any object … unless we know the intention of its owner in using it." It is by means of this subjective approach to capital that Marshall now attempted to formalize what he took to be the underlying ground of Mill's 1869 recantation. In the essay Marshall observes with approval that, in his 1869 review, Mill had "distinctly stated" the reasons that the wages fund was not in fact fixed in the short period. In other words, Marshall's starting point was Mill's 1869 declaration that the "real limit" of any rise in wages was "the practical consideration" by the capitalist of "how much would ruin him."

---

[83] *EEW*, I: 178, 48.
[84] *EEW*, I: 195.

Marshall follows this up, however, by insisting that it "is necessary however to supplement what [Mill] says by remarking that the phrase 'the amount of labourer's commodities in a country' is a very vague one." A stock of finished bricks, he explains, "may be used in building labourer's cottages or in enlarging a workshop or factory or in building an ornamental wall round a gentleman's park." What this means is that while wages might indeed be advanced out of the stock of commodities that constitutes capital, "there are at any time some commodities of which the destination is doubtful – whether for the consumption of the capitalist or for that of the labourers." Such indeterminacy means that we "cannot first find out what is the amount of labourer's commodities in existence and thence determine what wages must be."[85] In this way, Marshall's third period captures Mill's 1869 concession that, in the labor market, supply and demand theory might not establish a unique value.

Yet Marshall's strategy of diagrammatically formulating the orthodox theory of wages could work only if he could further show that, in the long period, the orthodox account was correct. His attempt to do so began with the assertion that we are justified in the longer period in assuming that on average the capitalist has "calculated tolerably rightly and caused those commodities to be produced for the consumption of labourers which actually are consumed by labourers."[86] But Marshall evidently lost faith in the ability of his diagrammatical approach to capture the orthodox theory of the determination of population growth, capital accumulation, and the natural rate of wages. At the head of the folio in which discussion of this fourth class of equilibrium wage commences, Marshall has written in pencil that the following folios "require to be *entirely rewritten*. The curves simply confuse matters if indeed any meaning attaches to them."[87] It is not altogether clear why Marshall came to the conclusion that the use of curves served to confuse rather than clarify economic ideas. Whitaker thinks that Marshall simply abandoned this paper after becoming acquainted with J. H. von Thünen's ideas, crucially the role of cost minimization in inducing factor substitution and of output as the source for the reward of all factors (both ideas, of course, being key steps toward a marginal-productivity

---

[85] *EEW*, I: 187–9.
[86] *EEW*, I: 189.
[87] M 4/9, f. 30, emphasis in original; see also *EEW*, I: 190. The period of this fourth class is said to be about a century. Note that in the discussion of the fourth class of equilibrium in "On Value," Marshall insists that there is an "upper limit to the periods which can be considered" (*EEW*, I: 139). This might be taken to suggest that this draft of "On Value" was composed only after the surviving draft of the essay "On Wages" was written.

theory).[88] To this conclusion, however, it seems possible to add two further observations.

First of all, the conception of the wages fund as determined by the subjective decisions of capitalists can, at least with the benefit of hindsight, be seen as a first step toward what would become a completely new theory of distribution. The recognition that the division of profits was determined by the subjective choice of capitalists suggested that the advance of wages from existing capital might be augmented by loans from abroad if the efficiency of labor was such that its employment raised expectations of increased future profits.[89] In other words, Marshall's early conclusion that the division between fixed and circulating capital was determined subjectively can be seen as a first step toward a view of wages as not paid out of existing capital at all, but rather paid out of the flow of output. In Chapter Seven we shall find Marshall, around 1872–3, advancing down precisely this path.

The development of Marshall's economic thinking after around 1871 can also be related to his continued reflection on the relationship between economics and education. It was suggested earlier that Marshall's subjective definitions of capital and such related terms as "wealth" and "value" were related to a revision of his earlier romantic separation of the spheres of economic life and higher education. We have also seen how, in "On Wages," Marshall would insist on the importance of technical education in determining the short-period cost of labor. When we turn to a detailed examination of Marshall's developing thought on education in Chapter Seven, we shall discover Marshall, in various notes from the early 1870s, coming to the conclusion that a liberal education produced efficient and trusted workers. This had obvious (and perhaps not so obvious) corollaries with regard to Marshall's thought on the relationship between labor supply and levels of output, but also, as we have just suggested, to his thought on the demand for labor. In a nutshell, Marshall gradually came around to the view that educated labor could be expected to generate that output which would (more than) pay its current high wages. The development of Marshall's economic

---

[88]   *EEW*, I: 178, 48.

[89]   The key point was made by Francis Walker in *The Wages Questions* (1876). Even granting that wages are "wholly advanced out of capital to supply the immediate necessities of the labourer," Walker writes, the questions "whether labour shall be employed at all" and "what wages shall be paid to labourers if employed ... are decided by reference to production and not to capital. It is the prospect of a profit in production which determines the employer to hire labourers; it is the anticipated value of the product which determines how much he can pay them" (Walker 1876: 144 [ML]). This passage, which is heavily marked in the margin of Marshall's copy of Walker's book, not only expresses the view that Marshall arrived at, but may very well have helped him arrive there.

thought in the few years that followed the composition of "On Wages" can thus be seen as bringing together elements of his treatment of the third class of equilibrium wages and his continuing concern with the relationship between higher education and economic production. As the remaining chapters of this book will show, this development occurred within the context of a philosophically grounded revision of Mill's organization of political economy.

PART III

NEO-HEGELIAN POLITICAL ECONOMY: 1872–1873

SIX

A Philosophy of History

SCIENTIFIC NATURALISM

In a public lecture on Babbage's calculating engines, delivered in 1872, Marshall's close friend W. K. Clifford mused on the connections between the evolution of life and the meaning of mechanism. Clifford dwelled on a feature of Babbage's working model of his difference engine that Babbage himself had made much of – the fact that the engine, in Clifford's words, "possesses the power of changing its law at a prearranged time" – for example, changing its performance from the successive addition of ones to the successive addition of twos.[1] Babbage had apparently derived great enjoyment from the surprise of his house guests when they watched the working part of his engine so change its behavior. But he had also drawn a serious philosophical lesson from this contrivance. In his famous *Ninth Bridgewater Treatise* (1837), Babbage argued that the programmed discontinuities of his calculating engines had corrosive implications for the belief that sudden catastrophes were responsible for the apparent discontinuities of the geological record.[2] Furthermore, at least in Clifford's opinion, Babbage had taken the analogy provided by his calculating engines one stage further and drawn the lesson that the mechanical laws governing inorganic matter are not, as at first sight they appear to be, "totally distinct from those of living bodies." To illustrate the point, Clifford imagined an observer of the "long series of ages" since the world's beginning:

We know that at one time the earth must have been entirely free from living things, because it was too hot to hold them; and that they appeared as it cooled down. If anybody could have watched the inorganic matter through a long series of ages, he

---

[1] Clifford ca. 1872. Unlike most of Clifford's public lectures, this talk was never published; the quoted extracts are taken from a manuscript of Clifford's notes for the talk (the manuscript can be found in the Babbage Collection in Cambridge University Library).
[2] On Babbage's *Ninth Bridgewater Treatise*, see Schaffer 1996.

would have observed it behaving according to certain definite laws; but then, at the appearance of life upon the earth, he would have seen this same matter suddenly behave according to laws apparently quite different.

If such an observer, continued Clifford, "should compare the molecules of matter to machines constructed by intelligence," one of two suppositions might be made: first, "that the original intelligence had stepped in and made an alteration" or, second, that the "constitution of the molecules had been originally so contrived that in virtue of it they made this step by themselves." It was this second supposition that Clifford took to be the argument of Babbage's *Ninth Bridgewater Treatise*, and he expressed deep admiration for the way that Babbage had been able to accept the appearance of discontinuities in nature, and yet "penetrate through" these discontinuities "to a deeper law and accept evolution as the true statement of the world's history."[3]

Clifford's lecture on Babbage's work reflects the ruminations of a mind that in the wake of the reception of thermodynamics and Darwin's evolutionary theory, now looked toward a unified science of matter, life, and consciousness. Such an aspiration, which brought him firmly into the camp of such "scientific naturalists" as Thomas Huxley and John Tyndall, was clearly set forth in Clifford's 1874 talk, "Body and Mind." In this talk he explained that the future progress of science would involve the combining "into a single string" of the three great divisions of knowledge: the sciences of inorganic matter, organic matter, and consciousness. Clifford presented "Body and Mind" as a commentary and elaboration on "Professor Huxley's admirable lecture delivered at Belfast before the British Association."[4] At this infamous meeting of the British Association for the Advancement of Science, Huxley had argued that human beings were merely "thinking machines," their thoughts no more than mental reflections accompanying but not influencing the body's actions.[5] In his own talk, Clifford endorsed Huxley's statement that the "brain is the organ of sensation, thought, and emotion" and himself declared that "we are to regard the body as a physical machine which goes by itself according to a physical law, that is to say,

[3]   Clifford's account of the history of life on earth was in many ways prefigured by Samuel Butler in "The Book of the Machines," part of his 1872 novel *Erewhon* (see Butler 1927: 233–70). For a discussion of the background of such speculation, see Schaffer 1989.
[4]   Clifford 1879, II: 31–70.
[5]   See Desmond 1998: 446. Already in 1870 Huxley had declared that "we shall sooner or later arrive at a mechanical equivalent of consciousness, just as we have arrived at a mechanical equivalent of heat" (Huxley 1970, I: 191).

is automatic."[6] More generally, and now switching his metaphor, Clifford explained that Huxley had outlined the "bridges" by means of which the three divisions of knowledge were to be – and to a significant extent already were – connected. The bridge between physical and biological science was constructed on Descartes's "conclusion that the science of organic bodies is only a complication of the science of inorganic bodies." The bridge between organic matter and mental science was in turn founded on the "great discovery of Descartes that the nervous system is that part of the body which is related directly to the mind." Together, these two Cartesian bridges connected the entire range of natural phenomena and, by so doing, established the grounds of a unified empire of science that is "in its great general features complete, and leaves nothing but more detailed explanations to be desired."

Marshall's third Grote Club paper, "Ye Machine," with its physicalist account of the mind and mechanical conception of "character," was eminently compatible with this unified vision of "scientific naturalism." Indeed, it seems very likely that hearing Marshall read this paper at the Grote Club provided Clifford with an important inspiration for his subsequent speculations (Clifford had joined the Grote Club in 1868 and, as Marshall later recalled, "had at that time read but little philosophy").[7] Certainly, it seems clear that both Marshall and Clifford came to think that Babbage's calculating engines pointed to a deeper continuity behind the apparent differences in kind in inorganic, organic, and at least some parts of psychological science.[8] Furthermore, there can be no doubt that Marshall would have agreed with Clifford's account of the natural history of the earth, including his argument that the emergence of life from inorganic matter was but an expression of an evolutionary law. Such materialist speculations as to the origins of life joined up, of course, with an evolutionary account of the subsequent course of life on earth, provided in the first instance by Darwin's *Origin of Species*. As we have seen, Marshall's "Ye Machine" was intended to fit into such an evolutionary history. Over time, an individual machine developed mental habits and routines, and these were passed on

---

[6]   Clifford 1879, II: 31–70. Proponents of the "automaton hypothesis" made much of William Carpenter's model of involuntary action (see pp. 125–7 above). In his attack on the automaton hypothesis of 1874, Carpenter declared, "I cannot regard myself, either Intellectually or Morally, as a mere puppet" (Carpenter 1889: 284). Clifford's 1874 talk can be read as containing an implicit reply to Carpenter when he insisted that, while an automaton, he was not a puppet.

[7]   Keynes 1925: 6.

[8]   See pp. 137–41 above.

from one generation to another according to a model of heredity that was shaped by a mechanical principle of selection. Furthermore, the two-level mechanical model of "Ye Machine" rested on the unstated assumption that, at some point in the evolution of animal life, the brains of the most advanced species had evolved a second mental circuit.

Nevertheless, Marshall's deep commitment to the postulate of self-consciousness entailed that he would resist the vision of a unified science, soon to be proclaimed by his friend Clifford. In Marshall's early psychological theory, humans were held to possess self-consciousness, and this spiritual agency was carefully placed outside of the evolutionary order in which the two mechanical circuits were seen to grow and develop. But such a postulate of self-consciousness did not sit easily with an evolutionary perspective. Indeed, and as Clifford effectively told Marshall, when placed within a wider natural history, which traced the history of the solar system from the cooling of the earth through the development of life on earth down to the descent of mankind, two suppositions were possible. Either human self-consciousness had, at some point, evolved out of the physical human body, or the natural processes of evolution had at some point been subject to a divine intervention that had imprinted the divine image on the hitherto purely natural human mind. We have good reason to suspect, then, that after 1868 Marshall's theological crisis became increasingly bound up with his speculations as to the origins – divine or natural – of a distinctly human self-consciousness. That is, given a naturalistic account of the evolution of life on earth, down to and including the descent of mankind from the apes, the question became at what point, if any, was it possible to identify the appearance of that element of human life that was not "natural." We may recall from Chapter Three Kingsley writing to Huxley that he fully accepted his descent from the apes and was concerned only about whether his moral nature was "nearer to God than to a Chimpanzee." The historical form of Marshall's theological and philosophical crisis could be said to have turned on the question of when, and how, Kingsley's ancestors had become moral beings more akin to God than to the apes.

READING SPENCER

Clifford's route to scientific naturalism lay through the evolutionary philosophy of Herbert Spencer. In his introduction to Clifford's posthumously published *Lectures and Essays* (1879), his university friend and fellow Apostle, Frederick Pollock, recalled "the knot of Cambridge friends of whom Clifford was the leading spirit," who, seeing in "Natural Selection" the "master-key of the universe," had been "carried away by a wave of Darwinian enthusiasm."[9] In fact, while Clifford's evolutionary enthusiasm was indeed unbounded, it is somewhat misleading to associate it so firmly with Darwin's theory of natural selection. In 1868, for example, Clifford published in the *Pall Mall Gazette* a discourse entitled "On Some of the Conditions of Mental Development."[10] His argument in this discourse was founded on an analogy between the laws of the development of the human mind and the laws of organic development as described by the "Evolution-hypothesis," which according to Clifford, while "much the same thing as the Darwinian theory," was "not by any means tied down to the special views of Mr. Darwin." The next issue of the *Pall Mall Gazette* carried a short note by Clifford in which he acknowledged the similarity of his own account of mental development to that already set down by Herbert Spencer. He had not previously been aware, he stated, of the extent to which his own argument "had already been worked out by Mr. Herbert Spencer."[11]

Clifford's 1868 discourse certainly reads as if he had deliberately set out to fuse Spencer's *First Principles* with Marshall's "Ye machine." The discourse essentially transposed the mechanical analogies of Marshall's third Grote Club paper into an organic framework. Clifford defined "mental development" as a "process of simultaneous differentiation and integration which goes on in the parts of consciousness, between the mind and external things, between the mind and other minds." "Differentiation" amounts to a proliferation of the wheels and circuits of Marshall's machine, as well as to the continual transformation of new upper-level connections into lower-level automatic habits, while "integration" amounts to the continuous building up of new circuits between diverse wheels by means of connecting bands. In this way the mechanical analogies of "Ye machine" became organic analogies. Such an approach was distinct from the Darwinian evolutionary mechanisms pointed to in "Ye Machine," in which random spinning of the machine's wheels led to chance contrivances and hence, by way of hereditary variation, the operation of a "purely mechanical" principle of natural selection. In a word, Clifford's evolutionary approach was not so much concerned with the causes of variation in the interaction of organism and environment as with providing a framework and a language in which the realms of nature were perceived as inherently in flux, engaged in a process that was at once a progression. To speak somewhat loosely,

[9] Clifford 1879, I: 41.
[10] Clifford 1879, II: 75–106.
[11] Clifford 1879, I: 106–8.

it was an emphasis on such a philosophical and conceptual – as opposed to scientific and empirical – approach to evolution that led to Spencer, as opposed to Darwin, as the more immediate source of Clifford's subsequent evolutionary enthusiasm.

Marshall certainly became a member of a "knot of friends" riding on a wave of Spencerian enthusiasm. In later life he would recall how, in his youth "a saying of Spencer sent the blood rushing through the veins of those who a generation ago looked eagerly for each volume of his as it issued from the press."[12] Such enthusiasm arose in Marshall only after the composition of his third Grote Club paper. Spencer's criticisms of Mill's empiricism had been referred to with approval in both of Marshall's first two Grote Club papers.[13] Yet as we have seen in Chapter Three, in the first of these papers Marshall had declared that only in Mansel's writings did he see any possible route to the derivation of an evolutionary account of consciousness. Spencer had not been mentioned in this context, which is to say that Spencer's evolutionary psychology had been dismissed out of hand. Quite why this was so at the time of composition of this first Grote Club paper is not readily discerned; but by the time of the second paper, at which point Marshall had come around to Grote's fundamental distinction between consciousness of phenomena and self-consciousness, Marshall's reasons for passing over Spencer's work are clear enough. By this time Marshall had embraced Grote's conception of a bifurcation of the subject matter and method of psychology, in which the objective idea of the self was placed within an evolutionary phenomenal order and studied by naturalistic science, while the subjective idea of the self was placed outside of the natural order and became the subject of a "higher" philosophical reflection. Spencer's monistic philosophy, which looked to a correlation between "internal" and "external" attributes of the mind, was incompatible with such a position.

In his *Principles of Psychology* (1855), Spencer described the mind in terms of "the continuous adjustment of internal relations to external relations." Seven years later, in his *First Principles*, he expanded this materialistic and developmental approach to psychology into an all-embracing evolutionary hypothesis. Spencer now presented the growth of all organisms, mind included, as a gradual development from simplicity to complexity – a

---

[12] Scott 1924–5: 499. For the relationship between Spencer's synthetic philosophy and the new incarnationalist theology, see Hilton 1988: 311–13. For a comparison (highly unfavorable to Spencer) between the work of Spencer and Darwin, see Moore 1979: 153–73. For Spencer's rather stormy relations with Huxley and other metropolitan agnostics, see Desmond 1998: 183–7, 591–9.

[13] *EPW*, 55, 64.

process of continuous differentiation and integration of separate parts in relation to the organism as a whole.[14] Thus, where Grote built up a dualistic philosophy by attempting to locate a "higher" point of view, from which the subjective (internal) self could be seen as expanding into the (external) "non-self" (and in doing so discovering the mind of God), Spencer saw internal change as correlated with external development, and so brought the entire realm of mental life within a framework that was grounded in what Grote considered to be purely phenomenological facts. Put another way, where Grote believed that, within any sensation, the philosophical mind could discover the nonphenomenological ground of reality, Spencer treated sensation as the mental corollary of nervous shock, and was therefore able to approach both internal and external components of the mind in terms of the interaction of the nervous system with its physical environment. Not surprisingly, Grote in his *Exploratio* charged Spencer with having denied Ferrier's proposition that self-consciousness is the ground of all cognition.[15]

Quite how Marshall came to a more appreciative view of Spencer's evolutionary philosophy must to some degree remain a matter of conjecture. There is a telling annotation in the margin of Marshall's 1867 edition of Spencer's *First Principles*, in which he writes that Spencer "does not evade Ferrier's position but, as supplementing it, & showing how the idea of the ego becomes developed it is very complete."[16] But, of course, we have no way of knowing when Marshall wrote this. Furthermore, the bald reference to "the idea of the ego" leaves Marshall's meaning in this annotation somewhat ambiguous (for Marshall, of course, drew a distinction between the objective and the subjective idea of the ego). Nevertheless, the assertion that Spencer *supplements* Ferrier's position suggests that Marshall believed that Spencer provided a "very complete" account of the development of the objective idea of the ego, while Ferrier's concern was with the subjective idea of the ego. In his second Grote Club paper, it will be recalled, Marshall had looked to Bain for an account of the education of the objective idea of the ego, but had pointed out that Bain considered only the development of the objective idea of the ego in the individual, and not the evolution of the objective idea of the ego within the race as a whole. This marginal annotation, then, suggests that at some point, presumably after the composition of the second and third Grote Club papers in 1868, Marshall began to look

---

[14] Spencer 1862: 79.
[15] Grote 1865: 54.
[16] Spencer 1867b: 157 [ML].

to Spencer for an evolutionary account of the collective education of the objective idea of the ego. We may well suspect Clifford's influence at work here.

From another perspective, we have some reason to suspect that the movement from Bain to Spencer was mediated by Marshall's study of Kant's *Critique of Pure Reason* and the English reception of non-Euclidean geometry. We know that in 1868 Marshall traveled to Germany in order to learn to read Kant's writings in the original, and we also know that in 1875 Marshall was extremely critical of the American philosopher Emerson for failing to grasp the implications of the new non-Euclidean geometries for his Kantian transcendentalism.[17] One conclusion that it was possible to draw from the new geometries was that what Kant took as the a priori had in fact evolved (Clifford went so far as to argue that non-Euclidean geometry compelled a turn from Kant's critical philosophy to an account of the evolution of our physiological apparatus of sensation).[18] There is some slight evidence that in the late 1860s, and before the English debate on the philosophical significance of non-Euclidean geometry had publicly commenced, such considerations were already leading Marshall to turn from Kant to Spencer. Marshall's fourth Grote Club paper, which has been dated to around 1869, is concerned with the axioms of geometry. In the first few folios of this essay, Marshall takes note of Kant's conception of a priori ideas as existing outside of space and time, and wonders what Kant would have made of Spencer's evolutionary conception of the a priori as that which evolves over long periods by way of the gradual inherited accumulation of empirical observations in the race. Raffaelli, in his introduction to this paper, suggests that in this comparison Marshall reveals an "unconfessed preference" for Spencer's evolutionary position.[19]

Although it is not impossible that his new interest in Spencer played a role in Marshall's continuing theological doubts, the evidence we have does not permit us to make such an inference. If we had reason to believe that Marshall moved from Grote's dualism to a position at least partially sympathetic to Spencer's monism, the obvious next step would be to inquire whether this had led Marshall into the kind of agnostic creed constructed by Spencer and Huxley out of Mansel's Kantianism. And it is, of course, entirely possible that between around 1869 and 1872 he did come close to

---

[17] On Marshall's trip to Germany, see Keynes 1925: 10–11; for a report of his conversation with Emerson, see *CAM*, I: 62. Marshall commended Clifford to Emerson as a representative of the new thinking on continuity.

[18] See my "Marshall and Psychology" in *ECAM* for further discussion.

[19] *EPW*, 75; see also pp. 71–3.

embracing such a form of agnosticism. Yet while the course of Marshall's theological doubts over these years is misty and shrouded in darkness, the marginal annotation quoted earlier concerning Spencer's treatment of Ferrier's first proposition does not imply that Marshall's reading of Spencer undermined his early commitment to Grote's form of dualism; it suggests rather that, in Spencer, Marshall found a way to supplement Bain's account of the evolution of the phenomenological side of that dualism. In this context it is worth noting that while Marshall may indeed have belonged to a university generation that eagerly purchased each of Spencer's volumes as they rolled off the press, such enthusiasm was not sufficient to motivate Marshall to read these volumes in their entirety. There are many uncut pages in Marshall's copies of both volumes of Spencer's *Essays* and even in the heavily annotated volume *Social Statics*. Furthermore, if we examine the content of the numerous annotations made throughout (the cut pages) of these volumes, it becomes clear that Marshall was not looking to Spencer to provide a light on his religious anxieties. Whatever the actual course of Marshall's theological crisis between 1868 and 1872, we would do well to resist the temptation to speculate on it.

Marshall's annotations of Spencer's various volumes reveal two primary concerns. First, he was evidently searching Spencer's writings, hunting for analogies between mental, organic, and inorganic evolutionary development. For example, in his copy of Spencer's *First Principles*, a discussion of political revolution as an "abnormal" change elicits the comment "Conf also mental disturbances ending in mania,"[20] while in Spencer's essay "The Social Organism," we find the interesting annotation "Capital & blood have strong analogies."[21] But in addition to this fascination with evolutionary analogies, Marshall was interested primarily in how Spencer applied his evolutionary

[20] Spencer 1867b: 363 [ML]. Next to a discussion in this volume of the "successive phases through which societies pass," we also find a marginal note about the process by which "suns attract asteroids & thence become bigger & so attract more" asteroids, which concludes with the following question: "Asteroids might increase the suns rate of rotation until it will [be] forced to throw off a new planet. Is there any analogy to this in [mental] associations?" (pp. 372–3). Again, in Marshall's copy of the first volume of Spencer's *Principles of Biology* (Spencer 1865 [ML]), we find next to Spencer's discussion of "Arguments from Embryology" the annotation "Analogies to this may be seen in the growth of mental, moral social & political conceptions, methods, & habits both in the race & in the individual" (p. 368). In the same edition a discussion of social evolution gives rise to the comment "The analogy to this in the intellectual world is symbolic reasoning" (p. 374), and a discussion of the occurrence of useless organs in organisms leads Marshall to write that "of course there are analogies to this in the mental world" (p. 385).
[21] Spencer 1868b, I: 411 [ML]. This annotation includes a reference to Spencer's subsequent comparison (pp. 413–14) of money to blood corpuscles.

philosophy to make sense of the historical evolution of human society. Thus the most heavily annotated of Spencer's various essays is "The Social Organism." In this essay, Spencer argues that the processes of historical development are not the product of either individual wills or legislative efforts, but are rather the consequence of "general natural causes," which, as is the case, for example, with the progress of the division of labor, have "arisen under the pressure of human wants and activities."[22] Just as with his approach to the mind, in which physical causes were seen to drive mental evolution, Spencer looked to natural social causes as the motor of social progress.

Spencer's *Social Statics* bears witness to Marshall's most careful reading. Here Spencer divides social philosophy "(as political economy has been) into statics and dynamics – the first treating of the equilibrium of a perfect society, the second of the forces by which society is advanced toward perfection."[23] For Spencer, "civilization" is the adaptation of the human constitution to the social state "that has already taken place," while "progress" is the "successive steps of the transition" toward a perfected state in which all human faculties are fit to this social state.[24] This perfect social state is one in which "each individual shall have such desires only, as may be fully satisfied without trenching upon the ability of other individuals to obtain like satisfaction," and what is more, it is a social state in which such equilibration between individual humans and their mutual needs and requirements renders void any need for central government. Spencer announces not only that the attainment of such a state is "logically certain" because progress toward it is "due to the working of a universal law," but also that such an inevitable destiny of the history of mankind is nothing less than the "realization" of "the Divine idea" that human society develop to a point at which the "greatest happiness may be attained."[25] Whatever he made of such an account of progress, Marshall would soon find in the work of Hegel a metaphysical philosophy that allowed him to assimilate, and in so doing to transform, Spencer's naturalistic account of both mental and social development. The journey from Spencer to Hegel, however, was made by way of Marshall's encounter with modern German socialism, his study of Adam Smith's *Wealth of Nations*, and his reading of Henry Maine's *Ancient Law*.[26]

---

[22] Spencer 1868b, I: 385 [ML].
[23] Spencer 1868a: 477 [ML]. All quotations in the paragraph in the main text are either marked by Marshall or found near marked passages.
[24] Spencer 1868a: 77 [ML].
[25] Spencer 1868a: 77, 78–9, 81–3 [ML].
[26] It is possible to discern the point at which Marshall's interest in Spencer's sociology began to overlap with his wider studies in political economy. For example, in his copy of

FROM NATURAL TO MORAL HISTORY

Marshall encountered modern socialism early in his academic career. Having spent time in Germany in 1868, he was there again in the winter of 1870–1 during the Franco-Prussian War.[27] While in Frankfurt on one of these visits, he attended what he later described as "a meeting advertised as of 'the working man's party,'" in which the speakers "persistently spoke of capital as 'the Enemy.'"[28] Marshall was evidently interested enough in the German socialist movement to have acquired some related literature, returning home with Marx's recently published *Das Kapital* (1867), Lassalle's *Arbeiterprogramm* (1863) and *Herr Bastiat-Schulze von Delitzch* (1864), and (obviously on his second visit) A. G. F. Schäffle's *Kapitalismus und Socialismus* (1870).[29] Marshall evidently studied carefully the historical arguments of the last section of *Kapital*, as well as the historical material scattered throughout the compendious footnotes of this volume. Furthermore, he was clearly disconcerted by Lassalle's claim that Ricardo, by showing that value is always determined by cost of production, which for labor supposedly amounted only to the bare necessities of subsistence, had demonstrated that under capitalism an "iron law" prevented the working class from ever sharing in the fruits of industrial development.[30] He was also impressed with the account of economic history that he found in Lassalle's writings.

In the second lecture of his advanced course in political economy, Marshall gave a brief sketch of economic history – a sketch informed mainly by his recent reading of German historical work. This outline began with the ancient world, moved through the feudal era, and appears

---

"The Social Organism," Marshall marks Spencer's several quotations from Guizot, while in a comment on book III of the *Wealth of Nations*, Marshall observes that Smith "points out the same distinction as Guizot does between the social relation of town and country in ancient [and] medieval times" (M 4/3, f. 22). I suspect that Bagehot's 1872 *Physics and Politics* [ML] also played a role in leading Marshall to think about political economy in relation to history and evolution. Marshall's copy is well marked (and, in light of the fact that I found two dried flowers and a gnat inside its leaves, was probably read in the summer).

[27] Keynes 1925: 10–11.
[28] *EEW*, II: 126.
[29] Marshall also purchased more orthodox works by, for example, Roscher, Rau, and Dühring.
[30] For Lassalle's account of history, see especially Lassalle 1864: ch. 4. Marshall cannot have failed to note Marx's claim, in the foreword to *Kapital*, that Lassalle had borrowed from him, without acknowledgment, all of his theoretical economics. Marx, however, was much more circumspect than Lassalle concerning the relationship between population growth and the determination of the wage rate.

to have culminated with seventeenth-century Europe.[31] In this brief historical outline, Marshall quoted from Lassalle's discussion of the ancient economy in his *Bastiat-Schulze* and referred to Lassalle's argument regarding the "absence of capitalism in feudal times."[32] But at the center of his sketch stands a summary of Schäffle's account of "the socialistic criticism" of economic history:

> The Greek Roman & Medieval society have the common characteristic that particular individuals, castes, callings & nationalities are privileged. The idea of the moral personal *per se* dignity of all was not recognised in theory let alone practice, but still slavery was not so bad a state as that of our undeveloped laborers.[33]

Schäffle's last point echoes an observation found in Marshall's notes on book III of the *Wealth of Nations*. As Marshall summarizes Smith's account of the transition from feudalism to modern commercial society, the feudal proprietors had consumed in "rustic hospitality" all of their income. But once the rise of commerce had provided these "masters of mankind" with a method of consuming the whole value of their rents, they came to spend on luxury consumption the price of the maintenance of a thousand men for a year. At this point Marshall makes the following comment: "It is precisely on this position that the modern socialists have founded their grossly exaggerated, but not altogether groundless, attacks upon the present form of society. The "reign of 'capitalism' is, they say the worst for the laboring classes that the world has known or shall know."[34] This "socialistic criticism" was a far cry from Spencer's claim of a natural evolution toward a perfect state. Yet German socialists presented such criticisms as founded on a scientific study of the natural development of economic relationships. The supposedly Ricardian iron law of wages, in particular, derived much of its force from a Malthusian population law which held that human beings, like all other animals, naturally bred up to the limit of the available means of subsistence.[35] Marshall's response to modern German socialism was, ultimately, to deny that modern economic life was a natural form of life. Such

---

[31] M 4/19, ff. 96–9. Note that there is clearly a folio missing (the narrative jumps from the ancient Greeks to feudalism). It is not impossible that other folios have also been lost and that the sketch continued past the seventeenth century.

[32] M 4/19, ff. 98–9. This brief historical sketch also makes reference to the historical discussions of McCulloch and Karl Heinrich Rau.

[33] M 4/19, f. 97. The source is Schäffle 1870: 134 [ML].

[34] M 4/3, ff. 25–6.

[35] Marshall's 1886 lecture notes on socialism contain, in addition to an acute theoretical criticism of Marx's account of surplus value, a general criticism of the modern socialists' "inconsistency: to assume at the same time the most intransigent form of the population

a position, however, inevitably entailed rejecting, or at least transforming, not only the socialist economics of Lassalle but also the social philosophy of Spencer. To trace the development of Marshall's thought that led to this position, however, we must begin with his initial musings on Smith's use of the term "natural."

From his early notes on Smith's *Wealth of Nations*, it is clear that Marshall was concerned about Smith's use of this term. On five separate occasions when quoting Smith in his notes on book IV, he wrote "[N.B.]" after the word "natural" or "naturally." The same comment also occurs once in the set of notes that Marshall made on Ricardo's *Principles of Political Economy*.[36] A clue to the nature of his discomfort with Smith and Ricardo's use of the term "natural" is provided by the fact that he also wrote "[N.B.]" after the word "fair" when quoting Buchanan's criticism of Smith's analysis of taxing wages in book V of the *Wealth of Nations*.[37] By contrast, we find at one point in the advanced lecture notes an asterisk placed after the word "natural" in a quotation from book I of the *Wealth of Nations* and a comment at the bottom of the page: "*natural* he had previously defined in this use as 'ordinary or average in a particular society or neighborhood.'"[38] Thus Marshall would appear to have been concerned that the term "natural" was ambiguous, as it could mean either average or ethically right (i.e., fair).

Now, a somewhat different concern with Smith's idea of the natural is noted in one of the folios on method intended for the first lecture in Marshall's advanced classes. The folio in question is headed "Induction or deduction," and it consists of a discussion of Cliffe Leslie's *Fortnightly Review* essay of 1870, "The Political Economy of Adam Smith." Marshall here noted Cliffe Leslie's opinion that, in contrast to the views of Buckle, two "schools one deductive the other inductive originated from A Smith" and that "on the deductive side" was a conception of "ye law of Nature," which included such ideas as "natural price," "natural liberty," and the "natural progress of opulence."[39] Yet neither in this folio, nor anywhere else in the advanced lecture notes, is there any hint that Cliffe Leslie's use of Henry Maine's scholarship in this article has any connection to Marshall's criticism

doctrine on the supposition of free contract; & the most intransigent denial of it on the collectivism hypothesis" (M 3/16, f. 42).

[36] M 4/5, f. 49. Cf. Foxwell's complaint in his 1887 essay that the "older school of English economists" deduced facts from assumptions that seemed to them to "be in some sense 'natural,' or common to all ages" (Foxwell 1887: 89).

[37] M 4/5, f . 49.

[38] M 4/19, f. 32.

[39] M 4/19, f. 6; and see Leslie 1870.

that Smith's use of the term "natural" conflates the ethical with the merely average. Put another way, what is perhaps most significant about this folio, at least with regard to Marshall's subsequent intellectual development, is less what it takes note of than what it passes over in Cliffe Leslie's paper. Marshall evidently did not see a reason to make any reference to Cliffe Leslie's further argument that, while Smith's inductive method derived from Montesquieu, the foundation of his deductive or a priori method was "that theory of Nature which, descending through Roman jural philosophy from the speculations of Greece, taught that there is a simple Code of Nature which human institutions have disturbed." Nor did he take note of Cliffe Leslie's passing remark that Maine had "explored the fallacies lurking in the terms Nature and Natural Law."[40] Within a short time after writing this note, however, Marshall had commenced a careful reading of Maine's *Ancient Law* and, subsequently, began to follow up precisely these latter aspects of Cliffe Leslie's essay.

In *Ancient Law*, Maine provided an outline of the history of jurisprudence from its primitive origins. Society in primitive times, he explained, "was not what it is assumed to be at present, a collection of *individuals*. In fact, and in the view of the men who composed it, it was *an aggregation of families*."[41] In such a society the relations between people are defined in terms of status, and law "has scarcely reached the footing of custom; it is rather a habit." An "epoch of Customary Law" emerges, however, as oligarchic rule is inevitably established within society. In the East such oligarchies assumed a religious status, in the West a political one; but in both cases these ruling groups were regarded as the depositaries and administrators of law. The next step, through which all the families of mankind must pass, is "the era of Codes," the most famous of them being the Roman Twelve Tables. In all the ancient codes, Maine explains, we find a mingling of religious, civil, and moral ordinances, "the severance of law from morality, and of religion from law, belonging very distinctly to the *later* stages of mental progress." It is at this point in history that, according to Maine, a fundamental division arises. Societies like those of India and China remain stationary at or around the "era of Codes," while others, such as the Roman and modern European societies, develop true legal systems. The latter are the progressive societies of history. A crucial element of the Roman legal system was the distinction between normal and inferior, easily movable commodities, with the latter alienable by simple contract as opposed to the "cumbrous

⁴⁰ Leslie 1870: 552.
⁴¹ Maine 1866: 126 [ML], emphasis in original.

solemnities" and "perplexed ceremonies" of archaic law. The history of the Roman law of property, insists Maine, is the history of the extension of the class of inferior commodities to all commodities, while the "history of Property on the European Continent is the history of the subversion of the feudalised law of land by the Romanised law of moveables."[42] Thus, Maine declared, "the movement of the progressive societies has hitherto been a movement from Status to Contract."

Marshall found in Maine's *Ancient Law* a historical explanation for Smith's use of the term "natural." Before turning to the application of this explanation to Smith (and, indeed, the history of political economy more generally), however, we must sketch one element of the historical framework that Marshall derived from Maine. We shall do so by turning to one of Marshall's early historical notes, headed "Rousseau." In this note we find a passage copied from Maine's fourth chapter, "The Modern History of the Law of Nature," which contrasts the "Historical Method" initiated by Montesquieu with the "counter-hypothesis" of a "Natural Law," which, we are told, was launched on a new career by Rousseau.[43] Behind this note stands Maine's discussion of the history of the natural law tradition. Maine explained that the Roman legal system was composed of Roman laws and customs, and what were regarded as laws common to all mankind (*Jus Gentium*). While initially the latter were regarded as inferior, under the influence of Stoicism and "the Greek theory of a Law of Nature," Roman lawyers came to hold that the *Jus Gentium* was in fact "the lost code of Nature." Now, Maine explains that the continuity between ancient Roman and modern European jurisprudence was broken by the Germanic invasions, which reintroduced into European societies a web of archaic usages and customs. But while in England the Roman legal tradition became all but extinct, it was revived and became extremely important in early modern continental Europe, particularly in France. But in the mid–eighteenth century, Montesquieu set forth that historical method which, Maine insists, has henceforth been "the great antagonist" of the natural law tradition. Montesquieu's challenge was soon countered by Rousseau's modern

---

[42] Maine 1866: 273 [ML]; see also M 4/14, f.3 and M 4/11, f. 76.

[43] M 4/13, f. 20. In a discussion of the education of women in his early notes on the division of labor, Marshall holds up the "one sided originality" of Rousseau as representative of the feminine mind, which, he tells us, broods long "over one leading thought, emotion, desire, or artistic enthusiasm ... without systematic firm-willed thinking out of difficulties" (M 4/26, ff. 62–3). Such a characterization seems to have been derived in part from Carlyle's *On Heroes*, in his copy of which Marshall marked the description of Rousseau as "morbid, excitable, spasmodic" and "intense rather than strong" (Carlyle 1872: 170 [ML]).

formulation of the natural law tradition, in which "the primary subject of contemplation" was "not the Law of Nature" as such, but rather "the State of Nature." In all of the speculations of Rousseau, explains Maine, "the central figure, whether arrayed in an English dress as the signatory of a social compact, or simply stripped naked of all historical qualities, is uniformly Man, in a supposed state of nature."[44] This contrast between Montesquieu's historical method and Rousseau's ideal of nature would provide Marshall with a key to the interpretation of the history of political economy.

If we turn to Marshall's *Principles of Economics*, the significance of Maine's contrast between the historical method and the natural law tradition is immediately clear. In what was initially an introductory chapter that sketched the growth of economic science (but later became Appendix A) and that Marshall claimed to have composed from the notes taken during his early historical studies,[45] we find these passages from Maine standing behind an analysis of the Physiocrats' "pursuit of natural laws of social life." The lawyers of eighteenth-century France, Marshall explains, "were full of the Law of Nature which had been developed by the Stoic lawyers of the later Roman Empire, and as the century wore on, the sentimental admiration for the 'natural' life of the American Indians, which Rousseau had kindled into flame, began to influence the economists. Before long they were called Physiocrats, or adherents of the rule of Nature." The work of the Physiocrats, however, "has but little direct value," and this is primarily because they "confused the ethical principle of conformity to Nature" with "those causal laws which science discovers by interrogating Nature."[46] Upon turning from the Physiocrats to Adam Smith, Marshall proceeds to explain that Smith himself "had not quite got rid of the confusion prevalent in his time between the laws of economic science and the ethical precept of conformity to nature." Smith's ambiguity over the meaning of the term "natural" led him, for example, to confuse the science of economics with the art of government.[47] In short, Marshall derived from Maine an additional thread to weave into his already complicated reading of the history of political

---

[44]   Maine 1866: 56, 85, 91 [ML]. Note that in his copy of Lecky's *History of European Morals*, Marshall marked a passage that discusses the influence of Stoicism on Roman legislation and the subsequent idea of a law of nature (Lecky 1869, I: 314–15 [ML]). For a contemporary discussion of Stoicism that illuminates Marshall's identification of Stoic moral philosophy as the root of eighteenth-century laissez-faire ideas, see Pollock 1879.

[45]   See "A Reply" (*Economic Journal*, September 1892), reprinted in *Principles*, II: 735; and for further discussion, see my introduction to *EHC*.

[46]   *Principles*, I: 756, n. 2.

[47]   *Principles*, I: 758, n. 1.

economy. This thread is also prominent in the introductory chapter of the theory of distribution in what became book VI of Marshall's *Principles*.

In the first part of this chapter of the *Principles*, Marshall sketched the history of the theory of distribution from Turgot through Ricardo. The Physiocrats are said to have held that wages were "kept at starvation limit" by a "natural law of population" and furthermore to have concluded that "the natural value of everything" was governed by the cost of production. Marshall proceeded to explain that both Smith and Ricardo had recognized to some degree that wages were not fixed at a starvation level, but were rather "determined by the ever-fluctuating conditions of demand and supply." Nevertheless, the writings of both Smith and Ricardo were marred by their continued use of Physiocratic modes of expression. Here, then, was an additional means by which Marshall separated true thought from badly chosen words. Smith, he explains, "when he is carefully weighing his words," makes clear that by "natural" he means simply the average value within a local environment. Nevertheless, he "sometimes falls back into the old way of speaking, and thus makes careless readers suppose that he believes the mean level of the wages of labour to be fixed by an iron law at the bare necessaries of life." Again, Ricardo was fully "aware that the necessary or natural limit of wages was fixed by no iron law, but is determined by the local conditions and habits of each place and time." Nevertheless, Ricardo's "language is even more unguarded than that of Adam Smith," and he "frequently adopts a mode of speaking similar to that of Turgot and the Physiocrats." What we see in this part of this introductory discussion, then, is the practical value that Marshall derived from his fundamental distinction between the roles of thought and language in the history of political economy. By attending to the words of Ricardo at the expense of his actual thought, Marshall explained, the German socialists had mistakenly concluded that Ricardo had formulated an iron law of wages, which they believe "is in operation now even in the western world."[48]

Thus Marshall supplemented his initial outline of the history of political economy with a much broader history of ideas. To his initial doctrinal history, Marshall now added the idea that the progress of economic science had involved a century-long process of discarding the vestiges of an eighteenth-century (but ultimately ancient and Stoic) language of "nature." Such language was itself the product of the natural law tradition, which in the nineteenth century had given way to a different, historicist and evolutionary understanding of society. Nevertheless, even in the nineteenth century

---

[48] *Principles*, I: 507–8.

truly economic doctrines were all too frequently formulated according to the older modes of expression. This extension of his narrative of the history of political economy led Marshall to purge his own economic thinking of the notion of the natural, just as it also prevented him from adopting, without serious modification, Spencer's sociological analysis. It also allowed him to firmly disassociate the iron law of wages from the economic thought of Ricardo. Already after his discussion of Turgot's implicit assumptions concerning the population principle in his early notes on the Physiocrats, Marshall had observed that the "more reckless Ricardians make all these assumptions."[49] From this point on, Marshall would insist that the iron law of wages was a Physiocratic rather than a Ricardian doctrine. Indeed, and as we shall see, armed with a historicist interpretation of the eighteenth-century conception of nature, Marshall would in fact take this one step further and declare that the belief that wages are fixed by a natural law at a subsistence level was a remnant of pre-modern pagan thought. Nevertheless, we have as yet uncovered only half of the ground on which Marshall raised this last criticism. To complete this picture we need to turn from Marshall's early reading of Maine to his early study of Hegel's *Philosophy of History*.

HEGEL AND MAINE

Around 1872 Marshall composed twenty-one folios of notes on Hegel's *Philosophy of History*. These notes begin with Hegel's identification of "spirit" and subjective freedom. "Spirit is the self-contained existence," notes Marshall, and such an existence that is not dependent on anything external "is *Freedom* exactly." But Marshall then takes note of a further, crucial identification: "This self contained existence of spirit is none other than self-consciousness."[50] Immediately, we are alerted to the fact that Marshall has found in Hegel a solution to that search for an evolutionary account of self-consciousness that he commenced in his first Grote Club paper. As Marshall proceeds to note, Hegel conceives of the development of self-consciousness

[49]	M 4/15, f. 45. Marshall observes that these "reckless Ricardians" differ from Turgot only in that they further assume that there exist "a number of highly salaried individuals who could be taxed." On Marshall's later identification of the iron law of wages with the Physiocrats, see, e.g., his 1886 lecture notes on socialism, in which he states that the iron law of wages as formulated by the socialists was not Ricardian and was "more truly to be called Physiocratic or Malthusian" (M 3/16, f. 41).

[50]	*EHC*, M 4/10, f. 4; and see Hegel 1991: 17. As is generally the case with Marshall's notes, his quotation is not exact (here he adds a definite article and changes the emphasis). For useful English-language discussions of Hegel's philosophy of history, see Beiser 1993, Forbes's introduction to Hegel 1975, and Riedel 1984.

as a "result of its own activity," which is to say, as a result of "the transcending of immediate simple unreflecting existence – the negation of that existence & the returning in to itself."[51] Thus Marshall found a way of placing within history the idea of the development (or education) of the subjective as well as the objective idea of the ego. Indeed, with the benefit of hindsight, it could be said that it is here that we find the real significance of Marshall's "unconfessed preference" for Spencer's evolutionary account of the a priori. Marshall may or may not have found himself drawn to Spencer's account of the correlation and externally driven evolution of internal and external attributes of mind. But the ultimate importance of Spencer's psychology was that it provided Marshall with a bridge that took him from Ferrier's first proposition to Hegel's metaphysics by way of an attempt to account for the evolution of the subjective as well as the objective idea of the self.

Such a bridge led not only from an initial postulate of self-consciousness to a dialectical history of self-consciousness, but also from psychology to social philosophy. At a certain point in the development of self-consciousness, argues Hegel, subjective freedom gives rise to that objective freedom which is manifested in the law and constitution of the modern state. As Marshall noted from Hegel's introduction, the "*state* is the realisation of *Freedom*; i.e. of the absolute final aim; and it exists for its own sake." The state is "that in which Freedom obtains objectivity & lives in the enjoyment of that objectivity. For *Law* is the objectivity of Spirit, volition in its true form. Only that will which obeys laws is free; for it obeys itself – it is independent & so free." Thus the subjective freedom of individuals finds its fruition in the objective freedom of the society to which they belong. Only through life in such a society is a human being "fully conscious, thus only is he a partaker of morality – of a just & moral social & political life."[52] The complete development of self-consciousness, in other words, cannot be understood without the perspective shifting from psychology to (a metaphysical form of) historical sociology. We should here recall how Spencer's *Social Statics* had presented Marshall with an anarchistic ideal of a social state that was defined purely in terms of relationships between individuals, as well as a materialist conception of progress toward that social state which was driven entirely by human wants, needs, and other natural causes.

---

[51] *EHC*, M 4/10, f. 7; and see Hegel 1991: 78.

[52] *EHC*, M 4/10, ff. 5–6; and see Hegel 1991: 39. As Marshall interprets Hegel in these notes, true freedom is realized when the law – the objectivity of spirit – is in accord with the "universal will." In short, a state is "well constituted & internally powerful when the private interests of the citizen is one with the common interests of the state; when the one finds its gratification & realisation in the other" (M 4/10, f. 4; see Hegel 1991: 24).

In Hegel's *Philosophy of History*, by contrast, Marshall found a conception of progress as driven by the internal dialectic of self-consciousness, which culminated in a state of "objective freedom" characterized by the rule of law and expressed in the constitution of the modern state. In terms of his own intellectual development, such a philosophy of history provided Marshall with a bridge between the idealist element of his earlier studies in psychology and his ongoing study of political economy.

Marshall's construction of a usable philosophy of history crucially involved the fusion of the historical narrative found in Hegel's *Philosophy of History* with that found in Maine's *Ancient Law*. This can be illustrated by three marginal annotations in his copy of *Ancient Law*. First of all we find, next to Maine's discussion of the juristic exclusion of children and lunatics from the law of contract, the following annotation: "This passage brings out the latent parallelism with Hegel."[53] Marshall's point is that both Hegel and Maine treat law as the product of progressive historical development, they draw a distinction between the customs of ancient societies and modern law, and they connect the development from one state to the other with a mental advance that gradually comes to separate religious, political, and moral spheres of social life. Only once the "primitive mind" has reached a sufficient level of maturity can legal principles (as opposed to customs or even habits) be established. The same point stands behind the annotation "Conf Hegels Beauty v. Law" written beside Maine's discussion of the tendency of the popular Athenian courts to confound law and fact. For Maine the "Greek intellect with all its mobility & elasticity, was quite unable to restrain itself within the strait waistcoat of a legal formula," and "the Greek tribunals exhibited the strongest tendency to confound law & fact."[54] Hegel, in his *Philosophy of History*, insists that Greek subjectivity and freedom were "adolescent" – advanced enough for the flowering of art and aesthetics, but not mature enough to engage in the abstract contemplation of law which is the mark of a modern self-consciousness that has advanced from subjective to objective freedom.[55]

A third marginal annotation, a laconic "Hegel's atonement," is found at the end of the first paragraph of Maine's chapter "The Modern History of the Law of Nature."[56] This last annotation merits careful exegesis. In the paragraph to which it is attached, Maine contrasts ancient and Christian conceptions of time. The "Law of Nature," he explains, is in practice "something

---

[53] Maine 1866: 170 [ML].
[54] Maine 1866: 75 [ML]. This sentence is transcribed in Marshall's historical notes (M 4/11, f. 78).
[55] See Hegel 1991: 225, 238–9, 250–4; see also *EHC*, M 4/11, ff. 3–4.
[56] Maine 1866: 74 [ML].

belonging to the present, something entwined with existing institutions";
and yet it also implies "a state of Nature which had once been regulated by
natural law" and which in the ancient world found "poetical expression in
the fancy of a golden age." This conception of the present as a corruption of
an ideal past is, according to Maine, a fundamentally ancient understanding of the direction of historical change. "The tendency to look not to the
past but to the future for types of perfection was brought into the world
by Christianity. Ancient literature gives few or no hints of a belief that the
progress of society is necessarily from worse to better." It is next to this last
sentence that Marshall wrote, "Hegel's atonement." If we turn to Marshall's
notes on Hegel we find that, for Hegel, Christ's atonement marks a pivotal
moment in the history that is the dialectical progress of the spirit and the
evolution of self-consciousness. In the early stages of the development of
self-consciousness, humanity does not grasp the fundamental difference
between itself and the natural world. But (to turn again to Marshall's notes
on Hegel) "sin is the discerning of good & evil as separation," and such discerning "brings with it the destruction of that which is alien & external in
consciousness & is consequently the return of subjectivity into itself. This
then adopted in the actual self consciousness of the world is the *reconciliation* (atonement) *of the World.*" Such reconciliation is at once the dawning
of a fully formed moral consciousness, the recognition of the inherent gulf
that separates moral autonomy from the natural world, and indeed the recognition of "the identity of the subject & God," all of which were made manifest in the Christian religion and were "introduced into the world when
the fullness of time was come."[57] What possible connection could Marshall
have perceived, then, between "Hegel's atonement" and Maine's discussion
of natural law?

Marshall discerned a "parallelism" between the work of Hegel and Maine
on a number of levels. In the first instance, both writers described history
as a progression that culminated in the development of the modern conception of the state, the individual, and the law. For Maine, the history of progressive societies involved a development from primitive society, in which
"all the relations of Persons are summed up in the relations of Family," to a
modern society in which "all these relations arise from the free agreement
of Individuals."[58] For Hegel, such a development involved the separation of
the individual from nature by the emergence of a moral consciousness and
the subsequent culmination of that development in the objective freedom

---

[57] *EHC*, M 4/11, ff. 10–11.
[58] Maine 1866: 169 [ML].

of the laws of the modern state. But as we have already seen, Maine also held that the progression from status to contract involved the mental development of mankind. Thus, for both Hegel and Maine, human history involved a series of steps in which religious, political, moral, and natural spheres of life were progressively differentiated and separated. For Hegel, the appearance of Christianity marked the moment at which subjective freedom (if not yet objective freedom) arrived at maturity. Maine, by contrast, was relatively indifferent to the historical significance of Christianity. Nevertheless, he pointed to a fundamental distinction between social thought before and after the appearance of Christianity. Before the Christian Era, society and law were readily associated with an ideal of an original natural order. After the Christian Era, however, social thought was founded on an ideal of progress toward a future state of grace. Marshall's third annotation, which connected this aspect of Maine's historical narrative with that of Hegel, thus pointed to the most crucial "parallelism" by means of which he sought to synthesize the historical narratives of Hegel and Maine. For Marshall, both Hegel and Maine had grasped the crucial fact that the hope of a better society was found only in the Christian Era, while the stoical acceptance of social ills as "natural" was an inherently pagan mode of thought. From this perspective, the eighteenth-century fascination with the natural law tradition now appeared to be atavistic and, ultimately, pagan.

THE HISTORY OF CIVILIZATION

Sometime in late 1872 or 1873, Marshall composed a long essay of more than 145 folios on the history of civilization. The essay began with the ancient world, in which East (China and India) and West (Greece and Rome) are distinguished, and the Persians and the Jews posited as forming something of a bridge between the two. The theme and most of the substance are provided by Hegel, and although Marshall quotes and refers to many other books and articles, his use of these other authorities is always subservient to the Hegelian narrative of the development of subjective freedom or self-consciousness. The turning point in the essay is the appearance of the Christian religion. The second half of the essay is concerned primarily with the development of objective freedom, first in the short-lived constitutional experiments of Charlemagne and then in the gradual emergence of modern forms of political and economic organization in the late Middle Ages. Marshall identifies three distinct forms taken by modern objective freedom: the French boroughs, the Italian trading republics, and the constitutional liberties that Magna Carta established for the English nation as a whole. In the second part of the essay

the influence of Maine, and also of a wealth of nineteenth-century constitutional and comparative scholarship, merges with and then takes over from
the initial Hegelian narrative. The essay concludes with a brief discussion of
English history in the century following Magna Carta.[59]

A familiar note is sounded in the introductory section of this long essay,
when Marshall insists that "I use the word history here in its highest & most
real sense." The echo of Grote (and ultimately of Coleridge) is spelled out
when Marshall explains that, to possess "real value," historical studies must
develop an "account of man[']s aims, of his spiritual life, of the life of his
moral nature, & also, as inseparable from them, of the development of his
intellectual faculties."[60] The actual account of such spiritual development,
however, is derived from neither Coleridge nor Grote, but from Hegel. Thus,
as we read through the essay, we learn the Hegelian lessons that "all the
Civilisations before the Christian Era much as they differ among themselves,
yet have in common striking points of difference from all those that have
come after this Era,"[61] that "in the Oriental World man had not separated
himself from Nature,"[62] and that in "the East moral freedom, freedom of
choice is not recognised."[63] We find also that "the grand distinction" between
the ancient and medieval worlds is that in the Middle Ages the "*Religious
element* stands in the same relation to all, and all are invested with an absolute value by religion. In India, the direct contrary is the case." Furthermore,
"in the Christian World" there is a "moral dignity which exists among us
in every class" and which is directly responsible for the fact that "equality before the law – rights of person and of property – are gained for every
class."[64] Contained in these and many similar Hegelian passages, of course, is
an implicit refutation of that "socialistic criticism" which denies that the idea
of universal moral dignity existed in the Middle Ages and claims that slavery
was not as bad a state as that of the modern working classes. Whatever the
material conditions of the modern poor may be, the real progress of civilization has endowed them with both dignity and equality before the law.

---

[59] Marshall's neo-Hegelianism certainly constituted a departure from the explicit conventions of English history writing in this period. Nevertheless, John Burrow has noted the
"underlying Hegelian metaphysic" of Bishop Stubbs's *Constitutional History* (1875–8) and
has suggested that in this period it was inevitable that German romanticism would sooner
or later become the organizing metaphor for a nineteenth-century Burkean tradition of
English historiography (Burrow 1981: 147–8).
[60] *EHC*, M 3/1, f. 11.
[61] *EHC*, M 3/1, f. 12.
[62] *EHC*, M 3/1, f. 17.
[63] *EHC*, M 3/1, f. 20.
[64] *EHC*, M 3/1, f. 23.

Such an adaptation of a Hegelian philosophy of history allowed Marshall to place his criticism of the term "natural" within a general historical framework. This is most readily seen if we turn to what appear to be introductory lecture notes to the long essay itself. Here Marshall draws an analogy between the "constitutions" of ancient civilizations and beehives, and points out that bees require neither education nor "pure thought."[65] India and China, the starting point of Marshall's narrative, while each in different ways exhibiting some embryonic stirrings of the spirit, are still in effect natural organisms like a beehive, the study of which might be undertaken by the biologist, or at least his fellow natural scientist, the Spencerian sociologist. What Hegel provides and Marshall closely follows – at least until the Christian Era – is an account of the stages whereby a moral order emerges, as it were naturally, out of the natural order, a narrative, that is to say, of the evolution of self-consciousness and freedom as man separates himself from nature. For Marshall as political economist, one key implication of such a rendering of Hegel's philosophical history is that, properly speaking, economic activity is not to be found in the ancient world.

As a consequence, then of this passive acquiescence in "Natural" arrangements we have an absence of the habit of determination of his conduct on the part of each individual so as to obtain most completely his own ends. Men do not seek to "buy in the cheapest market and sell in the dearest market." Trade, in any broad sense of the word does not exist. Division of labor is confined practically to the narrow sphere of one village, though very "rigid" within that sphere.[66]

Another way of putting this would be to say that political economy is a moral and not a natural science. Economic activity presupposes self-conscious and autonomous moral agents, whose actions are free, because self-determined. Ancient behavior, as Maine had insisted, is governed by habit and custom. The key event in the history of civilization was the revolution wrought by Christianity. Henceforth, a "deliberate appeal to conscience was recognised as the proper commencement of any course of action; custom was dethroned." Such a transformation was, ultimately, a moral revolution. Christianity proclaimed the individual as

a responsible being, the development of whose every action was, for good or evil, decided according to his free choice by a decision which was more momentous than any thing else which was not a moral decision. And since this was true of all

---

[65] *EHC*, M 4/10, f. 2. Marshall writes: "Instinct: bees require no instruction no pure thought; close analogy between constitution of a hive & constitution of ancient civilisation."
[66] *EHC*, M 3/1, f. 24.

men, since all were children of an impartial Father, since in the Kingdom of Heaven there was neither bond or free, since to every Human being there was attached, as it were, a hereditary portion of the Divine dignity, it was no longer possible with undisturbed complacency to trample underfoot the personality of the slave.[67]

One would thus suspect that both economic activity and economic theory commenced early in the Christian Era. Yet in this essay Marshall insists that anything "like a theory of Political Economy can scarcely be said to have existed before the end of the Middle Ages."[68] And, indeed, it does not seem that he thinks there is much that could be regarded as properly economic activity in the first millennium of the Christian Era. Three reasons can be given for what appears to be a delayed commencement of the modern world. First, continuity between ancient and modern history was interrupted by the Germanic invasions, which, as Maine argued, to various degrees replaced the principles of Roman jurisprudence with archaic customs and usages. We can approach the second cause of delay by turning to the last folio of Marshall's notes on Hegel's *Philosophy of History*. Here we find an account of Byzantine Christianity as "powerless on account of its very purity & intrinsic spirituality." "Religion is something internal having to do with conscience alone," and to it all passions and desires are opposed. In order that the heart, the will, and the intelligence "may become true, they must be *thoroughly educated*; right must become custom, habit; practical activity must be elevated to rational action; the state must have a rational organisation & then at length does the will of individuals become a truly righteous one."[69] There is, in short, a time lag between the moral insight proclaimed by Christianity and the practical realization of this lesson. We shall return to this "education" of the heart, will, and mind later in this chapter and again in the following two chapters, where we shall find that Marshall regarded his own day as still requiring a good dose of such education. Indeed, in later chapters we shall find that Marshall's reflection on the need for education in the modern world became ever more closely connected to the third and most straightforward reason for the fact that both economic theory and the modern economy itself are post-medieval institutions. This third reason is that objective as well as subjective freedom is a precondition of the modern state; for without the institutional protection

---

[67] *EHC*, M 4/12, ff. 1–3.
[68] *EHC*, M 3/1, f. 12.
[69] *EHC*, M 4/11. f. 13, emphasis in original – both Marshall and Hegel; and see Hegel 1991: 338.

of life, liberty, and property, neither free economic activity nor the science that studies it is likely to flourish.

The second part of the long essay is concerned primarily with the development of objective freedom in the modern world. Marshall is here interested mainly in the constitutional histories of the Italian city-state republics, the French charter towns, and the English Magna Carta. This last, of course, provides a model of objective freedom in a modern nation-state. Here Marshall departs significantly from Hegel, whose own history culminates in a constitutional monarchy. Marshall, by contrast, is determined to find the seeds of liberal democracy at the end of his historical narrative.[70] In light of this departure from Hegel's particular political conclusions, Marshall's historical narrative as a whole is perhaps best described as a "neo-Hegelian" or even a "Whig" narrative.[71] Furthermore, just as he had related subjective freedom to the appearance of trade in the earlier part of his essay, now in this second part he indicates that the legal and constitutional developments that are the manifestations of the emergence of objective freedom in the modern world are accompanied by the removal of institutional barriers to free competition. Thus the essay as a whole places this fundamental principle of political economy firmly within a Hegelian philosophical schema. If the potential for free competition arises only with the appearance in history of autonomous individuals who act independently in order to further their own ends, so such potentiality becomes actuality only once a social space or market environment emerges, in which contracts are regarded as sacred, and arbitrary intervention by external powers is held in check by the full force of the law.

[70] It would seem likely that Marshall was influenced here by J. S. Henderson's "Hegel as a Politician," an article in the *Fortnightly Review* of 1870 that, following Katia Caldardi's Herculean efforts in cataloging all of Marshall's bound periodical articles (Caldari 2000, 2003), we know to have been one of the first articles Marshall so collected. Henderson criticized Hegel's discussion of Britain's first Reform Bill, in which Hegel had argued for the need to strengthen the powers of the crown. For Henderson, Hegel's general insistence "on the necessity for an individual head or monarch" of the modern state was the product of an overly "local" point of view, which was apt to give rise to "defective and partial views regarding other nations" (see Henderson 1870: 265, 270–1 [BV, ML]).

[71] In my introduction to *EHC*, I commented that Marshall's "Whig" rendering of Hegel's narrative loses the symmetry of Hegel's neat dialectical circle from Chinese despotism to modern constitutional monarchy. Such a complaint overlooks the fact that Marshall observes at one point in his essay that had Hegel been acquainted with recent research showing the Indian village community to be the most ancient form of civilization, he would probably have put India before China (*EHC*, M 3/11, f. 18). A dialectical circle that begins with the village community might well be thought to close more neatly with a modern democratic or republican as opposed to monarchical form of government.

Properly speaking, then, the subject matter of Marshall's long historical essay is neither economic history nor the history of economic thought. Rather, the subject matter of the essay is the development of subjective freedom and objective freedom, which together constitute the preconditions of modern economic life and thought. The long historical essay, in short, is an account of the pre-history of both economic history and the history of economic ideas.

THEOLOGICAL RESOLUTION

Marshall's newly constructed philosophy of history provided him with an answer to the question of when Kingsley's ancestors first became more akin to God than to apes. To put the same point in different terms, Hegel provided Marshall with the means of recasting the continuity of evolution as it was presented by Clifford. As we have seen, Clifford posited a continual evolution of nature, from the formation of the solar system down to the emergence of intelligent life. Marshall would have assented to this account, and now he could also follow Spencer in adopting a naturalistic account of the development of primitive human society all the way to the ancient civilizations of China and India. But at this point in his historical narrative Marshall turned away from scientific naturalism. He had now found in the philosophy of Hegel metaphysical grounds for believing that the development of civilization past the point of the primitive Indian village community involved the gradual emergence of a moral order out of the natural realm. This moral evolution of individual autonomy culminated in the appearance of the Christian religion: from this moment onward humanity, no longer wholly constrained by inherited customs and instincts, was free to act according to the dictates of a fully developed self-consciousness. The moral order had thus evolved out of the natural world, but its evolution gave rise to a quite different kind of society. Where ancient civilizations had been natural organizations, modern civilizations were arenas of free moral action. And the "nature" of the inhabitants of such modern societies was, at least potentially, closer to God than to a chimpanzee.

In Marshall's Hegelian historical narrative, the appearance of the Christian religion was a turning point in the history of the world. We should not be led by this, however, to suspect that Marshall found his Christian faith anew in Hegel's metaphysics. Indeed, in his notes on Hegel's *Philosophy of History* we find, just after the notes on the Atonement discussed earlier, this comment on Hegel's text: "There follows a rationalistion of the Christian mysteries, not perhaps very happy."[72] What Marshall derived from Hegel was not a faith in the Christian religion, but rather a metaphysical faith in progress. History – "real history" – was an account of the intellectual and moral development that gave rise to social development. Within such a historical framework, the history of religion became a token for the real progress of self-consciousness. From animism, through polytheism, to the exclusive monotheism of the Jews, and culminating in the universal and abstract faith in God – and hence in mankind – proclaimed by Christianity, each form of religion was but an expression of the relative maturity of self-consciousness at any particular moment in the history of civilization, and as such was correlated with those forms of social organization and morality determined by that level of maturity. Christianity was a turning point of history because Christ proclaimed the religious and moral beliefs of a fully mature individual self-consciousness; this was a necessary condition (although as Byzantium showed, not a sufficient condition) of the subsequent development of objective freedom in the form of the modern state. In embracing such a philosophical history, Marshall's faith was no longer Christian as such, but rather metaphysical. His was no longer the active and vital Evangelical faith of his childhood, which looked to the Bible as the source of all spiritual truth and emphasized personal salvation through the acceptance of Christ's atonement.[73] Rather, this was a metaphysical faith that the history of the world had been, and would continue to be, a history of the progressive realization of freedom on earth.

Marshall's conversion to Hegel's philosophy of history brought him close to what might be described as a secular version of Maurice's incarnationalist theology. Indeed, to return to the theological dispute between Mansel and Maurice discussed in Chapter Three, it is important to note that Marshall's newfound enthusiasm for Hegel constituted a definitive rejection of Mansel's theological relativism. In his Bampton Lectures, Mansel had identified as the object of his attack that "Theology of Rationalism" which "identifies the shadow with the substance" and ultimately proclaims that "to know God as He is, man must himself be God."[74] Mansel regarded Maurice and Jowett as preaching this theology of rationalism, but he identified Hegel as its high priest.[75] In so associating his Anglican opponents with Hegel's philosophy, Mansel was drawing attention to an aspect of the

---

[72] *EHC*, M 4/11, ff. 9–11.
[73] For Marshall's childhood religion, see Groenewegen 1995: 25.
[74] Mansel 1859: 64–5.
[75] See, e.g., Mansel 1859: 65, 69, 86, and nn. 29 and 30 to this first chapter. Similar statements are also found in Mansel's *Metaphysics*.

new incarnationalist theology that was made explicit by Jowett, but not by Maurice. Jowett would, in fact, become an early English champion of the Hegelian philosophy (and, not by coincidence, also something of a mentor to Marshall in the 1880s). But Maurice himself was not particularly enthusiastic about Hegel. The index to his 1,250-page *Life and Letters* lists only three references to Hegel, and of these one is in passing and one is ambivalent.[76] Nevertheless, Mansel's implied suggestion that Maurice's theology was a form of Hegelianism was not altogether off the mark and indeed provides a useful perspective on the nature of Marshall's new metaphysical faith.

Maurice's incarnationalist theology emerged out of the Coleridgean thought on which the Broad Church movement had been founded in the first half of the nineteenth century. An important plank in this liberal Anglican theological edifice was set in the 1820s when Hare, Thirlwall, and, most importantly, Arnold constructed what Duncan Forbes has called the "liberal Anglican idea of history." According to Forbes, the origins of this idea of history are to be found in Coleridge's romantic philosophy of the mind, which, he says, "brought about of necessity a real revolution in historical thinking."[77] At the heart of the liberal Anglican philosophy of history was an idea of "real" moral and intellectual progress in the histories of the various nations of mankind. The emphasis on national as opposed to universal progress, Forbes explains, was a necessary corollary of the need to maintain a clear dualism between natural and moral forms of development, between natural evolution and providential moral progress. Thus, in his *Guesses at Truth*, Hare criticized Hegel for not clearly distinguishing between God and nature, and so proclaiming a pantheist historicism that failed to take due account of the fostering superintendence by which alone any real good is elicited.[78] And it was precisely on this ground that Thirlwall objected to what he perceived to be a monistic tendency in the infamous liberal Anglican volume *Essays and Reviews*.[79] The split within the Broad Church movement that followed the publication of *Essays and Reviews* in 1860 was thus very much a divide between the more orthodox theological dualism of an old guard of liberal Anglicans, represented by the likes of Thirlwall, and a new incarnationalist version of Coleridgean theology that

---

[76] For the third, see Maurice 1884, I: 467. Groenewegen suggests that Maurice directly encouraged Marshall to read Hegel's *Philosophy of History* (Groenewegen 1990: 67; 1995: 166n).

[77] Forbes 1952: viii; see also p. 126. For Hare and Thirlwall, see Searby 1997: 364–70.

[78] Forbes 1952: 65.

[79] See Forbes 1952: 85–6.

looked to Maurice for inspiration as it sailed close to the winds of a monistic heterodoxy. What Mansel had thus put his finger on, then, with his implicit association of Maurice and Jowett with Hegelianism, was the increasingly pantheistic implications of the recent development of a Broad Church theology that was associated particularly with Maurice and Jowett.

Maurice was a theologian. All his writings are colored by the intrinsically theological nature of his thought. Marshall, after 1872, definitively abandoned theology, both with regard to his own personal beliefs concerning God, salvation, and the afterlife, and also as a means of establishing the ground of scientific knowledge. In this respect the divide between Maurice and Marshall is pretty much absolute. But from the standpoint of today's more secular world, it is not at all clear that Marshall can really be said to have abandoned religious thought. Mansel's separation of the knowable and the unknowable, which with Spencer and Huxley became the separation of science from theology, is today recognizably modern. By the same token, however, Maurice's vision of a direct and inexpressible knowledge of the divine, like his vague pantheism, is distinctly echoed in the numerous varieties of "spiritual new age" beliefs that have been flourishing in ever more popular forms in Britain since at least the 1890s. Together, it is tempting to say, Mansel and Maurice established the two poles around which, as theological doctrine has progressively fallen away, British religious thought and spiritual feeling have hovered ever since. What today we have lost, what today is irrecoverable by either professional scientists or anarchistic "new agers," is a faith in the past and future progress of society. We have lost, in other words, precisely that element of Maurice's theological faith that was mirrored in Marshall's metaphysical faith.

Such a faith, however, was by no means an invention of the nineteenth century. Augustine long ago recognized the dangers of a prophetic religiosity that looked to contemporary social life for signs of those apocalyptic days foretold in the Bible. But from Eusebius through Joachim de Fiore and the medieval alliances of peasants, Franciscans, and German emperors, a Christian faith in contemporary history as the arena of social redemption had flourished. In the modern period, such an unorthodox strain of Christianity was given rationalistic philosophical form, and not only by Hegel.[80] As we saw in the introduction to this book, mainstream early modern philosophy was characterized by a belief that both God and His moral

---

[80] For a discussion of Hegel as a part of the Joachimite tradition, see Dickey 1987. On Marx's thought as a further stage in the history of rationalistic religious thought, see Gareth Stedman Jones's introduction to the *Communist Manifesto* (Marx, Engels, and Jones 2002).

ordinances for the world were knowable. In the hands of Reid and Stewart, this tradition of moral realism had been readily developed, first by Reid into a utopian ideal of a future political state and then by Stewart into a historicist vision of godly social progress toward that ideal. By way of his reading of Hegel, Marshall effectively aligned himself with this rationalistic, unorthodox, but quite distinctly Protestant tradition.

ECONOMIC FOUNDATIONS

A further word is in order here concerning the relationship between Marshall's early historical studies, his earlier philosophical studies, and his ongoing study of political economy. As we have seen, in his long historical essay Marshall effectively demonstrated that, properly speaking, both the economy and the science that studies it were products only of the modern world. Hence Marshall's neo-Hegelian philosophy of the history of modern social life stands at the very foundation of his mature conception of both the modern economy and modern economic science. Yet as will become clear in the last chapter of this book, the conception of modern history that Marshall had arrived at by late 1872, while providing the starting point for his mature vision of the progress of modern society, did not remain unaltered as his economic and philosophical thought developed. Furthermore, Marshall's adaptation of Hegel's philosophy of history strays farthest from the original when it comes to his account of the modern world, and it is by no means a simple task to discern the precise shape of his thinking on this period at this time. Thus, before turning in the last chapters of this book to the development of Marshall's economic and philosophical thought after 1872, it is important that we identify the basic elements of his *initial* neo-Hegelian conception of modern history.

We can approach this task by noting that in light of the exposition of Marshall's history of civilization given earlier, one might well conclude that a tension or even contradiction exists between Marshall's account of history before and after the Germanic invasions of Europe.[81] Marshall's account of modern European history was informed by recent comparative historical scholarship, which compared different peoples of the same racial family at different stages of social development; for example, Maine contrasted stationary Hindu with progressive Roman law, these two peoples being of the same Aryan stock. Consequently, such scholarship not

---

[81] Such, at any rate, was the premature conclusion that I drew in my initial interpretations of Marshall's historical essay (see *ECAM*, 35, and my introduction to *EHC*).

only defined progress as relative to a particular race, but indeed tended
to regard progress as confined only to the Aryan peoples. Such a conception of progress stood in direct opposition to Hegel's notion of "universal
history" and his narrative of the smooth development of subjective freedom across Chinese, Indian, and Israelite civilizations. Thus, despite the
"parallelisms" that Marshall discerned between the narratives of Hegel
and Maine, there would seem to be reason to believe that his synthesis of
these two narratives remained incomplete. That Marshall was aware of the
potential tension between these two historical approaches is demonstrated
by one of his early historical notes in which he records Max Müller's complaint that Hegel treats "religions as languages used to be treated." That is,
he classifies "them according to age, or place, or a stage of advancement.
They ought to be classified genealogically."[82] In fact, Marshall was able to
reconcile these two opposing perspectives on history, and the way that he
did so established the groundwork of his subsequent thinking on the philosophy of modern history.

Marshall's notion of historical progress as a whole is fully intelligible only
once we grasp that it was founded on a historical translation of his early
psychological project. That is, in his conception of historical progress, each
of the three levels of the psychological model (lower mechanical, spiritual,
and higher mechanical) is associated with a particular stage in the evolution of human civilization. Primitive societies, we should recall, are for
Marshall closely analogous to a beehive or an ant colony; as in the animal
world, behavior is there determined by inherited instincts, habits, and their
social equivalent, customs. From our earlier exegesis of "Ye Machine," it
should be clear that such behavior can be explained solely in terms of the
lower-level mechanical circuits of the mind. Thus the analysis of this stage
of social organization belongs to the natural scientist or (what is in fact the
same thing) the Spencerian sociologist. The second stage – the history of
civilization that Marshall traces from China and India to the appearance of
Christianity – is a history of the emergence of self-consciousness and moral
freedom; as such the study of this stage requires the a priori insights of the
philosopher. After these natural and spiritual stages of development, the
third phase of human evolution, which is coextensive with the Christian
Era, involves the initiation and ever-increasing use of the higher circuitry
of the mind, as individuals deliberate on particular courses of action. Such
deliberation presupposes the moral freedom that rests on self-consciousness
but can and of itself be analyzed mechanically. This last stage of human

---

[82] M 4/10, f. 24 (the passage is copied from Müller 1867: 21).

evolution thus brings together both self-consciousness and mechanism, and is the domain of the moral scientist.

This psychological underpinning of Marshall's philosophy of history gave rise to a conception of social evolution as necessarily gradual. It will be recalled that at the heart of Marshall's mechanical model of the mind is a notion of accumulated automatic routines, such that automatic lower-level circuits are gradually built up over time and then inherited by offspring. Thus each of these three stages inevitably shades into that which comes after. Early Christians, for example, might well have appealed to their newly discovered moral consciousness as a first step in their recently acquired ability to deliberate on different courses of action. Nevertheless, human beings are creatures of habit, and these early Christians could not escape the fact that, without constant self-conscious moral intervention, their inherited mental circuitry would automatically generate habitual actions and routines that had been formed in the distant pre-Christian past – hence the necessity for what Hegel had described as the thorough education of the heart, the will, and the intelligence before potentiality could become actuality. Thus the history of the Christian Era to date has consisted in a long and slow process of collective reeducation, whereby continued self-conscious reflection and moral deliberation have gradually had the effect of rewiring and reconnecting the lower-level, or automatic, "mental circuitry" of the human race. But reflection on this process of rewiring leads to the recognition that the course of reeducation might follow different paths among different peoples, and the implication of this is that universal history must give way to particular or racial history at the point where attention focuses on mechanical circuitry as opposed to moral freedom (which, to be clear, is the case both in primitive societies and in the Christian Era, but not in the history of the ancient world spanning the period between Indian and Chinese civilizations and the appearance of Christianity). In a word, the progress of the spirit is universal, but that of mechanical circuitry is local.

In the first instance, then, Marshall achieved his Coleridgean reconciliation of opposing historical narratives by placing his psychological model into a historical framework. From the perspective of this synthesis, Hegel had been right to sketch a universal history in the pre-Christian Era, but the diversity of collective customs and inherited habits in the Christian Era necessitated a comparative method of historical scholarship. Thus the means of reconciling opposing historical points of view is to be found in a division of the element of time, and we may suspect that Marshall was here inspired by his successful reconciliation of opposing theories of value but a year or so previously. The analogy, however, is not exact, for the division is now simply between ancient and modern modes of historical development (as opposed to short- and long-period perspectives). However, the reconciliation of historical approaches is not quite so straightforward. As we have seen, Marshall held that the history of the Christian Era is in part a history of the development of different institutional forms of objective freedom, which in themselves are but particular realizations of self-consciousness on the social level. Thus the Christian Era is the site of both mechanical and spiritual development. The moral scientist, who studies the present and the immediate past, and looks to the future, must therefore bring to bear on his studies an attention to *both* spiritual and mechanical factors.

For Marshall, the various histories of modern European nations were the result of different paths taken by the interaction of mechanical character, on the one hand, and political and legal institutions, on the other. These social institutions were, more or less, manifestations of objective freedom. Here, of course, we are brought up against the fact that, while it is evident that Marshall dissented from Hegel's identification of objective freedom with a constitutional monarchy, it is not clear how he did envisage objective freedom. In fact, and as will become apparent in the last chapter of this book, Marshall's thinking on modern history became fully clear only when he revised and refined his Hegelian terms in 1875 and in the process came to posit objective freedom as but a step along the way to a telos of modern history that he would come to describe as "collective freedom." Nevertheless, Marshall's mature ideas in 1875 developed out of an earlier characterization of the comparative political and social histories of modern France and England. To properly understand this early comparison, we must return to that point in his historical essay where Hegel's *Philosophy of History* meets up with, and then increasingly gives way to, the narratives of Maine and other more recent nineteenth-century historical authorities. This point is the invasion of the western Roman Empire by Germanic tribes.

In addressing this pivotal moment, Marshall first of all sets out Hegel's position that the Germans brought to a Roman civilization "an entirely new Spirit by which the world was to be regenerated, the Free Spirit – namely – which reposes in itself – the absolute self determination ... of subjectivity."[83] Marshall does not explicitly dissent from this position, but he nevertheless downplays the significance of the free Germanic spirit. He observes, for example, that the French historian "Guizot has taken the trouble to find for every German custom described by Tacitus, corresponding customs

---

[83] *EHC*, M 4/12, ff. 11–12; Hegel 1991: 356.

of North American Indians."[84] His conclusion, in fact, is that the Germans "seem distinguished from other barbarians only by personal independence combined with personal affection and fidelity. Custom ruled with them."[85] Such a conclusion allows Marshall, once he has moved from the ancient Teutonic mark to the feudal manor, to adopt Maine's analysis of feudalism as "a compound of archaic barbarian usage with Roman law." For Maine, the most striking characteristic of the "customs and institutions of barbarians" was "their extreme uniformity." But where archaic communities were held together by sentiment and instinct, feudal society was held together by a multitude of contractual ties and obligations left over from Roman law. It was this mixture of custom and Roman law, as opposed to some supposed spirit of Germanic freedom, that for Maine constituted the origin of "the irregular and various contour of modern civilisation."[86] Fusing Maine's position with that of Hegel, Marshall thus arrived at a perspective in which the origin of modern Europe was the product not merely of a universal development of spirit, but also of specific social institutions.

Now, passing over several areas of contention among nineteenth-century scholars (such as the extent of the development of feudalism in England before the Norman Conquest), we note that the various European feudal societies were generally considered to be fairly similar. It was in the transition from feudalism to modern commercial society that national divergences were seen to appear and develop, both on the level of objective freedom and on that of subjective character. In both France and England, the towns became islands of free commercial activity surrounded by a sea of feudalism. But according to the standard explanation of this time, the most immediate source of which was the writings of Guizot, French and English histories now diverged as a result of the different set of alliances formed between the crown, the feudal lords, and the new third estate. Thus, as the English positivist J. H. Bridges wrote of England in his study *France under Richelieu and Colbert* (1866):

In England the monarchical character of feudalism was exceptionally strong; here too there was a quasi feudal element, that of the Saxon gentry, who sharing the oppression of their countrymen in the towns shared too their resistance & were ultimately joined by the great Barons. Hence the peculiar character of the English constitution: aristocratic rather than monarchic, provincial rather than metropolitan, localised not centralised.[87]

---

[84] *EHC*, M 4/12, f. 18.
[85] *EHC*, M 4/12, f. 15.
[86] Maine 1866: 366 [ML].
[87] M 4/1, ff. 287, 289. The passage is a loose quotation from Bridges 1866: 13–14. It is taken from Marshall's loose-leaf book of the late 1860s (and therefore illustrates his historical

By contrast in France, Bridges explained, the burghers of the towns had formed an alliance with the crown against the feudal lords. Hence, where England had witnessed Magna Carta, a balanced national constitution in which Parliament exerted a check on the crown, and local government reflected the power of the lords and local gentry, France had followed a road that led to royal absolutism and political centralization. Marshall found a story in Maine that complemented this account (with English common law descending from Germanic codes, and the French legal system arising out of an alliance between natural lawyers and the crown).[88] But it was de Tocqueville who seems to have provided for Marshall the key to the crucial relationship between the political and legal institutions associated with objective freedom, on the one hand, and the mechanics of national character, on the other.

In his *Ancien Régime* (1856), de Tocqueville drew on the conclusions of his *Democracy in America* in order to explain the apparent continuity of French history before and after the Revolution. For de Tocqueville, the long period of pre-revolutionary absolutism and centralization had molded the feelings, habits, hearts, and minds of the French people in a manner that no mere political revolution could alter. An entrenched national character, which was marked by individual conformity and the absence of any sense of public duty, had produced a uniform society with an inherent tendency toward despotic rule and centralized administration. Thus, rather than the *philosophes* with their Anglophone ideas of political liberty, the true eighteenth-century spokesmen of the coming revolution were the Physiocrats, who combined a call for economic liberty with a celebration of political absolutism.[89] De Tocqueville's *Ancien Régime* was the source of many of Marshall's historical notes, both on modern French history in general (where it was used side by side with Bridges' *France under Richelieu and*

---

reading and interests in a period before his serious and systematic study of history, when, as is illustrated by many of his historical notes, Marshall would again turn to Bridge's book).

[88] Maine 1866: ch. 4. [ML].

[89] Note that in his copy of Mill's 1840 review of de Tocqueville's *Democracy in America*, Marshall marked, "Equality may be equal freedom or equal servitude. America is the type of the first; France [de Tocqueville] thinks, is in danger of falling into the second" (Mill 1859: 8 [ML]). Again, Marshall marked Mill's observation that de Tocqueville holds the condition of France to be one "in which the equalization of conditions has made greater progress than the spirit of liberty" (Mill 1859: 22 [ML]). On Tocqueville's *Ancien Régime*, see Herr 1962. For a critical appraisal of the distortions passed on to later generations of commentators by de Tocqueville's account of Physiocracy in his *Ancien Régime*, see Hochstrasser 2006.

Colbert) and as background on the Physiocrats. On a more abstract level, however, it can readily be seen how de Tocqueville provided Marshall with a means of relating objective freedom and national character. In England the decentralized constitution had fostered habits of political liberty and self-reliance that had become enduring features of the national character. In France, by contrast, a tradition of royal absolutism and political centralization had not only instilled habits and social instincts that were alien to free political life, but had given rise to the despotic ideology of the Physiocrats.

It was de Tocqueville who provided the key to Marshall's neo-Hegelian conception of the relationship between politics and economics. Marshall's "Whig" version of Hegel's philosophy of history, at least as set down in his long historical essay, identified objective freedom not with Hegel's ideal of a constitutional monarchy, but with the Italian trading republics, the free towns of the Middle Ages, and English parliamentary traditions. We can now see that this revision of Hegel's ideal of the constitution of the modern state was grounded in Marshall's psychological theory. Different constitutional arrangements are the product of, and also foster, different sets of mechanical habits. But not only does the national character direct the political arrangements of a modern nation, it also goes far toward determining the economic life of that nation. The nature of the English constitution, Marshall clearly believed, had hitherto fostered habits of free enterprise as well as personal liberty whereas, the Physiocratic belief in free trade notwithstanding, the French tendency toward social conformity was as corrosive to economic as it was to political liberty. Properly speaking, objective freedom had not existed in France before the Revolution, and its tumultuous and unstable existence in the nineteenth century was a consequence of the formation of a particular type of national character during a long period of absolutist and centralized government.

But if objective freedom was confined to democratic or republican forms of government, the examples of the Italian trading republics and French boroughs illustrated the fact that there could indeed be varieties of objective freedom in the modern world. The next stage in the development of this neo-Hegelian social philosophy came in 1875, when Marshall contrasted England not with France, but with America. What this contrast revealed was that modern freedom could take different forms and that these forms could be explained as the product of different economic conditions, which in turn gave rise to different types of national character. Such varieties of national character fostered different forms of political organization: for

Marshall, American industrial conditions contained the seed of true democracy, while English conditions fostered republican self-government and cooperative association – the seed of a further development of objective freedom. We must turn in the next chapter, however, to the economic and political lessons that Marshall drew in the period immediately following his intensive and extensive historical studies.

SEVEN

Missing Links: The Education of the Working Classes

INTRODUCTION

Mill's *Principles of Political Economy* was structured around a binary distinction between the doctrines of economic science and the moral applications of social philosophy. Yet as we have seen, in his 1876 essay on Mill's theory of value Marshall insisted on describing Mill's organization of the subject matter of political economy as a tripartite arrangement. As Marshall here presented the plan of Mill's *Principles*, the machinery of exchange stood side by side with the "natural laws" of production, on the one hand, and the particular "social arrangements" that determined the mode of distribution, on the other. For Mill, the machinery of exchange constituted a merely instrumental (i.e., noncausal) portion of political economy. For Marshall, this machinery was identified as "the proper province of 'pure' or 'abstract' economic investigations," and the tendency toward equilibrium of supply and demand was held up as the "central truth" of political economy. In the same essay, Marshall observed in passing that experience had shown that "in some details" Mill's tripartite arrangement was "not wholly successful."[1] In this chapter both the raising of the epistemic status of the theory of value and the criticism of Mill's arrangement of the subject matter of political economy will be related to Marshall's early encounter with Hegel.

If the various parts of this chapter do not form a rounded whole, this is because the chapter is concerned with the developments in Marshall's economic thinking that occurred in the immediate wake of his historical studies around 1873. At this time Marshall had not yet integrated the different social and economic lessons that he had learned from his study of Hegel. Already in his essay on the history of civilization, Marshall had identified subjective

---

[1] *MTV*, 126; and see p. 165 above.

freedom as the ground of economic action. What we shall discover in this chapter is that by 1873 Marshall had come to see social progress in terms of an education of mechanical character that allowed the self-conscious individual to realize his potential. In other words, Marshall looked to self-consciousness as the foundation and also as the end point of modern economic life. But between these two conceptions of self-consciousness, between, that is, self-consciousness as the foundation of market freedom and as the ground of social progress, Marshall was as yet unable to draw any clear connection. With the benefit of hindsight (or, at least, the arguments of the following chapter), this missing link in Marshall's social philosophy can be related to the fact that in 1873 he chose to pass over in silence the complicated relationship between mechanical character and political organization that, as we saw at the end of the preceding chapter, was already a part of his historical thinking. Instead, Marshall defined progress in terms of a simple contrast between the potential of self-consciousness and the actuality of mechanical mental circuitry, such that an extension and intensification of the education of the mechanical character of the working classes would propel British society toward an as yet unfulfilled potential.

Nevertheless, Marshall's achievements by 1873 were considerable. In revising his earlier Coleridgean division between the university and the economy, he was able to take several steps forward in his thinking about wages. In the early 1870s, Marshall came to believe that a liberal education fostered precisely those character traits that were the key to understanding the peculiar workings of the labor market. Employers would pay more for an educated worker, and they would do so in the knowledge that the resultant increase in output would more than recompense any increase in their present wage bill. Not only did such a perspective point the way to a new theory of wages, it also provided the grounds for a new liberal vision in which social progress was to be achieved by a massive injection of higher education into the political nation. The connection between education and productivity ensured that, in the long run, such a national investment would more than pay for itself. The vastly increased provision of higher education would also elevate the moral character of members of the working classes, transforming them into "gentlemen." But before examining how Marshall arrived at a political vision in which the universal provision of higher education ensured the realization of spiritual potential, we must first turn to the way in which, in the same period, he positioned subjective freedom as the foundation of modern economic life.

THE "CENTRAL DOCTRINE" OF VALUE

"After the primary necessities of food and raiment, freedom is the first and strongest want of human nature."[2] That Marshall marked this sentence in Mill's *The Subjection of Women* (1869) should not surprise us. Although his philosophical idea of freedom was very different from that held by Mill, both were nevertheless agreed not only on the vital social importance of liberty, but also on the notion that it was their capacity for free moral choice that distinguished humans from the rest of the natural world. Yet the economic doctrines presented in Mill's *Principles of Political Economy* were constructed around such brute facts of human existence as the necessity for subsistence, the animal instinct to procreate, and the self-regarding motivations that drove "economic man." Mill certainly had much to say about the role of free will in society, but what he said was derived from his social philosophy, not from his political economy. As a political economist, Mill was simply concerned to demonstrate certain hypothetical social tendencies that, other things being equal, could be expected to operate in a uniform law-governed manner. Such tendencies were deduced from a handful of initial assumptions, which themselves were derived from the physical sciences and from psychology. As De Marchi has pointed out, one great merit of this a priori method, as Mill called it, was that it allowed the political economist to claim the same demonstrative certainty, and hence the same authority in social matters, that the experimental method provided for the natural philosopher in the study of physical nature.[3] Such demonstrative certainty was established, however, by effectively removing free will from the subject matter of political economy.

Marshall very early on discarded Mill's methodological formulations. We have already seen that in his advanced lecture notes he not only insisted that the economist employed induction as well as deduction, but also provided an idealist and historical derivation of some of the "fundamental propositions" of political economy. His distance from Mill became insurmountable with the composition of "On Value." In this essay, the value in use of a commodity to an individual was defined simply as "the value of the things which must be given him in order that he may be induced to give it up"; in other words, value is publicly observable and physically measurable. As Marshall explained in his 1876 essay on Mill, a commodity should be "regarded as the embodiment of measurable efforts and sacrifices."[4] To measure such value

---

[2]   Mill 1869: 178 [ML] (*Mill CW*, 21: 336).
[3]   De Marchi 2002: 316–17.
[4]   See p. 165 above.

required observation of the market, and from this external perspective it was irrelevant whether the value in use of a commodity to an individual was the product of selfish, sympathetic, or even altruistic designs.[5] Analysis of the machinery of exchange did not rest on any introspectively derived principles supplied by the psychologist. A key step towards the discarding of Mill's a priori method was therefore taken when Marshall proclaimed that the "central doctrine" of the science of political economy was not some theory of efforts and sacrifices, but rather that instrument which allowed for the public measurement of those efforts and sacrifices.

But considerations arising from thoughts on methodology were reinforced by reflections on the philosophy of history. As we saw in the preceding chapter, in his historical essay Marshall insisted that trade, properly speaking, had come into being only at that moment in the history of civilization at which passive acquiescence to habits and customs was replaced by "the habit of determination of his conduct on the part of each individual so as to obtain most completely his own ends." This application to the economic realm of Hegel's notion of subjective freedom constituted a seminal step in Marshall's intellectual development. From this point onward, he would regard an ultimately metaphysical notion of moral freedom as describing the fundamental ground of modern industrial life. Of course, such characteristics as independence and self-determination of ends had already been implicitly ascribed to those hypothetical buyers and sellers who populated the markets of "On Value." But in conjunction with his reflections on methodology, Marshall's engagement with Hegel's *Philosophy of History* now led him to conceive of market behavior as founded on self-consciousness and to place a notion of moral freedom at the very foundation of his conception of modern economic life.

In his 1876 essay, Marshall insisted not only that Mill had held a subjective theory of value, but also that this theory constituted "Mill's central doctrine."[6] By arguing that Mill's carelessness of expression had given rise to the mistaken impression that he had explained value in terms of the material costs of production, as opposed to the subjective measure of those costs, Marshall was attempting to do more than merely recruit Mill posthumously in support of his own theory of value. He was also preparing the

---

5 The connection between measurement and the fact that economic motivations may be sympathetic as well as selfish was emphasized by Marshall in his 1885 inaugural lecture (Pigou 1925: 158–9), while the connection between measurement and the scientific status of economics was set out in the introductory pages of the *Principles of Economics* (*Principles*, I: 31).

6 *MTV*, 128.

ground for disassociating the theory of value from necessity and automatic behavior, and identifying it firmly with that which is most distinctly human in economics, that is, freedom. By commencing his essay with an overview of Mill's organization of political economy, Marshall thus prepared the way for his subsequent identification of value theory with the "human will" as opposed to "natural laws." And by claiming that Mill's theory of value was his "central doctrine," Marshall was in effect repositioning political economy firmly within the realm of freedom as opposed to the realm of necessity.

By the 1880s, it is worth noting, Marshall's meditation on the philosophy of modern history had led him to revise as well as to reinterpret Mill's economic legacy. Of particular importance in this context was his recasting of what for Mill had been a simple binary opposition between custom and competition. In his *Principles*, Mill argued that while custom had regulated social and economic relations throughout most of human history, nevertheless it had largely (but by no means entirely) been replaced by competition as the regulating principle of modern industrial life.[7] Through his historical studies, Marshall would eventually arrive at a more sophisticated conception of the relationship between competition and custom. Subjective freedom, as the internal ground of competition, had indeed arisen in opposition to those primitive habits and customs that replaced the need for "pure thought." But as we saw in the preceding chapter, such moral deliberations wrought new – more moral and civilized – habits and customs; and in fact it was possible for two different economic nations to both enjoy a basic liberty in the economic sphere and yet be characterized by fairly divergent patterns of political and legal institutions, local customs, and mental habits. The machinery of supply and demand analysis, which took a particular market as its unit of analysis, presupposed that subjective freedom which was the ground of competition and yet was flexible enough to take local variations of custom and habit in its stride. In the modern world, competition did not replace but rather cohabited with a variety of customs and habits (an increasing number of which were inculcated by way of economic activities).

By turning to Hegel, Marshall in his historical work had effectively answered the criticism of the deductive tradition of political economy that Cliffe Leslie had put forward in his 1870 essay on Adam Smith. As observed

---

[7] *Mill CW*, 2: 239–40. Mill argued that while in nineteenth-century Britain competition by no means exercised an unlimited sway, political economists nevertheless had a tendency to neglect custom and assume unlimited competition, because only by so doing was it possible to deduce hypothetical laws with regard to rents, profits, wages, and prices.

in Chapter One, Cliffe Leslie claimed that Smith's method of deduction was grounded on a discredited natural law tradition and argued that for this reason the entire tradition of deductive political economy from Smith through J. S. Mill must be rejected. By 1873 Marshall had come to accept the need to reject what he took to be the ancient and pagan modes of expression contained in the writings of not only Smith, but also Ricardo and even J. S. Mill. But for Marshall, deductive reasoning remained valid, provided, that is, that it abandoned the postulate of a universal human nature and was founded rather on a modern, moral, and historicist conception of character. Thus, in the 1879 *Economics of Industry*, the term "natural value" was decisively rejected in favor of "normal value."[8] The historicist foundations of the deductions involved in establishing "normal values," however, could be framed in two different ways. Both of these approaches can be found in the *Economics of Industry*, which Marshall co-authored with his wife, Mary Paley Marshall, and which was first published in 1879. In the third book of this volume, Cliffe Leslie's ongoing researches into local variations in prices, profits, and wages received close attention, and the Marshalls suggested that even within a single political nation there was not always free migration of capital and labor.[9] The implication of such local variation was that deductive methods could be applied only to limited ranges of economic phenomena. In the following years, Marshall would become increasingly convinced of the importance of local variations in customs and habits, and in his *Principles* he went out of his way to warn of the need for contextually sensitive and case-by-case applications of his deductive machinery of supply and demand analysis.[10]

---

[8] The connection between Marshall's substitution of "normal value" for "natural value" and his determination to free the language of economic science from "eighteenth century metaphysical notions as to Nature" is clearly spelled out in a footnote to Marshall's 1885 inaugural lecture (Pigou 1925: 157n). Note that, as Ian Hacking has pointed out, our "modern usage of the very word 'normal' evolved in a medical context" and derives from pathology by way of Comte (Hacking 1990: 165). Marshall was evidently well aware of this derivation (see, e.g., *Principles*, I: 34, 35–6), and he no doubt intended this term to suggest a link between his mechanical analysis of the market and his biological approach to production.

[9] See *EI*, bk III, ch. III; Dardi 1984; the discussion by Becattini and Dardi in *ECAM*, 56; and Becattini's essay "Economic Nations" in the same volume (pp. 203–9). In the early 1870s Marshall placed in his collection of bound periodical articles two papers by Cliffe Leslie dealing with these themes (Leslie 1872, 1874 [BV, ML]).

[10] Whitaker observes that after 1875 Marshall "increasingly repudiated" formal theory "as the proper path to useful economic knowledge, seeking instead to remain in close touch with economic reality and calling on formal arguments only to clarify restricted points" (*ECAM*, 42–3). For a useful summary of the conflicting interpretations offered by Whitaker and Dardi on Marshall's manuscripts of the late 1880s, see Raffaelli 2003: 40–3.

But Marshall's neo-Hegelianism also allowed for a less rigorously historicist approach to deductive political economy. This was in fact the route that he took in the immediate wake of his encounter with Hegel, when the primary moral drawn from Hegel and the study of history was simply that a postulate of universal human nature must be rejected. For the political economist, the derivative lesson was that economic laws are operative only across populations in which moral self-determination has become a dominant characteristic. In other words, the Hegelian lesson of history could be read solely in broad terms that assumed away any significance of the various regional divergences in local habits and customs that had developed since the Middle Ages. This broader reading of history clearly limited the range of deductive political economy to modern (i.e., post-medieval Christian) civilization. Nevertheless, it left deductive economics a free hand with regard to a fairly large swathe of modern history. From this point of view, the defining feature of modern economic life was not variation in local customs and habits, but the general play of free competition. Seen from this broader perspective, there was no reason that some version of traditional economic doctrines concerning long-period wage rates and accumulation should not be applicable to the present, the recent past, and the not too distant future. Of course, by 1873 Marshall was satisfied neither with Mill's formulation of the orthodox theory of wages nor with his own attempted reformulation of this theory in "On Wages." But from the perspective of this broad reading of the philosophy of history, it should have been possible, at least in theory, to improve on the essay "On Wages." That is, this broad historicism was eminently compatible with an intention to frame accounts of "normal wages" and "normal profits" by means of the old Ricardian doctrines, reformulated with the aid of supply and demand analysis. This was in fact what the Marshalls attempted to do in the second book of the *Economics of Industry*.[11]

Such differences and developments do not reflect a movement away from a notion of subjective freedom as foundational to modern economic life.

---

[11] The analytical distinction between the second and third books of the *Economics of Industry* (entitled "Normal Value" and "Market Value," respectively) would turn on the fact that perfect competition was assumed in the second and not in the third book. By the same token, the distinction between the analysis of normal values in the *Economics of Industry* and that in the *Principles of Economics* was that in the former book "normal value" was defined as that value which, other things being equal, competition would bring about in the long period, whereas in the *Principles* the term was explicitly defined independently of competition. See *EI*, 148, and *Principles*, I: 33–4. On the different formulations of normal values in these two books, see Vahabi's entry on normal value in *ECAM*, 273–80, and Whitaker 1982.

Rather, they are evidence of a growing tension between orthodox political economy and Marshall's increasingly sophisticated theoretical approach to the diverse local customs and habits that are found in the modern world. As we shall see in the concluding chapter of this book, the dawning recognition of the role played by local habits and customs in impeding the free circulation of commodities eventually found a parallel in Marshall's mature theory of production, in which modern industrial organizations were envisaged as training character, and hence engendering a limited range of habits, appropriate for the new industrial age. It was this twofold development that led Marshall to declare in the introduction to his *Principles* that the "fundamental character of modern industrial life is not competition," but rather a combination of self-reliance and independence, on the one hand, and a "habit of choosing one's own course" and a "habit of forecasting the future and shaping one's course with reference to distant aims," on the other.[12] Such a definition of modern industrial life brought together the economic manifestations of self-consciousness, on the one hand, and those particular mental habits that were the product of, rather than an impediment to, economic progress on the other, But further discussion of Marshall's mature thought must await the following chapter. For now, we must return to Marshall's more straightforward, not to say simplistic, historicist reading of modern history and explore how in 1873 he attempted to reformulate the theories of production and distribution in light of this reading.

Here we would do well to return, once again, to Marshall's 1876 discussion of Mill's tripartite division of the subject matter of political economy. Mill's theory of value was essentially an appendage to his grand theme of the confrontation of economic necessity with moral freedom. As we have seen, Marshall placed his own subjective theory of value firmly on the side of moral freedom. Nevertheless, the machinery of exchange by no means encompassed all aspects of Mill's social philosophy. As we saw in Chapter Five, a determination to bring the conditions of higher mental development within the province of the economist was one of the factors which ensured that, in his advanced lecture notes, Marshall would insist that political economy could not be narrowly defined as catallactics. As Marshall put it in his 1876 essay, a "chemist's balance takes not account of the medical properties of an ounce of arsenic; but the chemist does."[13] In other words, there was more to "the distinctly human element in economics" than the machinery of exchange and the measurement of motivations, and political

---

[12] *Principles*, I: 5.
[13] *MTV*, 125.

economy as a whole must include doctrines that pertained to the development of the human being. As already noted, in his 1876 essay Marshall had observed that "in some details" Mill's "arrangement is not wholly successful." What will be suggested in the following two sections is that Marshall here had in mind one specific element of the theory of production, which he had come to believe was as much a product of human will and social arrangements as it was of natural laws. This element was crucial to the mental and moral well-being of the individual, but in the early 1870s Marshall became convinced that it was also a vital, if hitherto overlooked, element of the doctrines of both production and distribution. This element was the production of educated human beings.

THE EDUCATION OF THE WORKING CLASSES

As noted briefly in Chapter Two, in the *Wealth of Nations* Smith had advised that some part of the primary education of the children of the common people should be paid for out of the public purse. As the division of labor in a nation intensifies, he had explained, so the employment of the great body of the people comes to be confined to a few very simple operations; and as the understandings of the greater number of men are necessarily formed by their ordinary employments, so the common people are liable to become "as stupid and ignorant as it is possible for a human creature to become."[14] In direct contrast to his conclusions concerning endowed institutions of higher education, Smith therefore counseled that there be established "in every parish or district a little school," the master being "partly, but not wholly paid by the public." Smith's reasons for calling for such public expenditure reflect the richness and complexities of his philosophical endeavor as a whole. A "man without the proper use of the intellectual faculties of a man" is "mutilated and deformed" in his nature, he explained, and therefore even if the state "was to derive no advantage from the instruction of the inferior ranks of people, it would still deserve its attention that they should not be altogether uninstructed."[15] But in addition, and as we saw in Chapter Two, civil society stood to gain much by educating the "inferior ranks" and thereby inoculating them against the public disturbances that were so often the fruit of the delusions of superstition and enthusiasm.

One of the folios of Marshall's early notes on the division of labor contains the following passage, translated and transcribed from Marx's *Kapital*: "In

[14] *WN*, 782 (V. i. f. 50).
[15] *WN*, 785–8 (V. i. f. 55–61).

order to prevent the complete deterioration of the masses wh[ich] would arise from division of labour A Smith recommends state instruction though in prudently homeopathic doses. G. Garnier his commentator consistently attacks this.... 'Education of the people conflicts with the first laws of the Division of labour & it would proscribe our whole social system.'"[16] But if in the early years of the nineteenth century French commentators had criticized Smith's "homeopathic" departure from the principles of laissez-faire, the consensus among mid-Victorian political economists was that in the case of the education of the nation's children, Smith had not gone nearly far enough in his call for state intervention. In an 1869 essay entitled "Endowments," for example, we find Mill arguing that "the capacity of free-trade to produce even the humblest article of a sufficient degree of goodness, depends on three conditions: First, the consumer must have the means of paying for it; secondly, he must care sufficiently for it; thirdly, he must be a sufficient judge of it. All three conditions are signally wanting in the case of national education."[17] Such arguments are already partly familiar to us from Chapter Two, where we saw Mill in 1835 utilizing the third – and perhaps also the second – of these conditions to support the case for endowed universities. In this essay of 1869, we find him arguing that in the case of national primary education, public support was also necessary because the working classes did not have sufficient means to pay for the education of their children. Like Smith, Mill believed that the education of the lower orders would constitute a good in itself. But Mill's nineteenth-century formulation of social philosophy also led him to look to universal education not as an antidote to religious enthusiasm, but as a means of raising a prudent and sympathetic population that would breed in moderation, that could be entrusted with the franchise in a representative democracy, whose improving character might eventually give rise to a reform of the social arrangements that determine the mode of distribution.

In the wake of the passage of the Second Reform Bill, Mill's conviction that the state must provide education for all children became mainstream in British politics. In 1870 Forster's Education Act established a national, and mainly free, system of compulsory state education for all children between the ages of five and twelve. Henceforth the national political debate was no longer whether education should be provided by the state, but rather what denominational form such state education would take. The national

---

[16] M 4/26, f. 35; Marx 1867: 348 [UL]. Germain Garnier published a French translation of the *Wealth of Nations* in 1802.

[17] *Mill CW*, 5: 622.

education debate, in other words, merged into a debate over the future of the established church.[18] For the academic liberals attending the meetings of the Cambridge Reform Club in the early 1870s, however, the underlying concern now became the need to extend the provision of higher, in addition to primary, education. As we saw in the first chapter of this book, these academic liberals were preoccupied with the political role of education in a democratic society. As Moulton explained in the first talk delivered at the Reform Club, the British, proud of their ancient liberties, would "rebel at the thought of a Bismarck's rule, even though we knew that his administration would be vastly more efficient than anything that we could hope to substitute for it." But while the British "trust and trust rightly to voluntary action and self-government," nevertheless the nation "must be educated if it is to act aright and be capable of self-government."[19] Such sentiments identify Moulton and other speakers at the Cambridge Reform Club as the political heirs of J. S. Mill. But the specific political concerns that informed the discussions of these Cambridge liberals in the early 1870s were quite different from the neo-Malthusian fears that had molded Mill's thinking on education earlier in the century. Consequently, in political economy as well as in political thought, this new generation of academic liberals moved decisively beyond Mill's analysis of the immediate benefits to be expected from the increased provision of education.

We have already noted Marshall's desire in his advanced lectures that political economy encompass the conditions of development of the "higher faculties." In his essay on the history of civilization, this concern was expressed in a more general form when he observed that "an uncultivated class" had existed in "all previous civilisations" and questioned whether such need be the case in "all those which are to come."[20] Both the concern with higher cultivation and the interest in the education of the working classes had clear roots in Mill's various writings. Yet Marshall's concern with cultivating the higher faculties of the working classes constituted a shift in emphasis from the basic tone of Mill's *Principles*; for while Mill had indeed looked forward to a future state in which the population as a whole devoted itself as much to culture as to making a living, his overriding concern had

---

[18] See Biagini 1995: 31–2.

[19] *RCP*, 3–5. Cf. de Tocqueville's statement in *Democracy in America* that if democracy "does not confer the most skillful kind of government upon the people," it nevertheless produces activity, energy, and force that "the most skilful governments are unable to awaken" (Tocqueville 1862, I: 295 [ML]). In his copy of de Tocqueville's book, Marshall marked this passage and wrote "NB" in the margin.

[20] *EHC*, M 3/1, f. 14.

been with providing a sufficient dose of primary education among the working classes as would lead to reproductive prudence, fostering the self-restraint of their animal passions. In other words, Mill looked to working-class education primarily as a remedy for Malthusian population pressures. As fears of overpopulation receded in the second half of the century and as agitation for franchise reform increased, so liberal discussions of the education of the working classes shifted focus.[21] By the early 1870s, and in the wake of the academic liberal concern over the results of the 1868 general election, capacity for citizenship had decisively replaced sexual prudence as the underlying concern of academic liberals. Cambridge liberals now began to look to national education to cultivate the higher faculties of members of the working classes, as opposed to merely subduing their animal instincts. As will become clear, such an elevation of the social role of national education would inspire Marshall with the conviction that it would ultimately be possible to bridge the cultural and material gulf that existed between the social classes of the nation.

The new academic liberal concern with education found practical expression in the university extension movement of the early 1870s, the origins of which can be traced in no small measure to the early discussions of the Cambridge Reform Club. The extension movement saw young Oxbridge dons touring the provincial centers of Britain with the object, as Marshall later put it, of causing "a desire for a collegiate education in the places in which the lectures were delivered."[22] By a "collegiate education," Marshall meant a liberal or general education, as opposed to merely a technical one. His early enthusiasm for providing such a liberal education to the working classes is evident in his own talk to the Cambridge Reform Club. But before turning to his thoughts on the education of the working classes, we should note that by the early 1870s he had come to revise his earlier conviction that the realms of commerce and culture related to different components of the mind and that political economy had no purchase on the higher realm of culture. Indeed, it is by first examining his reassessment of the economics

---

[21] For a sense of the state of Malthusian concerns around this time, see Newman 1871 [BV, ML].

[22] Groenewegen 1996: 21; 18, 185. A general history of the university extension movement can be found in Harrison 1961: ch. 6; the history of the Cambridge extension lectures is given in Roberts 1891 and Welch 1973. The extension teaching of political economy is described in Kadish 1993; for a discussion of the aims and successes of the extension movement with regard to working-class education, see also Kadish 1989: 107–8. For Marshall's account of the extension movement, see Groenewegen 1996: 21, 18, 185. In 1877 Foxwell credited Marshall with training the extension lecturers in political economy (*CAM*, I: 356).

of university education in the early 1870s that we can best understand a crucial development in his thinking about the labor market. Marshall in this period came to believe that wages reflected the relative efficiency of labor as opposed to its cost of production. The foundations of this belief were laid when he generalized to all ranks of labor a position that he first arrived at as an explanation of the wages of liberally educated labor.

As we saw in Chapter Two, Marshall insisted in his notes on Smith's article on education that "true men of learning" were motivated by selfless enthusiasm as opposed to the expectation of pecuniary reward. Such a position, we subsequently discovered, turned on the dualism between bodily and spiritual motivations that he had articulated in his early psychological project. But we should now note that this early commitment to a Coleridgean separation of culture from commerce went beyond the lessons actually provided by his psychological project. The division between mechanical thought and self-consciousness did indeed support the distinction between "ordinary" and "scholarly" minds that informed Marshall's writings on education in the late 1860s. Yet it did not support a distinction between two basic types of people so much as a distinction between two different states of mind that might coexist within any one person. Marshall never contemplated the possibility that some one individual might dispense entirely with mechanical routines; even the most enthusiastic scholar invariably relied on mental mechanisms for the vast majority of day-to-day activities. Furthermore, any person engaged in the ordinary business of life might, at some moment or other, engage in self-conscious reflection. And by the same token, while a scholarly mind might be self-motivated in terms of scientific research, it did not follow that the same scholar would inevitably be fueled by altruism in all other aspects of university life. In fact, and as Marshall gained more experience as a moral sciences lecturer, he evidently came to realize that even the most nobly minded research scientist might occasionally require some external stimulation when it came to finding the motivation required to teach undergraduates.

In a letter of 1871 to the *Cambridge University Reporter*, entitled "Celibacy in the University," Marshall effectively recanted a key argument of his earlier notes on Smith's article on education. He now pointed out that most college fellows regarded their fellowships as a temporary stage between graduation and finding a clerical living that enabled them to marry. Yet a "thorough knowledge" of any particular study could "be fully acquired only in a lifetime" (a lifetime involving much mechanical mental labor, we might add). The position of most fellows was therefore "similar to that of a farmer who has a short lease and who expects no compensation for improvements."

Yet "while the value of the Fellowships would be increased" if the celibacy requirement were abolished, the rate at which vacancies became available would drastically decrease. Furthermore, the pursuit of tripos success would become "even more intoxicating" than it was at present and consequently "the tendency to reaction after it even greater;" however, "there would be no possibility of removing those who fell into comparative lethargy." The solution Marshall proposed was that the period of a college fellowship should be limited and that at the end of this period fellows who wished to remain teachers and scholars should pass before a board composed of specialists in the candidate's chosen field of research. The income of the selected senior lecturers, Marshall further suggested, should derive from their original college fellowships, from a fixed annual sum from the college or university, and "as in Germany, part of his income would depend upon the number of his hearers and he would be kept up to his work by the competition of younger lecturers."[23] Not only could competition for monetary reward provide a spur to academic motivation, but Marshall had apparently decided that ordinary students might actually be capable judges of at least some aspects of professorial efforts.[24]

Such a change of opinion suggests a retreat from his early Coleridgean ideal of the university, but not a revision of his psychological theories; for while it might indeed be advisable (as Marshall claimed in his notes on Smith) for enthusiastic researchers whose work was extending the boundaries of knowledge to be engaged in teaching advanced classes, the business of even such advanced education was unlikely to be much more than a mechanical affair, in which the teacher showed the students how to work their brains so as to think like budding scientists.[25] Thus between 1869 and 1871 we can see Marshall moving away from the Coleridgean ideal of a liberal education as informal conversation held by Maurice and toward the more robustly physical ideal of education held by Fawcett and Stephen.

---

[23] *CAM*, I: 8–10.

[24] We cannot, however, conclude that Marshall had revised his initial agreement with Mill that, in the case of education, the public cannot form a proper judgment of the product; for the competition between lecturers is a competition that takes place between teachers who have already been stamped with an official seal of approval by the university itself; the situation is not analogous to that of the private coaches of earlier years.

[25] In his 1880 testimony to a parliamentary committee on education, Marshall made it clear that he believed that there was a conflict between research and the time taken up with reading examination papers (see Groenewegen 1996: 44, 59). Marshall's early lack of concern with the competition between teaching and research reflects the fact that in the late 1860s and early 1870s, moral science lecturers such as Venn and Marshall were able to use their teaching in order to develop their own research.

Like Fawcett and Stephen, Marshall held that competition in the tripos was itself an education in athletic character.[26] In other words, by 1871 Marshall had come to believe that the business of education was related as much, if not more, to that hardheaded and "masculine" ideal of character embraced by academic liberals like Fawcett and Stephen as it was to the romantic ideal of "manly character" as spiritual self-cultivation espoused by liberal Anglicans like Maurice. Of course, Marshall went beyond Fawcett in holding that lecturers at the university could also benefit from some external stimulation to effort. Indeed, the key point here is that such a revision of his former views provided Marshall with a crucial conceptual link between the business of education and the ordinary business of life.

In another letter of 1871, this time to the *Cambridge University Reporter*, Marshall argued that a Cambridge education must supply for students "the missing link between their school work and the business of their lives."[27] His argument was couched in terms of the need to forge a bridge between theory and practice. He complained that "while we have in England able practical men and able scientific men, we are lamentably deficient in practical men who understand science". Thus Marshall insisted that "it should be the special privilege of a highly educated man to be master of his rules." Such mastery was to come from knowledge taught by the university. This kind of knowledge would entail that each new rule that in later life the student encountered in his profession

would find its proper place in his system: his rules would increase his grasp of principles, his principles would enable him to understand his rules. Soon he would feel strong enough to modify old rules and to make new ones, to promote practice by applying it to science, and to promote science by supplying it with inductions.[28]

In this passage we find a very clear statement of what would henceforth provide the underlying philosophical framework of Marshall's conception of the relationship between the university and the wider society.[29] In a word,

---

[26] Note that in 1901 Marshall would complain that Maurice's disparagement of competition had tended to "emasculate character" (Pigou 1925: 394). It is possible that an identification of Cambridge examinations and masculine strength of character stands behind some of Marshall's later opposition to the granting of degrees to women students.

[27] *CAM*, I: 11.

[28] *CAM*, I: 11.

[29] This absorption of his arguments for education reform into his developing ideas on economic matters continued when in 1872 Marshall sent an untitled printed fly sheet to the Cambridge Senate. "We live amid a readily growing 'ardour of industrialism,'" he informed the Senate, and the result is that however "great his intellectual vigour," the "man engaged in practical life" finds that the "bustle of his practice makes it difficult for him unaided to

mechanical thinking establishes the connection, while the spiritual nature of inductive research maintains a dividing line. The student who has been educated mechanically is now capable of applying scientific principles to practical life, and even of modifying the old rules concerning such practice. Furthermore, his practical experiences benefit science by supplying new observations for scientific inductions. But the inductive leap from such new facts to the modification of scientific principles, or indeed the induction of new principles, is no part of his business. This last stage of the circuit must remain the monopoly of the scientific researcher, for it is the one link in the chain that necessarily requires self-consciousness as opposed to merely mechanical deliberation. The intermingling of commerce and culture is not complete, and for the rest of his life Marshall would continue to believe that self-conscious creativity and altruism in research separated the university from the main part of the ordinary business of life. Nevertheless, he did not hold that self-consciousness was found exclusively within the walls of the academy, nor did he believe that the manly characteristics associated with it had no place outside of those walls. We may recall that in a letter of 1868 Marshall had commended the Cambridge Mathematical Tripos for promoting thoroughness and thereby achieving "what art can do to create genius."[30] Such genius could be found in all ranks of life, but it was fostered by a thorough liberal education, and as such it was the duty of the suppliers of higher education to prepare the future leaders of an industrial society.

In one of Marshall's notes on education from the early 1870s, the following parable is found: "A youth with athletic mind sent out say to superintend building of railway at first a mere child in hands of men; but soon becomes their real leader." That Marshall believed that such an athletic mind was the product of education as opposed to heredity or even chance is made clear in the following sentences in this folio: "And yet what a little thing this education is! Workmen can gain it themselves if they will."[31] But until they do gain this education, their wages must remain below that of the athletically minded managerial classes. In another set of folios from this period, all of which are headed "*Education* as a remedy for low wages," Marshall explains how the "gymnastics" of education enable "a man not so much to be a highly skilled specialist as to be quick in adapting himself to changing circumstances adopting new ideas." As such, a liberal education supplies a

---

commence the study of the principles of the sciences which bear upon it" (see *CAM*, I: 14–15).

[30] See p. 149.

[31] M 4/25, f. 29. For the background to the notion of an "athletic mind," see Chapters Two and Four of this book.

man with "most of the requisites for enterprise." But in addition to this, the "more pliable his mind the more ready he is to enlarge his narrow circle of ethical precepts growing up into instincts notably that of the duty of the parents to bring up their children properly." The benefits of education are then summarized and their effects noted: "Enterprise, pliability, information, trustworthiness are the four elements which separate the wages of labor receiving classes from the wages of superintendence receiving class."[32]

The two sets of early notes just quoted mark a position intermediate between the essay "On Wages" and that set out in a course of lectures on political economy that Marshall gave to a class of women students in 1873. In "On Wages," it will be recalled, Marshall had avoided the implications of Lassalle's rendering of a Ricardian iron law of wages by arguing that the cost of production in the case of labor meant not simply the cost of subsistence, but also the cost of the "preparation required" for entering any particular trade. Indeed, in this essay Marshall had attempted to formulate the relationship "between the ratio of the average wages of a skilled labourer of any 'rank'… [and] those of unskilled, and the ratio of their costs of production."[33] In the 1873 lectures to women, however, we find Marshall insisting that the "remuneration for labor amongst the manual working classes depends almost entirely upon … whether these people in their childhood had slight sacrifices made for them, and not on the cost of production. It depends on efficiency of work and that again on one small point, on the amount of education that the man received as a child."[34] This point is explained further when Marshall asks what it is that workers are paid well for: not for technical skills, he insists, for these "may easily be acquired." Rather, high wages are paid by employers "for trustworthiness, pliability of intellect, rapidity in managing things, and power of managing men"; and "all these qualities come by education."[35] Thus, in these lectures of 1873, the elements that had but recently been singled out as distinctive to the wages of superintendence were generalized to form part of an explanation of wage differentials across the whole spectrum from unskilled to professional labor. Marshall's thinking on education and character, though developing out of the position set out in "On Wages," was leading him to a novel view of the labor market.

---

[32] M 4/25, ff. 24–5. Marshall adds, "Even his 'specialistic' technical knowledge will be made more thorough if his habits of intellectual enterprise are increased."
[33] *EEW*, I: 195. Note that in "On Wages" Marshall twice asserted, without explanation, that higher wages would increase efficiency (see *EEW*, I: 186, 192).
[34] *LTW*, 105.
[35] *LTW*, 105.

By 1873 Marshall had established most of the foundations on which he would subsequently develop a marginal-productivity theory of distribution, but it does not seem that he had as yet a clear idea of how such construction might proceed. Whitaker has suggested that Marshall moved gradually from a wages-fund approach to a marginal-productivity theory of distribution, "arriving at a fully-conscious and coherent stand by about 1875." For Whitaker, an abandoned volume on international trade, on which Marshall began work around 1874, illustrates a transitional stage in Marshall's thinking. In the surviving chapters of this projected volume, the earnings of labor are treated according to a wage-advance approach, observes Whitaker, but the wages of superintendence are governed "by what appears to be a vestigial marginal-productivity theory."[36] What Whitaker seems to have in mind with regard to the latter approach is Marshall's insistence, in this projected volume, that economists have not sufficiently emphasized that the supply of capital within a country is dependent on the number of men within that country "who have the sagacity, the energy, the firmness of character and the technical skill that are required for the successful conduct of business." Such qualities, Marshall here explains, are "the exclusive property of no one grade of society," for they in part depend on "natural genius" and in part may be "acquired by almost any man who has a good general education."[37] A key step here is, of course, the treatment of labor demand as flexible because wages are no longer conceived of as paid out of a fixed sum of capital. But such a position builds on the analysis of the economics of education that Marshall had worked through by 1873; by this date he had concluded that his initial analysis of the wages of superintendence could be generalized into an account of the causes that govern the wages of labor in general.

If in 1873 Marshall still approached the "wages question" along wages-fund lines, he had nevertheless arrived at the conviction that it was the efficiency and not the cost of production of labor that was of crucial

---

[36] *EEW*, I: 47–8. As Whitaker points out, the analogy between the wages of labor and the wages of management would be firmly stressed in the 1879 *Economics of Industry*.

[37] *EEW*, II: 22–3. This argument would appear to have grown out of the discussion of high wages and capital in the 1873 Reform Club talk (see *FWC*, 112–13). However, the key development of Marshall's thought seems to have coincided with his 1875 trip to America, where, as we shall see in Chapter Eight, he discovered that the conditions of American industry fostered the same kind of subjective freedom as did a good English liberal education. Thus we may speculate that the industrial conditions that he encountered on his American tour subsequently led Marshall to the conclusion that his account of the wages of superintendence might be generalized into a complete theory of distribution, at first with regard to a relatively new nation like America and then, ultimately, with regard to any modern national economy. For the culmination of this line of thought, see *EI*, 205.

importance. It was from this perspective that he denied that any interpretation of the wages-fund doctrine gave (in the words of his 1876 essay) "countenance to the notion that the distribution of the produce of industry between capitalists and wage-receivers is governed by a 'natural' and 'immutable law,' and is not capable of being modified by a readjustment of 'the arrangements of society.' "[38] As we shall see, for the more skilled grades of labor, such an adjustment might perhaps be achieved by trade unions. Nevertheless, it was to the extension of higher as well as primary education that Marshall looked to achieve a comprehensive shift within the existing order of production and distribution. "Promote education at the expense of capital," he told his women students in 1873;[39] for the present drag on progress consisted in the fact that "each generation consumes as it were the capital of the next," and "the advance of the world depends almost entirely on the extent to which parents will sacrifice themselves for their children." But the will to so sacrifice present rewards for the sake of the future of one's offspring was itself a product of a liberal education: "educated classes have always done this; uneducated never."[40] Thus the "best investment of the present capital of the country is to educate the next generation and make them all gentlemen."[41] Here, then, was the "detail" that marred Mill's identification of the realm of production and the existing system of distribution with "natural laws." Here too, as we shall now see, was the kernel of the political vision that arose out of Marshall's reformation of the doctrines and arrangements of political economy.

FUTURES OF THE WORKING CLASSES

In November of 1873 Marshall gave a talk to the Cambridge Reform Club entitled "The Future of the Working Classes." He introduced his talk by referring to the chapter in Mill's *Principles* entitled "On the Probable Futurity of the Labouring Classes." In this chapter Mill had argued that whether or not wealth increased was not important, at least not after "a certain point." But that it "should increase relatively to the number of those who share in it, is of the utmost possible importance"; and whether or not this was to occur, according to Mill, must depend on "the opinion and habits of the most numerous class, the class of manual labourers."[42] Mill's hope, of

---

[38] *MTV*, 123, n. 2.
[39] *LTW*, 98.
[40] *LTW*, 104–5.
[41] *LTW*, 107, 106.
[42] *Mill CW*, 3: 758.

course, was that the "increase of intelligence, of education, and of the love of independence among the working classes" could not but give rise to a "corresponding growth of the good sense which manifests itself in provident habits of conduct, and that population, therefore, will bear a gradually diminishing ratio to capital and employment."[43] He looked to school education, public debate, and the reading of newspapers and political tracts as the instruments of a hoped for improvement of working-class character, while he considered economic competition to be a vital bulwark against the ever-present dangers, within a mass society, of mental stagnation and dull habitual thought. But in this chapter of his *Principles*, Mill also looked beyond basic moral and social improvement and cast his sights on the just society of the future. The only just society, he insisted, is one where all are laborers. In such a society, improvement of character, and the resultant predominance of the sympathetic over the selfish sentiments, might give rise to various schemes of industrial partnership, cooperative businesses, and profit sharing.

In the prefatory comments of his 1873 talk "The Future of the Working Classes," Marshall explained that the "course of inquiry" that he would follow, while never straying far from Mill's chapter, "will seldom exactly coincide with it."[44] His intention, in fact, was to utilize his recent studies in political economy, as well as history and mental philosophy, in order to provide for his contemporaries an updated liberal image of the future of the working classes. Marshall was not the first to attempt to revise Mill's image of the future in light of contemporary concerns and knowledge claims. In 1869 Edward Beesly, member of the Positivist Society, professor of ancient history at University College, friend of Karl Marx, and active supporter of the trade union movement, had published an essay in the *Fortnightly Review* entitled "The Social Future of the Working Class."[45] Although we cannot be certain whether Marshall was familiar with Beesly's paper, the textual similarities of the two essays suggests that if Marshall had one eye on Mill's chapter, he had the other on Beesly's essay. Beesly situated his social reading of the future in direct opposition to the "middle-class"

---

[43] *Mill CW*, 3: 765. In his copy of Mill's *Principles*, we find a marginal summary of this part of Mill's chapter: "The future well being of the labouring classes principally dependent on their own mental cultivation" (Mill 1865: 458 [UL]).

[44] *FWC*, 101–2.

[45] On Beesly, positivism, and the trade union movement, see Harrison 1965; and for an account of the relationship between Beesly's political radicalism and his revisionist work on the Roman Revolution, see Wiseman 1998: ch. 11. Note that in Marshall's early notes on the guilds he refers to an 1867 paper by Beesly in the *Fortnightly Review* (M 4/13, f. 50; and see Beesly 1867).

radicalism of J. S. Mill and the academic liberals of Fawcett's generation. The liberalism of these political economists, Beesly explained, is founded on two principles: "Politically, we are still to be governed by Parliament. In industry we are to have the reign of free competition."[46] In the political sphere, Beesly continued, these liberals regard the recent Reform Bill as a major step forward and "sincerely believe that the series of political changes which they commenced in England forty years ago is nearly completed." What these liberals failed to understand, however, is that "for the first time" in history, social questions are "contesting precedence with political questions," that "there has been in truth but one revolution, which began in 1789 and has been going on ever since, and that the year 1848 marks the transition from the purely political to the social phase."[47] The social future of the working classes was to be decided not by Parliament, but by the working classes themselves as they combined and organized within the trade union movement.

In his essay, Beesly suggested that we "picture to ourselves" the condition of the working class when society shall approximate more nearly its "normal state." To imagine such a future state was not to indulge "in Utopias," for the picture that he presented of the future was drawn by way of a study "of the steady, continuous progress of society in the past."[48] According to Beesly, an examination of "the whole history of our race in Western Europe" demonstrated "the unbroken continuous progress of society" by means of which the "labouring class have steadily advanced in dignity and influence." The working masses were once "slaves, with no more rights than horses and oxen. Then they were serfs, with certain rights but still subject to grievous oppression and indignity. Then they became free hired labourers, nominally equal with the upper class before the law, but in practice treated as an inferior race, and themselves looking on the rich with much deference and awe." Marshall, we might note, would have assented without question to the first two stages of this account of social progress. But for him the equality before the law that arose with freedom of contract in the labor market was the key to subsequent progress. The next step in the evolution of society, in Marshall's view, must be the education of the characters

---

[46] Beesly 1869: 345. Mill had eulogized the cooperative movement in his chapter "The Probable Futurity of the Working Classes." Beesly insisted that cooperatives, which he regarded as but a variant of the joint-stock company, were not the solution to the social problem: "The world is not to be regenerated by the old dogma of the economist masquerading in modern dress" (Beesly 1869: 350).

[47] Beesly 1869: 344.

[48] Beesly 1869: 357.

of the working classes so that they might make the most of that freedom and equality which was potentially already their birthright. Such character improvement, Marshall maintained, must be achieved primarily by way of an education provided by those who were already gentlemen. Here is the parting of the ways, for Beesly looked to the working class to effect its own improvement. In the present day, Beesly declared, "we have come to a time when the workmen are almost everywhere standing on their rights, and resisting what they deem unfair or oppressive. They have learnt the secret of combination."[49] It is by means of the social force of such associations, and not by means of external direction, that the working class will educate itself and propel society toward a "normal state."

Thus the trade union movement was for Beesly the agent of social change. Trade unions contributed to the more equitable distribution of income, but even more importantly, they served to educate the members of the working class and so prepare them for their future elevated status. Yet if Beesly and Marshall differed with regard to the means of working-class education, their visions of the ultimate end point of such an education were not dissimilar. Indeed, educated Victorians did not in general regard working-class culture as intrinsically different from middle-class culture; rather, they simply held that the working class was lacking in culture.[50] Like the members of the Cambridge Reform Club, Beesly assumed that a population educated enough to reason would recognize the authority of sound reason when they encountered it. As a follower of Comte, Beesly expressed this conviction by stating that in the final stages of social progress a positivist religion of humanity would be established, and henceforth public opinion would be rationally directed. Such rationally directed public opinion, he insisted, would dictate that the rewards, presently won from employers by the struggles of the unions, would be given voluntarily. Nor would such public opinion tolerate the present state of affairs in which "an idle class" lives "by the sweat of others." Furthermore, it would lead the state to carry out sanitary regulations, ensure a liberal provision of medical assistance, place education within the reach of the poor, and ensure the construction of "an adequate supply of free libraries, museums, and picture galleries."[51] In general, there would be a diminution in the hours of work, and workmen would own their own homes. Nevertheless, Beesly warned, it was "highly

---

[49] Beesly 1869: 347–8.
[50] See Jones 1983: 183. Jones observes that it "was only at the beginning of the twentieth century" that "middle-class observers began to appreciate that the working class was not simply *without* culture or morality, but in fact possessed a 'culture' of its own."
[51] Beesly 1869: 360–1.

improbable" that "the position of the workman will ever be as desirable as that of the wealthier classes," for necessity required a certain amount of hard work in any society. Such hard work "*must* be done by some; and those to whom it falls to do it will inevitably have a less pleasant life than others."[52] In Beesly's imagined future the trade union movement will have educated the working masses, established a rational religion of humanity to direct public opinion, and vastly improved the position of the laboring class, but it will not have created a classless society.

It is against these two visions of the future of the working classes, one a midcentury liberalism, the other a new positivist social radicalism, that Marshall's "The Future of the Working Classes" should be placed. Just as Beesly had reflected on the fact that for the common people "life is absolute misery from birth to death … their dull round of toil occupies the whole day,"[53] so in his talk Marshall dwelled on "those vast masses of men who, after long hard hours of unintellectual toil, are wont to return to their narrow homes with bodies exhausted and with minds dull and sluggish."[54] But where for Beesly such endless toil was an evil in itself, Marshall now connected such physical overwork with mental exhaustion and so pointed to a physiological barrier to the improvements of the "opinions and habits" of the working classes. Mill had insisted that the just society was one in which all were laborers, and he looked to a moral improvement of the working classes in order to bring such a society into being. But Marshall defined a working man with properly educated opinions and habits as a gentleman – so long as his present occupation did not tend to degrade those habits and opinions. Hence Marshall asked whether the "education in youth" and "occupation in after-life" that "we are now wont to consider proper to gentlemen" might not in the future be extended to all.[55] In answering this question in the affirmative, Marshall proceeded to set out a vision of the future of the working classes that was in effect a vision of the abolition of the working classes, as successive rungs of the population were raised to the cultural and material level of gentlemen.

Marshall's future state as presented to the Cambridge Reform Club is one in which all are gentlemen. A gentleman is defined in terms of his character, and character is held to be primarily a product of youthful education and present occupation. While Marshall's 1873 talk can be read as simply calling

[52] Beesly 1869: 358.
[53] Beesly 1869: 345.
[54] *FWC*, 105. Marshall's early knowledge of the conditions of the working classes owed much to Ludlow and Jones 1867 [ML].
[55] *FWC*, 102.

for the transformation of the members of the working classes into members
of the middle class, his ideal of gentility embodies values that are as much
aristocratic as they are commercial.[56] Indeed, at the heart of Marshall's talk
is a vision of an intellectual aristocracy that is educated enough to perceive
its chivalrous duty to educate the lower orders. Such a vision was, of course,
informed by his recent psychological and historical studies. Earlier in 1873
he had told his women students that a gentleman is

> a man with an agile cultivated mind, but beside that he is self-reliant, impatient of
> being a burden on society. But further, he is willing to bear and to forbear to do and
> to suffer for the welfare of those around him. But this many people are willing to do
> who are not gentlemen. Yes, they have the will; but they have not the instinct to feel
> that what they are doing is jarring on society.[57]

For Marshall, a gentleman has both the will and the ability to do good, and
the social problem is essentially one of bridging the gap, among those who
are not gentlemen, between spiritual intentions and mechanical habits and
instincts. To illustrate this point, it is helpful to turn to the Marshalls' discussion of the "supply of skilled labour" in the 1879 *Economics of Industry*.
What we find here is that while the "poor are moved as much as any other
parents by the sight of the sufferings of their children," nevertheless they
"have not a vivid imagination" and so are "careless about the distant future
both of their children and of themselves." The spirit may be willing, but
the flesh – in the form of the deliberative circuitry of the brain – is weak.
Consequently, the poor are unable to see "the benefits that they may confer on their sons by investing … in their education."[58] The social problem,
then, is not that spiritual evolution is confined to the educated few, but
rather that self-consciousness remains a mere potential unless mechanical
character – the product of education – has evolved to make it an actuality.
As we saw in the preceding chapter, Marshall took note of, and absorbed
into his own psychological framework, Hegel's statement that if character
was to "become true," it "must be *thoroughly educated*." Hence Marshall's
1873 vision of social progress was founded on an ideal of an intellectual

---

[56] Historically, the social distinction between gentlemen and others predates the nineteenth-
century division of society into three classes; it belongs rather to an era in which no distinction was made between the middling and the "lowest sorts" of people, all of whom
were lumped together as plebeians in contrast to a patrician aristocracy. See Clark 2000:
165; but on the emergence of a non-patrician gentility in the late eighteenth and nineteenth centuries, see Hilton 2006: 125.

[57] *LTW*, 107,

[58] *EI*, 107.

aristocracy that saw that it was its duty to educate the physiological habits of the lower orders.

In this formulation of the social problem, we see the full implications of Marshall's revision of his earlier Coleridgean criticisms of Smith's article on education. In the late 1860s Marshall distinguished between mechanical commercial activity, which he considered "ordinary," and self-conscious cultural activity, which he termed "scholarly." By 1871, as we have seen, he had come to see that mechanism was involved in much cultural activity. By 1873 and in the wake of composing his long historical essay, he had come to insist that self-consciousness was a general attribute of modern humanity. What distinguished the "true scholar" and "gentleman" from the working masses was simply the development of mental machinery. In taking this last step, we might note, Marshall was in fact moving closer to Maurice's formulation of Coleridge's thought. Coleridge, we may recall from Chapter Three, held that only few men were capable of self-conscious philosophical reasoning. Such a distinction between the philosophical few and the nonphilosophical many naturally lent itself to the view that an endowed clerisy should be formally charged with preserving and disseminating the cultural creations of the few philosophical souls. But Maurice, the foremost Coleridgean within the church of England and without doubt the primary source of Marshall's encounter with Coleridgean ideas, departed from Coleridge on precisely this point. For Maurice, the faculty of reason was universal. The unskilled laborer, Maurice insisted, was as able to engage in self-conscious reasoning as an Oxford philosopher (and indeed was likely to do so with more success, as he was less likely to confuse reason with understanding and to be content with empty opinions rather than direct knowledge of God). Maurice, in other words, pointed Marshall toward a version of romanticism that was far more in keeping with Mill's liberal political vision than anything that could be found in the writings of Coleridge.

In his 1873 talk, Marshall identified the conditions of the present that prevented the progress of society toward such a future state and insisted that we "picture to ourselves the state of a country in which such circumstances have been excluded."[59] That picture revealed a society in which no one has an "occupation which tends to make him anything else than a gentleman," in which "everyone is to have in youth an education which is thorough while it lasts, and lasts long," and in which everybody, present gentlemen included, is to engage in a certain share of the necessary

---

[59] *FWC*, 109.

manual work.[60] This last detail was imperative because Marshall believed that a day of heavy manual labor exhausted the body as a whole, and therefore rendered the mechanical mind unfit for education after work.[61] Against this classless image of the future, Marshall painted a picture of the present, a key element of which was a characterization of the labor market as divided according to four basic grades of labor: liberal professional, highly skilled manual labor, less skilled manual labor, and unskilled labor. Social evolution was possible because, between an unskilled worker and a gentleman, "the chain is absolutely continuous and unbroken." The links of such an unbroken chain were composed of ever more complicated mechanical circuits. Thus, even at the present time, members of the more skilled artisan class were "steadily becoming gentlemen."[62] Political intervention, however, was necessary if this progress was to be extended to include the unskilled toiling masses. Such political intervention would take the form of the extension of education and impose the sharing of the necessary manual work among the population as a whole. In this way, the habits and minds of the entire population would be improved, while the manual work would be shared by all and therefore, for each individual, lessened, and so would not coarsen the habits or deaden the spirit.

Marshall's revision of Mill's "On the Probable Futurity of the Labouring Classes" was achieved by way of a careful development of another chapter from Mill's *Principles*, entitled "Of the Differences of Wages in different Employments." In the latter chapter Mill had divided labor into the four basic grades adopted by Marshall in his talk. He had further argued that two factors had hitherto prevented competition between these different types of labor. First, the expense of the course of instruction necessary to ascend the scale had created a "natural monopoly" that excluded "the great body of the labouring people" from competing in the more skilled labor markets. Second, the vestigial influences of ancient customs effectively closed many professions to those who were not already of sufficient social rank. For these two reasons, Mill argued, the line of demarcation between the different grades of labor had until recently been so strong "as

---

[60]   *FWC*, 110.
[61]   See pp. 283–5 below for an outline of the physiological basis of Marshall's position. Such a position was by no means unusual at this time. For example, in Marshall's copy of Thomas Brassey's *Work and Wages*, we find a marginal marking next to the statement that the "leisure which they enjoy is the highest privilege of the wealthy. The want of opportunity for thought and cultivation is the greatest privation of those who are compelled to pass the greater portion of their lives in manual or mental toil" (Brassey 1872: 152 [ML]). For another statement to similar effect, see Bagehot 1900: 9.
[62]   *FWC*, 105.

to be almost equivalent to an hereditary distinction of caste; each employ-ment being chiefly recruited from the children of those already employed in it." Consequently, the wages of each grade had been "hitherto regulated by the increase of its own population, rather than of the general population of the country." Yet Mill was also adamant that at the present moment a combination of changes in "usages and ideas" and the "increased facilities of education" was in the process of removing the barriers between these dif-ferent grades of labor.[63] Marshall's talk was essentially an argument that by means of a strong and general dose of higher education, the rate of progress of both of these changes could, and should, be speeded up.

On the level of "usages and ideas," Marshall's 1873 talk amounted to a public declaration that the authority of political economy must henceforth be directed against any argument that the existence of the lower orders was a natural or necessary feature of society. Any such interpretation of Ricardian doctrines to this effect, whether in Lassalle's form of an iron law of wages or in the more orthodox English form of the wages-fund doctrine as con-ventionally interpreted, was identified by Marshall with "a Pagan belief not very different from the old one – the belief that it is an ordinance of Nature that multitudes of men must toil a weary toil, which may give others the means of refinement and luxury, but which can afford to themselves scarce any opportunity of mental growth."[64] In short, the educated classes must be shown that it was indeed possible to elevate the lower orders, and because it was possible, it was therefore their social duty to do so. Marshall had made precisely the same point in his lectures to women students earlier in the year. The ancient world, he had then explained, had been founded on the institution of slavery. But while in the preceding century "the powers of production have increased immensely, man has yet been left so completely a slave to production that habits of action which have compelled people to grow up utterly destitute of mental and moral wealth have been insisted on as necessary."[65] The reason for this mistaken analysis of the social ques-tion was that while the free circulation of labor and capital was a prod-uct of but one short century, the nineteenth, people were still governed by modes of action that had descended from a time when labor and capital did not circulate freely.[66] Indeed, public discussion of the condition of the working classes was still governed by pagan modes of expression. "Aristotle

---

[63] *Mill CW*, 2: 387–8. Cf. *EEW*, II: 373, and see Marshall's summary in *MTV*, 122–3.
[64] *FWC*, 109.
[65] *LTW*, 125.
[66] *LTW*, 125–6.

said: 'Slavery is natural. Nature intended some men should be slaves' and the modern world has said that a proletarian class is necessary and natural. This they say in spite of their professing to be followers of a person [i.e., Jesus] who maintained with the most unflinching audacity the doctrine that a proletariat was not necessary."[67] In a word, political economy rightly proclaimed the social message that inequality of rank was not a natural feature of social life, and this message was sanctioned by Hegelian philosophy, by Maine's historical method, and by a Mauricean interpretation of the moral teachings of Christianity.

On the level of the economic significance of education, Marshall's talk rested on an argument that went considerably beyond the analysis of Mill's *Principles*. Marshall was not simply arguing that the extension of education would remove the monopolistic barriers between the grades of labor. The core argument on which the 1873 talk rested was that a liberal education cultivated not only the social habits of a gentleman, but also the plasticity of mind and moral uprightness that guaranteed the efficiency of labor. Hence an educated workforce would be a more efficient workforce, and any state expenditure on the extension of education would more than pay for itself over the course of a generation. Ultimately, however, Marshall's position was grounded on a set of three-way connections between education, labor efficiency, and a sense of social duty; for the fundamental problem facing modern society was that, in contrast to all other classes, the class of uneducated and unskilled laborers not only continued to reproduce itself improvidently but subsequently failed to educate its numerous offspring. Consequently, "competition for food dogs the heels of progress, and perpetually hinders it."[68] But if these offspring were to be educated, this root problem would be removed: Not only would an "educated man have a high conception of his duty toward his children, he would be deeply sensitive to the social degradation that he and they would incur if he failed in it."[69] Education, then, not only increased efficiency, but also elevated moral character and so inculcated that sense of duty that was necessary if the class of unskilled laborers was not to reappear in a subsequent generation. In other words, Marshall's vision of the future brought together economic arguments with what today we might call ideology. It was on this fusion of the economic with the realm of ideas and usages that Marshall rested his rejection of any interpretation of economic doctrines that suggested that

[67] *LTW*, 126.
[68] *FWC*, 117.
[69] *FWC*, 114.

poverty was a natural condition of capitalist society. It was on this synthesis of political economy and wider social philosophy that Marshall based his reinterpretation of Mill's division of political economy in terms of natural laws, human will, and social arrangements.

By means of such a reinterpretation of Mill's basic division of political economy, Marshall was able to advance a political vision that went beyond Mill's chapter "On the Probable Futurity of the Labouring Classes" and yet remained true to the spirit of the tradition of liberal political thought that Beesly had spurned in his essay "The Social Future of the Working Class." Marshall made no mention of trade unions in his 1873 talk, but it is clear from his early statements concerning unions that at this time he was in broad agreement with Beesly's conviction that they could provide an instrument of working-class education. In May 1874, for example, Marshall spoke at a meeting at Barnwell in Cambridge in support of the attempts of local farm workers to unionize. He argued that a union could make a man aware of the world beyond his parish boundary and show him where his labor was needed. Wages would rise and, *if wisely spent*, would increase the efficiency of labor.[70] Again, in the summing up of a discussion of unions that Whitaker dates to 1874 or 1875, Marshall concludes that trade unions "do or do not benefit working men as a whole" according to whether they "do or do not make the working classes more intelligent and more capable of governing themselves and of performing those functions which educated the citizens of small cities of Greece."[71] A similar statement can be found in the 1875 talk he gave following his recent visit to America (and which will be discussed in some detail in the next chapter). Following de Tocqueville, Marshall noted that local government in New England imposed moral responsibilities on each citizen, "as did the small republics of ancient Greece or medieval Europe. But the same may be said of that admirably organised republic: a first class English trades union."[72] Clearly, in the early and middle 1870s, Marshall believed that trade unions could play a useful role in the education of the working classes.

One key to Marshall's political differences with Beesly at this time can be found in the respective titles that they gave to their two essays. Where Beesly's title announced an investigation of the social future of the working *class*, Marshall's pointed to a discussion of the future prospects of the various components of the working *classes*. It was Marshall's differentiation

---

[70] See Tullberg 1973: 80–1.
[71] *EEW*, II: 351.
[72] *EEW*, II: 364; see pp. 268–71 below for further discussion.

of the four grades of labor, which was itself indebted to Mill's analysis of
wage differentials, that led him to distinguish between that section of the
working class whose progress appeared to be guaranteed by existing social
forces and that section of the working class that appeared to be in danger of
being left behind. The middle rungs of society, within which were included
the skilled members of the working classes, could be confidently left to rise
of their own accord. In the last part of his 1869 review of Thornton, Mill
had in fact expressed concern that trade unions might benefit the more
advanced sections of the working class at the expense of those unskilled
laborers who were not members of a union.[73] Trade unions, for Mill, could
work to increase the barriers that separated the various sections of the
working population. Such a concern was not only taken up by Marshall,
but was made the foundation of a new liberal vision of political intervention on behalf of the weakest and most vulnerable members of society. In
this chivalrous ideal is contained a kernel of what historians have heralded
as the "new liberalism" that emerged in the last decades of the nineteenth
century. As Gareth Stedman Jones puts it, the "counterpart of wooing the
respectable working class, in this new type of liberalism, was the espousal of
a more coercive and interventionist policy towards the 'residuum.'"[74] Jones
is here referring to Marshall's discussions of the London poor in the 1880s,
but it should now be clear that the roots of Marshall's new version of liberalism are to be found in his 1873 talk at the Cambridge Reform Club.

In Marshall's case, this revised form of liberalism arose in the context of
the concerns of academic liberals in the wake of the passage of the Second
Reform Bill and was the product of a neo-Hegelian reading of Mill's *Principles
of Political Economy*. The label "neo-Hegelian" is particularly appropriate
with regard to Marshall's political vision of 1873. Marshall had certainly
not read Hegel's *Philosophy of Right*, and whatever notion he had of Hegel's
political philosophy was gleaned from the introduction and the discussion
of the modern world in the last pages of Hegel's *Philosophy of History*. As
we saw in the preceding chapter, in his early historical essay Marshall had
decisively rejected Hegel's identification of the modern state with constitutional monarchy. Nevertheless, his deep engagement with Hegel's metaphysical positions gave his revised form of liberalism a distinctly Hegelian
feel. There is no explicit contrast of the state with civil society in Marshall's
writings or any identification of a state bureaucracy with Hegel's "universal
class." Nevertheless, Marshall's basic political vision embodies a version of

[73] See *Mill CW*, 5: 662–8.
[74] Jones 1984: 303.

what Marx once described as Hegel's conception of the "universal class" as mediating between the "materialism of civil society" and the "idealism" of the modern state.[75] In Marshall's vision, this "universal class" is that class of society composed of "gentlemen." These gentlemen are distinguished from the rest of the population not by virtue of any monopoly of a spiritual faculty, but because their education allows their particular physiological apparatus to make full use of this spiritual faculty. But Marshall's class of gentlemen is by no means equivalent to a modern state bureaucracy or coextensive with the ranks of Britain's civil service, and consequently his conception of the political extends beyond the state to include the voluntary intervention of educated individuals who actively participate in public work out of a sense of duty. Here Marshall's neo-Hegelianism was informed by more typical features of traditional mid-Victorian liberalism.

From Mill's reviews of de Tocqueville's *Democracy in America* onward, the call to social duty and civic participation had been understood both as safeguarding society from the potential conformity of democracy and as providing an antidote to the debilitating consequences of a wholly self-absorbed life.[76] As Mill had written in his 1840 review of de Tocqueville, "The spirit of a commercial people will be, we are persuaded, essentially mean and slavish, wherever public spirit is not cultivated by an extensive participation of the people in the business of government in detail."[77] It should be no surprise that Marshall marked this sentence in his copy of Mill's review. If such a "republican" emphasis on self-government seems incongruous with our notions of classic Victorian liberalism as a celebration of "negative liberty" and a "night watchman state," this is simply a reflection of the fact that we have lost sight of the realities of Victorian liberalism; in the words of Eugenio Biagini, "Victorian liberalism was both individualistic *and* republican at one and the same time."[78] That Biagini is quite correct, at least with regard to the academic liberalism with which we have been concerned in this book, can be demonstrated simply by returning to Moulton's 1872 paper "Primary Political Education," the first talk delivered at the Cambridge Reform Club. Moulton's message to his fellow Cambridge liberals was not just that the nation must be educated if it was to be capable of self-government, for he further suggested that participation in

---

[75] See Marx and Engels 1976: 164.
[76] See Chapters One and Two of this book.
[77] *Mill CW*, 18: 169.
[78] Biagini 2000: 58.

local politics could provide a perfect training ground for civic personality.[79] In Marshall's talk of the following year, the focus had shifted from general political participation to the civic duties of the elite. Both talks were delivered at what Moulton described as "the political day school of the Liberals in Cambridge."[80] Both took it for granted that civic participation was both a duty and a vital key to the success of Britain's democratic experiment.

MARSHALL'S EARLY REFORMATION OF POLITICAL ECONOMY

Biagini has characterized Marshall's 1873 talk as "utopian."[81] The charge rests on the observation that Marshall did not explicitly prescribe the mechanism that would bring his radical ideal into the realm of practical politics. With regard to Marshall's belief that the necessary manual work could be shared by everybody in the future, such an objection is certainly valid (as Beesly would no doubt have pointed out). Furthermore, one could readily argue that once this particular proposal is removed, the rest of Marshall's vision of social progress collapses. Nevertheless, the dismissal of the 1873 talk as a whole as utopian suggests a failure to grasp either its context or the intentions that stood behind it. "The Future of the Working Classes" was, first and foremost, a statement to the members of the Cambridge Reform Club in support of the extension movement, which at just this moment many members were in the process of inaugurating. An unstated but fundamental assumption of the talk, which would have been readily perceived by Marshall's audience, was that the extension of higher education to the working classes constituted precisely the mechanism that would generate the kind of social progress to which Marshall in his talk looked forward. But on an even more fundamental level, the charge of utopianism misses the basic point of Marshall's talk. By 1873 Marshall was no longer an apprentice political economist, and there should be no mistaking the fact

---

[79] *RCP*, 6. Compare the sentence, marked by Marshall in his copy of de Tocqueville's *Democracy in America*: "Political associations may therefore be considered as large free schools, where all the members of the community go to learn the general theory of association" (Tocqueville 1862, II: 140 [ML]). Compare Moulton's ideal of participation in local government with Marshall's 1875 comments on English trade unions, discussed in the next chapter.

[80] *RCP*, 6.

[81] See Biagini 1995: 25, 27. Part of the problem with Biagini's criticism is that he builds his argument by comparing only the supposed radicalism of Marshall with the *political* radicalism of J. S. Mill and Fawcett. In other words, Biagini entirely passes over the possible significance of the *social* radicalism of positivists like Beesly.

that he presented himself to the Reform Club as one who possessed the authority to interpret the laws of society as discovered by political economy. In his talk Marshall proclaimed a new gospel. This new gospel did not negate the old bible of political economy so much as to provide the key to its interpretation. This interpretation had already been worked out by Marshall in the lecture course for women students that he delivered earlier in the year, but it was in November of 1873, in his address to the Cambridge Reform Club, that Marshall publicly proclaimed that political economy lent its authority to the belief that political intervention, in the form of an extension of the provision of higher education, would generate social progress.

Marshall's new gospel of political economy can be seen as an attempt to carry to its logical conclusions that moralizing of political economy which Mill had begun in midcentury. As we saw in the first parts of this book, in the years after midcentury, England experienced a simultaneous retreat from the orthodoxies of both Evangelical theology and laissez-faire politics. As we have also seen, the new social optimism of Mill was achieved by way of a divorce between economic doctrine and that social philosophy through which such doctrines were interpreted. Thus whatever equivalence might have existed between the optimism of Maurice and that of Mill rested on the social philosophy and not the political economy of the latter. It was Marshall who reformulated political economy itself so that it proclaimed a secular version of Maurice's theological vision of continual progress. Between Marshall's Hegelian association of economic competition with subjective and objective freedom and Maurice's contrast between a morally debilitating competition and a Christian ideal of cooperation, there was, of course, a fundamental gulf. Nevertheless, and as will be recalled from Chapter One, in 1837 Maurice had declared that "political economy is not the foundation of morals and politics, but must have them as its foundation or be worth nothing." By 1873 Marshall's psychological, philosophical, and historical studies had led him to place moral philosophy at the foundation of political economy. Marshall can be regarded as the heir of Maurice as well as of Mill.

Marshall's achievement in 1873 amounted to a decisive break with the conventional orthodoxies of English social thinking, orthodoxies that had arisen in the wake of the French Revolution. By positioning an analysis of the economic effects of education at the center of his thinking about the wages question, Marshall broke with any interpretation of economic doctrines that appeared to suggest that the "natural value" of wages condemned the working classes to a life of poverty. But in so placing an ideal of education at the heart of his formulation of political economy, Marshall was also turning the page on that long chapter of English social thought in which an Evangelical conviction of mankind's fallen nature helped shape and sustain a widespread belief that poverty and economic misfortune were the inevitable providential consequences of moral failing. Marshall did not break the connection between moral character and economic fortune. What Marshall did break was the coupling of an Evangelical conception of human nature with a Malthusian population principle that had provided the bulwark of the orthodox rejection of social reforms proposed by republicans like Antoine-Nicolas Condorcet and Thomas Paine.[82] In denying that the poverty of the many was a natural and necessary consequence of the irredeemable corruption of human nature, Marshall was, of course, following the leads of both Maurice and Mill. Marshall's particular achievement was to situate the ideal of manly character, which by the 1860s was embraced by both liberal Anglicans and academic liberals, at the center of his reformulated political economy.

Such an interpretation of Marshall's significance in the history of political economy diverges from the historical self-image forged by Marshall himself. Crucially, this interpretation is informed by the tendency of recent scholarship to interpret the reaction to the French Revolution as marking an epochal discontinuity between the worldviews of the Scottish Enlightenment and those of early-nineteenth-century English political economists.[83] From this perspective, Marshall's optimistic rendering of political economy stands in direct opposition to the orthodoxies of early-nineteenth-century Evangelical and Benthamite social thought. But Marshall belonged to a generation that was just discovering a contrast between modern evolution and the historical method, on the one hand, and the natural law tradition of earlier centuries, on the other. Hence Marshall contrasted his moralized and historicized formulation of political economy with what he took to be an ultimately ancient identification of the moral and the natural worlds. From Marshall's perspective, Smith had inherited an ancient pagan form of expression from Turgot and the Physiocrats, and the conflation of moral freedom with natural necessity had remained an entrenched feature of political economy until Marshall's own day. Marshall's revision of Mill's division of the subject matter of political economy was thus, in his own eyes, a final step in that moral reaction of the nineteenth century against

---

[82] For late-eighteenth-century readings of Smith's *Wealth of Nations* as supporting broad measures of social reform, see Jones 2004.
[83] See Chapter One of this book.

the amoral thought of the eighteenth, a reaction in which Mill himself had played a crucial role.

Mill had utilized his own nineteenth-century formulation of social philosophy in order to derive a moralistic but also optimistic lesson from Ricardian doctrines. In his *Principles of Economics*, Marshall would point out "the care with which" Mill had "set himself to emphasize the distinctly human element in economics."[84] Marshall's underlying intention in 1873 was to locate just such a "human element" firmly within the realm of political economy, and he attempted to do this by inserting his own formulation of social philosophy into the heart of economic science. It would seem likely that Marshall saw himself here as doing no more than bringing out the latent meaning of Mill's general intellectual legacy. It will be recalled that Marshall's early reading of Mill's essays on Bentham and Coleridge gave rise to an enduring commitment to what he took to be Mill's uncompleted synthesis of liberal and romantic thought. By 1873 Marshall was able to approach political economy by means of a social philosophy that, if not as yet fully worked through, nevertheless synthesized elements of the schools of both Bentham and Coleridge. Viewed from this perspective, Marshall's 1876 criticism of the details of Mill's organization of political economy can be seen as the work of a loyal disciple of Mill. Yet what Marshall remained loyal to was not so much Mill's presentation of political economy as what he took to be the underlying spirit of Mill's incomplete philosophical project.

[84] *Principles*, I: 509.

EPILOGUE

"A ROUNDED GLOBE OF KNOWLEDGE"

EIGHT

Social Philosophy and Economic Science

INTRODUCTION

The aim of this final chapter is to sketch the broad outlines of Marshall's mature social philosophy and to identify its relationship to his mature formulation of economic doctrines. The chapter provides an epilogue to the detailed study of Marshall's early intellectual development that has occupied us until now in this book. Our business here is no longer to engage in close contextual readings, but rather to present in bare outline the key steps that took Marshall from "The Future of the Working Classes" in 1873 to the *Principles of Economics* – first published in 1890 but continuously revised as Marshall reorganized and redrafted his text over the course of seven subsequent editions. This chapter will argue that the development of Marshall's philosophical ideas after 1873 did not involve the derivation of completely new ideas so much as the revision of preexisting elements of his thought. Such revision, however, did direct Marshall toward a new evolutionary concept of economic organization. Together, these revised philosophical ideas and the new scientific concept of organization constituted the basic elements of that "rounded globe of knowledge" that was Marshall's mature social philosophy.

This chapter has four main sections. In the first we will discuss the seminal revision of Hegelian categories that Marshall enacted upon his return from a visit to America in 1875. As we shall see, Marshall now suggested that neither subjective nor objective freedom had yet reached its final stage of development and that their subsequent evolution was dependent on economic conditions. The second section examines the genesis of Marshall's mature conception of industrial organization in 1879. What we shall find is that this concept was derived initially from his philosophy of history, subsequently transposed into physical terms, and that both historical and physical accounts of organization found their place in Marshall's *Principles of Economics* – a historical introduction providing the metaphysical foundations of a physical science. The third section identifies the limits of Marshall's physical science of economics as they appear in his discussions of the progress of both character and knowledge in the *Principles*. In both cases, we will find that physicalist, economic analysis provided but a partial picture of Marshall's vision of social progress, the other part being of a non-physical nature. Having thus identified as metaphysical both the foundations and the limits of economic analysis, we will turn in the fourth section to Marshall's mature conception of the relationship between the economic and the metaphysical elements of modern social life. It will be argued that Marshall conceived of society as comprising physical and metaphysical elements and that economic science analyzed the causal relationships existing within the physical element alone. Marshall's mature social philosophy, it will be suggested, was composed of a dialectical conception of the relationship between the physical and the metaphysical elements of modern society.

HISTORIES OF THE PRESENT AND THE FUTURE

Marshall's 1873 talk to the Cambridge Reform Club had been founded on a vision of a gap between the potential freedom and the actual mechanical mental capabilities of a large part of the population – a gap that was to be overcome by the educational activities of a cultural vanguard or intellectual aristocracy. Following a summer tour of America in 1875, however, Marshall revised key aspects of his thinking. In the lecture notes that he composed in the wake of this visit, Marshall explained that he had crossed the Atlantic because he "wanted to see the history of the future in America."[1] In his lecture notes, as well as in the paper on American industry that he read to the Cambridge Moral Science Club in November of 1875, Marshall affirmed that education formed the basis of national character. He now insisted, however, that the most important education people received was supplied not by schools and colleges, but by the ordinary business of modern life:

It is being found that the influences of association and habits of action to which a man is subject during most of his waking hours during at least six days in the week,

---

[1]   *EEW*, II: 345. Marshall's vision of America's pioneering role in "the history of the future" was clearly inspired by Hegel's assertion that America is "the land of the future, where, in the ages that lie before us, the burden of the World's History shall reveal itself" (Hegel 1991: 86).

are, generally speaking, so incomparably more powerful in the formation of his character than any other influences, that those who have attempted to guide man's destinies, but have neglected the influences which his daily work exerts on him, are like children who have tried to determine the course of a ship, not by controlling her rudder and properly trimming her sails; but by merely blowing on her sails with their breath.[2]

"At the same time," he continued, "and in consequence in part of the same set of causes, Political Economy has to some extent changed its method." Political economists had once confined themselves "to deducing conclusions" from "a few simple premises." Now, however, they were "getting to regard human nature as more complex and the present condition of human life as more variable, than they once had thought them." Consequently, and because the economist could not utilize the experimental method of the natural sciences, it was necessary to employ "the Comparative Method":

> By the Comparative Method, I mean the method of comparing corresponding phe-nomena at different times and places, and under the operation of different disturb-ing causes. ... Thus economists have been led to investigate history; the history of the past, and the more accessible history of the present ... it appears that many of the changes that are being worked out in England, America has with more rapid steps gone through before us, and that by a study of the present of America we may learn much directly about the future of England.[3]

Echoing Mill's 1840 review of *Democracy in America*, Marshall recalled how de Tocqueville had warned "that democracy might entail over-centralisation, social despotism, and even loss of energy." Such a warning, Marshall now proceeded to argue, had been exaggerated. De Tocqueville, he explained, had not "regarded it as within his province to examine minutely the influence which the daily occupations of men exert on their charac-ter," and so had "spent little of his time, where I spent most of mine; in American workshops."[4] In fact, Marshall's discovery did not originate from his observation of life within these workshops, but from his observation of the circulation of labor between workshops. As Marshall saw, American workers migrated easily and frequently from one job to another. Not only did the restless and migratory lives of American workers, he explained, teach Americans to rely on their own individual judgment in economic matters, it also trained them to be good citizens of the American republic. An American, he asserted, will use "his own individual judgment, more

[2]   *EEW*, II: 354.
[3]   *EEW*, II: 354–5.
[4]   *EEW*, II: 357.

consciously and deliberately, more freely and intrepidly, with regard to Ethics than an Englishman uses his."[5] Marshall painted America as a society in which nearly "all receive nearly the same school education" and "where the incomparably more important education which is derived from the business of life, however various in form it be, yet is for every one nearly equally thorough, nearly equally effective in developing the faculties of men." Given such conditions, he concluded, in America "there cannot but be true democracy."[6]

In America, then, the extreme mobility of labor provided an education in self-reliance, independence, and trust in one's own judgment. But what Americans gained in subjective freedom, they lost in objective freedom. Mechanical routines were constantly interrupted and mechanical bonds of sympathy broken as individuals changed trades and locations. Consequently, American workers did not form stable associations. In England, by contrast, a relatively settled way of life fostered mutual trust and sympathy among workers, the result being a flourishing cooperative movement and many well-organized trade unions. In England, where the "happiness and general well-being" of the working man "depend largely upon the esteem and trust of his fellow men," a trade union could provide "an admirably organized republic." Such a republic would educate the workman in both "the virtues and the vices of patriotism."[7] But such local patriotism need not be the ultimate purpose of these worker associations:

Unions generally are showing signs of beginning to ask themselves whether any republic can be justified in adopting regulations, the general adoption of which by the surrounding republics would be injurious to all. In asking themselves this question they are giving themselves a great education. From this particular education the American working man is almost debarred.[8]

Because they were learning from experience, Marshall suggested, English trade unions were gaining insight into their moral duties, not just to their own members, but also to others (they were, in fact, learning to recognize the moral force of Kant's idea of the categorical imperative). Participation in trade union and cooperative organizations, then, fostered those mechanical bonds of sympathy that were a precondition of spiritual insight into a

---

[5]   *EEW*, II: 358.
[6]   *EEW*, II: 373. Note that in this talk Marshall insisted that both academy and republic foster spiritual autonomy: "the commonwealth of letters," he remarks in passing, "in many particulars strikingly resembles the American republic" (*EEW*, II: 360).
[7]   *EEW*, II: 365.
[8]   *EEW*, II: 366.

moral – as opposed to merely legal – sense of social duty. Such voluntary self-restraint on behalf of trade unions, their willingness to sacrifice their own interests for the sake of the wider society, can be seen as a projection onto the English working classes of that sense of social duty that, in his 1873 talk to the Cambridge Reform Club, Marshall had identified as characteristic of the "gentleman." As noted in the preceding chapter, Marshall's class of gentlemen has some affinity with, but cannot be identified with, Hegel's conception of a universal class. The divergence from Hegel is even more apparent in 1875; for the education that English trade unions were "giving themselves" went beyond either the moral autonomy of subjective freedom or the submission before a self-determined legal code that was objective freedom. This departure from Hegel, however, was fully in keeping with Marshall's declaration that, in this talk of 1875, he was looking not to the philosophy of history, but to the philosophy of the present and the future.

Positioning himself as one who was working his way "towards that ethical creed which is according to the Doctrine of Evolution,"[9] Marshall told his audience that "there are two principal factors of ethical growth." On the one hand, there is that "education of a firm will" that occurs when every action of the individual is submitted to the judgment of reason. This form of education, which Marshall saw to be dominant in America, he declared to be a precondition for what "I take Hegel to mean by 'subjective freedom.'" In other words, moral autonomy is not merely the ground of individual deliberation; such deliberation is itself a precondition of moral autonomy. On the other hand, there is that "peaceful molding of character into harmony with the conditions by which it is surrounded" that occurs as individuals' habits and customs are modified by participation in modern social organizations. This second form of education, which Marshall held to be dominant in England, he declared to be the precondition of what "I take Hegel to mean by 'objective freedom.'"[10] These interpretations of Hegel's meaning were far from identical with those around which the earlier historical essay had been woven; for if the central narrative strand of this earlier essay had been provided by Hegel's notion that "Spirit is essentially the result of its own activity,"[11] Marshall's central claim now was that the further progress of spirit was dependent on economic activity. Behind Marshall's 1875 comparison between England and America, we can thus discern an attempt to

---

[9] *EEW*, II: 377. Marshall's evolutionary ethics can instructively be compared with the approach of his friend Clifford. See Clifford 1875 [BV, ML], 1877 [BV, ML], and Clifford and Harrison 1876 [BV, ML].
[10] *EEW*, II: 375–6.
[11] Quoted by Marshall in his early notes on Hegel's *Philosophy of History* (*EHC*, M 4/10, f. 47).

revise and redeploy the categories of Hegel's *Philosophy of History* in order to frame a social philosophy appropriate to modern conditions. Such revision did not necessarily entail a rejection of the conclusions drawn in the earlier essay. This is because Marshall was now concerned with (as he put it) the history of the present and the future, and he evidently regarded progress as proceeding by way of a more complicated dialectic than that which had driven the development of humanity earlier in the world's history.

Marshall's identification of self-consciousness with Hegel's notion of freedom had provided the starting point of his early essay on the history of civilization. It will be recalled how, in his early notes on Hegel's *Philosophy of History*, Marshall had identified freedom and self-consciousness with "the self-contained existence" that is "not dependent upon anything external."[12] What we find in the 1875 talk, however, is a new insistence that both subjective and objective freedom have preconditions and that such preconditions are not themselves manifestations of the dialectical unfolding of spirit. The departure from the pure dialectic of self-consciousness is most striking with regard to objective freedom, whose further development is now said to rest on what are ultimately physical processes. What Marshall was arguing in 1875 was that participation in self-governing workers' organizations fosters particular physiological habits of thought and action, and that the formation of such habits constitutes the precondition of a spiritual education in social duty. Where the early essay on the history of civilization had presented the internal dialectic of spirit as generating the preconditions of truly economic behavior, Marshall in 1875 was asserting that modern economic life establishes the preconditions of future spiritual progress. Furthermore, Marshall was now pointing toward a new telos of modern history. For Hegel, as for Marshall in his earlier essay, history culminates in that objective freedom that manifests itself in a self-conscious equality of individuals before the law of the modern state. The education that Marshall in 1875 declared could be provided by English trade unions and cooperatives, however, goes beyond this stage of self-consciousness. Marshall, in fact, was suggesting that the telos of modern history would be arrived at when social duty and moral autonomy were fully reconciled.

Marshall's contrast between the individualist and collectivist tendencies fostered by American and English economic conditions grew out of his earlier historical thought. In the last section of Chapter Six, we looked briefly at Marshall's early comparison of the post-feudal histories of England and France. In that comparison we find the germ of the basic comparative lesson

---

[12]   See p. 206 above.

drawn in 1875. In the earlier comparison of England and France, Marshall had explored how a modern nation-state might follow a path to either liberty and decentralization or absolutism and centralization. Broadly speaking, however, both the England and America of his own day could be characterized as liberal democracies. As the terms were used in his early essay on the history of civilization, then, England and America were already possessed of both subjective and objective freedom; nor did Marshall in 1875 deny this – what he now claimed was that in such modern democracies an examination of economic conditions showed that the *further* development of freedom was to be expected. Just what the end point of this future development might look like he did not specify, although his paper suggests that both America and England would have to pass through the stage at present exemplified in the other. In other words, Marshall's paper suggests that modern progress could come to an end only when both individualistic and collectivist tendencies were not only worked out in full, but also reconciled. Thus Marshall was not so much revising Hegel's philosophy of past history as constructing a neo-Hegelian philosophy of present and future history. In so doing he was, in effect, engaged in the process of constructing a social philosophy of the modern age.

In contrast to his earlier philosophy of history, Marshall's mature social philosophy contains two distinctive features. The first is that, in terms of the Hegelian dialectic of self-consciousness, Marshall points to a new telos of modern history, which as yet he neither names nor explores but which he will ultimately hail as "collective freedom." This telos, we shall discover, constitutes the reconciliation of the opposing tendencies to individualism and to collectivism manifested in modern history. Arrival at this end point completes a historical cycle, which commenced with primitive humans, devoid of self-conscious individuality, who worked for the common good by following instinctual habits and customs. The second distinctive feature is that Marshall now posits economic in addition to purely spiritual conditions of historical progress. In Marshall's mature social philosophy, progress arises from a dialectical interplay between the spiritual and the physical elements of social reality. In this dialectical relationship, spiritual factors provide the precondition of those physical organizations that compose modern economic life, and the development of those organizations in turn generates the conditions of spiritual growth. But Marshall came to define economics as a physical science, and as such the spiritual components of social progress fell outside the limits of what he came to consider the proper province of economics. Thus Marshall's mature social philosophy is rendered essentially invisible within his economic writings. What is more, Marshall's

1875 paper on America constitutes the last of what we have described in this book as Marshall's "early philosophical writings." Hence the task that we face in the remainder of this chapter is to show the relationship between Marshall's economic science and a dialectical social philosophy whose nature was largely, if by no means entirely, passed over in silence.

THE GENESIS OF ORGANIZATION

Alongside period analysis, an investigation of economic organization is the most distinctive element of Marshall's mature economic science. The concept of organization stands at the heart of the theory of production set out in book IV of the *Principles of Economics*. As we shall see, this concept is framed in terms of biological analogies, as opposed to the mechanical analogies found in the discussion of period analysis in book V. The study of industrial organization is thus a study of economic development, or progress. Nor is such a form of progress limited to the sphere of production – for Marshall, a market can be more or less organized.[13] In all cases, the development of organization entails, for Marshall, an increased integration of the various mechanical parts of the modern "economic organism," combined with a greater differentiation between these separate parts. As such, the concept of organization provides the economic scientist with a view of the machinery of modern economic life from the same perspective from which, in 1868, Clifford had derived an evolutionary rendering of Marshall's mechanical model of the mind. In both cases, the development of a system of interconnected mechanical parts is explained in terms of the mutual processes of separation and closer connection between parts and whole.[14] At the same time, however, Marshall's conception of industrial organization provides a reflection within the economic sphere of that relationship between increased individual autonomy (i.e., differentiation of parts) and higher sense of social duty (i.e., connection to the whole) that Marshall in 1875 described as constituting ethical evolution.

Marshall's mature conception of economic organization is of considerable interest to us because it provides a crucial component of his mature social philosophy. That is to say, a model of the development of modern economic organizations amounted to a model of the evolution of those economic conditions that fostered the further progress of subjective and

---

[13] *Principles*, I: 327; see also p. 325.
[14] See p. 193 above. Note that Marshall refers to Clifford's paper in his 1879 manuscript "Course of Lectures on Economic Progress (Mill Book IV)."

(potentially) objective freedom and thereby generated social progress. As markets became more highly organized, so participation in those markets could be expected to provide an ever more rigorous education in subjective freedom. At the same time, the evolution of modern business enterprises demanded from their employees an ever more complicated series of mechanical habits and routines. The organization of modern economic life was, for Marshall, a phenomenon of the utmost historical significance. The evolution of mental habits and customs in primitive times had been essentially open-ended. Once self-consciousness appeared in the world and actions were preceded by an appeal to conscience, a slow process of reeducation of the mechanical heart and mind was set in motion. But even in the world of post-feudal Europe, as the examples of French and English history showed, such education could follow different paths. Modern economic life, however, provided a unifying education. As the reach of the market extended into more remote corners of the world, as hitherto isolated areas of England were transformed into local centers of production for particular industries, so the inhabitants of these regions were called on to exercise individual judgment in the market and to exercise responsibility in their operation of specialized machinery in the workplace. Myriad personal habits and ancient customs were being transformed into a small set of modern routines and sympathetic bonds appropriate to the new industrial age.

The genesis of Marshall's conception of economic organization can be traced to 1879, in which year we find him setting out two distinct accounts of organization. In a chapter of the *Economics of Industry*, Marshall and Mary Paley derived a definition of "industrial organization" from Marshall's earlier historical studies. Shortly after composing this chapter, however, Marshall framed a biological account of organization in a set of lecture notes. Versions of both formulations can be found in the *Principles of Economics*. His development of the concept of organization at the end of the 1870s, then, constitutes a crucial transition point between Marshall's philosophical and scientific thought. By tracing the genesis of this concept, from historical metaphysics through biological analogy, and examining the respective places that these two distinct accounts – the historical and the biological – later came to occupy in the *Principles*, it is possible to establish a facet of the relationship that Marshall envisioned between social philosophy and economic science.

In his early essay on the history of civilization, Marshall made no mention of organization. Nevertheless, it was in a version of this essay – adapted, pruned, and extended – that Marshall first introduced this notion. This occurred in chapter VII of the *Economics of Industry* (1879), entitled, appropriately enough, "Organization of Industry." The chapter begins with Mary Paley and Marshall attempting to extend Marshall's earlier historical inquiries back to the period before the advent of civilization. They achieved this by reworking the stadial history found in Smith's *Wealth of Nations*. Beginning with an account of savage tribes, the Marshalls explain that society first advanced when animals were domesticated and that this stage was followed by the ownership and working of the land. Drawing on the recent work of Henry Maine and other comparative scholarship, the Marshalls now introduce the "Village Community." This community, we are told, was once prevalent in most of Europe and much of Asia, and is still to be found, albeit in modified form, in Russia and India. The distinctive feature of the village community is that it fosters "a network of customary rules" that not only checks agricultural improvement, but also "hampers the freedom and enterprise of individuals."[15] In the village community, then, there was usually a hereditary division of labor among the inhabitants, yet there was "scarcely any freedom in the choice of their occupations." And because of this lack of freedom, the Marshalls conclude, "there is as yet nothing that can properly be called organization."[16]

Before tackling the question of how freedom, and hence organization, first appeared in history, the Marshalls engage in an exercise in nineteenth-century comparative history. The purpose of this exercise is to show that the "fixed customs" of the primitive village communities were perpetuated in the earliest civilizations. These fixed customs "have been especially powerful in the East," where "Oriental custom" not only "decides the Caste or rank in society to which a man belongs," but also "regulates the wage of each kind of service, and the price of every commodity with an inflexible rule." But in Greece and Rome it was also believed that "there were multitudes of men whom nature had consigned at their birth to weary toil" in order that others could have the time for culture and the discharge of their duties as citizens. Not only did such habits of belief, we should note, choke enterprise and freedom, they were in themselves socially corrosive: "for when a race has lived for several generations among the excitements of civilised life, but scorning work and despising those who work, it has become heartless and frivolous and therefore weak."[17] This part of the *Economics of Industry* amounted to an abridged version of the first half of the essay on the history of civilization.

---

[15] This account of the village community is supplemented by material drawn from a subsequent chapter, "Tenure of Land" (see *EI*, 60–1).

[16] *EI*, 43–4.

[17] *EI*, 44–5.

In the *Economics of Industry*, modern economic history is said to begin in the towns of the middle ages. In contrast to the ancients, the "Teutonic races that peopled Western Europe" after the fall of the Roman Empire had "a reverence for man as man, and this reverence was promoted by the Christian religion." Thus the early Germanic independence and love of freedom, as described by Tacitus, were combined with the equality of souls before God proclaimed by Christianity, and the result was the dissolution of those fixed habits of thought that regarded either caste or slavery as in some way natural. Teutonic attitudes and Christian dogma unlocked the mind from its long inheritance of fixed customs and, in doing so, opened up a freedom of occupation and the free circulation of labor, commodities, and, ultimately, capital, giving rise to modern organization. It was only in the medieval towns, however, that these spiritual forces manifested themselves in the birth of organization. In these towns the workers began, of their own free will, to specialize in particular occupations and trades, and so "the industry of the towns became highly organized."[18]

It is only on reaching this point in their historical narrative that the Marshalls are prepared to offer a definition of organization: "A body is said to be highly *organized* when each part has its own work to perform, when by performing this work it contributes to the well-being of the whole, so that any stopping of this work injures the whole; while, on the other hand, each part depends for its own well-being on the efficient working of the other parts."[19] Thus we learn that it is a physical body that is subject to organization, and the argument of the chapter as a whole becomes clear: the Marshalls are telling us that the emergence of higher forms of physical organization is dependent on spiritual preconditions. With spiritual freedom, the physical structure of medieval urban industry became highly organized, and such a physical structure is the product of a metaphysical freedom. In the early historical essay, Marshall had pointed to the institutional forms of the modern state – the manifestations of objective freedom – as arising in the Middle Ages. Implicit in this earlier essay was the idea that these modern manifestations of freedom included the free circulation of economic entities. Now, in 1879, this point is made explicit, and the emergent economic order is characterized as an "organization" of diverse human practices. The Marshalls have now set the stage for an advance into "more modern times," where they find "a continual growth of the specialisation or division of labour," the result of which is that industry has become

---

[18] *EI*, 44–5.
[19] *EI*, 45–6, emphasis in original.

localized and a variety of manufacturing districts are now connected by the railway, the steamship, the printing press, and the telegraph.[20] The history of the modern world is essentially a story of how, from the medieval town, the whole world is becoming highly organized.

But only a short while after composing this chapter, Marshall set out the first sketch of the framework that would be developed into a biological account of organization in his *Principles of Economics*. This sketch forms the kernel of some manuscript notes headed "Course of Lectures on Economic Progress (Mill Book IV)," which Marshall appears to have composed in Bristol in 1879. In these notes Marshall defines progress as an "increased power" to make nature serve our wants and claims that such "increased power" depends on (a) increased knowledge and (b) increased organization, and finally divides the second into (i) "changes in human habits & even character" and (ii) "changes in the methods of production."[21] The rest of the notes are occupied exclusively with the last element, and Marshall proceeds to construct a biological analogy of the development of the methods of production in human history. Biology, he explains, allows us "to arrange living beings in order of the complexity of their physiological organization"; he gives a progression from "fishes" through "sharks," followed by "mammals" and culminating with "men with feet and hands." Such an arrangement of living beings according to complexity of structure, he now asserts, has been made by biologists "in connexion with a doctrine of descent, which whether true or not with regard to animals is true certainly with regard to societies."[22] Marshall's arrangement of societies according to a doctrine of descent begins with "stone men," passes to "hunt stage bronze men" and "iron men," but then stops, and he announces that after this last stage society was "for a long time homogenous or at most divided into a few castes as the bees."[23] The development of organization, Marshall appears to suggest, was stagnant between the dawn of the Iron Age and the new age of steam-driven machines, picking up again only when in the nineteenth century cheap transportation and "freedom from custom" gave rise to a new "economy of skill & labour."[24]

It seems safe to assume that the manuscript notes on progress were composed later than the chapter on organization. Marshall, then, was using his

---

[20] *EI*, 46–7.

[21] M 3/2, ff. 2–3.

[22] Between his arrangements of animals and societies according to a doctrine of descent, Marshall writes, "Some account of Clifford's paper & its relation to H Spencer." "Clifford's paper" is presumably the 1868 "On Some of the Conditions of Mental Development."

[23] M 3/2, ff. 5–6.

[24] M 3/2, f. 10.

lectures on economic progress to move his category of organization out of his neo-Hegelian historical framework and to formulate it as a scientific category. On the surface, these two accounts appear to diverge significantly, yet many of the apparent differences can be dismissed as matters of presentation as opposed to substance. Thus, although in the manuscript's arrangement of social descent Marshall now echoes Huxley rather than Smith, this descent is still compatible with the earlier stadial theory. The "hunt stage bronze men" correlate with Smith's hunter-gatherer savages, and given that this descent of social structure is identified with a development of complexity in the methods of production, we can assume that "iron men" are using their iron as ploughs as well as swords, which is to say that we have here arrived at the agricultural stage of Smith's stadial scheme. In the lecture notes, we no longer have any kind of comparative history, but this means simply that we are no longer treated to the various dead ends of progress to be found in ancient Indian, Greek, and Roman society. (These various societies are now summarily dismissed with the observation that, for a long period of history, societies were "divided into a few castes as the bees.") There is, however, one crucial divergence: when jumping from the Iron Age to the nineteenth century in his notes, Marshall passes over what, in the *Economics of Industry*, was pinpointed as the crucial metaphysical moment when, in post-Roman Europe, Christian dogmas and Teutonic attitudes gave rise to the freedom and hence organization of the medieval towns. This difference points to the fact that the relationship between these two accounts is not contradictory, but rather complementary. The biological sketch deals only with the development of physical organization itself, while the historical account deals primarily with the preconditions of the higher development of organization. Only with the aid of the historical sketch can we fully explain the fact, illustrated in the scientific account, that the modern age has been marked by the advent of higher forms of physical organization.

Both accounts of organization found their way into the *Principles*. Marshall's neo-Hegelian narrative was reiterated in the introductory historical chapters of this volume, while a biological account of organization was placed at the center of Marshall's theory of production. Organization was now proclaimed as a fourth factor of production, alongside land, labor, and capital, and a chapter entitled "Industrial Organization" stood as the kernel of book IV, which dealt with "the agents of production."[25] Marshall here introduced the category of organization by invoking what he described as "a fundamental unity of action between the laws of nature in the physical

[25] *Principles*, I: 323; and see *Principles*, II: 268.

and in the moral world." Such unity consisted in the "general rule" that "the development of the organism, whether social or physical, involves an increasing subdivision of functions between its separate parts on the one hand, and on the other a more intimate connection between them." Following both Spencer and Clifford, Marshall labeled these processes of subdivision and connection "differentiation" and "integration," respectively.[26] Industrial differentiation manifested itself in "such forms as the division of labour, and the development of specialized skill, knowledge, and machinery"; integration, in "such forms as the increase in security of commercial credit, and of the means and habits of communication by sea and road, by railway and telegraph, by post and printing-press."[27] Much of this discussion had its germs in the *Economics of Industry*, but, of course, many pages now separated the historical and metaphysical discussion of freedom from the scientific account of organization. What are we to make of the way that Marshall so organized his *Principles*?

The harmony of the historical and the biological sections of the *Principles* turns on a dual conception of freedom. In the historical chapters, we find the now-familiar sketch of the genesis of a substantive metaphysical conception of freedom as the product of self-consciousness, individual moral agency, and the separation of humanity from the natural order. In the properly economic (mechanical and biological) parts of this treatise, however, freedom means simply that mechanical mental habits are fluid rather than fixed and that the circulation of commodities is not impeded. This distinction provides the clue to the organization that Marshall gave to his *Principles*. If the business of book IV of the *Principles* was to outline a unity of physical development, we can infer that it was the business of the introductory historical chapters to establish the distinction between the physical organisms of the natural world and the higher social organisms of the moral world. Here we should note the way that in introducing his biological formulation of economic organization, Marshall drew a distinction between the "physical" and the "moral" worlds at the same time as he pronounced that the same rule of organic development applied to both. What the historical chapters tell us, in other words, is that modern economic organizations are fundamentally different from natural organizations, even if the general rule of their development is the same. The difference is twofold: first, modern organizations exist in a moral and not a natural environment, in an environment, that is to say, characterized by objective freedom. Second, they are

[26] Cf. Spencer 1862: 79; for Clifford, see p. 193 above.
[27] *Principles*, I: 241.

composed of individuals who have at least the potential for self-conscious action, and not mere animals driven only by automatic habits and instincts. The introductory sections of the *Principles* thus establish the metaphysical foundations of that form of physical organization that is distinctive to modern social life.

For the mature Marshall, physical freedom is founded on metaphysical freedom, but its manifestations may be analyzed separately. In the introductory pages of the *Principles*, Marshall declares that economic science "aspires to a place" in the group of "progressive physical sciences."[28] In light of such an aspiration, it is hardly surprising to find a physical formulation of organization separated from the introductory historical account of its metaphysical preconditions. As was noted in the preceding chapter, in the introductory comments to this volume Marshall would also insist that spiritual characteristics, like self-reliance and independence, were fundamental characteristics of modern industrial life. The introductory historical sketches perform a similar function, pointing to the spiritual or moral foundations of those physical processes that make up modern industrial life and that will be analyzed scientifically in the main body of the volume. Thus the introductory book points to subjective freedom or self-consciousness as the ground of individual economic behavior and to objective freedom as the ground of modern industrial organization. This introductory book serves, in other words, to identify modern economic life as the product of a particular moment in history, whose spiritual conditions did not always exist. In the main body of the volume, however, modern economic life is defined in terms of a variety of physical processes amenable to mechanical analysis and biological analogy. In a word, Marshall tells us in his *Principles* that a metaphysical notion of freedom stands at the foundation of the physical science of economics.

THE LIMITS OF ECONOMIC SCIENCE

The limits of economic science are also its foundations. Ultimately, for Marshall, almost any entity found within the domain of material life could be described as a physical organization. Within the modern world,

---

[28] *Principles*, I: 31. Such a classification is not quite as simple as it appears to be at first sight. Marshall proceeds to identify exact measurement as the key to the progress of the science, thereby pointing to the machinery of exchange as the progressive element of economic science. But not all of economic science, he confesses, is as yet capable of rigorous quantitative statement. If not yet quantitative, however, these facets of economic science are nevertheless resolutely physical.

individual mechanical minds and modern research universities constitute forms of physical organization as much as do modern businesses. In
all cases, the distinctly *modern* form of the organization of these physical
entities follows from the metaphysical conditions of their development.
Modern brains, businesses, and scientific laboratories are highly organized,
and a precondition of their complexity is that they have developed within a
world of subjective and objective freedom. As we have just seen, Marshall
in his introduction pointed to this spiritual foundation of higher physical
organization, but his scientific analysis is concerned only with the physical
structure and development of such organizations. Such analysis, however,
of necessity arrives at a limit, for there are certain developments in modern life that cannot be attributed to physical mechanism alone. A scientific
research organization, for example, may organize its inductive investigations and construct machinery of deductive analysis, and this will aid the
progress of scientific knowledge. But no amount of physical organization
will in itself generate those constructive ideas that are supplied by the
self-conscious mind. Of the latter source of progress, the practitioner of a
physical science of economics can take no account; the springs of creative
thought lie beyond his horizons. Self-consciousness stands not only at the
foundation but also at the limits of the analyses of a physical science of
economics.

In this section we shall examine Marshall's later scientific analysis of the
progress of character and the growth of knowledge. Our discussion will be
greatly simplified by the fact that, as we shall see, Marshall employed the
same basic model to relate the development of organization to both the
improvement of character and the growth of knowledge. Standing behind
this shared model is Marshall's argument in the *Principles* that the replacement of human labor by machinery is an inevitable consequence of the
growth of organization. With regard to ordinary business, this argument
was established in the chapter on the division of labor in book IV. Here
Marshall first of all rendered into physiological form Smith's argument that
specialization improves manual dexterity. "Anyone who has to perform the
same set of operations day after day," he writes, "gradually learns to move
his fingers ... by almost automatic action and with greater rapidity than
would be possible if every movement had to wait for a deliberate instruction of the will." But this formation of automatic nervous mechanisms is
but a first step in the process that, by breaking down the production process
as a whole into a series of routines, leads inevitably to the substitution of
human for machine production; for it is "a general rule" that "any manufacturing operation that can be reduced to uniformity ... is sure to be taken

over sooner or later by machinery."[29] This general rule, however, applied equally to the manufacture of knowledge as it did to the manufacture of commodities.

"Organization aids knowledge," Marshall wrote in the *Principles*.[30] It does so by means of the same principle of differentiation that gives rise to specialized machinery in the production of material commodities. Turning to a discussion of methodology elsewhere in the *Principles*, we find that just as in industry it "pays to make a machine" when "the same operation has to be performed over and over again," so when processes of reasoning must be repeated in science, "it is worth while to reduce the process to system, to organize methods of reasoning and to formulate general propositions to be used as machinery for working on the facts as vices for holding them firmly in position for the work."[31] Organization thus assists the progress of science, but it does not in itself produce new constructive ideas. What it does do, in both industry and the academy, is free up mental attention from routine tasks and thus allow attention to be brought to bear on higher-level tasks and problems. This process leads to the development of ever more complicated forms of machinery and entails that human labor not only is freed from basic routine drudge work, but is also continually called to perform more demanding and responsible operations in supervising machinery. Hence, with regard to industry in general, the development of organization leads to the improvement of working-class habits and therefore character. Thus, to borrow a phrase from Marshall's discussion of the Cambridge Mathematical Tripos in one of his early letters to the *Cambridge Gazette*, while organization cannot produce new creative scientific ideas, it does as much as "art can do to create genius."[32]

The new category of organization helped clarify the nature of the conceptual bridge that Marshall was building between the academy and industry. It was now possible to describe the modern university in economic terms without necessarily introducing the terminology of the marketplace. In 1880, for example, we find him setting out before a parliamentary committee a vision of the organization of national higher education in terms of the simultaneous integration and differentiation of the component parts of the system. Differentiation in such a system meant, for Marshall, the proliferation of local colleges, while integration was to be achieved by means of the

[29] *Principles*, I: 253–5.
[30] *Principles*, I: 138.
[31] *Principles*, I: 779.
[32] See p. 149 above.

centralization of examinations.[33] On a parallel path, by 1885 Marshall was insisting that economic research itself must be properly organized. In his inaugural lecture as the new Cambridge Professor of Political Economy, he proclaimed the existence of an "economic organon," which was "not a body of concrete truth, but an engine for the discovery of concrete truth."[34] In an address to the Silver Jubilee meeting of the Statistical Society that same year, he discussed some of the inductive machinery that constituted this organon. Marshall here described a method of statistical curves that "if properly organized" could become "a great engine of scientific inquiry."[35] But the production of books of such curves was a costly business, and the key to the success of the organization of statistical research was the establishment of "a standard gauge for the thickness of the strip allotted to each year" (he proposed a depth of five millimeters); the "system of standard gauges and interchangeable parts has recently revolutionized many industries; and I think that it may do great good in the statistical industry."[36] The integration of production by means of the establishment of international standards generated economies associated with large-scale production, both in the ordinary business of life and in the academy.

But again, if the organon of economic science can aid the economist, it does not in itself produce new fundamental economic ideas. The organization of statistical curves, for example, may perhaps aid the mind in noticing correlations and possible connections between phenomena, but only by an inductive leap of the self-conscious mind can one arrive at a general law that ties together a series of particular facts. Whewell's philosophy of the inductive sciences had informed Marshall's earliest theoretical advances in political economy. The same idealist philosophy also informs his mature conception of the spiritual origin of those "real ideas" that are embodied in machines and serve to increase the productivity of both industry and academy. Of course, such constructive ideas do not constitute the whole domain of knowledge, and much of the business of scientific life consists of the derivation of particular items of knowledge, including both general propositions and particular facts, from existing ideas. By the same token, much new industrial machinery is generated not by the material embodiment of a new idea, but by the transformation of existing physical operations into mechanical form. Organization is in large part the efficient development

[33] Groenewegen 1996: 44; see also p. 59.
[34] Pigou 1925: 159.
[35] See Pigou 1925: 175–87; and for a correction of Pigou's description of this paper as delivered to the International Statistical Congress, see Whitaker 1996: 25–43.
[36] Pigou 1925: 178–9.

and utilization of just such forms of knowledge and machinery, and the analysis of precisely this kind of physical process falls neatly within the province of the economic scientist. But just as in Marshall's 1871 formulation of the relationship between industry and academy, in this mature vision there is a "missing link" in the circuits that flow back and forth between self-conscious theory and practical activity.[37] Self-consciousness continues to play a vital role in the discovery of new ideas that are subsequently embodied in both the machinery of science and the processes of production; the invisible spring of the spirit continually bubbles up at the very center of the visible realm of physical organization, generating new ideas that are subsequently embodied in innovative mechanical appliances. However, the analysis of precisely this aspect of modern life falls outside the proper province of the economic scientist.

Marshall's conception of the relationship between organization and character was similar if not identical to his conception of the relationship between organization and knowledge. As we have seen, in the *Principles* Marshall outlined a "general rule" that any laboring process that could be broken down into uniform components would inevitably become mechanized. One of Marshall's favorite examples was the manufacture of standardized watches. In what was surely intended to stand as an implicit parallel with Smith's famous pin factory, he described one small part of the production of such watches, which involved "a beautiful machine" that was used to make "tiny screws of exquisite form." This machine was "intricate and costly," and "the person who minds it must have an intelligence, and an energetic sense of responsibility, which go a long way towards making a fine character."[38] Before the development of this machine, the requisite mechanical parts were produced by skilled artisans, "who lived sedentary lives, straining their eyesight through microscopes, and finding in their work very little scope for any faculty except a mere command over the use of their fingers."[39] Clearly it is not simply a quantitative saving of labor power that Marshall is here celebrating; it is also the improvement in character that such industrial progress draws forth. Indeed, it is striking to observe the way that Marshall here contrasts the bodily labor of the craftsmen of old, who worked with eyes and fingers, with the almost managerial efforts of the machine operative, whose work provides an education in intelligence and responsibility. In other words, in Marshall's mature conception of economic

[37] See pp. 241–2 above.
[38] *Principles*, I: 257–8.
[39] *Principles*, I: 253–8.

progress, the development of the organization of industry, as manifested in the mechanization of labor, provides an automatic education that develops the character of the working classes.

Behind this mature vision of the improvement of the working classes stands the 1875 declaration that the ordinary business of life is also the most important form of education. This declaration was, in fact, a crucial step in the gradual process whereby Marshall came to see an increasing (but never complete) connection between those realms of culture and commerce that he had initially regarded as separate. As we saw in the preceding chapter, by 1871 Marshall had come to believe that competition might improve university teaching practices. Nevertheless, at this time he was still convinced that education itself was the predominant preserve of the school or university; this indeed was the underlying premise of his 1873 talk to the Cambridge Reform Club. This position had in fact been supported by a very particular analysis of the social cost of the division of labor. In some notes from the early 1870s, we find Marshall using the physiological terminology found in "Ye Machine" to argue that increased specialization within industry saved "cerebrum work," as "cerebellum work or even to some extent nerve-centre work is substituted for it."[40] In other words, the upper-level mechanical circuit (the cerebellum) was freed up as operations increasingly came under the control of the lower-level circuit (cerebrum), or even became quasi-instinctual automatic nervous reflexes. Specialization is here associated not with higher-level management of complicated machinery, but simply with increased physical dexterity as routines become automatic. This early position was the product of placing Smith's analysis of the division of labor within a psychological framework. Marshall's mature position, however, arose when he arrived at an evolutionary account of the mechanization of productive processes.[41]

Marshall's analysis of the physical side of production led him to turn upside-down Smith's bleak picture of the social cost of increased specialization. Opposition to Smith's analysis of the social costs of the division of labor was already present in the early 1870s, when Marshall argued that

[40] M 4/26, f. 51. Once again, the earliest expression of this approach is found in Marshall's copy of Mill's *Principles*. In a lengthy discussion written on a blank page of chapter 8 of book I, Marshall writes of specialized skill "saving cerebrum work" and extending the "range of application of nerve-center & cerebellum work" (Mill 1865: 72 [UL]).

[41] Marshall's evolutionary model of the mechanization of production was derived with the aid of Charles Babbage's reformulation of Smith's principle of the division of labor. For reasons of space, however, this aspect of Marshall's conception of organization is not addressed in this book.

"when the work is in itself light & the hours of work are not long," then "a rigid monotony need not be extremely injurious." In itself, monotonous work "will not stimulate thought," but it will "leave the brain every possible opportunity of thought." Here is the ground of Marshall's 1873 vision that social progress is to be achieved by a lessening of the hardships of labor and the utilization of leisure for self-improvement and higher education. From this early perspective, monotonous work is a problem only when "the work is of a kind to absorb the whole of a man[']s attention while engaged on it & sufficiently heavy to allow a man little energy for thought after it is over." In such cases "monotony is an unmitigated evil."[42] Here we see why, in the 1873 talk to the Cambridge Reform Club, Marshall's picture of the problems of the present emphasized the weary toil of the masses rather than (as Smith had emphasized) the stupefying effects of the monotony of their daily grind. By 1875, however, Marshall was prepared to consider any process that engaged the workers' whole attention as educative of character, in and of itself. Once this point of view was coupled with the belief that routine labor would inevitably become mechanized, the result being that monotonous routine would give way to responsible machine management, the way was open to a vision of character development as an endogenous component of economic progress. Education was projected from the sphere of leisure consumption into the sphere of machine production.

But the economist's analysis of the economic education of character did not embrace all aspects of moral improvement. On the theoretical plane, the limits of the economic analysis of the education of character are identical to the limits of the economic explanation for the progress of science. In both cases, the economist arrives at, and indeed points toward, but cannot use the physicalist language of economic science to speak about the self-consciousness that is the source of progress. Just as organization can aid knowledge, so machine minding can "go a long way towards making a fine character" – a long way, but not all the way. As with ideas and knowledge, so with character; while maintaining a vision of social progress as dependent on spiritual as well as economic improvement, Marshall nevertheless saw the study of spiritual factors as falling outside the province of the economic scientist. But Marshall's investigation of the social education of character was also limited by practical considerations. In 1875, and in a manner reminiscent of Beesly, Marshall described trade unions as self-governing republics and looked to collective action by workers to build the mechanical bonds of sympathy that would foster that sense of social duty

<hr>

[42] M 4/26, f. 47.

that he identified with the future evolution of objective freedom. As we shall see, the basic claim that objective freedom might develop into "collective freedom" can indeed be found in Marshall's *Principles*. Nevertheless, in the *Principles*, Marshall in the main passed over collective organizations such as trade unions and focused almost exclusively on private business enterprises. For this reason, his analysis of the education of character consistently emphasizes only those economic and physiological developments that are the preconditions of the development of subjective freedom. The preconditions of the development of objective freedom are not brought into focus in Marshall's picture of modern economic life. We shall turn to the explanation of this apparent lacuna in Marshall's *Principles* in the following section.

ECONOMIC SCIENCE AND SOCIAL PHILOSOPHY

For Marshall, economic science formed one part of a wider, dialectical social philosophy. As we have seen, in the introductory book of the *Principles*, Marshall pointed to subjective freedom as the ground of individual economic actions and to objective freedom as the ground of modern industrial organization. Once this metaphysical foundation was laid, Marshall embarked in the main part of his volume on a scientific investigation of the various physical processes that constitute modern economic life. Such an investigation was, however, necessarily curtailed when it arrived at the limits of the physical dimension of modern social reality. In reaching such limits, economic science had, so to speak, returned to its foundations; for what lay beyond the limits of a physical science of society were self-consciousness, its manifestations, and its further development – the spiritual elements on which modern economic life was founded. Yet from the 1875 talk on America, we know that Marshall believed that the development of certain aspects of economic life formed a precondition of the further evolution of subjective and objective freedom. In other words, from a perspective wider than that of the economic scientist, the physical and the spiritual components of modern social life might be correlated. From the perspective of the social philosopher, the evolution of the modern economic organism might be seen to generate the conditions of such spiritual developments as serve to transform the foundations and thereby also the nature of modern economic life.

Marshall's economic science and his social philosophy frame modern social life in two different ways. Economic science utilizes a range of scientific techniques to isolate and identify the causes of economic phenomena.

Social philosophy, however, deals with elements of social reality between which a conception of causation is not appropriate. Between a metaphysical conception of freedom and a principle of physical organization, no causal connection can be specified. The relationship between such philosophical opposites is dialectical. This dialectical relationship does not correspond to any particular economic relationship. It is a mistake, for example, to identify the market as the domain of freedom and suppose that, from the point of view of social philosophy, a dialectical relationship exists between the freedom of the market and the physical organization of a modern business enterprise; as already noted, a market itself can be more or less organized. More generally, both physical organization and subjective freedom play vital roles in both markets and organizations. It will be helpful to illustrate further how this is the case before delineating the dialectical relationship that stands at the heart of Marshall's mature social philosophy.

As Marco Dardi has observed, Marshall conceived of individual market behavior as directed primarily by the lower-level mechanical circuitry of the brain.[43] That is, ordinary market behavior involves routine mechanical responses to normal run-of-the-mill events. Only when some unprecedented event occurs do Marshall's market agents find themselves forced to engage the higher faculties of their minds. Put in the terms of Marshall's 1875 paper, it is only in the latter kinds of situation that the market provides an education in subjective freedom, fostering such moral characteristics as self-reliance and independent judgment. But whether individuals are acting mechanically or self-consciously, they are always acting so as to achieve ends that they themselves have decided on in the first place. Thus we may say that, for Marshall, subjective freedom remains the precondition of the existence of a market; everyday market life is a predominantly mechanical affair, but when, as inevitably happens, a spanner is thrown into the works in the form of an unprecedented market event, at this point the market provides an education that develops subjective freedom.

A similar combination of self-consciousness and mechanical routine can be discerned in Marshall's mature theory of production. For Marshall, a modern business organization is in the first instance a mechanism that develops and harnesses particular sets of mechanical routines among the workforce. From machine supervision through managerial superintendence, most work within an established business organization is the work of routine. Such routines, of course, can be created only once ancient customs have been undermined by the emergence of self-consciousness and once

[43] See Dardi 2003.

an environment characterized by objective freedom has come into being. But an originally innovative modern business runs the risk of new routines becoming rigidly entrenched and therefore obsolete, or at least uncompetitive, industrial practices. The survival of a business in a market environment thus depends on its ability to adapt to new market situations, and individuals and businesses that are incapable of adapting their mechanical operations will sooner or later be pushed aside by more vigorous economic organisms.[44] But this emphasis on adaptation is not the random variation of natural Darwinian evolution. It is a variation that arises through self-conscious deliberation and also creative insight. Ultimately, the modern business organization, though it organizes a host of particular mechanical routines, must also foster subjective freedom among its employees if it is to survive and flourish.

From the point of view of Marshall's social philosophy, markets and organizations are but two sides of the same coin. Both operate by means of physical mechanisms, but both are not only founded on, but also generate, subjective freedom. A single dialectical relationship between physical organization and freedom thus characterizes modern social life as a whole.[45] This dialectical relationship generates social progress, but not by way of a totalizing reconciliation of two abstract historical forces. Social progress, for Marshall, is rather the outcome of a continuing and ongoing interplay between spirit and matter that occurs in myriad local situations. Simply put, Marshall's vision is of a varied but continuous interplay between self-consciousness, on the one hand, and mechanical habit and social organization, on the other, whose product is a continual transformation of traditional customs into modern industrial habits, of traditional and simple social organizations into highly organized modern businesses, and the gradual spread of moral autonomy throughout all sections of the economy. Physical routines and self-consciousness thus interact in a continual process of dialectical advance, and in this way economic progress transforms the natural and the traditional into the moral and the free, thereby establishing the foundation of future economic progress. In this way we can see that Marshall achieved the reconciliation of the philosophical opposites of mind and matter not as

---

[44] Brian Loasby has shown how, at a number of levels, Marshall's analysis of the individual firm replicates or develops his analysis of the human mind. See especially Loasby's chapter on industrial organization in *ECAM*, 371–8, but also Loasby 1989, 1990.

[45] At this point my exegesis would seem to converge with the more recent writings of Tiziano Raffaelli, who approaches what I take to be the same point but by way of an exploration of Marshall's materialistic mental science and physicalist economic science. See especially Raffaelli 1994, 1995.

a psychologist, but as a social philosopher. The reconciliation of mind and matter that occurs in modern life is what Marshall conceives of as social progress.

Yet as already suggested, such a vision of social progress does not generate the philosophy of modern history that Marshall outlined in his 1875 talk on America. In theory, the concept of organization could encompass worker associations as readily as private business enterprises. Again, in theory the economic scientist could account for those mechanical bonds of sympathy fostered by participation in worker republics, which provided the physical preconditions of the further evolution of objective freedom. In practice, however, Marshall directed his reader's attention to the character traits of responsibility and intelligence that arose by way of employment within a hierarchical, privately owned business venture, which, like the market, provided an education only in subjective freedom. Thus the social philosophy that is bound up with Marshall's economic science leans toward individualism as opposed to collectivism. Hence the dialectic of modern economic life as framed by social philosophy does not, in itself, lead to that dialectical resolution of subjective and objective freedom that in the 1875 paper was implicitly formulated as the telos of modern history. A piece of the whole is now missing.

At some point, very late in his life, Marshall made some critical comments on one of the privately printed copies of his talk "The Future of the Working Classes." Writing of his present views in reference to those of his younger days, he declared, "Don't regard Utopia as likely to come soon: or as likely to come ever unless 'self-forgetting virtues' become common. Argue only that not *economically* impracticable."[46] This annotation captures precisely the gap that can be found between his social philosophy as conceived in 1875 and his practical work as an economic scientist. This gap does not reflect an abandonment of idealist commitments and a turn to the physicalist monism of scientific naturalism. It reflects simply a decision, the result of which is manifest in almost every page of the *Principles*, not to discuss the economic road to utopia. There can be no doubt that Marshall believed for all of his life that altruistic behavior constituted the highest form of life and that the cultivation of a self-conscious sense of social duty was the key to a transformation of society, a transformation not dissimilar

---

[46] M 6/41/2, emphasis in original. Marshall also writes of his earlier talk: "Too much stress on leisure for adults. This only one of many movements: would in many ways do harm at present: machinery takes off excessive strain: Education of children far more important." The script suggests to me a date later than 1900. I would speculate that Marshall wrote these comments while preparing his last and uncompleted book on progress.

to that which Mill had hoped for in his *Principles of Political Economy*.[47] But as Marshall's second sentence in the quotation indicates, after 1875 he came to the conclusion that the economic scientist should refrain from discussing the preconditions of the further progress of objective freedom. This was not a theoretical conclusion. It reflected rather a growing sense of unease concerning the modern socialist movement that began to emerge in Britain around 1885. Marshall increasingly feared what he considered to be a one-sided doctrine of collectivism, that "failed to properly analyze the nature of competition" and therefore was, in the present state of social development, likely to lead only to "the tyranny and the spiritual death of an ironbound socialism."[48] As we shall see, Marshall by no means abandoned his metaphysical faith that one day individualism and collectivism would be reconciled in a higher form of social life. But he also remained convinced that the evolution of self-consciousness toward this goal must proceed not by way of a reaction against the conditions of subjective freedom, but by way of competition and the further development of moral autonomy.

CONCLUSION

While Marshall came to classify economics as an aspiring physical science, the introductory book of his *Principles* emphasized the real value of the nonphysical elements of modern life. In Chapter Four we saw Marshall insisting that "the source of all progress," vigor, was a moral as opposed to a physical energy. Vigor, for Marshall, was an expression of the free moral energy of self-consciousness, and it was the source of great thoughts, deeds, and feelings. Economic science itself was the product of vigor. This becomes apparent when we turn to the introductory pages of his *Principles*, where Marshall set down a brief summary of the moral history that had informed his 1873 talk to the Cambridge Reform Club.

Slavery was regarded by Aristotle as an ordinance of nature, and so probably was it by the slaves themselves in olden times. The dignity of man was proclaimed by the Christian religion: it has been asserted with increasing vehemence during the last

---

[47] Marshall's writings from the mid-1880s onward contain numerous statements regarding the importance of altruistic self-sacrifice in modern social life. See, e.g., Pigou 1925: 152, 174, 225, 251, 228–9, 342.

[48] Pigou 1925: 284, 291. For an extended discussion of the way that Marshall's social philosophy informed his mature attitude toward socialism and his construction of an alternative ethos of chivalry, see Cook 2008. For Marshall's early attitude toward socialism, see Tullberg 1973, and for his response to Henry George in the early 1880s, see Stigler and Coase 1969.

one hundred years: but only through the spread of education during quite recent times, are we beginning to feel the full impact of the phrase. Now at last we are setting ourselves seriously to inquire whether it is necessary that there should be any so called 'lower-classes' at all: that is, whether there need be large numbers of people doomed from their birth to hard work in order to provide the requisites of a refined and cultured life; while they themselves are prevented by their poverty and toil from having any share or part of that life.[49]

Economic science, as Marshall presented it from 1890 onward, was to serve the moral aim of eradicating poverty and raising the material and cultural conditions of the working classes. Thus in this passage Marshall effectively characterized economic science as the product of a culminating moment in the history of morality. Economic science was not in itself an ethical science, and as we have seen in this chapter, in his mature thought Marshall was careful to separate the physical science of economics from the "higher" studies of ideas and ideals. Nevertheless, the various techniques and the scientific machinery of economics served an ethical purpose. Those techniques and methods, like the subject matter they were employed to examine, might indeed be confined purely to the realm of the physical. But the ultimate motivation of the economic scientist in studying the ordinary business of life lay beyond the physical realm. Here, then, is a version of that Coleridgean conception of the relationship between academy and commercial society that had informed Marshall's early notes on Smith's article on education. As we have seen, from his initial separation of culture and commerce, Marshall came to perceive many connections and shared characteristics between industry and university; indeed, his mature vision of modern economic life was in many ways a vision of the education of different aspects of character by different parts of the economic system. Nevertheless, his classification of economics as a physical science served to highlight one aspect of his first formulation of the nature of this relationship that remained constant throughout his intellectual life, namely that the real man of learning was motivated in his studies not by an ordinary expectation of personal reward, but rather by an enthusiasm for a higher good.

Vigor, according to Marshall, manifests itself in great thought as well as great deeds and feelings. With regard to the former, Marshall insisted in the *Principles* "[i]deas, whether those of art and science, or those embodied in practical appliances, are the most 'real' of the gifts that each generation receives from its predecessors."[50] Economic science is not only the

---

[49] *Principles*, I: 3.
[50] *Principles*, I: 780.

handmaiden of ethics; as we saw earlier, it is also founded on the epistemic fruits of self-consciousness. For example, and as Marshall explained in the preface to the *Principles*, the theory of supply and demand constitutes "a Fundamental Idea running through the various parts of the central problem of Distribution and Exchange."[51] These, and the other "Fundamental Ideas" out of which the science of economics is constructed, are not derived by the inductive and deductive machinery of science; rather, they are born of self-consciousness. Indeed, not only does the the spiritual component of a manly character, vigor, provide the ethical ideals that motivate the economic scientist and the "constructive ideas" employed by him, it also generates that culture which is the foundation of industrial prosperity. As Marshall explained the real value of constructive ideas:

The world's material wealth would quickly be replaced if it were destroyed, but the ideas by which it was made retained. If however the ideas were lost, but not the material wealth, then that would dwindle and the world would go back to poverty. And most of our knowledge of mere facts could quickly be recovered if it were lost, but the constructive ideas of thought remained; while if the ideas perished, the world would enter again on the Dark Ages.[52]

Here, then, is Coleridge's idealism as filtered through the medium of Whewell's ideal of a scientific clerisy, and here too is an indication of the distance that political economy had traveled since the days of the Scottish Enlightenment. Between Smith's *Wealth of Nations* and Marshall's *Principles*, we can identify a whole series of intellectual transformations. In the second chapter of this book, it was noted that in the last decade of the eighteenth century Edmund Burke had reversed the standard Scottish Enlightenment formulation of the relationship between commerce and civilization. Where Smith saw commerce as leading to the improvement of tastes and manners, Burke now proclaimed the church and the nobility to be the foundations of polite society, and hence the preconditions of commercial society. As Burke explained his conception of this relationship in his *Reflections on the Revolution in France* (1790):

Where trade and manufactures are wanting to a people, and the spirit of nobility and religion remains, sentiment supplies, and not always ill supplies their place; but if commerce and the arts should be lost in an experiment to try how well a state may stand without these old fundamental principles, what sort of a thing must be a nation of gross, stupid, ferocious, and at the same time poor and sordid barbarians,

---

[51] *Principles*, I: viii.
[52] *Principles*, I: 780.

destitute of religious honour, possessing nothing at present, and hoping for nothing hereafter?[53]

By formulating Burke's position in the language of German idealism, Coleridge shifted the focus of subsequent discussion from the manners and mores of civilized society to the "real ideas" that constituted the culture and manly character of those who became cultured. Furthermore, Coleridge now amalgamated Burke's two ideals of church and aristocracy into his peculiar yet extremely influential notion of a clerisy, whose duty it was to preserve and disseminate the cultural heritage of the nation. With Whewell the professors and dons of mid-Victorian Cambridge became the guardians, and also the discoverers, of the fundamental ideas of a culture that was understood to include both the natural and the moral sciences. In his own way, Marshall continued this tradition. If those who comprised Marshall's intellectual aristocracy were masters of secular science as opposed to doctors of divinity, his 1873 vision of the social role of this secular clerisy was nevertheless firmly in the tradition of Burke, Coleridge, and Whewell. By advancing scientific knowledge and disseminating that knowledge throughout society, this intellectual aristocracy was charged not only with promoting culture, but also with establishing the conditions of material prosperity. Thus, where Smith had taken for granted that civilization was the daughter of commerce, Marshall now assumed that the progress of culture was the key to the development of industry.

But between the talk of 1873 and the position set down in the *Principles of Economics* stand three further, crucial transformations. The first of these occurred within a year or two of his Reform Club talk, while the second and third would take Marshall two decades to work out in full. The first transformation in Marshall's thought occurred when he decided that the ordinary business of life constituted a school of character at least as important as anything that could be provided by formal education. The second arose when he formulated a model of the development of what he called "industrial organization," one implication of which was that the progress of industry entailed the eventual mechanization of operations initially performed by hand. This meant that industrial machinery had a tendency to become increasingly complicated and so demanded greater responsibility from its operatives. Together, these first two developments in Marshall's thinking allowed him to conceive of the modern economy as an evolving organism, whose development necessarily entailed an ever more intensive working

[53] Burke 1987: 69–70.

education of the character of the laboring classes – an education that would, in the normal course of things, occur during the ordinary business of life. If Marshall the economic scientist put the physical preconditions of the "self-forgetting virtues" out of sight, he nevertheless presented his readers with a vision of the continuing improvement of mechanical character and the suggestion of a further development of self-conscious autonomy and responsibility.

By means of his mature vision of economic progress, Marshall attempted to draw to a close the tradition, which had commenced with Adam Smith, of highlighting the negative social effects of modern productive methods. Although Smith had indeed celebrated commerce as an agent of civilization, he had nevertheless pointed to the increasingly intensive division of labor as responsible for stupefying and brutalizing the modern laborer. The problem as Smith saw it, at least in the first instance, was that the monotonous repetition of a few basic operations deforms and mutilates the personality as a whole. But behind Smith's analysis of the social effects of the division of labor stands a long tradition of humanist political thought, in which civic personality was understood as founded on the ownership of land and the bearing of arms. From this perspective the underlying problems with modern commercial society began with the division of labor between professional soldier and taxpayer; and it is no coincidence that in addition to recommending state support of primary education, Smith in his article on education also counseled the establishment of a citizen militia.[54] By the 1870s, however, the civic humanist challenge to modern commercial society was not remembered even by historians of thought. Hence for Marshall in the early 1870s the social effects of the division of labor were to be analyzed according to a different conception of personality, and the resulting analysis, when coupled with an evolutionary account of the mechanization of production, was resoundingly optimistic.

But Marshall did not see the economic education of character purely as a consequence of participation in the processes of production. In 1875, we should recall, he had argued that American workers obtained their training in subjective freedom not from any one specific trade, but from the fact that they moved from one trade to another with astonishing frequency. The distinctive traits of the American character were formed through participation in a multitude of labor markets, rather than through labor itself. The third transformation in Marshall's thought after 1873 was the shift in his early conception of an opposition between the realms of culture and commerce,

---

[54] See *WN*, 786–8 (V. i. f).

and between self-consciousness and mechanism, to a notion of a dialectical relationship between freedom and physical organization. In his intellectual youth, Marshall learned from liberal Anglican followers of Coleridge the method of reconciling opposites, but the opposition that stood at the center of his mature social thought was Hegelian. Such an opposition did not give rise to a stable new synthesis, but to the extent to which his social philosophy informed his economic writing, generated an irresolvable creative tension, as Marshall attempted to give formal expression to a philosophical idea that defied any comprehensive scientific articulation; for behind all of Marshall's discussions of economic progress stands a vision of real social progress. Such a vision was neither mechanical (as was the machinery of partial equilibrium analysis) nor biological (as was the analysis of industrial organization); it was dialectical.

It is hard to imagine that, had he lived to read Marshall's *Principles*, Karl Marx would have made a polite, let alone a sympathetic, reader. In the afterword to the second German edition of *Kapital*, Marx praised Hegel for being the first to present the general form of the working of the dialectic. Nevertheless, following Feuerbach he declared that with Hegel the dialectic "is standing on its head." In this mystified and inverted form, the dialectic served "to transfigure and to glorify the existing state of things." Turned right-side-up, however, the dialectic shows every developed social form to be in "fluid motion," thereby revealing the transient nature of such forms, as well as their momentary existence.[55] That Marshall's conception of the dialectic served to justify an existing social order there can be no doubt; nor is there any question that Marshall's philosophy of history celebrated a gradual as opposed to a revolutionary transformation of the present state of society. And yet, while in the main he went out of his way to pass over the economic preconditions of the development of objective freedom, there can be no question that Marshall's idea of the dialectic of modern history also led him to look forward to the dawning of a new era of human history. Consider, for example, the following passage from the account of "the growth of free industry and enterprise" in the *Principles*, in which Marshall asserts that

by the aid of the telegraph and the printing-press, of representative government and trade associations, it is possible for the people to think out for themselves the solution of their own problems. The growth of knowledge and self-reliance has given them that true self-controlling freedom, which enables them to impose of their own

---

[55] Marx 1954: 29.

free will restraints on their own actions; and problems of collective production, collective ownership and collective consumption are entering on a new phase.

Any attempt at a revolutionary leap into the future, Marshall continues, is "foredoomed to fail"; for "we cannot move safely, if we move so fast that our new plans of life altogether outrun our instincts." Nevertheless,

gradually we may attain to an order of social life, in which the common good overrules individual caprice, even more than it did in the early ages before the sway of individualism had begun. But unselfishness then will be the offspring of deliberate will; and though aided by instinct, individual freedom will then develop itself into collective freedom: – a happy contrast to the old order of life, in which individual slavery to custom caused collective slavery and stagnation, broken only by the caprice of despotism or the caprice of revolution.[56]

Whatever side up the form of Marshall's dialectic, he took from Hegel the same notion of the shape of history as a whole as did Marx. For both Marx and Marshall, the present is indeed but a transient moment in a dialectical process that leads from one form of collectivity, through the individualism of the present, to another. Marx, of course, rendered this dialectic of history in terms of the collective or private ownership of property, history as a whole thus entailing a transformation from primitive to future communism via the various stages of private ownership of property (of which the present stage of capitalism was the last). Marshall, by contrast, rendered this dialectic in ultimately psychological and metaphysical terms (and hence, from the point of view of Marx, employed an idealistic and mystical form of the dialectic). For Marshall, the dialectical circle of history begins with collective custom and culminates in collective freedom, while history itself consists of the gradual development of subjective or individual freedom and its physical corollaries. Within this total dialectic of history, both Marx and Marshall posit particular dialectics of historical progress, the engines, as it were, that drive society through a series of stages from the beginning to the end of history. Marx's particular dialectic, which he called "historical materialism," was conceived in terms of a series of contradictions between the forces and the relations of production in any one of the intermediate stages between primitive and industrial communism. Marshall did not have such a monolithic vision of the whole of human history. But with regard to the present period of modern history, his particular dialectic involved an interplay that had begun to emerge in the towns of the Middle Ages, between freedom and physical organization. With the aid of industrial technologies

---

[56] *Principles*, I: 751–2.

such as the telegraph and moral technologies such as sympathetic habits, subjective and objective freedom would one day develop into that ultimate form of freedom, collective freedom.

Both Marxist and Marshallian forms of the dialectic posit an ultimate state of society in which self-consciousness and material conditions are in full harmony with one another. In fact, the key difference between the two perspectives is actually incidental to the respective forms of their dialectic. For orthodox Marxism, revolutionary vision is firmly fixed on the total dialectical synthesis that must at some point create a new utopia. Yet after the Russian Revolution, the Bolsheviks were confronted with the reality that the road from post-revolutionary socialism to true communism was not a short one, and they were of necessity forced to engage with the practical realities of the nebulous stage that must be traversed between political revolution and the arrival of utopia. As for Marshall, his dialectical thought when taken in its entirety certainly points to an eventual state of total reconciliation of subjective and objective freedom. In other words, it is true that the logic of his thought points to the fact that the present stage of history will come to an end eventually, as the material and spiritual components of modern economic life gradually become one harmonious self-conscious whole. But such a state is little more than a theoretical ideal, which in practice serves Marshall by mapping out a theoretical period between the beginnings of the modern age (i.e., the point at which freedom and mechanical organization begin to enact a dialectical engagement with one another) and the end of the present stage of history. This current period is by definition a period of flux, during which a continual dialectical interplay between subjective freedom and physical organization moves society ever nearer to an ultimate and total reconciliation of subjective and objective freedom. This philosophical insight into the ultimate shape of modern history as a whole is the ground on which the economic scientist constructs a scientific study of mankind, engaged in the ordinary business of modern life. So where the Marxist looks to the ultimate dialectical resolution of social contradictions, but in practice is forced to engage with the slow process of arriving at this future state, the Marshallian economist conceives of the dialectic as a whole simply in order to fix his analytical gaze on the complicated and, for practical purposes, endless paths of the present.

In so doing, the economic scientist loses sight of the telos of modern history and proceeds by means of the analysis of particular and local periods that are abstracted from the dialectical flux of modern life. Furthermore, the economist qua economist abstracts not only from the totality of social relations but also from the totality of mental life; for as we have seen, the economic scientist focuses not on the dialectical interplay of subject and object, but simply on the observable and the physical. These last two are not the same, at least for practical purposes, for there is much that occurs in the physical world that lies beyond the gaze of the economic scientist. The limits of economic science are not the limits of economic observation, but the limits simply of physical reality. Looking to the whole of this physical reality, the economist takes within his province not only the gradual evolution of industrial organizations, but also the gradual evolution of mechanical character as it adapts to an evolving physical environment. But while recognizing that such social evolution is grounded on subjective freedom, and aware that the manifestations of self-consciousness play a continual role in the progress of society, the economist stops short of discussing any but the most liminal of such manifestations. Nor does he concern himself with the role of economic – or for that matter political – progress in fostering the development of self-consciousness. Finally, and for what would seem to be political reasons, Marshall himself refrained from discussing even the physical preconditions of the evolution of collective freedom. Hence the last passage from the *Principles* quoted above is written in the conditional tense. The economic scientist declares only that "we may" arrive at a social order in which subjective freedom has become collective freedom, for he knows that the arrival of utopia is conditional on the development of those "self-forgetting virtues" that are the fruit of the self-consciousness born of collective action, and of these he will not speak. In short, a crucial piece of the dialectic is removed from the province of the economist. It is because of the removal of this piece of his social philosophy as a whole, and not because his form of the dialectic was inverted or mystical, that Marshall the political economist derived from Hegel not a dialectical philosophy of modern society, but a science of ordinary economic life. Marshall's intentions were never revolutionary; the ideal of social progress, which from first to last inspired his search for truth, was to be reached through the path of reconciliation and consensus.

Bibliography

Marshall's Manuscripts

All of the following manuscripts are to be found in the Marshall Archive of the Marshall Library in Cambridge.

M 3/2: Lectures on Economic Progress
M 3/16: Lecture Notes on Socialism
M 4/1: Loose-Leaf Book
M 4/3: Notes on Smith's *Wealth of Nations*
M 4/4: Notes on Smith's *Wealth of Nations*
M 4/5: Notes on Smith's *Wealth of Nations*
M 4/9: Lecture Notes on *Wages*
M 4/10: Historical Notes
M 4/11: Historical Notes
M 4/12: Historical Notes
M 4/13: Historical Notes
M 4/14: Historical Notes
M 4/15: Notes on the Physiocrats
M 4/19: Advanced Lecture Notes
M 4/25: Notes on Education
M 4/26: Notes on the Division of Labour
M 4/29: Statistics
M 4/32: Essay on Value
M 6/41/2: Privately printed copy of "The Future of the Working Classes" (1873, with late annotations in Marshall's hand)
M 7/5: Red Book

Other Manuscript Sources

Clifford, William K. ca. 1872. Untitled and undated mss. Add. 8795, Babbage Collection, folder 33, Cambridge University Library.
Venn, John. ca. 1903. "Autobiographical Sketch." Venn Papers, Church Missionary Society Archives, Special Collections, University of Birmingham.

Marshall's Books and Articles

The following abbreviations indicate where a book or article is now located: ML, Marshall Library, Cambridge; UL, University Library, Cambridge. In addition, BV indicates that an article was collected and bound by Marshall (see Caldari 2000, 2003).

Bagehot, Walter. 1872 [1869]. *Physics and Politics, or, Thoughts on the Application of "Natural Selection" and "Inheritance" to Political Society.* London: Henry King. [ML]

Brassey, Thomas. 1872. *Work and Wages Practically Illustrated.* London: Bell and Daldy. [ML]

Buckle, Henry T. 1867 [1857–61]. *History of Civilization in England.* 3 vols. London: John W. Parker & Son. [ML]

Carlyle, Thomas. 1872 [1842]. *On Heroes, Hero-Worship and the Heroic in History.* London: Chapman and Hall. [ML]

Carpenter, William B. 1875. "On the Doctrine of Human Automatism." *Contemporary Review* 25: 397–416, 940–62. [BV, ML]

Clifford, William K. 1875. "Right and Wrong: The Scientific Ground of Their Distinction." *Fortnightly Review* 24: 770–800. [BV, ML]

  1877. "The Ethics of Belief." *Contemporary Review* 29: 289–308. [BV, ML]

Clifford, William K., and Frederick Harrison. 1876. "On the Scientific Basis of Morals." *Contemporary Review* 26: 650–60. [BV, ML]

Henderson, J. Scot. 1870. "Hegel as a Politician: His Views on English Politics." *Fortnightly Review* 14: 262–76. [BV, ML]

Jevons, William S. 1871. *The Theory of Political Economy.* London: Macmillan & Co. [ML]

Lecky, William E. H. 1869. *History of European Morals from Augustus to Charlemagne.* 2 vols. London: Longmans, Green, and Co. [ML]

Leslie, T. E. C. 1872. "The Gold Question and the Movement of Prices in Germany." *Fortnightly Review* 18: 554–71. [BV, ML]

  1874. "The Movements of Agricultural Wages in Europe." *Fortnightly Review* 21: 705–19. [BV, ML]

Ludlow, John M., and Loyd Jones. 1867. *Progress of the Working Class, 1832–1867.* London: Alexander Strahan. [ML]

Maine, Henry. S. 1866 [1861]. *Ancient Law: Its connection with the early history of society, and its relation to modern ideas.* London: John Murray. [ML]

Marx, Karl. 1867. *Das Kapital: Kritik der politischen Oekonomie.* Buch I: Der Produktionsprocess des Kapitals. Hamburg: Otto Meissner. [UL]

Mill, John S. 1859. *Dissertations and Discussions Political, Philosophical, and Historical Reprinted chiefly from the Edinburgh and Westminster Review.* Vol. 2. London: John W. Parker and Son [ML].

  1865 [1848]. *Principles of Political Economy with Some of Their Applications to Social Philosophy.* People's edition. London: Longmans. [UL]

  1869. *The Subjection of Women.* London: Longmans, Green, Reader, and Dyer. [ML]

  1871 [1861]. Utilitarianism. London: Longmans, Green, Reader, and Dyer. [ML; inscribed: "Mary Paley Cambridge 1872"]

Newman, Francis W. 1871. "Malthusianism, True and False." *Fraser's Magazine* 3 (83 o.s.): 584–98. [ML, BV]

Sargant, William L. 1867. *Recent Political Economy*. London: Williams and Norgate. [ML]

Schäffle, Albert G. F. 1870. *Kapitalismus und Socialismus, mit besonderer Rücksicht auf Geschäfts- und Vermögensformen. Vorträge zur Versöhnung der Gegensätze von Lohnarbeit und Kapital*. Tübingen: H. Laupp. [ML]

Senior, Nassau. W. 1863 [1850]. *Political Economy*. London: Charles Griffin and Company. [ML]

Sidgwick, Henry. 1877. "Bentham and Benthamism in Politics and Ethics." *Fortnightly Review* 27: 627–52. [BV, ML]

    1879. "The Wages-Fund Theory." *Fortnightly Review* 25: 401–13. [BV, ML]

Smith, Adam. 1871. *An Inquiry into the Nature and Causes of the Wealth of Nations*. With notes by J. R. McCulloch. 5th ed. London: Ward, Lock. [UL]

Spencer, Herbert. 1865, 1867a. *The Principles of Biology*. 2 vols. London: Williams and Norgate. [ML]

    1867b [1862]. *First Principles*. London: Williams and Norgate. [ML]

    1868a [1851]. *Social Statics: or, The Conditions essential to Happiness specified, and the First of them Developed*. London: John Chapman. [ML]

    1868b. *Essays, Scientific, Political, and Speculative*. 2 vols. London: Williams and Norgate. [ML]

Tocqueville, Alexis de. 1862 [1835–40]. *Democracy in America*. 2 vols. London: Longman, Green, Longman, and Roberts. [ML]

Walker, Francis. 1876. *The Wages Question: A Treatise on Wages and the Wages Class*. New York: Henry Holt and Company. [ML]

General Bibliography

Aarsleff, Hans. 2006. "Philosophy of Language." In *The Cambridge History of Eighteenth-Century Philosophy*. Edited by Knud Haakonssen, pp. 451–95. Cambridge: Cambridge University Press.

Allen, Peter. 1985. "S. T. Coleridge's Church and State and the Idea of an Intellectual Establishment." *Journal of the History of Ideas* 46: 89–106.

Annan, Noel G. 1984. *Leslie Stephen: The Godless Victorian*. New York: Random House.

Babbage, Charles. 1864. *Passages from the Life of a Philosopher*. London: Longman & Co.

    1971 [1832]. *On the Economy of machinery and manufactures*. New York: M. Kelley.

Backhouse, Roger E. 2004. "History of Economics, Economics and Economic History in Britain, 1824–2000." *European Journal of the History of Economic Thought* 11: 107–27.

    2006. "Sidgwick, Marshall and the Cambridge School of Economics." *History of Political Economy* 38: 15–44.

Bagehot, Walter. 1900 [1867]. *"The English Constitution," and other political essays*. New York: D. Appleton.

Bain, Alexander. 1882. *John Stuart Mill. A Criticism: with Personal Recollections*. London: Longmans, Green, & Co.

    1977 [1855]. *The Senses and the Intellect*. Washington, D.C.: University Publications of America.

Ball, W. W. Rouse. 1889. *A History of the Study of Mathematics at Cambridge*. Cambridge: University Press.

Beesly, Edward S. 1867. "The Amalgamated Society of Carpenters." *Fortnightly Review* 7: 319–34.

1869. "The Social Future of the Working Class." *Fortnightly Review* 5: 344–63.

Beiser, Frederick C. 1993. "Hegel's Historicism." In *The Cambridge Companion to Hegel*. Edited by Frederick Beiser, pp. 270–300. Cambridge: Cambridge University Press.

Berman, David. 1990. *A History of Atheism from Hobbes to Russell*. London: Routledge.

Bharadwaj, Krishna. 1989. *Themes in Value and Distribution: Classical Theory Reappraised*. London: Unwin Hyman.

1995. "The Anglican Ethic and the Spirit of Citizenship: The Political and Social Context." In *Alfred Marshall's "Lectures to Women": Some Economic Questions Directly Connected to the Welfare of the Laborer*. Edited by T. Raffaelli, E. Biagini, and R. Tullberg, pp. 24–46. Aldershot: Edward Elgar.

2000. "Neo-Roman Liberalism, 'Republican' Values and British Liberalism, ca. 1860–1875." *History of European Ideas* 29: 55–72.

Bicknell, John W. 1962. "Leslie Stephen's 'English Thought in the Eighteenth Century': A Tract for the Times." *Victorian Studies* 6: 103–20.

Bridges, John H. 1866. *France under Richelieu and Colbert*. Edinburgh: Edmonston & Douglas.

Bristed, Charles A. 1852. *Five Years in an English University*. New York: G. P. Putman & Co.

Brose, Olive J. 1971. *Frederick Denison Maurice: Rebellious Conformist*. Athens, Ohio: University Press.

Burke, Edmund. 1987 [1790]. *Reflections on the Revolution in France*. Edited by J. G. A. Pocock. Indianapolis: Hackett Publishing Company.

Burrow, John W. 1981. *A Liberal Descent: Victorian Historians and the English Past*. Cambridge: Cambridge University Press.

1988. *Whigs and Liberals: Continuity and Change in English Political Thought*. Oxford: Clarendon Press.

Burrow, John W. (ed.). 1993. *The Limits of State Action*. By Wilhelm von Humboldt. Indianapolis: Liberty Fund.

Butler, Samuel. 1927 [1872]. *Erewhon: Or Over the Range*. London: Jonathan Cape.

Butterfield, Herbert. 1959. *George III and the Historians, rev. ed.*. New York: Macmillan.

Caldari, Katia. 2000. "A List of the Essays Collected in Bound Volumes by Alfred Marshall: Part 1." *Marshall Studies Bulletin* 7. http://www.dse.unifi.it/marshall/welcome.htm.

2003. "A List of the Essays Collected in Bound Volumes by Alfred Marshall: Part 2." *Marshall Studies Bulletin* 8. http://www.dse.unifi.it/marshall/welcome.htm.

Campanelli, Giuliana. 1982. "W. Whewell's Contribution to Economic Analysis: The First Mathematical Formulation of Fixed Capital in Ricardo's System." *Manchester School of Economic and Social Studies* 53: 404–31.

Campbell, Lewis. 1901. *The Nationalisation of the Old English Universities*. London. Chapman and Hall.

Capaldi, Nicholas. 2004. *John Stuart Mill: A Biography*. Cambridge: Cambridge University Press.

Carpenter, William. 1889. *Nature and Man: Essays Scientific and Philosophical*. New York: Appleton and Company.

Carr, Robert. 1962. "The Religious Thought of John Stuart Mill: A Study in Reluctant Scepticism." *Journal of the History of Ideas* 23: 475–95.

Clark, John C. D. 2000. *English Society, 1660–1832: Religion, ideology and politics during the ancient regime*, 2nd ed. Cambridge: Cambridge University Press.

Clayton, James. 1972. "Reason and Society: An Approach to F. D. Maurice." *Harvard Theological Review* 65: 305–35.

Clifford, William K. 1879. *Lectures and Essays*. 2 vols. Edited by L. Stephen and F. Pollock. London: Macmillan.

Coats, Alfred W. 1954. "The Historicist Reaction in English Political Economy, 1870–1890." *Economica* 21:143–53.

Cochrane, James L. 1975. "William Whewell's Mathematical Statements of Price Flexibility, Demand Elasticity and the Giffen Paradox." *Manchester School of Economics and Social Studies* 43: 396–400.

Coleridge, Samuel T. 1969 [1818]. *The Friend*. 2 vols. Edited by B. Rooke. Princeton, N.J.: Princeton University Press.

    1976 [1830]. *On the Constitution of the Church and State*. Edited by J. Colmer. Princeton, N.J.: Princeton University Press.

    1983 [1817]. *Biographia Literaria, or Biographical Sketches of My Literary Life and Opinions*. Edited by James Engell and Walter Jackson Bate. Princeton, N.J.: Princeton University Press.

    1993 [1825]. *Aids to Reflection*. Edited by John Beer. Princeton, N.J.: Princeton University Press.

Collini, Stefan. 1975. "Idealism and 'Cambridge Idealism.'" *Historical Journal* 18: 171–7.

    1989. "'Manly Fellows': Fawcett, Stephen, and the Liberal Temper." In *The Blind Victorian: Henry Fawcett and British Liberalism*. Edited by L. Goldman, pp. 41–59. Cambridge: Cambridge University Press.

    1991. *Public Moralists: Political Thought and Intellectual Life in Britain, 1850–1930*. Oxford: Clarendon Press.

Collini, Stefan, Donald Winch, and John Burrow. 1983. *That Noble Science of Politics: A Study in Nineteenth-Century Intellectual History*. Cambridge: Cambridge University Press.

Cook, Simon J. 2004. "Missing Links in Alfred Marshall's Early Thoughts on Education." *European Journal of the History of Economic Thought* 11: 555–78.

    2005. "Minds, Machines, and Economic Agents: Cambridge Receptions of Babbage and Boole." *Studies in the History and Philosophy of Science* 36: 331–50.

    2008. "Poetry, Faith and Chivalry: Alfred Marshall's Response to Modern Socialism." *History of Economics Review* 47: 20–38.

Cooper, Charles H. 1861. *Annals of Cambridge*. Vol. 2. Cambridge: University Press.

Corsi, Pietro. 1987. "The Heritage of Dugald Stewart." *Nuncius: Annali di Storia della Scienza* 2: 89–144.

Crary, Jonathan. 1999. *Suspensions of Perception: Attention, Spectacle, and Modern Culture*. Cambridge, Mass.: M.I.T. Press.

Cunynghame, Henry H. 1904. *A Geometrical Political Economy*. Oxford: Clarendon Press.

Dardi, Marco. 1984. *Il giovane Marshall. Accumulazione e mercato*. Bologna: Il Mulino.

2003. "Alfred Marshall's Partial Equilibrium: Dynamics in Disguise." In *The Economics of Alfred Marshall: Revisiting Marshall's Legacy*. Edited by R. Arena and M. Quéré, pp. 84–112. London: Palgrave Macmillan.

Daston, Lorraine J. 1978. "British Responses to Psycho-Physiology." *Isis* 69: 192–208.

De Marchi, Neil. 1974. "The Success of Mill's *Principles*." *History of Political Economy* 6: 119–57.

1983. "*The Case for James Mill.*" In *Methodological Controversy in Economics; Historical Essays in Honour of T. W. Hutchison*. Edited by A. W. Coats, pp. 155–84. Greenwich, Conn.: JAI Press.

2002. "Putting Evidence in Its Place: John Stuart Mill's Early Struggle with 'Facts in the Concrete.'" In *Fact and Fiction in Economics: Models, Realism and Social Construction*. Edited by U. Mäki, pp. 304–28. Cambridge: Cambridge University Press.

Desmond, Adrian. 1998. *Huxley: From Devil's Disciple to Evolution's High Priest*. London: Penguin.

Dickey, Laurence. 1987. *Hegel: Religion, Economics, and the Politics of Spirit, 1770–1807*. Cambridge: Cambridge University Press.

Donoghue, Mark. 2004. "William Thomas Thornton and John Stuart Mill: A Victorian Friendship." In *History and Political Economy: Essays in Honour of P. D. Groenewegen*. Edited by T. Aspromourgos and J. K. Lodewijks, pp. 76–96. London: Routledge.

Ellens, Jacob P. 1987. "Lord John Russell and the Church Rate Conflict: The Struggle for a Broad Church, 1834–1868." *Journal of British Studies* 26: 232–57.

Fawcett, Henry. 1860. "Strikes: Their Tendencies and Remedies." *Westminster Review* 18: 1–23.

Fisch, Menachem, and Simon Schaffer. 1991. *William Whewell: A Composite Portrait*. Oxford: Clarendon Press.

Fontana, Biancamaria. 1985. *Rethinking the Politics of Commercial Society: The "Edinburgh Review," 1802–1832*. Cambridge: Cambridge University Press.

Forbes, Duncan. 1952. *The Liberal Anglican Idea of History*. Cambridge: Cambridge University Press.

1982. "Natural Law and the Scottish Enlightenment." In *The Origins and Nature of the Scottish Enlightenment*. Edited by R. H. Campbell and A. S. Skinner, pp. 186–204. Edinburgh: John Donald.

Foxwell, Herbert S. 1887. "The Economic Movement in England." *Quarterly Journal of Economics* 2: 84–103.

Garland, Martha M. 1980. *Cambridge before Darwin: The Ideal of a Liberal Education, 1800–1860*. Cambridge: Cambridge University Press.

Gibbins, John R. 1988. "John Grote and Modern Cambridge *Philosophy*." *Philosophy* 73: 453–77.

2001. "Constructing Knowledge in Mid-Victorian Cambridge: The Moral Sciences Tripos, 1850–70." In *Teaching and Learning in Nineteenth-Century Cambridge*. Edited by Jonathan Smith and Christopher Stray, pp. 61–89. Rochester, N.Y.: Boydell Press.

2007. *John Grote, Cambridge University and the Development of Victorian Thought*. Exeter: Imprint Academic Books.

Gibbon, Edward. 1984 [1796]. *Memoirs of My Life*. Edited by Betty Radice. New York: Penguin.

Groenewegen, Peter D. 1995. *A Soaring Eagle: Alfred Marshall, 1842–1924*. Aldershot: Edward Elgar.

Groenewegen, Peter D. (ed). 1990. *Alfred Marshall on the Method and History of Economics*. University of Sydney: Department of Economics.

(ed). 1996. *Official Papers of Alfred Marshall, A Supplement*. Cambridge: Cambridge University Press.

Grote, John. 1865. *Exploratio Philosophica: Rough Notes on Modern Intellectual Science*. Pt. 1. Cambridge: University Press.

Haakonssen, Knud. 1981. *The Science of a Legislator: The Natural Jurisprudence of David Hume and Adam Smith*. Cambridge: Cambridge University Press.

1982. "What Might Properly Be Called Natural Jurisprudence?" In *The Origins and Nature of the Scottish Enlightenment*. Edited by R. H. Campbell and A. S. Skinner. pp. 205–25. Edinburgh: John Donald.

1996. *Natural Law and Moral Philosophy: From Grotius to the Scottish Enlightenment*. Cambridge: Cambridge University Press.

2004. "Protestant Natural Law Theory: A General Interpretation." In *New Essays on the History of Autonomy: A Collection Honoring J. B. Schneewind*. Edited by Natalie Brender and Larry Krasnoff, pp. 92–109. Cambridge: Cambridge University Press.

2008. "Natural Law Without Metaphysics: A Protestant Tradition." In *Contemporary Perspectives on Natural Law: Natural Law as a Limiting Concept*. Edited by Anna Marta González, pp. 67–86. Aldershot: Ashgate.

Haakonssen, Knud. (ed.). 2006. *The Cambridge Companion to Adam Smith*. Cambridge: Cambridge University Press.

Hacking, Ian. 1990. *The Taming of Chance*. Cambridge: Cambridge University Press.

Haley, Bruce. 1978. *The Healthy Body and Victorian Culture*. Cambridge, Mass.: Harvard University Press.

Hampsher-Monk, Ian. 1992. *A History of Modern Political Thought*. Oxford: Blackwell.

Harrison, John F. C. 1961. *Learning and Living, 1790–1960*. London: Routledge & Kegan Paul.

Harrison, Royden. 1965. *Before the Socialists: Studies in Labour and Politics, 1861–1881*. London: Routledge & Kegan Paul.

Harvie, Christopher. 1976. *The Lights of Liberalism: University Liberals and the Challenge of Democracy, 1860–1886*. London: Allen Lane.

Hegel, Georg W. F. 1975. *Lectures on the Philosophy of World History – Introduction: Reason and History*. Translated by H. B. Nisbet with an introduction by D. Forbes. Cambridge: Cambridge University Press.

1991 [1857]. *The Philosophy of History*. Translated from the third German edition by J. Sibree. New York: Prometheus Books.

Henderson, James P. 1985. "The Whewell Group of Mathematical Economists." *Manchester School* 53: 404–31.

1990. "Induction, Deduction and the Role of Mathematics: The Whewell Group versus the Ricardian Economists." *Research in the History of Economic Thought and Methodology* 7: 1–36.

1996. *Early Mathematical Economics: William Whewell and the British Case*. Lanham, Md.: Rowman & Littlefield.

Herr, Richard. 1962. *Tocqueville and the Old Regime*. Princeton, N.J.: Princeton University Press.

Hilton, Boyd. 1988. *The Age of Atonement: The Influence of Evangelicalism on Social and Economic Thought*. Oxford: Clarendon Press.

   1989. "Manliness, Masculinity and the Mid-Victorian Temperament." In *The Blind Victorian: Henry Fawcett and British Liberalism*. Edited by L. Goldman, pp. 60–70. Cambridge: Cambridge University Press.

   2006. *A Mad, Bad, and Dangerous People? England, 1783–1846*. Oxford: Clarendon Press.

Hitchcock, Henry C. 1891. "Broad Church Theology." *Bibliotheca Sacra* 48: 630–51.

Hochstrasser, Tim J. 2006. "Physiocracy and the Politics of Laissez-Faire." In *The Cambridge History of Eighteenth-Century Political Thought*. Edited by M. Goldie and R. Wokler pp. 421–2. Cambridge: Cambridge University Press.

Hofstetter, Michael J. 2001. *The Romantic Idea of a University: England and Germany, 1770–1850*. London: Palgrave.

Hollander, Samuel. 1985. *The Economics of John Stuart Mill*. 2 vols. Oxford: Basil Blackwell.

Hont, Istvan. 1983. "The 'Rich Country–Poor Country' Debate in Scottish Classical Political Economy." In *Wealth and Virtue: The Shaping of Political Economy in the Scottish Enlightenment*. Edited by Istvan Hont and Michael Ignatieff, pp. 271–316. Cambridge: Cambridge University Press.

   2005. *Jealousy of Trade: International Competition and the Nation-State in Historical Perspective*. Cambridge, Mass.: Harvard University Press.

Hont, Istvan, and Michael Ignatieff. 1983. "Needs and Justice in the *Wealth of Nations*." In *Wealth and Virtue: The Shaping of Political Economy in the Scottish Enlightenment*. Edited by Istvan Hont and Michael Ignatieff, pp. 1–44. Cambridge: Cambridge University Press.

Hort, Anthony F. 1896. *Life and Letters of F. J. A. Hort*. 2 vols. London: Macmillan.

Houghton, Walter E. 1957. *The Victorian Frame of Mind, 1830–1870*. New Haven, Conn.: Yale University Press.

Howard, Henry F. 1935. *An Account of the Finances of the College of St. John the Evangelist in the University of Cambridge, 1511–1926*. Cambridge: Cambridge University Press.

Huber, Victor A. 1843. *English Universities*. Abridged translation by F. W. Newman. 2 vols. London: William Pickering.

Hume, David. 1983 [1754–62]. *The History of England from the Invasion of Julius Caesar to the Revolution in 1688*. 6 vols. Indianapolis: Liberty Fund.

Hunter, Ian. 2001. "The Recovery of Natural Law: Hochstraser's History of Morality." *Economy and Society* 30: 354–67.

Hutchison, Terrence W. 1953. *A Review of Economic Doctrines, 1870–1929*. Oxford: Clarendon Press.

Huxley, Thomas H. 1970 [1893–4]. *Collected Essays*. 9 vols. New York: Hildesheim.

Hyman, Anthony. 1982. *Charles Babbage: Pioneer of the Computer*. Oxford: Oxford University Press.

Jones, Gareth S. 1983. *Languages of Class Studies in English Working Class History, 1832–1982*. Cambridge: Cambridge University Press.

   1984 [1971]. *Outcast London: A Study in the Relationship Between Classes in Victorian Society*. New York: Pantheon Books.

   2004. *An End to Poverty? A Historical Debate*. London: Profile Books.

Jones, Tod E. 2003. *The Broad Church: A Biography of a Movement*. Lanham, Md.: Lexington Books.

Kadish, Alon. 1982. *The Oxford Economists of the Late Nineteenth Century*. Oxford: Clarendon Press.

1986. *Apostle Arnold: The Life and Death of Arnold Toynbee, 1852-1883*. Durham, N.C.: Duke University Press.

1989. *Historians, Economists, and Economic Historians*. London: Routledge.

1993. "The Teaching of Political Economy in the Extension Movement: Cambridge, London and Oxford." In *The Market for Political Economy: The Advent of Economics in British University Culture*. Edited by Alon Kadish and Keith Tribe, pp. 78-110. London: Routledge.

Keynes, John M. 1925 [1924]. "Alfred Marshall, 1842-1924." In *Memorials of Alfred Marshall*. Edited by A. C. Pigou, pp. 1-65. London: Macmillan.

Kingsley, Charles. 1877. *His Letters and Memories of his Life*. 2 vols. London: Kegan Paul & Co.

Knights, Ben. 1978. *The Idea of the Clerisy in the Nineteenth Century*. Cambridge: Cambridge University Press.

Koot, Gerard M. 1975. "T. E. Cliffe Leslie, Irish Social Reform, and the Origins of the English Historical School of Economics." *History of Political Economy* 7: 312-36.

1977. "H. S. Foxwell and English Historical Economics." *Journal of Economic Issues* 11: 561-86.

1980. "English Historical Economics and the Emergence of Economic History in England." *History of Political Economy* 12: 173-205.

1987. *English Historical Economics, 1870-1926: The Rise of Economic History and Neomercantilism*. Cambridge: Cambridge University Press.

Lassalle, Ferdinand. 1864. *Herr Bastiat-Schulze von Delitzch, der ökonomische Julian, oder: Capital und Arbeit*. Berlin: R. Schlingmann.

Leavis, Frank R. 1952. *The Common Pursuit*. London: Chatto & Windus.

Leavis, Queenie D. 1947. "Henry Sidgwick's Cambridge." *Scrutiny* 15: 2-11.

Leslie, T. E. C. 1870. "The Political Economy of Adam Smith." *Fortnightly Review* 8: 549-63.

1969 [1888]. *Essays in Political Economy*. New York: Augustus M Kelley.

Lightman, Bernard. 1987. *The Origins of Agnosticism: Victorian Unbelief and the Limits of Knowledge*. Baltimore: John Hopkins University Press.

Lingard, Jno T. 1877. "Dr. Carpenter's Theory of Attention." *Mind* 2: 272-3.

Loasby, Brian J. 1989. *The Mind and Method of the Economist: A Critical Appraisal of the Major Economists in the 20th Century*. Aldershot: Edward Elgar.

1990. "Firms, Markets, and the Principle of Continuity." In *Centenary Essays on Alfred Marshall*. Edited by John K. Whitaker, pp. 108-26. Cambridge: Cambridge University Press.

Maas, Harro. 2005. *William Stanley Jevons and the Making of Modern Economics*. Cambridge: Cambridge University Press.

Macleod, Henry D. 1863. *A Dictionary of Political Economy: Biographical, Bibliographical, Historical and Practical*. London: Longman, Green, Longman, Roberts, and Green.

Maloney, John. 1976. "Marshall, Cunningham and the Emerging Economics Profession." *Economic History Review* 29: 440-51.

1985. *Marshall, Orthodoxy, and the Professionalisation of Economics.* Cambridge: Cambridge University Press.

Malthus, Thomas R. 1976 [1798]. *An Essay on the Principle of Population.* Edited by P. Appleman. New York: W.W. Norton and Company.

Mansel, Henry L. 1859 [1858]. *The Limits of Religious Thought Examined in Eight Lectures Delivered Before the University of Oxford.* Boston: Gould and Lincoln.

1875 [1860]. *Metaphysics or the Philosophy of Consciousness Phenomenal and Real.* Edinburgh: Adam and Charles Black.

Marshall, Alfred. 1895 [1890]. *Principles of Economics,* 3rd ed. Vol. 1. London: Macmillan & Co.

1919. *Industry and Trade: A Study of Industrial Technique and Business Organization; and of their Influences on the Conditions of Various Classes and Nations.* London: Macmillan & Co.

Marx, Karl. 1954 [1867; 1887 first English translation]. *Capital: A Critique of Political Economy. Book One: The Process of Production of Capital.* Translated by Samuel Moore and Edward Aveling. London: Lawrence and Wishart.

Marx, Karl, and Engels, Frederick. 1976. *Collected Works [of] Karl Marx [and] Frederick Engels [1845-7],* [vol. 5]. Edited by Clemens Dutt, W. Lough, and C. P. Magill. London: Lawrence & Wishart.

Marx, K., Engels, F., and Jones, G.S. 2002 [1848; 1888 English translation]. *The Communist Manifesto.* London: Penguin Books.

Maurice, Frederick. 1842. T*he Kingdom of Christ; or, Hints to a Quaker, respecting the Principles, Constitutions, and Ordinances of the Catholic Church. 2 vols.* London: James Clark.

1859. *What is Revelation? A series of sermons on the epiphany; to which are added Letters to a student of theology on the Bampton lectures of Mr. Mansel.* London: Macmillan & Co.

1860. *Sequel to the Inquiry, What is Revelation? In a series of letters to a friend containing a reply to Mr. Mansel's "Examination of the Rev. F. D. Maurice's strictures on the Bampton lectures of 1858".* London: Macmillan & Co.

1862. *Modern Philosophy; or, a Treatise of Moral and Metaphysical Philosophy from the Fourteenth Century to the French Revolution, with a Glimpse into the Nineteenth Century.* London: Griffin, Bohn, and Company.

1884. *The Life of Frederick Denison Maurice. 2 vols.* London: Macmillan & Co..

Millar, Alan. 1998. "Mill on Religion." In *The Cambridge Companion to Mill.* Edited by John Skorupski, pp. 176–202. Cambridge: Cambridge University Press.

Miller, Edward. 1961. *Portrait of a College: A History of the College of Saint John the Evangelist, Cambridge.* Cambridge: Cambridge University Press.

Mirowski, Philip. 2002. *Machine Dreams: Economics Becomes a Cyborg Science.* Cambridge: Cambridge University Press.

Moore, Gregory. 1995. "T. E. Cliffe Leslie and the English Methodenstreit." *Journal of the History of Political Economy* 17: 57–77.

2003. "John Neville Keynes's Solution to the English Methodenstreit." *Journal of the History of Economic Thought* 25: 5–38.

2006. "The Cambridge Millites and the Early Economic Writings of Leslie Stephen." *History of Political Economy* 38: 596–615.

Moore, James R. 1979. *The Post-Darwinian Controversies: A Study of the Protestant Struggle to Come to Terms with Darwin in Great Britain and America, 1870-1900.* Cambridge: Cambridge University Press.

Moore, James. 2006. "Natural Rights in the Scottish Enlightenment." In *The Cambridge History of Eighteenth-Century Political Thought.* Edited by Mark Goldie and Robert Wokler, pp. 291-316. Cambridge: Cambridge University Press.

Morris, Jeremy. 2005. *F. D. Maurice and the Crisis of Christian Authority.* Oxford: Oxford University Press.

Morrow, John. 1986. "The National Church in Coleridge's Church and State: A Response to Allen." *Journal of the History of Ideas* 47: 640-52.

1990. *Coleridge's Political Thought: Property, Morality and the Limits of Traditional Discourse.* London: Macmillan & Co.

Morus, Iwan R. 2000. "'The Nervous System of Britain': Space, Time and the Electric Telegraph in the Victorian Age." *British Journal for the History of Science* 33: 455-75.

Müller, Max. 1867. *Chips from a German Workshop.* London: Longmans, Green.

Newsome, David. 1961. *Godliness and Good Learning: Four Studies on a Victorian Ideal.* London: Murray.

Norton Wise, Matthew. 1989-90. "Work and Waste: Political Economy and Natural Philosophy in Nineteenth Century Britain, (I)-(III)." *History of Science* 27, 28: 263-301, 391-449, 221-261.

Paley, Frederick A. 1869. "Religious Tests and the Nationalizing of the Universities." *Fortnightly Review* 5: 322-39.

Palfrey, David S. 2003. "The Moral Sciences Tripos at Cambridge University, 1848-1860." Unpublished Ph.D. thesis, Cambridge University.

Phillipson, Nicholas. 1983. "The Pursuit of Virtue in University Education: Dugald Stewart and Scottish Moral Philosophy in the Enlightenment." In *Universities, Society, and the Future: A Conference Held on the 400th Anniversary of the University of Edinburgh, 1983.* Edited by N. Phillipson, pp. 82-101. Edinburgh: Edinburgh University Press.

Pigou, Arthur C. 1935. *Economics in Practice: Six Lectures on Current Issues.* London: Macmillan & Co.

Pigou, Arthur C. (ed.). 1925. *Memorials of Alfred Marshall.* London: Macmillan & Co.

Pocock, John G. A. 1983. "Cambridge Paradigms and Scotch Philosophers: A Study of the Relations Between the Civic Humanist and the Civil Jurisprudential Interpretation of Eighteenth-Century Social Thought." In *Wealth and Virtue: The Shaping of Political Economy in the Scottish Enlightenment.* Edited by Istvan Hont and Michael Ignatieff, pp. 235-52. Cambridge: Cambridge University Press.

1985. *Virtue, Commerce, and History: Essays on Political Thought and History Chiefly in the Eighteenth Century.* Cambridge: Cambridge University Press.

1995. "Within the Margins: The Definition of Orthodoxy." In *The Margins of Orthodoxy: Heterodox Writing and Cultural Response, 1660-1750.* Edited by Roger Lund, pp. 33-53. Cambridge: Cambridge University Press.

1999. *Barbarism and Religion: Volume 1: The Enlightenments of Edward Gibbon.* Cambridge: Cambridge University Press.

2003. *Barbarism and Religion: Volume 3: The First Decline and Fall.* Cambridge: Cambridge University Press.

Pollock, Frederick. 1879. "Marcus Aurelius and the Stoic Philosophy." *Mind* 4: 46-68.

Pryme, George. 1870. *Autobiographical Reflections of George Pryme*. Cambridge: Deighton, Bell, and Co.

Raffaelli, Tiziano. 1991. "The Analysis of the Human Mind in the Early Marshallian Manuscripts." *Quaderni di Storia dell'Economica Politica* 9: 30–58.

——— 1994. "Marshall on Machinery and Life." *Marshall Studies Bulletin* 4: 9–22. http://www.dse.unifi.it/marshall/welcome.htm.

——— 1995. "Order and Creativity in Marshall's Views of Social Progress." *Kwansei Gakuin University Annual Studies* 44: 199–207.

——— 2003. *Marshall's Evolutionary Economics*. London: Routledge.

Raphael, David D. 2007. *The Impartial Spectator: Adam Smith's Moral Philosophy*. Oxford: Oxford University Press.

Rashid, Salim. 1977. "William Whewell and Early Mathematical Economics." *Manchester School* 45: 381–91.

Reid, Thomas. 1863 [1846]. *The works of Thomas Reid, D.D., now fully collected, with selections from his unpublished letters* ... Edited by W. Hamilton, D. Stewart, and H. Mansel. Edinburgh: MachLachlan and Stewart & Co.; London: Longman, Brown, Green and Longmans.

Ricardo, David. 2004 [1817]. *The Principles of Political Economy and Taxation*. Mineola, N.Y.: Dover Publications.

Richards, Joan. 1988. *Mathematical Visions: The Pursuit of Geometry in Victorian England*. New York: Academic Press.

Riedel, Manfred. 1984. *Between Tradition and Revolution: The Hegelian Transformation of Political Philosophy*. Translated by W. Wright. Cambridge: Cambridge University Press.

Riley, Jonathan. 1998. "Mill's Political Economy: Ricardian Science and Liberal Utilitarian Art." In *The Cambridge Companion to Mill*. Edited by John Skorupski, pp. 293–337. Cambridge: Cambridge University Press.

Roberts, Robert D. 1891. *Eighteen Years of University Extension*. Cambridge: University Press.

Robertson, John. 1983. "Scottish Political Economy Beyond the Civic Tradition: Government and Economic Development in the Wealth of Nations." *History of Political Thought* 4: 451–82.

Robertson, William. 1825 [1768]. *Charles V*. Vol. 1. Oxford: Talboys and Wheeler; London: W. Pickering.

Romano, Richard M. 1982. "The Economic Ideas of Charles Babbage." *History of Political Economy* 14: 385–405.

Rosenberg, Nathan. 1994. *Exploring the Black Box: Technology, Economics and History*. Cambridge: Cambridge University Press.

Ross, Ian S. 1995. *The Life of Adam Smith*. Oxford: Clarendon Press.

Rothblatt, Sheldon. 1968. *The Revolution of the Dons: Cambridge and Society in Victorian England*. New York: Basic Books.

Rothschild, Emma. 1994. "Adam Smith and the Invisible Hand." *American Economic Review, Papers and Proceedings of the Hundred and Sixth Annual Meeting of the American Economic Association* 2: 319–22.

——— 2001. *Economic Sentiments: Smith, Condorcet and the Enlightenment*. Cambridge, Mass.: Harvard University Press.

Rule, Philip C. 1964. "Coleridge's Reputation as a Religious Thinker: 1816–1972." *Harvard Theological Review* 67: 289–320.

Ryan, Alan J. 1970. *John Stuart Mill*. New York: Pantheon Books.

Sachs, William L. 1993. *The Transformation of Anglicanism: From State Church to Global Communion*. Cambridge: Cambridge University Press.

Sanders, Charles R. 1936. "Coleridge, F. D. Maurice, and the Distinction between the Reason and the Understanding." *Proceedings of the Modern Language Association* 51: 459–75.

   1938. "Maurice as a Commentator on Coleridge." *Proceedings of the Modern Language Association* 53: 230–43.

   1940. "Sir Leslie Stephen, Coleridge, and Two Coleridgeans." *Proceedings of the Modern Language Association* 55: 795–801.

   1941. "Coleridge, Maurice, and the Church Universal." *Journal of Religion* 21: 31–45.

Schaffer, Simon. 1989. "The Nebular Hypothesis and the Science of Progress." In *History, Humanity and Evolution: Essays for John C. Greene*. Edited by James Moore, pp. 131–64. Cambridge: Cambridge University Press.

   1994. "Babbage's Intelligence: Calculating Engines and the Factory System." *Critical Inquiry* 21: 203–27.

   1996. "Babbage's Dancer and the Impresarios of Mechanism." In *Cultural Babbage: Technology, Time and Invention*. Edited by F. Spufford and J. Ugloq, pp. 53–80. London: Faber and Faber.

Schneewind, Jerome B. 1977. *Sidgwick's Ethics and Victorian Moral Philosophy*. Oxford: Clarendon Press.

Schultz, Bart. 2004. *Henry Sidgwick: Eye of the Universe – An Intellectual Biography*. Cambridge: Cambridge University Press.

Schumpeter, Joseph. 1986. *History of Economic Analysis*. London: Allen & Unwin.

Schwartz, Pedro. 1972. *The New Political Economy of John Stuart Mill*. Durham, N.C.: Duke University Press.

Scott, Walter R. 1924–5. "Alfred Marshall, 1842–1924." *Proceedings of the British Academy* 11: 446–57.

Searby, Peter. 1997. *A History of the University of Cambridge*. Cambridge: Cambridge University Press.

Shove, Gerald. 1942. "The Place of Marshall's Principles in the Development of Economic Theory." *Economic Journal* 52: 294–329.

Sidgwick, Henry. 1876. "The Theory of Evolution in Its Application to Practice." *Mind* 1: 52–67.

   1886. "The Historical Method." *Mind* 11: 203–19.

   1887 [1883]. *The Principles of Political Economy*. London: Macmillan & Co.

   1890 [1874]. *The Methods of Ethics*. London: Macmillan & Co.

Sidgwick, Arthur, and Eleanor Sidgwick. 1906. *Henry Sidgwick: A Memoir*. London: Macmillan & Co.

Skorupski, John. 1999. *Ethical Explorations*. Oxford: Oxford University Press.

Smith, Crosbie. 1998. *The Science of Energy: A Cultural History of Energy Physics in Victorian Britain*. London: Athlone Press.

Sonenscher, Michael. 2007. *Before the Deluge: Public Debt, Inequality, and the Intellectual Origins of the French Revolution*. Princeton N.J.: Princeton University Press.

Spencer, Herbert. 1862. *First Principles*. London: Williams and Norgate.

Stephen, Leslie. 1873. *Essays on Freethinking and Plainspeaking*. London: Longmans, Green and Co.

1885. *Life of Henry Fawcett*. London: Macmillan.

1903 [1893]. *"An Agnostic's Apology" and other essays*. New York: G. P. Putnam's Sons.

1962 [1876]. *History of English Thought in the Eighteenth Century*. 2 vols. London: Harbinger Books.

Stigler, George J., and Ronald H. Coase (eds.). 1969. "Alfred Marshall's Lectures on Progress and Poverty." *Journal of Law and Economics* 12: 181–226.

Teichgraeber, Richard. 2000. "Adam Smith and Tradition: The Wealth of Nations Before Malthus." In *Economy, Polity, and Society: British Intellectual History, 1750–1950*. Edited by Stefan Collini, Richard Whatmore, and Brian Young, pp. 85–105. Cambridge: Cambridge University Press.

Thomas, William. 1979. *The Philosophical Radicals: Nine Studies in Theory and Practice, 1817–1841*. Oxford: Clarendon Press.

Thomson, William, and Peter Tait. 1879 [1867]. *Treatise on Natural Philosophy*. 2 vols. Cambridge: University Press.

Thornton, William T. 1866. "A New Theory of Supply and Demand." *Fortnightly Review* 6: 420–34.

1870 [1869]. *On Labour: Its wrongful claims and rightful dues, its actual present and possible future*. London: Macmillan & Co.

Tuck, Richard. 1987. "The 'Modern' Theory of Natural Law." In *The Languages of Political Theory in Early-Modern Europe*. Edited by Anthony Pagden, pp. 99–122. Cambridge: Cambridge University Press.

1993. "The Contribution of History." In *A Companion to Contemporary Political Philosophy*. Edited by Robert Goodin and Philip Petit, pp. 72–89. Oxford: Blackwell.

Tullberg, Rita. 1973. "Marshall's 'Tendency to Socialism.' " *History of Political Economy* 7: 74–111.

Venn, John. 1866. *The Logic of Chance: An essay on the foundations and province of the theory of probability, with especial reference to its application to moral and social science*. London: Macmillan & Co.

von Arx, Jeffrey P. 1985. *Progress and Pessimism: Religion, Politics, and History in Late Nineteenth Century Britain*. Cambridge Mass.: Harvard University Press.

Ward, William R. 1992. *The Protestant Evangelical Awakening*. Cambridge: Cambridge University Press.

Waterman, Anthony M. C. 1991. *Revolution, Economics and Religion: Christian Political Economy, 1798–1833*. Cambridge: Cambridge University Press.

Warwick, Andrew. 1994. "The Worlds of Cambridge Physics." In *The Physics of Empire: A Guide to the Exhibition*. Edited by R. Staley, pp. 57–86. Cambridge: Whipple Museum of the History of Science.

1998. "Exercising the Student Body: Mathematics and Athleticism in Victorian Cambridge." In *Science Incarnate*. Edited by C. Lawrence and S. Shapin pp. 288–326. Chicago: University of Chicago Press.

Weintraub, Roy. 2002. *How Economics Became a Mathematical Science*. Durham, N.C.: Duke University Press.

Welch, Edwin. 1973. *The Peripatetic University: Cambridge Local Lectures, 1873–1973*. Cambridge: Cambridge University Press.

Whewell, William. 1835. *Thoughts on the Study of Mathematics as a part of a Liberal Education*. Cambridge: J. & J. J. Deighton.

1837. *On the Principles of English University Education*. London: John W. Parker; Cambridge: J. and J. J. Deighton.

1845. *Of a Liberal Education in General; and with particular reference to the leading studies of the University of Cambridge*. London: J. W. Parker.

1858. *Novum Organon Renovatum: Being the second part of the philosophy of the inductive sciences*. London: John W. Parker and Son.

1862. *Six Lectures on Political Economy Delivered at Cambridge in Michelmas Term, 1861*. Cambridge: University Press.

Whitaker, John K. 1982. "The Emergence of Marshall's Period Analysis." *Eastern Economic Journal* 8: 15–29.

1994. "Marshall's Third Review." *Marshall Studies Bulletin* 4. http://www.dse.unifi.it/marshall/welcome.htm.

1996. "How Far do the Memorials Versions of Marshall's Essays Correspond to Their Original Texts?" *Marshall Studies Bulletin* 6: 25–43. http://www.dse.unifi.it/marshall/welcome.htm.

White, Michael. 1990. "Invention in the Face of Necessity: Marshallian Rhetoric and the Giffen Good(s)." *Economic Record* 66: 1–11.

1994. "The Moment of Richard Jennings: The Production of Jevons's Marginalist Economic Agent." In *Natural Images in Economic Thought: "Markets Read in Tooth and Claw."* Edited by P. Mirowski, pp. 197–230. Cambridge: Cambridge University Press.

2002. "Doctoring Adam Smith: The Fable of the Diamonds and Water Paradox." *History of Political Economy* 34: 659–83.

2004. "Sympathy for the Devil: H. D. Macleod and W. S. Jevons's Theory of Political Economy." *Journal of the History of Economic Thought* 26: 311–29.

Williams, Perry. 1991. "Passing on the Torch: Whewell's Philosophy and the Principles of English University Education." In *William Whewell: A Composite Portrait*. Edited by Menachem Fisch and Simon Schaffer, pp. 117–47. Oxford: Clarendon Press.

Wilson, Fred. 1998. "Mill on Psychology and the Moral Sciences." In *The Cambridge Companion to Mill*. Edited by John Skorupski, pp. 203–54. Cambridge: Cambridge University Press.

Winch, Donald. 1978. *Adam Smith's Politics: An Essay in Historiographic Revision*. Cambridge: Cambridge University Press.

1983. "Adam Smith's 'Enduring Particular Result': A Political and Cosmopolitan Perspective." In *Wealth and Virtue: The Shaping of Political Economy in the Scottish Enlightenment*. Edited by Istvan Hont and Michael Ignatieff, pp. 253–70. Cambridge: Cambridge University Press.

1991. "Adam Smith's Politics Revisited." *Quaderni di Storia dell'Economica Politica* 9: 3–27.

1992. "Adam Smith: Scottish Moral Philosopher as Political Economist." *Historical Journal* 35: 91–113.

1996. *Riches and Poverty: An Intellectual History of Political Economy in Britain, 1750–1834*. Cambridge: Cambridge University Press.

2004. "Review Essay: Mill as Romantic Idealist." *Journal of the History of Economic Thought* 26: 543–55.

Winstanley, Denys. 1935. *Unreformed Cambridge: A Study of Certain Aspects of the University in the Eighteenth Century*. Cambridge: University Press.

1947. *Later Victorian Cambridge*. Cambridge: University Press.

Wiseman, Timothy P. 1998. *Roman Drama and Roman History*. Exeter: University of Exeter Press.

Yeo, Richard R. 1979. "William Whewell, Natural Theology and the Philosophy of Science in Mid Nineteenth Century Britain." *Annals of Science* 36: 493–516.

1993. *Defining Science: William Whewell, Natural Knowledge, and Public Debate in Early Victorian Britain*. Cambridge: Cambridge University Press.

Index

Marshall, Alfred (*cont.*)
his synthesis of Hegel and Maine, 208–10
his theory of language, 5–6, 141, 162, 205–6
his trip to America, 266
his use of Maine's *Ancient Law*, 205
his vision of moral development compared with Smith's, 10–12
his visits to Germany, 128, 171, 196, 199
influenced by Whewell's pedagogy, 61
on Babbage's engines, 138–40
on difference between sympathy and altruism, 148
on economic history, 199, 212, 213–15, 219, 225
on evolution of social conventions, 11, 273
on organization, 272–79, 293
on productive and unproductive labour, 168
on relationship of custom and competition, 231–32
on the method of political economy, 173, 281
on the real value of ideas, 291–92
origin of his mature theory of wages, 242–45
swelling of his right foot, 143
the aim and tragedy of his life's work, 10
the method of his earliest economic research, 160
Marshall, Mary Paley, 146, 232, 273, 274
Marx, Karl, 176, 199, 246, 257, 296–98
Das Kapital, 170, 199, 235, 295
Mathematical Tripos, 60, 61, 71, 72, 74, 87, 89, 281
1868 reform of, 130
and undergraduate identification with machinery, 132
as moral training, 70, 73
emphasis of upon physical mechanism, 129
intensification of competition in, 72
Marshall's view of, 146, 149, 242
pressure of on undergraduates, 88

Maurice, Frederick Denison, 40, 44, 46, 58, 68, 75, 76, 78, 92, 93, 94, 96, 97, 98, 99, 100, 102, 104, 107, 113, 119, 148, 175, 216, 217, 218, 240, 241, 251, 259, 260
and spiritual ideal of manliness, 149
as missing from Keynes's narrative, 92
enthuses over Mill's demolition of Mansel, 107
his attitude to Darwin, 93
his aversion to system, 59
his Coleridgean methodology, 47
his Coleridgean theology, 97–99, 259
his conception of society as domain of religious duties, 7, 259
his conception of the church, 28
his conversational pedagogy, 59
his dispute with Mansel, 92, 102
his ideal of political economy, 27–28
his revision of Coleridge's elitism, 98
his theology as Hegelian, 217
introduces Mill to Coleridge, 67, 89
Marshall's conversations with, 118
Sidgwick and Marshall's relation to, 46
Stephen's hostility to, 94
why a true Coleridgean, 46
Maxwell, James Clerk, 130
McCulloch, John Ramsay, 174, 175
his edition of Smith's *Wealth of Nations*, 163, 168
Memory
as related by Coleridge to fancy, 142
Marshall on role of in perception, 123
Mill's problems with, 110
Mercantilism, 168, 172
Mid-century shift of conventions, 26, 99, 259
Middle Ages, the, 255, 275, 277
as cradle of modern economic life, 275, 296
no science of political economy previous to, 213
spiritual equality of, 211
Mill, James, 20, 24, 65, 68

Other books in the series *(continued from page iii)*

David Laidler *Fabricating the Keynesian Revolution: Studies of the Inter-War Literature on Money, the Cycle, and Unemployment*

Odd Langholm *The Legacy of Scholasticism in Economic Thought: Antecedents of Choice and Power*

Harro Maas *William Stanley Jevons and the Making of Modern Economics*

Philip Mirowski *More Heat Than Light: Economics as Social Physics, Physics as Nature's Economics*

Philip Mirowski (ed.) *Natural Images in Economic Thought: "Markets Read in Tooth and Claw"*

D. E. Moggridge *Harry Johnson: A Life in Economics*

Mary S. Morgan *The History of Econometric Ideas*

Takashi Negishi *Economic Theories in a Non-Walrasian Tradition*

Heath Pearson *Origins of Law and Economics: The Economists' New Science of Law, 1830–1930*

Malcolm Rutherford *Institutions in Economics: The Old and the New Institutionalism*

Esther-Mirjam Sent *The Evolving Rationality of Rational Expectations: An Assessment of Thomas Sargent's Achievements*

Yuichi Shionoya *Schumpeter and the Idea of Social Science*

Juan Gabriel Valdes *Pinochet's Economists: The Chicago School of Economics in Chile*

Karen I. Vaughn *Austrian Economics in America: The Migration of a Tradition*

E. Roy Weintraub *Stabilizing Dynamics: Constructing Economic Knowledge*

Printed in the United States
by Baker & Taylor Publisher Services